Bastian Lange, Martina Hülz, Benedikt Schmid, Christian Schulz (eds.)
Post-Growth Geographies

Social and Cultural Geography | Volume 49

With special thanks to Kevin Brendler, Joyce Gosemann and Vanessa Mena Arias (all ARL, Hannover) for the effort and commitment and Katharine Thomas (Kempen) for the translation work.

Bastian Lange studied human geography in Marburg/Lahn and Edmonton. He received his PhD at Johann-Wolfgang-Goethe-Universität Frankfurt am Main in 2006. Since 2017, he has been teaching at the University of Leipzig (habilitation in 2017) . He is conducting research in the field of alternative economies, transition studies, creative placemaking and governance processes. He spearheads Multiplicities, an urban development office that analyzes transition processes, moderates stakeholder processes, and advises municipalities and cities on user-driven local and urban development processes.

Martina Hülz studied geography, sociology and urban planning in Berlin, Bonn and Southampton. She researched and lectured at the universities of Dortmund, Duisburg-Essen and Luxembourg on spatial learning processes, knowledge economics as well as knowledge and technology transfer. After completing her doctorate at the University of Luxembourg, she worked for several years as a project manager in a regional consulting office. Since 2012, she has headed the "Economy and Mobility" department at the Academy for Spatial Research and Planning.

Benedikt Schmid holds a doctorate in geography from the University of Luxembourg and is currently a post-doctoral researcher at the chair Geography of Global Change at the University of Freiburg. His research focusses on the role of community initiatives and social enterprises in the transition towards a post-growth economy.

Christian Schulz studied geography in Saarbrücken/Germany, Québec/Canada und Metz/France. He obtained his PhD from the University of the Saarland (1998), and then worked as a PostDoc/Assistant Professor at the University of Cologne (habilitation in 2004). Since 2006, he has been holding a full professorship for sustainable spatial development at the University of Luxembourg, where he does research primarily on alternative economies and post-growth regimes from an economic geography perspective.

Bastian Lange, Martina Hülz, Benedikt Schmid, Christian Schulz (eds.)
Post-Growth Geographies
Spatial Relations of Diverse and Alternative Economies

[transcript]

We acknowledge financial support by the University of Luxembourg for the English translation of this book, support for the Processing Charge by ARL – Academy for Territorial Development in the Leibniz Association and the Open Access Publication Fund of Leipzig University.

Bibliographic information published by the Deutsche Nationalbibliothek
The Deutsche Nationalbibliothek lists this publication in the Deutsche Nationalbibliografie; detailed bibliographic data are available in the Internet at http://dnb.d-nb.de

This work is licensed under the Creative Commons Attribution 4.0 (BY) license, which means that the text may be remixed, transformed and built upon and be copied and redistributed in any medium or format even commercially, provided credit is given to the author. For details go to http://creativecommons.org/licenses/by/4.0/
Creative Commons license terms for re-use do not apply to any content (such as graphs, figures, photos, excerpts, etc.) not original to the Open Access publication and further permission may be required from the rights holder. The obligation to research and clear permission lies solely with the party re-using the material.

First published in 2022 by transcript Verlag, Bielefeld
© **Bastian Lange, Martina Hülz, Benedikt Schmid, Christian Schulz (eds.)**

Cover layout: Maria Arndt, Bielefeld
Cover illustration: Katharina Günther (Thinking Visual), Berlin
Sketchnotes: Viola Schulze Dieckhoff (TU Dortmund University), Dortmund and Joyce Gosemann (ARL), Hannover
Translation: Katharine Thomas, Kempen
Copy-editing: Katharine Thomas, Kempen, Kevin Brendler, Joyce Gosemann and Vanessa Mena Arias (all ARL), Hannover
Proofread: Bastian Lange (University of Leipzig), Leipzig, Martina Hülz (ARL), Hannover, Benedikt Schmid (University of Freiburg), Freiburg, Christian Schulz (University of Luxembourg), Luxembourg
Typeset: Mark-Sebastian Schneider
Printed by Majuskel Medienproduktion GmbH, Wetzlar
Print-ISBN 978-3-8376-5733-3
PDF-ISBN 978-3-8394-5733-7
https://doi.org/10.14361/9783839457337
ISSN of series: 2703-1640
eISSN of series: 2703-1659

Printed on permanent acid-free text paper.

»What if we were to accept that the goal of theory is not to extend knowledge by confirming what we already know, that the world is a place of domination and oppression? What if we asked theory instead, to help us see openings, to provide a space of freedom and possibility?«

Gibson-Graham, J. K. (2008). Diverse economies: performative practices for ›other worlds‹. Progress in Human Geography , 5(32), 613–632. (quote p.619)

Inhalt

Post-growth geographies
Conceptual and thematic cornerstones of this book
Christian Schulz, Bastian Lange, Martina Hülz, Benedikt Schmid 15

I. Spaces of Perspective

Using socio-spatial concepts of situatedness to explain work processes in the context of post-growth economies
Hans-Joachim Bürkner, Bastian Lange 39

Spatial strategies for a post-growth transformation
Benedikt Schmid 61

Reducing working hours in small enterprises as a post-growth practice?
Hubert Eichmann 85

Lessons from Practice

The emancipatory project of degrowth
Andrea Vetter, Matthias Schmelzer 99

Degrowth
A kind of pragmatic utopian thinking, re-politicising humanistic debates
Helen Jarvis 107

II. Spaces of Possibility

Growth independence through social innovations?
An analysis of potential growth effects of social innovations in a Swiss mountain region
Pascal Tschumi, Andrea Winiger, Samuel Wirth, Heike Mayer, Irmi Seidl 115

Criteria for post-growth residential development:
The example of the city of Zurich
Olivia Wohlgemuth, Marco Pütz 137

Makerspaces
Third places for a sustainable (post-growth) society?
Matti Kurzeja, Katja Thiele, Britta Klagge 157

Performing gaps
The relationship between alternative economies and urban planning in Dortmund
Le-Lina Kettner, Samuel Mössner 173

Town and countryside in flux
The significance of urban functions for the vitality of rural areas and the importance of individual and systemic solutions for the realisation of a growth-critical way of life
Anna Szumelda 189

Lessons from Practice

The role of interstitial spaces in the growing urban region of Hamburg
Michael Ziehl 205

'Hobbyhimmel' – an open workshop in the context of post-growth
Martin Langlinderer 211

Neighbourhood farms as new places for participation and grow-your-own
Heike Brückner, Jan Zimmermann 217

III. Spaces of Conflict

Provincialising degrowth
Alternatives to development and the Global South
Antje Bruns 225

Financing post-growth?
Green financial products for changed logics of production
Sabine Dörry, Christian Schulz 241

'Status quo avant-gardists' and 'prevention innovators'
Food for thought for the geographical post-growth debate
Bastian Lange, Hans-Joachim Bürkner 263

The growth fixation of the European Union
A commentary on the draft Green Deal
Christian Schulz 287

Lessons from Practice

We have a responsibility to be a bit more pragmatic
Yvonne Rydin 297

We should continue this dialogue with the EU institutions
Tom Bauler 303

IV. Spaces of Design

Spatial transformations: Process, goal, guideline?
Markus Hesse 311

Cornerstones and positions of a precautionary post-growth economy
The end of the growth-based model of prosperity
Ulrich Petschow, Nils aus dem Moore, David Hofmann,
Eugen Pissarskoi, Steffen Lange 323

New roles in collective, growth-independent spatial organisation
Christian Lamker, Viola Schulze Dieckhoff 347

The Bauhaus as a designer of transition
Post-growth approaches in East Germany after reunification –
between false growth and unwanted non-growth
Heike Brückner 363

Lessons from Practice

Post-growth perspectives for the Lausitz lignite mining region? – Opportunities and challenges
Carel Carlowitz Mohn 391

Hacking Ulm
Open data, digital literacy and coding as practices creating space in the city
Stefan Kaufmann 399

Designing living spaces together in open-ended approaches
Participation in spatial development for a good life
Torsten Klafft 407

Opening up spaces of possibility with artistic experiments
Viola Schulze Dieckhoff, Hendryk van Busse 417

Authors 423

'Questioning the meaningfulness of continuous material growth should become an integral part of spatial sciences and planning.'

Christian Schulz, Martina Hülz, Bastian Lange, Benedikt Schmid

About this book

The idea for this book arose from the collaboration of the editors and a number of the contributors in the working group 'Post-Growth Economies'[1] of the Academy for Territorial Development in the Leibniz Association (*Akademie für Raumentwicklung in der Leibniz-Gemeinschaft, ARL*[2]). The working group involved more than a dozen geographers, economists and spatial and landscape planners from Germany, Switzerland and Luxembourg. From mid-2017 to mid-2020, the group members met every six months at workshops in different locations and systematically tackled the topic of post-growth economies from the perspective of the spatial and planning sciences.

Exchanges with post-growth actors on the ground were always an integral part of the workshops and a source of inspiration for further work. In addition to this book, the working group has been involved in various other activities. Members of the group were instrumental in preparing the 2019 ARL annual congress on 'Post-growth and Transformation' in Kassel. In addition, they contributed to the conception and content of an issue of the journal *politische ökologie* entitled '*Möglichkeitsräume. Raumplanung im Zeichen des Postwachstums*' ('Spaces of opportunities. Spatial Planning and Post-growth'; also see https://www.arl-net.de/de/postwachstum, 28.02.2020).

All the chapters in this book are direct translations from the German original (Lange et al. 2020) and authorised by the respective authors. The introduction has been updated for an international audience. As the original work was sent to the publisher in early 2020, the implications of the Covid-19 pan-

---

[1] Goals, activities and membership of the ARL working group 'Post-Growth Economies': https://www.arl-net.de/de/projekte/postwachstumsökonomien (28.02.2020)

[2] The ARL – Academy for Spatial Research and Planning, Leibniz Forum for Spatial Sciences, adopted a new name at the beginning of 2021: ARL – Academy for Territorial Development in the Leibniz Association. This new name has not been used in the articles of this volume.

demic had not yet been addressed. The revised introduction includes observations on the pandemic from a post-growth perspective.

The editors would like to thank all contributors and interviewees for their commitment and participation. Special thanks go to the ARL, the University of Luxembourg and the University of Leipzig for its financial support and to the staff of the ARL Headquarters for their all-round support of the working group and this publication. We would also like to thank the team at transcript for including us in the series Social and Cultural Geography and for their consistently professional support and encouragement of the project. We hope that this publication will inspire as many people as possible and look forward to further discussions, comments and reactions.

Berlin/Hannover/Freiburg/Luxembourg, May 2021
Bastian Lange – Martina Hülz – Benedikt Schmid – Christian Schulz

Illustrations

The cover design and the pages separating the main parts of the book are based on a graphic recording of the 2019 ARL Congress in Kassel, designed by Katrina Günther of 'Thinking Visual', Berlin.

The quotations on the rear sides of the dividing pages are taken from a video project with compiled interview sequences, produced in the run-up to the 2019 ARL Congress. Viola Schulze Dieckhoff and Joyce Gosemann drew the portrait sketches of the individuals quoted.

Post-growth geographies
Conceptual and thematic cornerstones of this book

Christian Schulz, Bastian Lange, Martina Hülz, Benedikt Schmid

Post-growth: Context and current debates

In the last ten to fifteen years, there has been a rapid increase in the importance of debates held under the headings of degrowth or post-growth, considering the consequences of systemic growth imperatives and possible alternatives to dominant economic practices.

The enhanced significance of such discussions is linked, first, to the so-called 'economic and financial crisis' of 2007/2008, which revealed the culmination (Jorberg, 2010) of global crises (the financial, climate, migration, hunger and biodiversity crises) and their mutual interdependencies.

Second, the growth of social inequality, both globally and between and within regions and cities, and the intensified deregulation and financialisation of the economy, e. g. in the property sector, has led to broad media coverage of their causal interrelationships.

Third, new social movements such as Extinction Rebellion, Fridays for Future and associated groups have recently managed to establish a socio-ecological framework for their climate policy demands, the effectiveness of which seems to be only temporarily overshadowed by the Covid-19 pandemic, as demonstrated by current campaigns for the German 2021 federal elections. Indeed, the pandemic is seen as having the potential to accelerate post-growth policy approaches, for instance in the context of regional resilience, shortened supply chains and security of supply (further discussion of this below).

In the aftermath of the 2007/2008 'economic and financial crisis', a number of growth-critical approaches were taken up by international organisations that had not previously addressed the issue of growth limits. Examples include the European Commission and their strategy paper 'GDP and beyond' (European Commission, 2009) and the Organisation for Economic Co-operation and Development with their 'Better Life Index' (OECD, 2011). These organisations thus started to engage with conventional measurements of economic development and prosperity.

Subsequently, both organisations attempted to link growth management and sustainability goals: the EU in its 'Strategy 2020', using the concept of 'Sustainable Growth' (European Commission, 2010), and the OECD, who adopted the principle of 'Green Growth' (OECD, 2014, 2009). The concept of the 'Green Economy' propagated by the United Nations (UNEP, 2011) has a similar focus. Indeed, among the Sustainable Development Goals (SDGs), which are currently subject to much discussion, SDG 8 calls for the promotion of 'sustained, inclusive and sustainable economic growth, full and productive employment and decent work for all'. This is to be achieved through explicit adherence to GDP growth targets[1] and a development policy that focuses on technology, efficiency and diversification[2]. The aim is that economic growth and environmental degradation should be decoupled by 2030[3]. Similarly, the 2019 'Green Deal' called for by the new EU Commission also discusses a 'new growth strategy' based on a 'modern, resource-efficient and competitive economy where there are no net emissions of greenhouse gases in 2050 and where economic growth is decoupled from resource use' (European Commission, 2019, 2).

None of these approaches fundamentally question the material growth logic of the dominant economic system. However, they do see it as causing negative social and ecological externalities and, in order to minimise these externalities, are thus in favour of the ecological modernisation of the current production system. Technology is intended to improve efficiency in the

---

1 Target 1: 'Sustain per capita economic growth in accordance with national circumstances and, in particular, at least 7 per cent gross domestic product growth per annum in the least developed countries'

2 Target 2: 'Achieve higher levels of economic productivity through diversification, technological upgrading and innovation, including through a focus on high-value added and labour-intensive sectors'

3 Target 4: 'Improve progressively, through 2030, global resource efficiency in consumption and production and endeavour to decouple economic growth from environmental degradation'

production and use of goods (e. g. smart homes) and, coupled with greater recycling of resources (e. g. the circular economy), is expected to support sustainability and open up new possibilities for economic development and diversification in the field of environmental technology or eco-technology.

However, it is already apparent that such technology-based modernisation approaches are insufficient to address the prevalent ecological and social problems. Indeed, the one-sided focus on improving resource efficiency through technological progress encourages us to assume that current patterns of consumption and behaviour can be maintained in the long term. In this context, Kenis and Lievens (2016, 221) speak of the 'royal road to saving capitalism'. Three important points of criticism can be identified here.

First, it has not yet proved possible to decouple economic growth from resource consumption, either globally or at a national level. Thus, despite all the efforts to improve efficiency in the 2000s and 2010s, resource consumption has continued to rise with economic output (Giljum & Lutter, 2015). At best, it is possible to recognise a degree of *relative* decoupling whereby economic output has risen somewhat faster than resource requirements. However, in absolute terms, consumption of materials and energy has continued to grow steadily (Jackson, 2009, Haberl et al., 2020, Paech, 2010).

Second, this lack of decoupling can only be partially attributed to demographic trends (e. g. global population growth) and socio-economic developments (the emergence of a high-consumption 'middle class' in emerging economies). It is also due to the fact that improved efficiency is associated with financial savings (e. g. reduced heating costs), which then lead to additional purchases (e. g. energy-intensive electrical equipment) or activities (e. g. increased air travel). In terms of resource ecology, this is counterproductive and produces a 'rebound effect' (also known as the 'Jevons paradox'; W.S. Jevons, 1865). In view of recent increases in material intensity in certain industries, there has even been talk of 'recoupling' (Hickel & Kallis, 2019).

Third, 'smart' technologies and the 'Internet of Things' are viewed with increasing scepticism (Kerschner et al., 2018), not only in terms of data protection or the potential vulnerability of such technologies ('critical' infrastructures), but also from a resource perspective. The introduction of high-tech solutions, e. g. in building technology, always involves new materials and energy requirements, which in some cases outweigh the desired efficiency gains or even lead to new environmental and resource problems (as with the example of rare earths).

Post-growth as an emancipatory critique of growth promises

In addition to asking whether economic growth can be decoupled from resource consumption, feminist and postcolonial critiques problematise growth, measured as gross domestic product (GDP), as a political economy objective in itself. GDP fails to capture significant and fundamental elements of social relations – such as private care work, household labour, free exchange and production for personal use. Focusing economic policy on growth therefore provides an incentive to repress such social relations in favour of formal markets. This not only limits what is recognised as work and the economy (Gibson-Graham & Dombroski, 2020), but also leads to the undermining and destabilisation of traditional communities and economic activities under the pretext of (economic) progress (Kothari et al., 2019).

Discussions about the limits of economic growth and resulting prosperity and satisfaction are conducted primarily by those who have already achieved a certain level of material prosperity, a position from which it is hardly possible to achieve happiness and fulfilment through further material growth. It is therefore extremely important to problematise global relations of exploitation (Brand & Wissen, 2021), questions of responsibility and distributive justice, for instance in relation to the reduction of greenhouse gas emissions.

Justified doubts about the technology and market focus of approaches favoured by the political sphere have fed a vibrant post-growth debate that is seeking options for fundamental change (see the overview in Schmelzer & Vetter, 2019). This discussion presents the idea of sufficiency as a counterpoint to one-sided, strongly growth-oriented efficiency approaches (Schneidewind & Zahrnt, 2014). However, more recent debates (Kerschner et al., 2018, Pansera et al., 2019, Lange and Santarius, 2020) also include consideration of whether and how technological developments (under the keywords of 'digitalisation' and 'automation') can be positively managed in social and ecological terms.

Post-growth researchers discuss not only what and how we consume but also the ways in which we organise production, how much time we devote to paid work, and how we measure the importance of non-market and non-GDP-relevant economic activities (home care, neighbourhood help and voluntary work). Behind this is the larger issue of the purpose and focus of our economic system (profit maximisation versus a focus on the common good) and the attempt to overcome material growth imperatives – for example in the sense of the *décroissance*/degrowth approach (Latouche, 2006, Kallis, 2018) or the search for 'prosperity without growth' (Jackson, 2009, Lange, 2018).

Post-growth in spatial and planning sciences

Against the backdrop of the lively debates on post-growth approaches that are currently being conducted primarily in civil society forums and organisations, spatial and planning sciences are also beginning to pay attention to the topic (Zademach & Hillebrand, 2013, Krueger et al., 2017, Schmid, 2019, Schulz & Bailey, 2014, Lamker & Schulze Dieckhoff, 2019, Demaria et al., 2019, Lange, 2017). In some cases this involves drawing on approaches which are not explicitly post-growth but are critical of capitalism, such as the concept of diverse economies (Gibson-Graham, 2008).

It seems surprising that spatial sciences and planning have not become involved in the debate sooner. After all, it is some time since the spatial sciences pointed out the limits to growth and there has been extensive research and many publications on the negative consequences of global resource consumption from within the discipline. In turn, spatial planning has traditionally addressed the scarcity of land, landscapes, habitats and resources and is concerned with channelling or limiting land consumption.

However, most prevailing concepts, models and theoretical approaches in the spatial sciences continue to draw on an unquestioned growth paradigm. For example, common indicators and models in regional development are based on the assumption that quantitative growth (e. g. of labour markets, population, company turnover and infrastructure investment) is the most important driver of any positive development. The negative externalities of this development paradigm – such as environmental and health impacts – are problematised and efforts are made to reduce and manage such impacts, but there is generally little fundamental questioning of the purpose and desirability of continuous growth.

Paradoxically, this also applies to recent research on shrinking cities and on demographic change in rural areas. Here the focus tends to be on the problems and possible ways of returning to growth paths rather than on the opportunities presented by change.

To ensure there is no misunderstanding here: post-growth is not synonymous with shrinkage (e. g. of the population) or recession (e. g. of economic output). Rather, it is about abandoning the illusory notion that technological innovations and improved efficiency can ensure the long-term global growth of current production systems and consumption patterns, thereby improving living conditions for all.

Furthermore, post-growth does not mean that material growth should no longer be possible. Most post-growth approaches rather assume that spatial differentiation is necessary (e. g. pro-poor growth in economically disadvantaged regions). In essence, it is about adjusting understandings of growth and re-evaluating it, examining the long-term meaningfulness of certain developments and, if necessary, looking for possible alternatives within free social conditions. Meaningfulness refers here not only to the environment but also to individual and social needs, i.e. a focus on the common good rather than individual economic profitability.

In this context, a broader understanding of 'economy' is also relevant. This includes not only formally constituted enterprises operating according to market principles, but also forms of the social and solidarity economy, private pursuits (e. g. home care) and community activities (e. g. neighbourhood help, swap shops). This is by no means to say that all forms of human activity should be assessed and quantified according to market logics. Rather, authors like Seidl and Zahrnt (2019) argue that the creation of social prosperity should be recognised as being just as valuable as GDP-relevant activities (see the article by Brückner in this volume).

The spatial sciences, with their established interest in sustainability issues, are particularly called upon to critically engage with the current debates on green growth, the circular economy, smart cities and the sharing economy. At the same time, more systematic engagement with alternative forms of economic activity is urgently needed in order to understand such approaches, some of which remain ephemeral while others are clearly gaining in relevance (e. g. Community Supported Agriculture). This will then allow their transformative potential to be evaluated.

Concepts for a geographical perspective on post-growth processes

Common spatial concepts such as scale, network, territory and place, along with other terms such as terrain, landscape and border, have a long tradition in spatial science research. The former are cited by various authors as fundamental concepts of space, as they each stand for different logics of how space is produced in social practice and can be examined (Jessop, Brenner & Jones, 2008). The way in which space and spatial relations may be socially produced (Lefebvre) and grasped is also of great importance for transformation research (see the article by Schmid in this volume).

A recurring topic in many of the empirical articles in this volume is, for example, the question of the scaling of civil society initiatives. This reflects the central importance of issues of scaling in current debates on post-growth (Buch-Hansen, 2018). However, understandings of scaling vary considerably and include range, relevance, professionalisation or institutionalisation. Attempts to overcome structural distinctions between the local and global (Marston, Jones & Woodward, 2005, Massey, 2005) play a role here, as does distinguishing between bottom-up and top-down strategies of social change (Gallo-Cruz, 2017).

Inspired by non-hierarchical, rhizomatic and horizontal ontologies – as proposed, for example, by practice theory or actor-network approaches – change is increasingly imagined and conceived as the shifting of diverse practices in more than human contexts (Joutsenvirta, 2016, Lange & Bürkner, 2018, Rodríguez-Giralt, Marrero-Guillamón & Milstein, 2018, Schmid & Smith, 2020).

Similarly, governance and planning-related contributions raise questions about the reference areas, spaces of action and territoriality of post-growth processes (see the article by Bürkner/Lange in this volume). While spatial science approaches repeatedly point out the constructed nature of territorial entities (Agnew, 1994, Cox, 2003), administrative and planning territories are usually presented as one way (among several) of describing 'reality' for transformative policies.

With the help of more recent urban research approaches in urban geography and cultural studies, it is possible to identify subject-oriented and scale-critical perspectives as an extension of transition theory approaches. The subjectively configured spatial frame of reference of actors and its relevance for actors' roles, functions and expectations in post-growth processes are examined more closely by Smith, Voß and Grin (2010) and Coenen, Benneworth and Truffer (2012) as transition geographies (see the articles by Lamker/Schulze Dieckhoff and Kettner/Mössner in this volume).

At the same time, debates on digitalisation have detected the increasing dissolution of spatial boundaries. However, it is easy to overlook the fact that social practice is bound to specific places and materialities even in the digital age. The multifaceted spatial relations and translocal linkages of online and offline communities therefore require approaches that capture spatial interconnections and links to places of social practice.

Developments around open workshops (Lange, 2017) and the maker movement (Davies, 2017) are a case in point (see the article by Kurzeja/Thiele/Klagge in this volume). While supra-regional organisations (such as the *Verbund Offener Werkstätten* [Association of Open Workshops]) and online platforms play an important role in the diffusion of open workshops, the actual places themselves are charged with specific meanings, shaped by communities and temporary, so that they cannot easily be expanded or replicated (scaled). Thus, interaction between different forms of space – e. g. scale, place and network – is also an important prerequisite for understanding transformation processes and potentials (Schmid, 2020).

Concrete examples of post-growth economic activities, consumption, planning and construction can thus neither be considered in isolation from superordinate levels of action and policy nor detached from their relational connections to other practices and actors, be they regional or more extensive. It is this interplay of levels, scopes and relationships that creates new geographies of post-growth. We refer here to geographies in the plural in order to include not only the structural and thematic diversity of geographical articulations of post-growth, but also the current dynamics and volatility of emergent patterns. Considering and reflecting upon these developments provides both opportunities and challenges and requires the constant questioning of established models and explanatory approaches. It is to be hoped that the present and future findings of spatial post-growth research will soon be reflected in textbooks and policy recommendations. This book aims to make a contribution here (Oekom, 2020, ARL, 2021a, 2021b).

Challenges for the spatial sciences

From a spatial science perspective, many of the post-growth phenomena are clearly highly relevant and require intensive scientific monitoring so that we can learn from the early phases of the initiatives and draw conclusions for future projects and policy advice (see below).

While, for example, alternative energy concepts (Klagge & Meister, 2018) and aspects of communal urban farming (Rosol, 2018) have already received great attention, the empirical study of other approaches oriented towards post-growth is still in its infancy. The following topics serve as examples.

Land

Land ownership and land policy are not new topics for the spatial sciences or spatial planning (see Hertweck, 2020). However, current debates on rising property prices and housing shortages are bringing the issue of land ownership back into the spotlight (Difu & vhw, 2017). There are a number of links here to the post-growth debate such as the commodification of public land, the question of re-municipalising formerly privatised property (e. g. for public welfare housing) and – closely related to this – the issue of democratic participation in decision-making about the socially desirable use of land (Hesse, 2018).

Housing

Concerns about a lack of control over settlement development in times of progressive privatisation and financialisation are closely linked to the question of what kinds of growth are desired (e. g. what kind of housing for whom). In addition to social factors and design aspects (including sustainable building standards), this also involves ways of enabling and promoting types of housing that offer space for post-growth lifestyles and modes of production (Jarvis, 2017, Nelson & Schneider, 2019). One option is, for example, to combine (comparatively) small private living spaces with spaces for communal use (office spaces, workshops, play and sports areas and gardens). Also of relevance are collective forms of planning, investment and housing provision (e. g. cooperatives) (see the article by Wohlgemuth/Pütz in this volume).

Work

Aspects of settlement design are in turn closely linked to the development of new forms of urban production. In addition to urban farming, this includes open workshops and makerspaces (Lange & Bürkner, 2018), forms of communal or temporary office use (co-working spaces – increasingly in combination with childcare, housing and catering services) and a variety of other types of cooperative and shared functions.

As well as the issue of new places of work, the post-growth debate also raises the far more fundamental question of the role of work (Grenzdörffer, 2021, McKinnon, 2020, Seidl & Zahrnt, 2019). This is, first, about the general importance of work for social well-being, with a particular focus on improving (formal) recognition of care work, which has mostly gone unpaid and unnoticed by economic statistics. Second, discussion focuses on how the temporal balance between gainful employment and other forms of socially and personally important activities can be changed on an individual basis – not least in order to facilitate more resource-efficient lifestyles with time for gardening, handicrafts/repairing, food preparation, etc.

Sharing

Not every form of the sharing economy is per se post-growth-oriented or more sustainable than conventional forms of use. On the contrary, a whole range of commercial services run under this label only involve sharing on a superficial level or in part, e. g. large car sharing providers or the online accommodation marketplace Airbnb. Such services are increasingly subject to critical scrutiny (Belk, 2017, Martin, 2016). However, sharing practices that focus on conserving resources and the community – so-called 'transformative sharing' – provide important impulses for post-growth economies (Schmid, 2020).

Agriculture

Alongside the focus on changing consumption patterns and a return to regional food production, new forms of active or passive participation are also particularly important, for example contributing financial resources or labour in the context of community supported agriculture (CSA). Social science research is interested not only in the ecological aspects of land conversion and spatial patterns of changed supply relationships, but also in the socio-economic questions of cohesion, participation and co-production.

Rural areas

CSA initiatives are not only found in the environs of urban agglomerations but are increasingly shaping rural areas as well. Here, too, the focus is on adaptability, security of supply and social cohesion. In addition to farming, there are a wide variety of growth-critical approaches in rural areas (e. g. neighbourhood shops, co-working spaces, swap shops, local currencies, energy cooperatives) that are often brought together under the umbrella of Transition Town initiatives.

Transdisciplinary perspectives on post-growth

All of the thematic areas discussed above involve new forms of social relations and specific forms of organisation. The latter often go beyond conventional understandings of private-sector enterprises or public institutions and include diverse types of hybrid organisations. These include constellations of economic, public and civil society actors, such as those that have emerged in fair trade initiatives or in the decentralised production of renewable energies (Dufays & Huybrechts, 2016). Social enterprises or '(eco-)social enterprises' (Defourny, 2014, Johanisova & Franková, 2017) are examples of hybrid organisations that combine economic, social and ecological concerns in very different ways. So far, they have only received marginal attention from the spatial sciences (e. g. economic geography).

Post-growth can be taken into account more or less explicitly at all levels of planning. Especially in urban planning and architecture, there are numerous examples of approaches that are creating design and infrastructural conditions intended to promote or enable post-growth activities (see the articles by Kettner/Mossner and Lamker/Schulze Dieckhoff in this volume). Including particular design features in residential and commercial buildings or public areas can proactively create spaces for sharing (e. g. co-working, community gardens) and necessary infrastructures (e. g. workshops, car/bike sharing). In this context, reference should also be made to the idea labs of the ARL's Post-Growth Society Initiative (*Initiative Postwachstumsgesellschaft*), which experimentally engage with approaches to post-growth planning (Schulze Dieckhoff & Lamker, 2017).

Last but not least, we should also consider the question of how intensively the spatial sciences want to participate in these political and social debates.

There is a large gap between, on the one hand, a position of defensive observation, which addresses post-growth phenomena primarily from empirical or conceptual interest, and, on the other hand, an explicitly activist role with socially engaged researchers who see themselves as part of a movement (Participatory Action Research, see Kindon, Pain & Kesby, 2007).

It seems clear that examining the topics presented here from a spatial science perspective is relevant and necessary. This edited volume provides examples that demonstrate how the spatial sciences can continue to serve as descriptive and analytical research disciplines and also develop a role as a body for action and implementation in planning practice. In both cases, far-reaching imperatives for action emerge in the context of a post-growth analysis of society.

A valuable contribution could also be made to the increasingly dynamic debate on fundamental economies (Foundational Economy Collective, 2018). Starting from a critique of the neo-liberal state's withdrawal from public services and welfare, the concept has identified a set of foundational infrastructures and services that is considered indispensable for societal well-being (public utilities, education, health services and care). The authors argue that these services and infrastructures should be distributed and accessible to all members of a society with the same high-quality standards and reliability. They should be counted as citizen rights and not subject to privatisation, speculation or profit-oriented market dynamics. Rather, they should become (or remain) public services financed by the state and decided upon in democratic, transparent and inclusive decision-making processes that serve the common good (Nygaard & Hansen, 2021). This pledge resonates with recent geographical contributions to the role of infrastructures in the socio-ecological transition (Moss & Marvin, 2016, Becker, Naumann & Moss, 2016).

Post-growth in times of pandemic

Both the importance of foundational infrastructures and services for societal well-being and their vulnerability in a growth-based market economy have become very clear in the recent months which have been greatly influenced by Covid-19. In lieu of a detailed analysis, many of which have been offered by scholars across the social sciences (see for example the Special Issue 'The Geography of the COVID-19 Pandemic' of the Tijdschrift voor Economische en Sociale Geografie, KNAG, 2020), we want to highlight a number of observations that are particularly important from a post-growth perspective.

The pandemic has impressively demonstrated the vulnerability of economic relations that depend on highly distributed global value chains and the continuous intensification of market exchange. Even in the absence of real demand – as mass events, holiday travel and many indoor and outdoor leisure activities had to be put on hold – the economy needed to be kept going at all costs. This led to balancing the health of 'the economy' against the health of people (e. g. by failing to significantly restrict contacts in offices and factories or by subsidising the automobile industry instead of investing in better public transportation). Higher demands in other areas, in particular the hospital, medical and healthcare sector, in turn, led to the overload and breakdown of basic services which had been streamlined towards market efficiency. Key workers, who were most affected by the pandemic and at the same time crucial for the maintenance of basic supply, received symbolic appreciation (clapping for care workers) but neither monetary nor professional improvement of their structural position.

States, meanwhile, mobilised impressive financial, administrative and discursive resources and implemented a wide range of measures – ranging from comprehensive restrictions on public and private life to massive vaccination programmes. This raises the question of whether this astonishingly rapid execution of power could not be transferred to more diffuse but no less dangerous crises, such as climate change or species extinction? From a post-growth perspective, there needs to be (finally) recognition of the scientifically proven urgency of ecological crises, leading to a decisive redirection of political and economic processes. At the same time, the forces of inertia have been amply demonstrated in the massive subsidies awarded to carbon-intensive industries such as airlines and the automobile sector. In the face of intensifying climate crises, many states have squandered a unique opportunity to 'build back better'.

In sum, Covid-19 has deepened existing fault lines and socio-ecological challenges, but also made them more visible. Alternative discourses and practices that emancipatory groups and movements were already implementing before the pandemic have acquired new meanings and dynamism. Amidst attempts to get back to 'normal', the viability and urgency of alternative forms of economic activity and notions of prosperity have gained traction in social debates. New practices that address social and ecological challenges have emerged at a speed that would have been unimaginable without the rupture caused by Covid-19. These range from neighbourhood initiatives with a wide variety of people offering help to others, especially those in 'risk groups', to pop-up bike lanes in large cities that would otherwise have taken years to implement.

The pandemic has intensified structural issues but also given impetus to certain discussions, some of which have long been part of the post-growth debate. These include the measurement of prosperity by GDP, the growth-oriented incentives of tax and interest rate policy, the limits of markets as an allocation mechanism, the (re)evaluation of waged labour and non-waged labour, and the purposes of business activities. Covid-19 has magnified both the structural inequalities within and across regions and countries, and the severe limitations of existing instruments and approaches intended to address them. Post-growth research therefore has to (continue to) develop alternative visions and discourses that address the roots of socio-environmental crises – of which the current pandemic is but one dimension.

Objectives of the publication

Against this backdrop, the key concern of this book is to provide answers to the following questions:

1. How does a spatial perspective contribute to an understanding of post-growth economies?
2. In which relations of place, network connections and positionings do practices and processes of the post-growth economy become visible?
3. How can established terms and concepts of spatial and planning sciences be fruitfully operationalised for post-growth research?
4. How do the possibilities and problems of institutionalising and scaling post-growth organisations and practices appear from a spatial science perspective?
5. Which consequences and design options emerge for spatial and urban planning?
6. Which explanations of social change that include a spatial perspective prove analytically helpful and applicable to practice?

These questions can only be answered through critical consideration of the established terms and concepts of the spatial and planning sciences. This includes identifying the latent influences of growth-oriented regional and spatial analysis and, if necessary, providing modified heuristics.

For example, our analytical understanding of regional development processes is generally inextricably linked to conventional methods of measuring or evaluating them. Despite long-standing and manifold criticism of the use of purely quantitative monetary indicators (e. g. GDP, productivity, direct investment, expenditure on research and development), these indicators continue to dominate scientific analysis and political debates. Alternative approaches to assessing sustainability, life satisfaction and the extent of social cohesion/solidarity already exist. However, these approaches – not least because of their greater complexity – have so far been confined to the margins of academia.

Our prevailing understanding of innovation is similarly one-sided or narrow. Although the concept of social innovation has found its way into spatial science research in recent years (Avelino et al., 2017), most work remains linked to a more technical-organisational understanding of innovation. The focus tends to be primarily on researching the spatial effects of incremental improvements in production processes (e. g. efficiency increases through new manufacturing processes, the optimisation of logistical processes) rather than on the consequences of disruptive innovations or inventions, such as the so-called Internet of Things. However, an expanded spatially situated understanding of innovation would allow us to additionally capture societal change and related innovations in the areas of, for example, political participation, local communities, models of working hours, lifestyles and consumption patterns (see Lange/Bürkner and Tschumi/Winiger/Wirth et al. in this volume).

Furthermore, not only do the spatial sciences mostly use a narrow concept of the economy, they also take a traditional view of enterprises as central actors. As a rule, enterprises are understood as formally constituted organisations that are subject to the rules of the market and pursue targets related to monetary profitability. Public enterprises (e. g. municipal utilities) or social and solidarity enterprises (e. g. cooperatives and non-profit organisations) are also primarily seen from the perspective of market logic. This understanding of enterprises leaves little room for hybrid or temporary constellations of actors, public welfare-oriented initiatives and other heterodox ways of organising everyday economic activity, developments to which the post-growth debate attaches particular importance.

Structure of the edited volume

The book is structured around the key questions listed above and the associated disciplinary and interdisciplinary strands of discussion. The questions are addressed in four thematic sections (I-IV) in which the individual articles are grouped. On the one hand, these articles reflect the breadth of current debates in academia and practice and, on the other hand, highlight conceptual and factual problems that have been somewhat neglected in discussion to date.

In the first thematic section 'Spaces of Perspective', the articles explore how a spatial perspective can contribute to understandings of post-growth. What are the relations of place, network connections and positionings in which practices and processes of the post-growth economy become visible? What spatial strategies and social innovations underlie such post-growth economic practices and processes?

Section II presents 'Spaces of Possibility' and discusses how actors in the field of the post-growth economy assess their environmental, spatial and place relations. How do they deal with the expectations of transition and transformation directed towards them? Which concrete practices, concepts and visions create new geographies of post-growth?

The third thematic section 'Spaces of Conflict' addresses selected fields of tension, considering, for example, the global dimension or the North-South dimension of socio-ecological transformation and the role of the financial sector.

Finally, thematic Section IV is dedicated to 'Spaces of Design' and considers questions such as: What are the consequences for spatial and settlement planning? What impulses, topics and methodologies should be incorporated in training and teaching? What action is required from spatial development policy? What options does civil society have for intervention and co-design?

The four thematic sections are accompanied by practical examples, interviews and case studies. The intention is to present the specific stories, practices, processes and perceptions of activists and actors directly in their own words. This polyvocality thus includes practitioners as defining promoters of post-growth geographies – even if they rarely use the term post-growth, their practices nevertheless display concrete links to the movement.

The book aims to provide conceptual stimuli and arouse curiosity about a new thematic field. Rather than presenting conclusive answers, the objective is to trace and synthesise the diversity and potentials of post-growth geographies. Open questions are also identified and hence goals for continued debate are derived. A further emphasis is on questioning familiar ways of thinking and working and initiating new thematic collaborations across disciplines. The concluding interview on the potential role of art and creative experimentation in post-growth spatial development exemplifies this approach. We encourage an open and dynamic process between activist and academic discussions on post-growth. Spatial sciences and planning should contribute here by developing a geographical perspective on post-growth processes, taking a differentiated view of the spatial dimensions of societal, socio-economic and ecological change dynamics. This is particularly called for in the context of current debates on the socio-economic and ecological consequences of the Covid-19 pandemic.

Cited literature

Agnew, J. (1994). The territorial trap: The geographical assumptions of international relations theory. *Review of International Political Economy, 1*(1), 53–80.

ARL – Akademie für Raumentwicklung in der Leibniz-Gemeinschaft (Ed.) (2021): *Postwachstum und Raumentwicklung – Denkanstöße für Wissenschaft und Praxis.* Positionspapier aus der ARL 122.

ARL – Akademie für Raumentwicklung in der Leibniz-Gemeinschaft (Ed.) (2021): Themendossier: *Postwachstum und Raumentwicklung* https://www.arl-net.de/de/postwachstum (2021, September 02.).

Avelino, F., Wittmayer, J. M., Pel, B., Weaver, P., Dumitru, A., Haxeltine, A., Kemp, R., Jørgensen, M. S., Bauler, T., Ruijsink, S., & O'Riordan, T. (2017). Transformative social innovation and (dis)empowerment. *Technological Forecasting and Social Change, 145,* 195–206.

Becker, S., Naumann, M., & Moss T. (2016). Between coproduction and commons: understanding initiatives to reclaim urban energy provision in Berlin and Hamburg. *Urban Research & Practice, 10*(1), 63–85.

Belk, R. (2017). Sharing versus pseudo-sharing in Web 2.0. *The Anthropologist*, 18(1), 7–23.

Brand, U., & Wissen, M. (2021). *Imperial mode of living: Everyday life and the ecological crisis of capitalism*. Verso Books.

Buch-Hansen, J. (2018). The preresquisites for a degrowth paradigm shift: Insights from critical political economy. *Ecological Economics*, 146, 157–163.

Coenen, L., Benneworth, P., & Truffer, B. (2012). The geography of transitions. Addressing the hidden spatial dimension of sociotechnical transformations. *Research Policy*, 41(6), 955–967.

Cox, K. R. (2003). Political geography and the territorial. *Political Geography*, 22(6), 607–610.

Davies, S. R. (2017). *Hackerspaces: Making the maker movement*. Polity.

Defourny, J. (2014). From third sector to social enterprise. In J. Defourny, L. Hulgard, & V. Pestoff (Eds.), *Social enterprise and the third sector: Changing European landscapes in a comparative perspective*. Routledge, 17–41.

Demaria, F., Kallis, G., & Bakker, K. (2019). Geographies of degrowth: Nowtopias, resurgences and the decolonization of imaginaries and places. *Environment and Planning E: Nature and Space*, 2(3), 431–450.

Difu, & vhw (2017). *Bodenpolitische Agenda 2020-2030. Warum wir für eine nachhaltige und sozial gerechte Stadtentwicklungs- und Wohnungspolitik eine andere Bodenpolitik brauchen*.

Dufays, F., & Huybrechts, B. (2016). Where do hybrids come from? Entrepreneurial team heterogeneity as an avenue for the emergence of hybrid organizations. *International Small Business Journal*, 34(6), 777–796.

European Commission (2009). *GDP and beyond. Measuring progress in a changing world*. COM (2009) 433 final.

European Commission (2010). *Europe 2020. A strategy for smart, sustainable and inclusive growth*.

European Commission (2019). *The European Green Deal*. COM(2019) 640 final 11.12.2019.

Foundational Economy Collective (2018). *Foundational economy. The infrastructure of everyday life*. Manchester University Press.

Gallo-Cruz, S. (2017). The insufficient imagery of top-down, bottom-up in global movements analysis. *Social Movement Studies*, 16(2), 153–168.

Gibson-Graham, J. K. (2008). Diverse economies: performative practices for 'other worlds'. *Progress in Human Geography*, 32(5), 613–632.

Gibson-Graham, J. K., & Dombroski, K. (2020). Introduction to the handbook of diverse economies: Inventory as ethical intervention. In J. K. Gibson-Graham, & K. Dombroski (Ed.), *The handbook of diverse economies*. Edward Elgar Publishing, 1–24.

Giljum, S., & Lutter, S. (2015). Globaler Ressourcenkonsum: Die Welt auf dem Weg in eine Green Economy? *Geographische Rundschau, 67*(5), 10–15.

Grenzdörffer, S. M. (2021). Transformative perspectives on labour geographies – The role of labour agency in processes of socioecological transformations. *Geography Compass*.

Haberl, H., Wiedenhofer, D., Virág, D., Kalt, G., Plank, B., Brockway, P., Fishman, T., Hausknost, D., Krausmann, F., Leon-Gruchalski, B., Mayer, A., Pichler, M., Schaffartzik, A., Sousa, T., Streeck, J., & Creutzig, F. (2020). A systematic review of the evidence on decoupling of GDP, resource use and GHG emissions, part II: Synthesizing the insights. *Environmental Research Letters, 15*(6), 065003.

Hertweck, F. (2018). Hans-Jochen Vogels Projekt eines neuen Eigentumsrechts des städtischen Bodens. *Arch+, 51*(231), 46–53.

Hertweck, F. (2020). *Architecture on common ground. The question of land: Positions and models*. Lars Müller Publishers.

Hesse, M. (2018). In Grund und Boden. Wie die Finanzialisierung von Bodenmärkten und Flächennutzung Städte unter Druck setzt. *Arch+, 51*(231), 78–83.

Hickel, J., & Kallis, G. (2019). Is green growth possible? *New Political Economy, 25*(4), 469–486.

Jackson, T. (2009). *Prosperity without growth? The transition to a sustainable economy*. Sustainable Development Commission.

Jarvis, H. (2017). Sharing, togetherness and intentional degrowth. *Progress in Human Geography, 43*(2), 256–275.

Jessop, B., Brenner, N., & Jones, M. (2008). Theorizing sociospatial relations. *Environment and Planning D: Society and Space, 26*(3), 389–401.

Jevons, W. S. (1865). *The coal question*. Augustus M. Kelley Publishers.

Johanisova, N., & Fraňková, E. (2013). Eco-social enterprises in practice and theory. A radical vs. mainstream view. In M. Anastasiadis (Ed.), *ECO-WISE. Social enterprises as sustainable actors: Concepts, performances, impacts*. 1. edition. Europäischer Hoschulverlag, 110–129.

Jorberg, T. (2010). Finanzmärkte und Aufgaben der Banken. In I. Seidl, & A. Zahrnt (Eds.), *Postwachstumsgesellschaft. Konzepte für die Zukunft.* Metropolis Verlag, 145–153.

Joutsenvirta, M. (2016). A practice approach to the institutionalization of economic degrowth. *Ecological Economics, 128,* 23–32.

Kallis, G. (2018). *Degrowth. Agenda.*

Kenis, A., & Lievens, M. (2016). Greening the economy or economizing the green project? When environmental concerns are turned into a means to save the market. *Review of Radical Political Economics, 48*(2), 217–234.

Kerschner, C., Wächter, P., Nierling, L., & Ehlers, M.-H. (2018). Degrowth and technology: Towards feasible, viable, appropriate and convivial imaginaries. *Journal of Cleaner Production, 197*(2), 1619–1636.

Kindon, S., Pain, R., Kesby, M. (2009). Participatory Action Research. In R. Kitchin, & N. Thrift (Eds.), *International Encyclopedia of Human Geography.* Elvesir, 90–95.

Klagge, B. & Meister, T. (2018). Energy cooperatives in Germany – an example of successful alternative economies? *Local Environment, 23*(7), 697–716.

KNAG - Royal Dutch Geograhical Society (Ed.) (2020): The Geography of the COVID-19 Pandemic. Utrecht. = *Journal of Economic and Human Geography 111*(3).

Kothari, A., Salleh, A., Escobar, A., Demaria, F., & Acosta, A. (2019). *Pluriverse: A post-development dictionary.* Tulika Book.

Krueger, R., Schulz, C., & Gibbs, D. C. (2017). Institutionalizing alternative economic spaces? An interpretivist perspective on diverse economies. *Progress in Human Geography, 42*(4), 569–589.

Lamker, C. & Schulze Dieckhoff, V. (2019). Mit oder gegen den Strom? Postwachstumsplanung in der Fishbowl. *RaumPlanung, 201*(2-2019), 48–54.

Lange, B. (2017). Offene Werkstätten und Postwachstumsökonomien: kollaborative Orte als Wegbereiter transformativer Wirtschaftsentwicklungen? *Zeitschrift für Wirtschaftsgeographie, 61*(1), 38–55.

Lange, B., & Bürkner, H.-J. (2018). Open workshops as sites of innovative socio-economic practices: approaching urban post-growth by assemblage theory. *Local Environment, 23*(7), 680–696.

Lange, S. (2018). *Macroeconomics without growth. Sustainable economies in neoclassical, keynesian and marxian theories.* Metropolis Verlag.

Lange, S., & Santarius, T. (2020). *Smart green world? Making digitalization work for sustainability.* Routledge.

Latouche, S. (2006). *Le pari de la décroissance*. Fayard.
Marston, S. A., Jones, J. P., & Woodward, K. (2005). Human geography without scale. *Transactions of the Institute of British Geographers*, 30(4), 416–432.
Martin, C. J. (2016). The sharing economy: A pathway to sustainability or a nightmarish form of neoliberal capitalism? *Ecological Economics*, 121(C), 149–159.
Massey, D. (2008). *World city (Reprint)*. Polity.
McKinnon, K. (2020). Framing essay: the diversity of labour. In J. K. Gibson-Graham, & K. Dombroski (Eds.), *The handbook of diverse economies*. Edward Elgar Publishing, 116–128.
Moss, T., & Marvin, S. (2016). *Urban infrastructure in transition: networks, buildings and plans*. Routledge.
Nelson, A., & Schneider, F. (2019). *Housing for degrowth: Principles, models, challenges and opportunities*. Routledge.
Nygaard, B., & Hansen, T. (2021). Local development through the foundational economy? Priority-setting in Danish municipalities. *Local Economy: The Journal of the Local Economy Policy Unit*, 35(8), 768–786.
OECD (2009). *Declaration on green growth (adopted at the council meeting at ministerial level on 25 June 2009)*. OECD Publishing.
OECD (2011). *How's life? Measuring well-being*. OECD Publishing.
OECD (2014). *Greener skills and jobs. OECD green growth studies*. OECD Publishing.
Oekom (Ed.) (2020). *Möglichkeitsräume. Raumplanung im Zeichen des Postwachstums*. Politische Ökologie 160.
Paech, N. (2010). Eine Alternative zum Entkopplungsmythos: Die Postwachstumsökonomie. *Humane Wirtschaft*, 2010(5), 12–14.
Pansera, M., Ehlers, M.-H., & Kerschner, C. (2019). Unlocking wise digital techno-futures: Contributions from the degrowth community. *Futures*, (114), 102474.
Rodríguez-Giralt, I., Marrero-Guillamón, I., & Milstein, D. (2018). Reassembling activism, activating assemblages. *Social Movement Studies*, 17(3), 257–268.
Rosol, M. (2018). Alternative Ernährungsnetzwerke als Alternative Ökonomien. *Zeitschrift für Wirtschaftsgeographie*, 62(3-4), 174–186.
Schmelzer, M., & Vetter, A. (2019). *Degrowth/Postwachstum zur Einführung*. Junius.

Schmid, B. (2019). Degrowth and postcapitalism: Transformative geographies beyond accumulation and growth. *Geography Compass*, 13(11), e12470.

Schmid, B. (2020). *Making transformative geographies. Lessons from Stuttgart's community economy*. transcript.

Schmid, B., & Smith, T. S. (2020). Social transformation and postcapitalist possibility: Emerging dialogues between practice theory and diverse economies. *Progress in Human Geography*, 45(1), 030913252090564.

Schneidewind, U., & Zahrnt, A. (2014). *The Politics of Sufficiency*. oekom.

Schulz, C., & Bailey, I. (2014). The green economy and post-growth regimes: Opportunities and challenges for economic geography. *Geografiska Annaler B*, 96(3), 277–291.

Schulze Dieckhoff, V., & Lamker, C. (2017). Junges Forum NRW diskutiert Postwachstumsplanung. *Nachrichten der ARL*, 2017(3), 33–34.

Seidl, I., & Zahrnt, A. (2019). *Tätigsein in der Postwachstumsgesellschaft*. Metropolis Verlag.

Smith, A., Voß, J.-P., & Grin, J. (2010). Innovation studies and sustainability transitions: The allure of the multi-level perspective and its challenges. *Research and Policy*, 39(4), 435–448.

UNEP (2011). *Towards a green economy: Pathways to sustainable development and poverty eradication*. www.unep.org/greeneconomy

Zademach, H.-M., & Hillebrand, S. (2013). *Alternative economies and spaces. New perspectives for a sustainable economy*. transcript.

I. Spaces of Perspective

'Is there really a lack of conceptual ideas for alternative development models that are not based on material growth indicators? Or is it only a question of not daring to act?'

Frank Gwildis

Using socio-spatial concepts of situatedness to explain work processes in the context of post-growth economies

Hans-Joachim Bürkner, Bastian Lange

1. (Post)capitalist understandings of work

1.1 Questions and objectives

Geographical discussions about the possible forms and effects of nascent post-growth economies have thus far strangely excluded the category 'work'. Economic geography in particular has paid little attention to concrete forms of work and their influence on production structures, networks and spatial constructs. This seems particularly strange given that work, as a central component of economic processes, should be an immediate focus of the discipline. It is therefore necessary to develop a perspective on post-growth that places the category 'work' and its particular socio-spatial implications at the centre of consideration.

Of especial relevance here are social innovations that penetrate economic fields in somewhat unpredictable ways. This extends considerably beyond the horizons of economic analyses. Such analyses have usually linked work directly with economic processes and structures, which in turn have been devised as subordinated to the basic logic of capitalist economic activity. This has remained accepted practice even when considering marginal areas of economics, irritating as they often are for economists. For example, although in recent years concepts of economic innovation have been discussed in terms of their receptiveness for further social impulses, the fundamental growth postulates of the current global economic system have remained unaffected by this. Viewed from this perspective, 'user innovation' or 'open innovation', with which ingenious enterprises use external knowledge and tap into low-cost resources, serves the continued pursuit of growth and unconditional profit maximisation (see Brinks 2019).

The problem of adequately describing changed work processes is thus more complicated than it may initially appear, since it involves nothing less than breaking up the traditional concepts of 'production', 'consumption' and 'market' as fixed points of convergence for capitalist economic activities. New forms of work, which have developed outside formal economic structures, have an experimental and often emancipatory character that requires attention to be paid to flexible arrangements and links between social practice, the economy and spatial development. What is needed here is an intensive examination of the diverse meanings and social consequences of the co-evolution of technological and social innovations (Blättel-Mink 2010).

Technological innovations reach far into social activities and transform almost all social spheres but are relatively easy to investigate, as they are close to traditional disciplinary concerns and require only a slightly different focus. In comparison, the analysis of social innovations, and their relevance for economic and technological innovation, is more difficult. They are highly dependent on context, so that the focus must clearly be on analysing social forms of practice (Howaldt/Schwarz 2010a: 30 ff., 66).

This chapter aims to provide some food for thought on tackling these tasks from the perspective of spatial socio-economic research. In light of the limited role played by social innovations in the theories of economic geography to date, we make this field the starting point of our considerations. We introduce the term 'situated social innovation' to refer to the linking of innovation processes to social communities and specific social constructs of space (Section 6). At the same time, we show that in the course of the quasi-natural and uncontrolled development of an everyday culture of post-growth (Hagen/Rückert-John 2016), work processes are also being redefined, and are in turn accompanied by changed situational constructs of space.

1.2 Structure of the discussion

Due to the comprehensive embedding of social innovations in social forms of practice, we adopt a context-oriented view on work. It not only focuses on original, new kinds of work processes, but also on mixed transitional forms located between classic gainful employment and 'atypical' work not subject to the pressure of profit. Accordingly, we pay particular attention to hybrid work practices, which can be recognised in the transitional area between hobbies, voluntary work, self-organised or freelance work and formalised gainful employment and its variants (part-time, full-time). These heterogeneous forms of work and their practices often do not follow a clear development logic. They emerge more or less contingently and unplanned in situ, i. e. in places where complex, multidimensional social practice is located. From the perspective of spatial science, the task is thus to capture their particular situatedness. We assume that work is always situated, i. e. embedded in certain spatial-social contexts that give it particular characteristics. Situatedness and concrete characteristics must therefore be established as central objects of the analysis of post-growth economies. Last but not least, this requires a change in approaches to spatial relations by the geographical sub-disciplines, especially economic geography.

2. Transformation of work: cornerstones and forms of practice

2.1 'New work'?

In current descriptions of societal futures, numerous concepts of work are being brought into position. On the one hand, there are the promises of a digitalised world of work, which should optimise existing industrial and technological structures. This primarily involves more flexibility and efficiency in the design of work processes, increased performance, the easy organisation of multilocal production and services, and technical omnipotentiality (Apt/Bovenschulte/Hartmann et al. 2016). Such notions are related to the first waves of digitalisation that swept through the core areas of industry and drove robotisation and automation within enterprises, known as 'Industry 4.0'. They also address more recent processes of digitalisation which appear as new forms of the internet-based platform and gig economy and as crowdworking, and penetrate deep into the organisation of individualised wage labour and pseudo self-employment outside of enterprises.

On the other hand, in accordance with the credo of 'new work' (Bergmann 2019 [1988]), alternative concepts of work are developing that are based on changed social premises. Thus in more recent post-growth debates, work is addressed in strikingly anti-technical and reductionist terms with an emphasis on self-sufficiency. It follows that work in the future should be freely chosen, socially embedded, community-oriented and people-centred, with independently scheduled working hours and a positive energy balance (Schmelzer/Vetter 2019; Chatterton/Pusey 2019).

Such ideas are influenced by the conviction that new arrangements of economic activities should relate to what is humanly desirable. The emancipatory project of post-growth economies not only criticises the materially and ecologically disastrous resource consumption of growth-oriented industrial production, it also calls for new, self-determined work processes. Critiques of economic growth imperatives therefore include consideration of the dominant working conditions in both the global South and the global North. Accordingly, discriminatory and exploitative work is increasingly organised digitally. It is thus the 'ground troops for globalisation' (Busche 2001, translated from German) who are primarily burdened with the social costs of technological change. Micro jobs, a lack of legal protection and the strategic exploitation of differences in prosperity weaken the position of those who in any case have little say in the purpose and organisation of work.

2.2 The emancipatory critique of dominant working conditions

As an emancipatory counterproposal, the post-growth debate bases the concept of work on the postulate of structural autonomy. The definition of work no longer focuses on profit and economic gain but rather takes heterogeneous forms and contexts of work into equal consideration. Liberation from the dictates of profit presupposes the existence of multiple counter-positions: they must be anti-consumerist, anti-neoliberal and anti-hegemonic and draw orientation from an appropriate pyramid of needs (Seidl/Zahrnt 2019, 924). At the same time, new technologies are seen as a way of achieving this liberation. Digitally organised access to resources, tools and knowledge seems to provide important bottom-up options for action. Another counter-position to the autonomy postulate propagates the transition to a societal state of post-work (Chatterton/Pusey 2019; Pitts/Dinerstein 2017). This is based on calls for the general abolition of industrial work, the safeguarding of livelihoods through a minimum income and the structural decoupling of work and the economy.

Such postulates abandon well-known social theory and risk theoretical paradoxes. Thus, on the one hand, the debate considers work as the abstract negation of a neoliberally distorted concept of work, which leads to calls to overcome capitalist principles of production. On the other hand, work – drawing on the evolutionary perspective of 'new work' – is elevated to a utopian instrument of liberation that does not necessarily have to free itself from the conventional rationality of the system. This makes the emancipation project of post-growth less and less clearly definable. Furthermore, the theoretical definition of 'work' and its functions for post-growth economies also runs the risk of getting caught in a maelstrom of speculation, eclecticism and epistemological arbitrariness. For contemporary social and spatial science, the focus is therefore primarily on understanding the way in which social practice is moving away from the affirmative and eclectic expectations of innovation and growth of the past. At the same time, the paths leading to alternative work processes must be empirically and theoretically reconstructed and their emancipatory substance analysed. It is, however, not enough to merely observe the practical consequences of political-normative demands on individuals ('Change your lifestyle!'). The onus is rather on taking the intrinsic logics and autonomy postulates of the workers themselves seriously. It is thus indispensable to obtain and develop reliable analytical approaches to the concrete starting points, characteristic features and social contexts of heterogeneous forms of work.

2.3 Work processes in post-growth spaces

In the 2010s, new phenotypes of work attracted increasing public attention. Work processes that are carried out in makerspaces, real labs, fab labs, open workshops and co-working spaces do not fit into the descriptive categories of economics and business studies. They can no longer be clearly assigned to traditional entrepreneurial or wage-dependent forms of work (in the sense of labour) (Krueger/Schulz/Gibbs 2017), nor can they be simply described by the attribute 'new' (as used in the term 'new work' in descriptions of post-industrial change undertaken by the social sciences; Bergmann 2019[1988]). It is also insufficient to view them it as an 'atypical' residual category of flexibilised industrial work (see Schiek/Apitzsch 2013), since this largely ignores their social contexts. Similarly, labelling such forms of work as unpaid, voluntary and personally motivated and classifying them under the heading 'amateur economy' misses the point, as this implies an ex-ante contrast to the category of a 'professional economy' with paid employment (see Sekulova/Kallis/Rodríguez-Labajos, 2013: 4). In fact, however, recent work processes of this kind are mostly situated in heterogeneous social practice contexts – located between hobbies, the flexible everyday appropriation of digital technologies, digitally based prototypical small-scale production, early forms of start-ups, and expanding economies of sharing and making (Carr/Gibson 2015; Chatterton/Pusey 2019).

2.4 The hybridisation of work

The 'new' open forms of work are de-standardised and autonomously organised. They are based on taking on manual tasks and handicrafts, freshly acquired digital expertise and informal elements of practice that were often previously viewed as unproductive or reproductive. As they cannot be understood as deviating from a specific standard but involve rather individual and collective explorations and experiments, they are not described here as 'atypical'.

Such 'open work' can be linked to gainful employment, but often exists independently of it. It is clearly a hybrid phenomenon with links to both the social and the economic. A key characteristic is the strong orientation of workers towards social communities and peer groups (Simons/Petschow/Peuckert 2016). They prioritise social motives and independent, non-hierarchical work contexts over organisations and their requirements. Actors largely develop their interests and abilities independently and enter into open communication with like-minded people. They negotiate the exchange of knowledge, materials and ideas. They tolerate different competences and the emergence of small organisational elites that set up and manage the various working environments. This community practice leads to the transformation of what were originally do-it-yourself attitudes into a kind of do-it-together attitude (Smith/Fressoli/Abrol et al. 2017). Collective discovery and practice create meaning and special social and symbolic rewards quite apart from the concrete results of the work.

The recent socio-economic hybridisation of work poses considerable conceptual problems for politics and spatial sciences. In areas characterised by the diffusion of forms of work that cannot be clearly located in economic terms, the social and economic fields involved are increasingly diffuse and changeable. Thus, for example, the collective search for new mobility infrastructures has become highly ambivalent. As the case of the ridesharing provider Uber shows, social goals (i. e. sharing with no profit) are undermined by the quasi-employment of drivers, while the economic side of such work develops outside of state security systems and fails to comply with minimum social standards (Rogers 2017). It is very hard to adequately categorise such phenomena; nevertheless, they have expanded the range of 'diverse' and pluralistic understandings of work beyond an income-oriented economic understanding (Gibson-Graham 2008; North 2016; White/Williams 2016).

It is therefore unsurprising that conventional ideas about the emergence of economic spatial constructs can no longer be viewed with conviction. We need only to refer here to the stagnating political discussions concerning regional innovation clusters, which in the past always assumed an extremely specialised and highly qualified workforce would be available within dynamic enterprises. Other innovative work contexts have only recently been considered relevant for development, e. g. in connection with 'open innovation', the appropriation of external innovation potential by commercial enterprises (Beise-Zee 2014). This draws the attention of the wider professional public to temporary clusters and also to changing aggregations of business-related communication processes.

3. Formal economies and work typologies

3.1 The spatial transformation of work

A similar fixation on formal economies and work typologies has been evident in the economic and social science debate on the transformation of economic spaces. Since the 1990s, economic geography in particular has adopted a more or less linear logic of space with reference to economic activity, one in which the spatial proximity or distance of economic actors to one another functions as an important causal and interpretative variable (Coenen/Raven/Verbong 2010). Only since about 2005 has the discussion increasingly recognised that digitalisation, virtualisation, globalisation, new production technologies and 'atypical' forms of work have led to the proliferation of possible relations of proximity and distance (Reichwald/Piller 2006; Ibert 2010; Ibert/Hautala/Jauhiainen 2015; Butzin/Meyer 2020). Not only has the new complexity of these relationships been noted, but doubts have also been expressed about whether such relations have general significance for spatial development. Proximity is now rather understood as processual, reflexive and often temporary. It is viewed as a phenomenon of practice with variable effects that is difficult to reliably address ex ante (Eckhardt 2019). Digitalisation and the emergence of online platform economies are thus creating new hybrid forms of work and an unexpected diversification of spatial relations (Autio/Nambisan/Thomas et al. 2018; Brettel/Friederichsen/Keller et al. 2014; Carr/Gibson 2015; Ravenelle 2017). This is also leading to new socio-spatial inequalities, asynchronous development and different degrees of political anticipation.

3.2 Multiplicity of spatial relations: a challenge for economic geography

Unexpectedly and often initially unnoticed, multiple relationships between actors and attributable spatialities have emerged – between the co-presence of actors at physically localised workplaces, focused communication in protected global data channels, the open interaction of heterogeneous actors in online social networks, activities on topic-related internet platforms, blogs and forums, and finally the temporary arrangement of projects and events within and outside organisations and social communities.

While inquiring into the nature of these relationships, the focus must also be on how the localisation processes of new forms of production and consumption can be conceived without – as so often in the past – immediately deriving or suggesting that physical spatiality has any kind of primacy simply because of the mere existence of a physical place of work (e. g. in a concrete urban neighbourhood). Although physical places should still be approached as a 'hard' condition of social and economic activities, they are nevertheless linked to other diverse conceptual, symbolic and material contexts (Butzin/Meier 2020). Their social and economic meanings must first be attentively ascertained before the theoretical relevance of a physical place can be asserted. All too often in the past, spatial research gave in to the temptations of appealing political catchwords: it adopted labels that were previously established by politicians and economic actors. The 'creative urban neighbourhoods' of the 2000s are only one well-known example of this uncritical adoption of crude spatial abstractions (see Merkel 2008). In this respect, spatial physicality is always to be understood as a phenomenon integrated in multiple disciplinary discourses and the ongoing interdisciplinary negotiation of spatial imaginaries (Watkins 2015).

4. Variants of post-capitalist forms of work

Although different crafts, e. g. screen printing, woodworking, digital printing, fabric processing, metalworking and software creation, may each represent a starting point for exploration, they have one feature in common: the individual design dimensions and forms of processing only emerge in the course of a collaborative process of discovery. The focus of everyday practice is on the gradually emerging 'product' development options and their modification, and on the practice of independently developed processing routines. It is not only local working communities that define themselves in this way, but also small social movements that propagate a transition from discovery to competent work and processing. In the USA, the actors involved often refer to themselves as 'ProAms' (Professional Amateurs) or regard themselves as part of a larger craftsmanship movement that focuses on rediscovering manual skills and crafting qualities in amateur, often urban, everyday realities (Sennett 2008).

4.1 Crafters, tinkerers, makers

To take the discussion a step further, this sort of community focus, which is clearly revealed in everyday practices of self-empowerment, self-organisation and self-direction, can be related to more fundamental post-capitalist and post-growth economic values (Baier/Hansing/Müller et al. 2016). Many actors understand their work as part of a countermovement to the growth ideology of currently dominant variants of capitalism, offering a contrast with an increased focus on discovery and the processual configuration of alternative forms of production, work and life. This is not always obvious. Thus, for instance, those involved in the newly popular maker-movement seldom tend to use blatant post-growth or degrowth rhetoric.

Nevertheless, the participants have a community-based and practical self-image with an unmistakable focus on exploring alternatives to the ubiquitous routines of generating growth. Here, the everyday routines of economic activity already involve repairing, maintaining, prolonging usage, sharing and exchanging without the use of money. These practices are directed towards social needs and the principle of sufficiency.

4.2 Universalists and prosumers

Furthermore, types of actors have emerged who see themselves as new universalists: as prosumers who take the development, production and distribution of products into their own hands or directly influence the production of goods by other actors (Hellmann 2010). These include creative freelancers engaged in translocal networking projects, spontaneous value creation and experimental discovery processes in mobile workspaces (co-working spaces, home offices, cafes etc.) (Bender 2013); niche actors engaged in DIY production and repair; and participants in a subculture of informally organised sharing – both in the local neighbourhood and across the globe as internet-based exchange systems and issue-oriented communities.

All these actors have not only tried out new things and often developed experimental forms of work, they have also formally reversed the supply-oriented logic of capitalist economies. Demand, which is largely socially defined, is the focus of the new activities and makes it possible to develop flexible starting points for new value creation processes. These processes are then no longer subordinated to universal competitive economic logic. The relevant socio-economic fields are often social communities with their particular collective values and needs rather than 'the market' with its monetary exchange mechanisms.

4.3 Post-growth work

The conceptualisation of post-growth work must therefore take into account that the focus is always on hybrid forms of work. Working within such social communities means assigning a subordinate position to profit and income generation in the individual and collective hierarchy of values. The social and economic purposes and objectives of work exist side by side. There are not necessarily any links between them, nor do they always compete with one another. Work need not be separated from processes of self-discovery and the associated self-positioning of actors in a group or a community of practitioners. At the same time, practices of do-it-together bring actors into locally interwoven but readily comprehensible contexts of communication, distribution and consumption. Compared to dependent wage labour, the new workers enjoy a high degree of autonomy and self-empowerment. This predestines them for social roles that in a capitalist economy are only granted to individual entrepreneurs, for example as agents of the 'trial and error' principle, of social innovation and of the creative invention of products and processes.

It is no coincidence that associations with Joseph Schumpeter's ideal type of creative entrepreneur spring to mind. However, this association cannot be pursued too far, because Schumpeter's entrepreneur must always avert economic ruin and, in the interest of growth, must channel creativity towards destroying the old and inventing the new, instead of using creativity for non-profit purposes like a social entrepreneur (Löffler 2013). There is of course another story here, in that even social entrepreneurs are required to submit to competitive pressures and market conditions. However, in protected realms of work, community-oriented workers can at least temporarily combine 'free and creative' making with the powerful environmental conditions of 'competition' and 'market survival'.

As promising as this perspective may be for further conceptualisation, the preconditions of actor constitutions must nevertheless be fundamentally addressed. More specifically, attention must be paid to the particular forms and logics of social innovations that enable active creators to influence the form and setting of their work. The aim is to determine more precisely the innovative content of the action focus on communities, alternative networks, social or economic niches and non-economic rationalities, and to trace its effects on forms of work and the attributable spatial constructs.

5. Social innovations as drivers of new forms of work and attributable spatial constructs

5.1 The embedding and practices of social innovations

Recent interdisciplinary approaches to the topic of social innovation question many of the sweeping assumptions about the direct sectoral effects of inventing and disseminating new goods or economic procedures. They draw attention to the fact that innovations need to be accepted by society and are therefore always socially mediated. This mediation can occur within industries, social communities, milieus or similar sub-fields of society. Economic innovations in the narrower sense are thus always linked to social innovations that involve a change in the purposes, uses, effects and socio-spatial ranges (i. e. scales) of goods and services (Howaldt/Schwarz 2010b).

Moreover, the fixed temporal sequencing of technical innovations (first the invention, then the actual innovation in the form of dissemination, acceptance and the discursive labelling of new or changed goods and technologies) is replaced by variable temporal relations. Socially initiated or mediated 'inventions' can occur at the same time as their implementation – i. e. in the actual execution of social practices. Thanks to their anchoring in practice, they do not necessarily need to be labelled as innovations before they are disseminated. In this respect, it seems that a variable co-evolution of technical and social innovations can be assumed, which leaves great scope for both the success and the failure of experiments.

The shift from a technicistic worldview focusing on the mastery of nature by technology to a mindset focusing on resource conservation and sustainability can be viewed as a macro-social innovation that affects the 'subordinate' spheres of society as well as the individual subjects. Exogenous, universal innovations of this kind require individuals and small collectives to creatively adapt to set development models, while endogenous innovations follow their own intrinsic logic to a greater extent. They invite further experimentation – in the sense of open-ended trial and error – and are less predictable (Brandsen/Evers/Cattacin et al. 2016: 310).

5.2 Post-growth economies as social innovations?

New ways of thinking, norms and moral standards have so far tended to be regarded as exogenous innovations. Such classifications have quickly become established in the rather fundamental debates held on post-growth and post-capitalism. However, at the grassroots level the concerns of the philosophical-ideological protagonists of the post-growth transformation (e. g. Paech 2012; Mason/Gebauer 2016) are often perceived as strange and somewhat detached from reality. The norms and values they formulate are received by the practitioners but must always be compared with their own factual everyday experience. Such exogenous innovations easily reach their limitations.

Degrowth and post-growth are then often no longer the main things but are rather almost side-effects of collective success in an open workshop or a 3-D printing lab. Problematic endogenous-exogenous couplings can thus be identified for every sub-area of society (e. g. a socio-economic field). It becomes difficult to bring together the local dynamics of change in forms of work, modes of production and consumption habits on the one hand and overarching ideological, economic and cultural changes on the other hand. As a result, the co-evolution and co-existence of different reference systems (grassroots practice as opposed to ideological superstructure) are more likely than convincing mediation and integration.

Social innovations and their couplings thus require the opening of conceptual approaches beyond the demand for new and better social theory (for instance in the sense of Howaldt/Schwarz 2010a). As Jaeger-Erben, John and Rückert-John (2017) have pointed out, a social theory approaches its subject matter with a logic of subsumption that inevitably leads to the misinterpretation of experiments, demands for freedom in the use of products and activities, seemingly independent testing and other social practices. It attributes actors with an intentionality that they perhaps do not possess, or not in the way assumed. The promise of a better future generally associated with the term 'social innovation' (Jaeger-Erben/John/Rückert-John 2017: 246) immediately leads to demands for this future to be politically controlled. However, this ignores the experimental character of innovations and the right of experimenters to freedom of scope and freedom from the external exploitation of what they have just discovered or found – not to mention their right to fail.

5.3 From the social niche to the entrepreneurial world?

Applied to the phenomenon of new forms of work, this means that not everything that society as a whole regards as a social innovation has to be one. It may rather be a case of attempting to tame norm-defying actors within a given set of power relations. To return to our current case: when makers and users of open workshops use their tinkering and experimentation to develop potential (or actual) business ideas with a public-good focus and to become (socially) entrepreneurial, this is often seen as a successful social innovation, since it represents economic upscaling out of a niche, which is in turn associated with economic innovations (Schmid 2019; Lange/Domann/Häfele

2016). However, what is seldom taken into account is that this can lead to the annexing of the lifeworld 'below' by outsiders, covertly denying that the social innovation is justified and advocating instead for 'correct' (i. e. institutionalised) paths of innovation.

Conceptual, symbolic and material expropriations of innovators may be undertaken by political institutions (economic development policy), scientific institutions (including economic geographers who claim that this upscaling is unexpectedly useful for urban and regional development) and economic actors (e. g. niche competitors who cannot draw on a specific innovation in a current debate). Others who may be involved in expropriation emerge in situ (in cities mostly in the form of city marketing with a focus on urban creativity) and under the influence of prominent elites (e. g. media leaders).

Social innovators are thus confronted with the necessity of defending from takeover the painstakingly defined socio-technical domains (e. g. digital competence), corresponding social spaces and especially the curating communities. This can be temporarily achieved by retreating into less accessible subcultures and exclusive practices. However, such a retreat is increasingly at odds with the post-capitalist demand for publicly accessible knowledge bases, procedures and blueprints (see the papers in Baier/Hansing/Müller et al. 2016). DIY (do it yourself) and DIT (do it together) technologies, the insistence on free access to public domains and the re(establishment) of technically advanced products fit for everyday use are all only possible in the public sphere. However, this public accessibility renders innovators vulnerable and easy to marginalise by institutionally established actors.

6. Cornerstones of the 'situated social innovations' perspective

In practice, makerspaces, open workshops and co-working spaces are open spaces. They encourage the actors involved to experiment within the community, to embark on self-discovery, to communicate openly with peers and to further develop a supportive community. Looking over each other's shoulders when exploring new things, sharing knowledge and also tolerating the temporary knowledge advantages of others may seem risky to many people who have been socialised in a neoliberal, competitive society, but it is also very enticing (Simons/Petschow/Peuckert 2016: 20 ff.).

Social spaces that emerge in the form of local communities at a specific location (e. g. meeting place, workshop) result from attempts to make targeted use of the work-specific materiality of crafts, tools, working spaces and visible labelling, as in the example of the 'Makerspace Rhein-Neckar'[1]. At the same time, they symbolically and materially safeguard what has been achieved, enable the dissemination of new working practices and bring together interested parties in a visible place. The socio-material elements of these places emerge in part through the working techniques and practices, but they also result from erratic searching and chance encounters. As open-source spaces, it remains possible to change them collectively and to simultaneously shape them individually.

This variability and the open-endedness of design is an expression of a process that we call 'situated social innovation'. New forms of work are situated when they relate to a social community that encourages individuals in their experimentation (cf. Rogowska-Stangret 2018) and protects them against appropriation from outside (for use in an established model or a political role, for example to showcase seemingly vibrant or diverse urban development). The collective adoption of attitudes and practices of experimentation is the real social innovation. It is always temporary and can be superseded or its importance relativised by the next community initiative. The approach focuses on social forms of practice in the context of work, especially those that draw on diverse, internet-based communication and everyday technological adaptation processes.

Due to the processuality and open-ended variability of social practices, the actors involved each develop temporary and context-related spatial constructs. These constructs are also fundamentally situated because in practice the actors each work in a concrete but changeable place, be this a social place (community, organisation, meeting place), a physical workplace (office, workshop, desktop) or an identifiable virtual communication node (virtual network, IP address).

Situatedness is made up not only of communalisation processes and their material safeguards in the form of physical spatial components; it also takes place through openings into virtual spaces, as exemplified by the

---

1 See https://www.makerspace-rheinneckar.de/ (21.02.2020)

maker movement. Makers, tinkerers and sharers have long since integrated the world of the internet, social networks and blog-based interaction with important makers into their own communication practice. The impulses for new fields of experimentation, community action and fairs (e. g. the emblematic Maker Fairs) originate largely from the USA and the first communities that popularised the maker idea (see the description by the US makerspace-guru Dale Dougherty[2]).

Here, individual users worldwide can still receive concrete support and advice. The situating is realised by selectively using virtual means to bring the relevant global communities and their members to a specific local point. Seen from the perspective of the local actors, the emerging spatial construct also extends variably into virtual spaces, driven by interest or curiosity. The continuous changing of this oscillating spatial construct, its expansion and contraction in line with the collective nurturing (curation) of the experimental (as a modus operandi), represents an important peculiarity and at the same time a central condition for the further development of the respective communities and their forms of practice.

In this sense, the task here is not to carefully observe the Marxian 'state of the productive forces', but rather the state and the continuous change of the 'experimental forces'. Important drivers, the directions of movement and the effects of experimental activities must be reconstructed empirically and theoretically. Jaeger-Erben/John/Rückert-John (2017) have already advocated the utilisation of a theory of social change rather than more static social theory. The extent to which such a theory already includes entrenched assumptions about social structures, relations and processes that stand in the way of the unconditional reconstruction of open experimentation has yet to be demonstrated in the concrete reconstruction of a specific case.

A spatial science that is primarily interested in Euclidean distances or even in the observation of structurally determined social distances will find few opportunities for engagement here. Only if structure-fixated thinking is abandoned in favour of variable, multidimensional and reflexive processes of spatial construction (beyond the geographical fix) will more satisfactory explanations emerge in the foreseeable future.

Even where it has already been recognised that social proximity does not necessarily correlate with physical proximity (e. g. in research on co-pres-

---

2 https://makezine.com/author/dalepd/ (21.02.2020)

ence and co-location, see Grabher/Melchior/Schiemer et al. 2018), it could be deceptive to hope that minimal course correction will suffice. The case of a makerspace will remain obscure if it is approached with harboured hopes of discovering physical correlates of the social or economic. The actors are then viewed as demonstrating apparently familiar patterns of 'innovation through physical proximity', although in reality the virtual spaces of reference to similar communities of enthusiasts are much more relevant for shaping their everyday work. Hence it is necessary to make a conscious decision to embark on a reconstruction of multidimensional spatial oscillations to get closer to the phenomenon.

7. The 'spaces of work' perspective and post-growth questions: an initial résumé

A decisive move towards work-related forms of practice allows economic determinisms in the descriptions and explanations of more or less fixed 'spaces of economic activity' to recede from the centre of attention. The focus then shifts to the social penetration of economic processes and activities. The diversity of forms of work is associated with the multiple ways in which actors deal with their social and material environment – including the apparent rejection of commercial exploitation when testing new technologies, the profit-free provision of products and services for a community, and even the transition of small-scale work and production concepts into entrepreneurial livelihoods and formalised employment relationships. This diversity and polymorphism of forms of work is linked to a fundamentally open socio-materiality of the constructs of place and space. New spaces stretch across temporary virtual places and spheres of communication on the one hand and physical places of co-present work on the other. This openness means that the constructs of space are fluid and cannot be conceived as static spatial structures or as a systematically generated spatial fix – in the sense of a spatial manifestation of social or economic processes.

In particular, ideas for products, services and work processes emerge from everyday post-growth practices and are communicated to actors through virtual, multilateral channels, but it is seldom that these ideas are clearly traceable to their places of origin. They are thus rarely localisable. Under these conditions, it is fairly clear that there is no such thing as 'the' location of 'the' post-growth innovation. Analogously, it must be assumed that we are dealing with spaces that are multi-dimensionally constituted, i. e. simultaneously virtualised, globalised and localised. They arise from situated innovation processes that also initiate translocal forms of post-growth. This must be addressed in detail by a modified analytical reconstruction of the diverse, processual constructions of space in the context of new post-growth forms of work.

Cited literature

Apt, W., Bovenschulte, M., Hartmann, E. A., & Wischmann, St. (2016). Foresight-Studie 'Digitale Arbeitswelt'. Research Report of the Bundesministerium für Arbeit und Soziales 463. https://www.ssoar.info/ssoar/handle/document/47039 (2016, June 14).

Autio, E., Nambisan, S., Thomas, L. D. W., & Wright, M. (2018). Digital affordances, spatial affordances, and the genesis of entrepreneurial ecosystems. *Strategic Entrepreneurship Journal*, 12(1), 72–95.

Baier, A., Hansing, T., Müller, C., & Werner, K. (Eds.) (2016). *Die Welt reparieren: Open Source und Selbermachen als postkapitalistische Praxis*. transcript.

Beise-Zee, M. (2014). Regionale Innovationscluster und internationale Netzwerkkompetenz. In C. Schultz, & K. Hölzle (Eds.), *Motoren der Innovation. Zukunftsperspektiven der Innovationsforschung*. Springer, 295310.

Bender, D. (2013). Mobile Arbeitsplätze als kreative Räume: Coworking Spaces, Cafés und andere urbane Arbeitsorte. transcript.

Bergmann, F. (2019). New work new culture: Work we want and a culture that strengthens us (Original word published 1988). transcript.

Blättel-Mink, B. (2010). Innovation und Kultur am Beispiel von Crowdsourcing. Herausforderung für die Innovationsforschung. In J. Howaldt, & H. Jacobsen (Eds.), *Soziale Innovation. Auf dem Weg zu einem postindustriellen Innovationsparadigma*. Wiesbaden, 127–142.

Brandsen, T., Evers, A., Cattacin, S., & Zimmer, A. (2016). The good, the bad and the ugly in social innovation. In T. Brandsen, S. Cattacin, A. Evers, & A. Zimmer (Eds.), *Social innovations in the urban context*. Springer, 303–310.

Brettel, M., Friederichsen, N., Keller, M., & Rosenberg, M. (2014). How virtualization, decentralization and network building change the manufacturing landscape: An industry 4.0 perspective. *International Journal of Mechanical, Aerospace, Industrial and Mechatronics Engineering, 8*(1), 37–44.

Brinks, V. (2019). 'And since I knew about the possibilities there ...': The role of open creative labs in user innovation processes. *Tijdschrift voor economische en sociale geografie 110*(4), 381–394.

Busche, A. (2001, July 17). Bodentruppen für die Globalisierung. *taz, die tageszeitung.* https://taz.de/Bodentruppen-fuer-die-Globalisierung/!1161619/.

Butzin, A., & Meyer, K. (2020). Urbane Produktion und temporäre räumliche Nähe in Produktionsprozessen. *Raumforschung Und Raumordnung Spatial Research and Planning, 78*(1), 5–20.

Carr, Ch., & Gibson, Ch. (2015). Geographies of making: Rethinking materials and skills for volatile futures. *Progress in Human Geography, 40*(3), 297–315.

Chatterton, P., & Pusey, A. (2019). Beyond capitalist enclosure, commodification and alienation: Postcapitalist praxis as commons, social production and useful doing. *Progress in Human Geography.* (2019, January 8).

Coenen, L., Raven, R., & Verbong, G. (2010). Local niche experimentation in energy transitions: a theoretical and empirical exploration of proximity advantages and disadvantages. *Technology in Society, 32*(4), 295–302.

Eckhardt, F. (2019). Technologie und Virtualität. In F. Kessl, & Ch. Reutlinger (Eds.), *Handbuch Sozialraum. Grundlagen für den Bildungs- und Sozialbereich.* 2nd edition. Springer, 243–258.

Gibson-Graham, J. K. (2008). Diverse economies: performative practices for 'other worlds'. *Progress in Human Geography, 32*(5), 613–632.

Grabher, G., Melchior, A., Schiemer, B., Schüßler, E., & Sydow, J. (2018). From being there to being aware: Confronting geographical and sociological imaginations of copresence. *Environment and Planning A: Economy and Space, 50*(1), 245–255.

Hagen, K., & Rückert-John, J. (2016). Teilen, tauschen, leihen – tragfähige Modelle zukünftigen Wirtschaftens? Editorial. *Vierteljahrshefte zur Wirtschaftsforschung, 85*(2), 5–12.

Hellmann, K.-U. (2010). Prosumer Revisited: Zur Aktualität einer Debatte. Eine Einführung. In B. Blättel-Mink, & K.-U. Hellmann (Eds.), *Prosumer Revisited. Zur Aktualität einer Debatte.* Springer, 13–48.

Howaldt, J., & Schwarz, M. (2010a). *»Soziale Innovation« im Fokus: Skizze eines gesellschaftstheoretisch inspirierten Forschungskonzepts.* transcript.

Howaldt, J., & Schwarz, M.(2010b). Soziale Innovation – Konzepte, Forschungsfelder und -perspektiven. In J. Howaldt, & H. Jacobsen (Eds.), *Soziale Innovation. Auf dem Weg zu einem postindustriellen Innovationsparadigma*. Springer, 87–108.

Ibert, O. (2010). Relational distance. Sociocultural and time-spatial tensions in innovation practices. *Environment and Planning*, A(42), 187–204.

Ibert, O., Hautala, J., & Jauhiainen, J. S. (2015). From cluster to process: New economic geographic perspectives on practices of knowledge creation. *Geoforum*, 65, 323–327.

Jaeger-Erben, M., John, R., & Rückert-John, J. (2017). Soziale Innovation: Verheißung oder Verführung? *GAIA - Ecological Perspectives for Science and Society*, 26(3), 245–248.

Krueger, R., Schulz, Ch., & Gibbs, D. C. (2017). Institutionalizing alternative economic spaces? An interpretivist perspective on diverse economies. *Progress in Human Geography*, 42(4), 569–589.

Lange, B., Domann, V., & Häfele, V. (2016): Wertschöpfung in offenen Werkstätten. Eine empirische Erhebung kollaborativer Praktiken in Deutschland. IÖW publication series, 213/16.

Löffler, M. (2013). Der Schumpeterianische Unternehmer als fragwürdiges Vorbild für Social Entrepreneurs. *Kurswechsel*, 2/2013, 16–27.

Mason, P., & Gebauer, S. (2016). *Postkapitalismus. Grundrisse einer kommenden Ökonomie*. Suhrkamp.

Merkel, J. (2008). *Kreativquartiere. Urbane Milieus zwischen Inspiration und Prekarität*. Springer.

North, P. (2016). The business of the Anthropocene? Substantivist and diverse economies perspectives on SME engagement in local low carbon transitions. *Progress of Human Geography*, 40(4), 437-454.

Paech, N. (2012). *Befreiung vom Überfluss. Auf dem Weg in die Postwachstumsökonomie*. oekom verlag.

Pitts, F. H., & Dinerstein, A. C. (2017). Postcapitalism, basic income and the end of work: A critique and alternative. *Bath Papers in International Development and Wellbeing* 55.https://www.econstor.eu/bitstream/10419/180927/1/100921179X.pdf (2020, January 1).

Ravenelle, A. J. (2017). Sharing economy workers: selling, not sharing. *Cambridge Journal of Regions, Economy and Society*, 10(2), 281–295.

Reichwald, R., & Piller, F. (2006). Interaktive Wertschöpfung. Open Innovation, Individualisierung und neue Formen der Arbeitsteilung. Gabler Verlag.

Rogers, B. (2017). The social costs of Uber. *University of Chicago Law Review Online*, 82(1), 85–102.

Rogowska-Stangret, M. (2018). Situated Knowledges. *New Materialism: Almanac.* https://newmaterialism.eu/almanac/s/situated-knowledges.html (2019, July 21).

Schiek, D., & Apitzsch, B. (2013). Doing Work. Atypische Arbeit in der Film- und der Automobilbranche im Vergleich. *Berliner Journal Für Soziologie*, 23(2), 181–204.

Schmelzer, M., & Vetter, A. (2019). *Degrowth/Postwachstum zur Einführung.* Junius Verlag.

Schmid, B. (2019). Degrowth and postcapitalism: Transformative geographies beyond accumulation and growth. *Geography Compass*, 13(11), 49.

Seidl, I., & Zahrnt, A. (2019). Neugewichtung von Erwerbsarbeit und Tätigsein für eine Postwachstumsgesellschaft. Ökologisches Wirtschaften - Fachzeitschrift, 33(1), 17.

Sekulova, F., Kallis, G., Rodríguez-Labajos, B. Schneider, F. (2013). Degrowth: from theory to practice. *Journal of Cleaner Production*, 38, 1–6.

Sennett, R. (2008). *The craftsman*. 2nd edition. Penguin Books Ltd.

Simons, A., Petschow, U., & Peuckert, J. (2016). *Offene Werkstätten – nachhaltig innovativ? Potenziale gemeinsamen Arbeitens und Produzierens in der gesellschaftlichen Transformation.* IÖW publication series 212/16.

Smith, A., Fressoli, M., Abrol, D., Arond, E., & Ely, A. (2017). *Grassroots innovation movements.* Taylor and Francis.

Watkins, J. (2015). Spatial imaginaries research in geography: Synergies, tensions, and new directions. *Geography Compass*, 9(9), 508–522.

White, R., & Williams, C. (2016). Beyond capitalocentrism: are non-capitalist work practices 'alternatives'? *Area*, 48(3), 325–331.

Spatial strategies for a post-growth transformation

Benedikt Schmid

1. Introduction

It becomes increasingly obvious that there is a disjuncture between the socio-economic developments that lead to increasing destabilisation and exploitation of ecological and social systems on the one hand and scientific concerns about these developments on the other hand. Research into possible forms of socio-ecological transformation is gaining corresponding significance in the social and spatial sciences. Aside from criticising social conditions, researchers and practitioners are exploring a range of alternative development options. Research into economic and political alternatives (Fuller/Jonas/Lee 2016; Leyshon/Lee/Williamet et al. 2003) comprises a series of complementary but also diverging concepts and research strands such as post-growth (Demaria/Kallis/Bakker 2019; Schmelzer/Vetter 2019), post-capitalism (Chatterton/Pusey 2019; Gibson-Graham 2006), commons (Helfrich/Bollier 2019), radical democracy (Barnett 2017), post-development (Kothari/Salleh/Escobar et al. 2019) and the solidarity economy (Exner/Kratzwald 2012; North/Cato 2017). All these approaches criticize political, economic and cultural practices that are based on increasingly severe encroachments in social and ecological systems and leading to the highly unequal destabilisation of communities and ecosystems.

Despite sound scientific knowledge about the consequences and effects of the prevailing lines of development and their contradictions, alternative concepts have received little attention, never mind implementation by (higher levels of) policy, planning or economic decision-making (Gills/Morgan 2019). Disillusioned by reforms 'from above', various forms of practice have emerged that address these deficiencies 'from the bottom up' (Chatterton 2019; Schmelzer/Vetter 2019). These alternative projects and organisations include civil society initiatives as well as socio-ecological enterprises and protest movements – which can be characterised by different approaches, strategies and objectives.

Transformation – profound changes in the form and structure of socio-ecological relations – meanwhile is a fundamentally spatial process. Social change occurs in concrete locations, is embedded in immediate and more far-flung networks of relations and challenges existing boundaries. Some publications have highlighted the significance of space in processes of transformation (including: Bouzarovski/Haarstad 2018; Chatterton 2016; Chatterton/Pickerill 2010; Coenen et al. 2012; Hansen/Coenen 2015; Longhurst 2015; Raven et al. 2012; Smith et al. 2010; Vandeventer et al. 2019). Nonetheless, there is a lack of genuine geographical concepts in the theorisation of transformation and transition. Hansen and Coenen (2015: 105), for instance, argue that most studies on the spatiality of transformation draw on existing transition literature and seldom venture beyond the addition of 'spatial sensitivity'. There is little research, according to Hansen und Coenen, that develops genuinely spatial perspectives to address questions of socio-ecological transformation.

This article tackles precisely this research gap. It endeavours to develop a decidedly spatial perspective for the investigation of transformation processes. Two key questions provide a focus here:

1. Which spatial concepts can be used to think about transformation?
2. What strategies for socio-ecological transformation can be derived from a spatial perspective?

In order to address these questions, the paper is structured as follows. Section 2 outlines the essentials of a post-growth transformation. On the basis of an overview of the concept of transformation and the post-growth discourse, this section considers different transformation strategies. It draws on the typology proposed by Erik Olin Wright (2010), which distinguishes between symbiotic, interstitial and ruptural strategies. Section 3 addresses the spatiality of transformation using the spatial concepts of territory, network, place and scale. Each of these concepts provides a specific perspective on transformation processes. Subsequently, section 4 links the spatial and strategic dimensions of transformation and develops spatial strategies for a post-growth transformation.

2. Post-growth transformation

Transformation

Transformation refers to fundamental changes in the form and structure of socio-ecological relations. At first, thereby, the term transformation does not indicate a specific direction in which these changes lead, nor which forces cause them. Transformation, therefore, can be specified along two lines. First, it must be determined whether transformation is viewed as a process that is to be actively shaped or as a change that emerges from largely undetermined forces (passive). In the latter, passive, sense, transformation describes diverse and interwoven social and biophysical processes of change like globalisation and climate change. Here the focus is primarily on determining which changes are occurring and how societies and communities can respond to them (adaptation and resilience). Considering transformation in a more *active* sense, meanwhile, foregrounds the individuals, organisations and institutions that affect change, or attempt to do so, for example in the context of social movements.

Second, the directionality of transformation must be determined. Transformation does not necessarily lead to more justice and sustainability. It is therefore particularly important that a critical perspective specifies which changes should be encouraged or prevented. As the direction of socio-ecological transformation should not be decided by a few while leaving out others, transformation research faces the challenge of using ecological, social and ethical principles for guidance while ensuring inclusive negotiation processes between different perspectives. The post-growth debate navigates this field of tension by combining collective decision-making and management processes with perspectives on global justice and ecological sustainability.

Post-growth

Post-growth brings together a range of theoretical and practical approaches that question the position of economic growth as the primary guiding principle of human societies. In doing so, post-growth perspectives call for a reflexive reorientation of economic, political and social institutions to enable temporally and spatially just, sustainable and dignified lives. Post-growth tackles the growth imperative of capitalist economies and takes seriously the notion that there are material and social limits to growth (Georgescu-Roegen 1977; Meadows/Randers/Meadows 2004; Rockström/Steffen/Noone et al. 2009). To date, there has been no sign of an (absolute) decoupling of economic growth from resource consumption, as postulated by green economy approaches – an option that appears increasingly unlikely (Fatheuer/Fuhr/Unmüßig 2015; Georgescu-Roegen 1977; Jackson 2017; Kenis/Lievens 2015; Paech 2013).

Regardless of whether further growth is possible, it stands to question how far it is even desirable.[1] Post-growth approaches point out the fact that prosperity cannot be reduced to market relations and therefore cannot be captured by the growth of economic indicators (Hayden/Wilson 2017; Rosa 2016; Rosa/Henning 2018). At the same time, growth and acceleration – when seen as an end in themselves – increasingly lead to conditions of physical and psychological exhaustion (ranging from dissatisfaction to burnout) (Fisher 2009), which are exacerbated by the continued fixation on growth. In contrast, post-growth posits satisfaction, frugality, moderation and leisure as basic positive qualities (Kallis 2019).

Various strands can be identified within the post-growth debate (for categorisations see van den Bergh 2011; Eversberg/Schmelzer 2018; Koepp/

---

1 Post-growth acknowledges that in certain contexts a further increase in material prosperity is required (especially in the Global South but also for socio-economically disadvantaged population groups in the Global North). However, it is becoming clear that this is, first, rather a question of wealth redistribution than a further increase in economic output. And that, second, an economy based on growth actually creates poverty (structural adjustment measures, volatility of the markets for food and raw materials due to financialisation, the break-up of traditional economic and social relations, focus on exports…). These and other issues are also discussed under keywords like 'imperial mode of living' (of the Global North) (Brand/Wissen, 2017), 'postdevelopment' (Kothari/Salleh/Escobar et al. 2019) and alternative visions of the good life (Gudynas 2011).

Schunke/Köhler et al. 2015) which adopt very different positions vis-à-vis existing institutions and which follow different visions and strategies of transformation. What they have in common is, however, that they all shift away from economism towards social and ecological justice (Latouche 2009; Martínez-Alier/Pascual/Vivien et al. 2010). Schmelzer and Vetter (2019) distinguish between three central objectives of post-growth.

Global ecological justice: first, lifestyles in the capitalist centres depend on the 'shaping of social conditions and natural conditions elsewhere' (Brand/Wissen 2017: 43). This 'imperial mode of living' (ibid.) is based on externalisation and 'cheapening' (Patel/Moore 2018: 22) and is neither generalisable (as it depends on an exploitable outside) nor just (as this exploitation creates and sustains asymmetric power relations) nor sustainable (as it destroys its own ecological and social foundations). Post-growth, therefore, does not aim simply for a shrinkage of the economy, but rather for a fundamental restructuring of economic relations to enable a just and sustainable way of life for all.

Good life: a second objective is basic material and social well-being that can in actual fact (and not just formally) be attained by all people. The 'good life' can only be defined via democratic and self-determined processes of negotiation and requires a re-politicisation of economic relations (Gibson-Graham 2006; Gibson-Graham/Cameron/Healy 2013). Fundamentally, this involves a radical redistribution of resources and wealth, the provision of accessible and comprehensive basic services and a renegotiation of economic objectives (Schmelzer/Vetter 2019).

Growth independence: these changes require, thirdly, that economic institutions and infrastructures become growth-independent. Economic structures, social institutions and even the subjects of capitalist societies are fundamentally oriented towards growth and can therefore only be 'dynamically stabilised' (Rosa/Dörre/Lessenich 2017). In other words, institutions, infrastructures and subjectivities can only be maintained in their prevailing constitution by continued growth. Within current institutional orders, recessions and stagnation, but also frugality, leisure and contemplation,[2] lead to crises. Post-growth aims for not less than the fundamental restructuring of economic, social, political and cultural relations consonant with social justice and ecological sustainability.

---

2 Except for when contemplation and leisure are used to increase efficiency (Purser 2019).

Transformation strategies

In addition to in-depth analysis and critique of existing conditions and the formulation of possible alternatives, transformation research also requires a transformation theory that encapsulates how fundamental changes to social conditions can occur and be actively shaped. In an influential piece of work, Erik Olin Wright (2010) distinguishes between three transformation strategies: symbiotic, interstitial and ruptural (see Figure 1).

Symbiotic strategies, first, aim to strengthen emancipatory transformation processes within existing power structures by striving to achieve synergies between socio-ecological aspects and the objectives of dominant interest groups. Symbiotic strategies pursue a largely reformist policy and attempt to fundamentally change socio-ecological conditions in cooperation with existing institutions.

Interstitial strategies, second, are based on producing alternatives in in-between spaces of the incumbent order. Instead of cooperation with politically and economically influential actors, interstitial activities, projects and organisations remain largely outside (and often under the radar) of capitalist institutions. Compromises are replaced by the (anarchist-inspired) principle of prefiguration – the anticipation of desired relations in the here and now (Loick 2017).

Ruptural strategies, third, focus on revolutionary notions of transformation and try to attain change through direct confrontation, protest and resistance. In contrast to the gradual approach of symbiotic and interstitial strategies, ruptural strategies aim to build an organised counterforce to achieve abrupt and comprehensive changes. The primary orientation of ruptural strategists is antagonistic, breaking with existing conditions first and creating alternatives second.

Wright himself sees the best prospect for advancing fundamental socio-ecological change in the countries of the Global North in a strategic orientation 'mainly organized around the interplay of interstitial and symbiotic strategies, with perhaps periodic episodes involving elements of ruptural strategy' (Hahnel/Wright 2016: 103). A bottom-up emancipatory transformation, Wright argues, needs not only to make use of the various strategies but must also coordinate them with one another.

Figure 1: Strategic dimensions of transformation

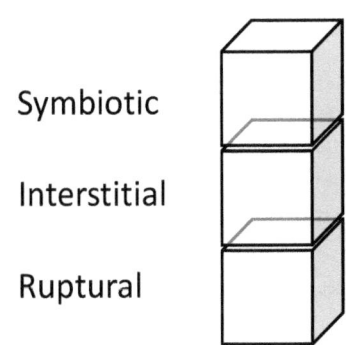

Source: the author

The actors of a post-growth transformation thus face the challenge of developing and implementing context-specific transformative strategies and of combining and harmonising different strategic orientations. I suggest that this can be supported by a resolutely spatial analysis of transformation processes. The following section specifies the spatialities of transformation using different concepts of space, before section 4 returns to the discussion of transformation strategies, further sharpening their focus through the addition of a spatial perspective.

3. The spatiality of transformation

This section discusses transformation processes in the light of different forms of socio-spatial relations (see Figure 2). In their much-quoted article *Theorizing Sociospatial Relations*, Jessop, Brenner and Jones (2008) distinguish between four concepts of space: territory, network, place and scale. Each of these concepts embodies:

> its own logic and perspectives on the way in which space is produced in social practice ... Place operates primarily with and through proximity, embeddedness and local differentiation. Networks are constituted by interdependences and connectivity, while scale indicates hierarchies and vertical differentiation. Territory is manifested though the drawing of boundaries,

subdivisions, inclusions and exclusions (Schmid/Reda/Kraehnk et al. 2019: 93 f., translated from German).

It is important to note that the discussion about socio-spatial dimensions is not exhausted by these four concepts. Nonetheless, they are particularly significant in geographical research and debate (Belina 2013). This section addresses key aspects of these four forms of spatiality and links them to the multifaceted transformation processes.

Figure 2: Spatial dimensions of transformation

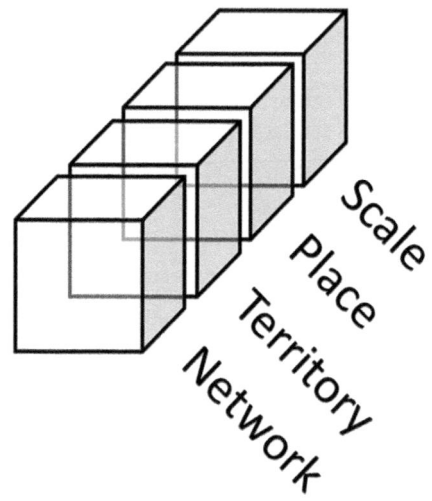

Source: the author

Place

Places are constituted by spatial encounters and interactions between bodies, artefacts, things, meanings and practices. They are meaningful locations in which historical paths of development meet, integrate, stabilise or transform. Place should not be understood as a spatially separate and self-contained unit, but as a locality with materialities, practices and meanings that always exist in relation to other places.

In light of the complex interactions between a place and 'elsewhere' it is easy to overlook the fact that this 'elsewhere' is also grounded in concrete places. Doreen Massey (2008), for instance, uses the City of London in her famous demonstration of how 'the global' is produced locally. Existing conditions as well as the potential for changing them do not lie in an abstract, placeless global sphere but start in specific places.

Just as far-reaching economic and political dynamics emerge from practices that are spatially and materially anchored, so too is the potential of emancipatory transformation interwoven in place-bounded contexts. Transformation, in this sense, does not occur in an a-spatial 'vacuum' but in concrete places. Longhurst (2015: 184), for example, underlines the significance of 'alternative milieus' as local concentrations of institutions and networks that promote alternative practices, experiments and new ideas. Authors who emphasise the importance of proximity also speak of 'informal local institutions' as central moments of transformative practice (Coenen et al. 2012; Hansen/Coenen 2015; Späth/Rohracher 2012) and point out how norms, values, trust, social networks and cooperation constitute alternative forms of economic activity and decision making. Many transformation initiatives, such as the Transition Town movement, therefore focus especially on the scales of neighbourhoods and municipalities, without being reducible to them (see below).

Network

A place-specific perspective is important for understanding the various constellations of values, communities and technologies from which transformative practices emerge. However, it is equally vital to capture the people, ideas and techniques that pass through the various places and create links between them. Through interactions between individuals, organisations and artefacts, horizontal relations emerge which can be comprehended as networked spatialities. Networks therefore are constituted by 'the horizontal links of entities and spaces created through their interactions' (Schmid/Reda/Kraehnk et al. 2019: 106, translated from German).

In transformation research, the horizontal spatiality of networks is a recurring figure of thought, particularly in approaches inspired by feminism and anarchism (Gibson-Graham 2006; Springer 2014; Chatterton/Pickerill 2010). Numerous projects and organisations are considered – such as food networks (Rosol 2018), housing projects (Chatterton 2016; Metzger 2017), repair initiatives (Baier/Hansing/Müller et al. 2016), neighbourhood initiatives (Gibson-Graham 2006) and social-ecological enterprises (Johanisova/ Fraňková 2017) – all of which are based on horizontal economic and political relations. Beyond individual projects, the possibility of building far-reaching networks is particularly relevant and has inspired many transformation narratives (Chatterton 2016; Habermann 2009; Mason 2016; Meretz 2014).

Although individual projects are usually strongly embedded in place-related contexts, their activities and impacts are by no means limited to the local. Places, as discussed above, should not be understood as independent and self-contained units but are linked to one another in diverse ways. Fair trade and sustainable production, for example, can improve living conditions and environmental conditions elsewhere (or rather initially simply reduce the negative impacts on other places). The places, people and communities involved in transformative practice are themselves linked with one another via umbrella organisations, urban networks, conferences and other cooperative formats and are thus involved in an exchange of ideas, values and technologies. The aforementioned Transition Town movement, for instance, comprises and links well over 1000 initiatives in more than 40 countries (Grossmann/Creamer, 2016).

Ultimately, the relationality of social conditions also affects large social phenomena like statehood or capitalist markets (Schatzki 2016a). Critical geographers challenge representations that portray states and markets as apparently coherent macrogeographical systems. These representations abstract from the multifaceted practices, processes and bodies that produce statehood or capitalist markets while differently positioned in their power structures (Gibson-Graham 2006; Marston/Jones/Woodward 2005; Springer 2014). Considering the concrete relations that produce social (macro-) phenomena at the same time reveals possibilities to break down existing institutions and to replace them with more emancipatory alternatives (Chatterton 2016).

Territory

Territories are another important form of social spatiality that are relevant in transformation processes. Territories are generally understood as bounded segments of space. Like places and networks, neither the boundaries nor the territories themselves are givens, but are rather the products of social practice. Geographers therefore particularly emphasise processes of territorialisation (Belina 2013; Painter 2010).

Territories are relevant for transformation processes, both in their production and in their effects. Administrative entities generally constitute a 'reality' for transformative practice that cannot be simply ignored. Indeed, violating laws and regulations can have forcible consequences, as in cases of civil disobedience (Braune 2017). Local, regional, national and supranational legislation can promote, hinder or prevent sustainable and postgrowth oriented practice. Simultaneously, actors can tactically resort to different administrative territories and scales to navigate political parameters, acquire funding and disseminate alternative practices. In doing so, they negotiate and transform the territorial dimension of society.

Scale

Scale refers to the vertical differentiation of social conditions. Traditionally, scale is related to different levels – from local to regional to national and on up to global – which, however, as will be shown, is conceptually problematic. Nonetheless, scale is of key significance for transformation research (Schmid 2019). Firstly, because the debate about scale is fundamental to an understanding of the possibilities and limitations of transformative practice. Second, because transformation inevitably includes forms of diffusion, dissemination and institutionalisation that are often discussed in a superficial manner. I briefly consider both these aspects in the following.

The debate about horizontal and vertical forms of spatiality is characterised by many misunderstandings – particularly by the conflation of ontological arguments and those concerned with existing social power relations (Moore 2008). Relational perspectives on space show that the a priori structuring of social relations in different scaler levels (local, regional, national, global) is not tenable (Jones/Woodward/Marston 2007; Marston/Jones/Woodward 2005). While horizontal perspectives are characterised by an inherent emancipatory moment, it is nonetheless important not to lose sight of the power relations that structure and limit the spaces and scope for action (Schmid/Smith 2020). This means that a critical scalar perspective requires both a spatial ontology that is not based on the presupposition of distinct structural levels, while at the same time recognising the socio-material conditions that enable or constrain (transformative) practice. Vertical differentiations then become visible not as predefined givens but rather as social products.

Nevertheless, different positions are adopted vis-à-vis the opportunities and limitations of transformative practice. A 'politics of hope' emphasises the opportunities made visible by a 'flat ontology' (Schatzki 2016b). More sceptical approaches, in contrast, highlight the influence of institutional arrangements that – although socially produced –, still condition transformative practice, which is inevitably embedded in the context of existing social relations (Buch-Hansen 2018; Joutsenvirta 2016).

Notwithstanding different positionings in relation to the possibilities and constraints of transformative practice, scale itself is fundamental to concepts of transformation. Upscaling, polycentric shifts, diffusion, expansion and dissemination express different views about how changes unfold. A critical understanding of scale suggests that simple notions of scaling socio-ecological innovations and niche experiments are insufficient. Instead, the linking of scalar and network spatialities allows an understanding of transformation to emerge that grasps social change as an emergent, non-linear, polycentric and complex process.

4. Spatial strategies for a post-growth transformation

Place, network, territory and scale capture the multi-layered spatialities of transformation. Although different socio-spatial dimensions overlap and condition one another, an analytical separation – as presented in Section 3 – sharpens the focus of the transformation strategies discussed in Section 2. This fourth section attempts a synthesis by developing spatial strategies for post-growth transformation. Three social fields are considered which are central for a socio-ecological transformation: the economy, politics and community. Although these deliberations remain incomplete and in no way exclude alternative readings, they are intended to encourage debate on transformation strategies to focus more closely on space.

Networked interstitial strategies for an economic transformation

The complexity and opacity of globalised economic relations represent a great challenge to socio-ecological transformation. Subjects, organisations and places that are very differently positioned in terms of resources, decision-making power and agency are brought into complex relations of dependency and exploitation by (peri-)capitalist value chains (Tsing 2015). These relationships remain largely invisible under the surface of formal economies.

In this context, symbiotic strategies may be very limited in scope as they themselves build on the existing non-transparent value chains. Symbiotic strategies are based on compromises and cooperation and must navigate a narrow line between the subversion of and reintegration in incumbent social relations. Social enterprises, for example, are themselves situated in economic relationships that actually force the continuation of exploitative conditions through competition.

Ruptural strategies, on the other hand, lack a centre against which to direct their resistance (important exceptions here are clearly localisable practices such as lignite mining in Germany and the protests against it organised by the resistance movement '*Ende Gelände*'). However, targeting the complex of transnational enterprises and (supranational) legislation as a whole seems inconceivable without a broad (revolutionary) movement (which does not currently exist in the capitalist centres).

In contrast, interstitial strategies aim to establish transformative networks to replace exploitative and unsustainable economic relations. Interstitial strategies react to the complexity of extractive value chains by building fairer and – wherever possible – more local alternatives. They are based on the possibility of creating potentially autonomous 'circuits of cooperation' (Hardt/Negri 2017: 145) and thus on finding a decentralised answer to the structural irresponsibility of capitalist and peri-capitalist value chains.

In order to have a transformative effect, interstitial processes should not, however, remain limited to the production and maintenance of niches and in-between spaces. Criticism (some justified and some based on misunderstandings) has been directed towards the focus of many interstitial projects on their immediate context (Srnicek/Williams 2016). Explicitly thinking of interstitial strategies in terms of networked spatialities reveals the potential of alternative circuits of value for economic transformations. The networking of alternative practices introduces the prospect of cooperative networks that gradually replace exploitative relations until they encompass entire fields of economic activity (Mason 2016).

Networked interstitial strategies for economic transformation, however, are often complicated and blocked by political parameters that focus on economic growth and thus prioritise profit over the common good – not to mention the fact that state structures in general are fundamentally dependent on growth-based politics. A simultaneous intervention in formal politics is therefore necessary. Interstitial strategies, thereby, match badly with the territorial organisation of political institutions, requiring the consideration of other spatial strategies.

Confronting territorially organised power

Territorially organised power jars with the networked character of dispersed and multiple economic exchange relations and dependencies. While political power is not only exercised territorially, legislative processes and their legal implementation generally play out in spatially bordered entities and have a fundamental role in the reproduction of existing social relations. The territoriality of political power formally precludes the option of interstitial spaces in which alternative forms of bureaucracy, administration and legislation could be tested and implemented. Grey zones of regulation and taxation, of course, provide important scope for counterhegemonic groups and socio-ecological organisations. However, the possibilities for extending and generalising alternative political and regulative mechanisms – in line with interstitial ideas related to economic practice – seem to be very limited.

Symbiotic strategies are *one* option for changing political parameters to ensure close attention is paid to social and ecological issues in regulation. In order to have a transformative effect, however, symbiotic strategies must 'interact to point beyond the capitalist, growth-oriented mode of production and defend and extend spaces where it can be overcome' (Schmelzer/Vetter 2019: 27, translated from German). In the current political sphere with its mostly reactive orientation, however, majorities supporting radical change are rarely found. The question thus arises as to whether and to what extent symbiotic strategies can lead on to overcome growth-based economic and social relations. Or are the changes possible in the context of these strategies so limited in their transformative effect that they ultimately contribute to the stabilisation of existing conditions?

Another option is provided by ruptural strategies. Although ruptural strategies are unable to locate an identifiable centre for confrontation in the context of the decentralised interactions described in Section 3, focusing on territorial power allows such a centre to become visible. Territories do not simply exist; they must rather be continuously produced and enforced. This work of reproduction reveals the centres from which the regulative, controlling and enforcing exercise of territorial power emanates – e. g. the government district of a capital city or the seat of an important financial institute. This opens options for place-based action and confrontation aiming to change the (territorially organised) political conditions.

Post-growth coalitions – the place-relatedness of symbiotic strategies

Ruptural strategies have a crucial disadvantage however: they have a divisive effect, distinguishing between 'us' – those who put up resistance and denounce injustices – and 'them' – who must be held accountable. This can lead to aggressive accusations, social disintegration and entrenched positions and even trigger counter movements based on a shared identity of being 'accused'. The antagonistic orientation of ruptural strategies can therefore lead to the reproduction and deepening of opposition rather than to solidarity and the joint tackling of socio-ecological wrongs. The abstract nature of territorial power and its distance from the populace may well require the exercising of ruptural strategies, but this type of strategy seems less appropriate for specific place-related problem solving.

Symbiotic strategies, on the other hand, are challenged by the fact that coalitions operating with and through the existing institutional landscape require a great deal of reflexivity, knowledge and trust to have transformative effects despite the compromises they have to make. Place, thereby, offers a possible strategic entry point for symbiotic transformative practice. While determinist and romanticised images of proximity and the local should be avoided, direct contacts, trust, personal relations and mutual knowledge are important resources for reflexive and emancipatory cooperation. On that basis, the selective perpetuation of unsustainable and unjust conditions caused by compromise can be assessed collectively and transparently.

Places where transformative practices are concentrated – alternative milieus (Longhurst 2015) – can act as central sources of further impulses and changes. This may involve specific establishments like a neighbourhood office or an open workshop (Smith 2019), but also includes beneficial (for a socio-ecological transformation) relationships between different actors from the sphere of politics and civil society (Barnes 2015). In this way, places also offer a shared frame of reference that promotes the forging of transversal coalitions. Post-growth discourses discuss the fundamental need for intact and liveable socio-ecological conditions that are not limited to specific political groups. Places offer experimental spaces for prefigurative practices and immediate experiences, which can then in turn have a positive effect on the transformative potential of these places.

5. Conclusion

Post-growth demands fundamental social-ecological transformation away from political, economic and cultural practice that leads to an increasing destabilisation and exploitation of ecological and social systems. The institutional restructuring implied by post-growth is so far-reaching that it challenges both our notions of what is feasible and encounters a great deal of resistance from people who feel afraid or want to maintain their privileges. As a consequence, it is insufficient to formulate convincing alternatives. What is required, furthermore, is a strategic orientation to push for a social-ecological transformation.

The typology drawn up by Erik Olin Wright with symbiotic, interstitial and ruptural transformation strategies offers a framework for the systematic investigation and organisation of different transformative practices. Compromise-based, interstitial and antagonistic approaches, thereby, must be scrutinised in terms of their social and spatial manifestations and interactions. By combining these strategic approaches with different spatial concepts, particularly robust socio-spatial post-growth strategies can be identified (see Figure 3).

Figure 3: Socio-spatial post-growth strategies

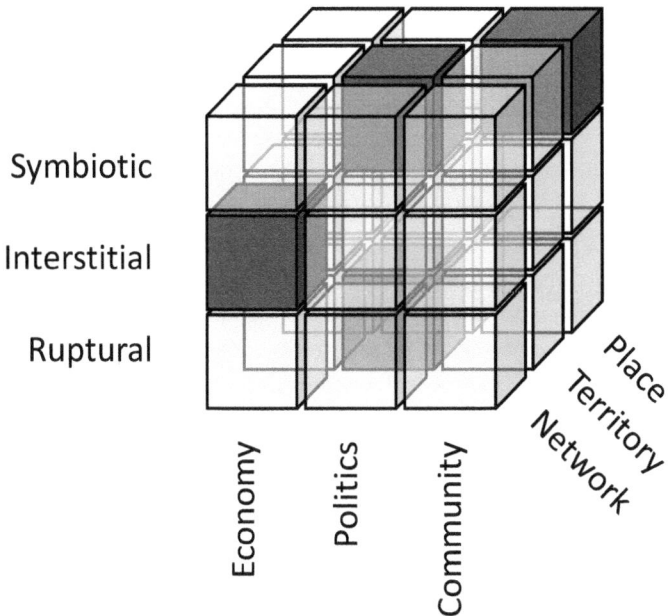

Source: the author

An economic transformation primarily requires a long-term focus on interstitial strategies aimed at creating alternative circuits of value. In the context of 'structural irresponsibility', ruptural strategies find it difficult to identify an economic centre against which resistance can be directed. Symbiotic strategies, in contrast, are themselves subjected to economic constraints and often appropriated.

Interstitial strategies, however, quickly reach their limits when faced with growth-oriented framework conditions and are less suited to confront political institutions. Ruptural strategies, on the other hand, can find a 'target' in the centres from which territorial power is exercised. Such an antagonistic approach may, however, be problematic, as it generates opposition where more solidary ways of living are envisioned. Particularly in contexts where proximity and trust can be established, symbiotic strategies in their attempts to achieve reasonable compromises are important.

The interplay of the various strategies discussed here supports Wright's assessment that a fundamental (emancipatory) restructuring of social conditions requires a combination of symbiotic, interstitial and ruptural strategies. A robust spatial perspective clarifies which roles can be assigned to the different strategic orientations in the context of a post-growth transformation. The elaboration of these three socio-spatial strategies is intended to encourage different socio-ecological developments, organisations, actors and practices to be considered in relation to one another. In concrete terms this involves focusing on the fact that while social movements, alternative economic organisations and socio-ecological initiatives demonstrate very different strategic orientations, there is also significant convergence in their objectives. Spatial strategies for post-growth transformation can provide an analytical framework for the better understanding and systematic organisation of these struggles.

Cited literature

Baier, A., Hansing, T., Müller, C., & Werner, K. (2016). Die Welt reparieren: Eine Kunst des Zusammenmachens. In A. Baier, T. Hansing, C. Müller, & K. Werner (Eds.), *Die Welt reparieren. Open Source und Selbermachen als Postkapitalistische Praxis.* transcript, 34–63.

Barnes, P. (2015). The political economy of localization in the transition movement. *Community Development Journal*, 50(2), 312–326.

Barnett, C. (2017). *The priority of injustice: Locating democracy in critical theory.* University of Georgia Press.

Belina, B. (2013). *Raum. Zu den Grundlagen eines historisch-geographischen Materialismus.* Springer.

Bouzarovski, S., & Haarstad, H. (2018). Rescaling low-carbon transformations: Towards a relational ontology. *Transactions of the Institute of British Geographers*, 44(2), 256–269.

Brand, U., & Wissen, M. (2017). *Imperiale Lebensweise: Zur Ausbeutung von Mensch und Natur im globalen Kapitalismus.* oekom.

Braune, A. (2017). *Ziviler Ungehorsam: Texte von Thoreau bis Occupy.* Reclam.

Buch-Hansen, H. (2018). The prerequisites for a degrowth paradigm shift: Insights from critical political economy. *Ecological Economics*, 146, 157–163.

Chatterton, P. (2016). Building transitions to post-capitalist urban commons. *Transactions of the Institute of British Geographers, 41*(4), 403–415.

Chatterton, P. (2019). *Unlocking sustainable cities: A manifesto for real change.* Pluto Press.

Chatterton, P., & Pickerill, J. (2010). Everyday activism and transitions towards post-capitalist worlds. *Transactions of the Institute of British Geographers, 35*(4), 475–490.

Chatterton, P., & Pusey, A. (2019). Beyond capitalist enclosure, commodification and alienation: Postcapitalist praxis as commons, social production and useful doing. *Progress in Human Geography, 44*(1), 27–48.

Coenen, L., Benneworth, P., & Truffer, B. (2012). Toward a spatial perspective on sustainability transitions. *Research Policy, 41*(6), 968–979.

Demaria, F., Kallis, G., & Bakker, K. (2019). Geographies of degrowth: Nowtopias, resurgences and the decolonization of imaginaries and places. *Environment and Planning E: Nature and Space, 2*(3), 431–450.

Eversberg, D., & Schmelzer, M. (2018). The degrowth spectrum: Convergence and divergence within a diverse and conflictual alliance. *Environmental Values, 27*(3), 245–267.

Exner, A., & Kratzwald, B. (2012). *Solidarische Ökonomie & Commons. Intro – eine Einführung.* Mandelbaum.

Fatheuer, T., Fuhr, & L., Unmüßig, B. (2015). *Kritik der Grünen Ökonomie.* oekom.

Fisher, M. (2009). *Capitalist realism: Is there no alternative?* John Hunt Publishing.

Fuller, D., Jonas, A. E. G., & Lee, R. (2016). *Interrogating alterity. Alternative economic and political spaces.* Routledge.

Georgescu-Roegen, N. (1977). Inequality, limits and growth from a bioeconomic viewpoint. *Review of Social Economy, 35*(3), 361–375.

Gibson-Graham, J. K. (2006). *Postcapitalist politics.* University of Minnesota Press.

Gibson-Graham, J. K., Cameron, J., & Healy, S. (2013). *Take back the economy. An ethical guide for transforming our communities.* University of Minnesota Press.

Gills, B., & Morgan, J. (2019). Global climate emergency: after COP24, climate science, urgency, and the threat to humanity. *Globalizations, 17*(6), 885–902.

Grossmann, M., & Creamer, E. (2016). Assessing diversity and inclusivity within the Transition movement: An urban case study. *Environmental Politics*, 26(1), 161–182.

Gudynas, E. (2011). Buen Vivir: Today's tomorrow. *Development*, 54(4), 441–447.

Habermann, F. (2009). *Halbinseln gegen den Strom: Anders leben und wirtschaften im Alltag*. Ulrike Helmer Verlag.

Hahnel, R., & Wright, E. O. (2016). *Alternatives to capitalism: Proposals for a democratic economy*. Verso Books.

Hansen, T., & Coenen, L. (2015). The geography of sustainability transitions: Review, synthesis and reflections on an emergent research field. *Environmental Innovation and Societal Transitions*, 17, 92–109.

Hardt, M., & Negri, A. (2017). *Assembly*. Oxford University Press.

Hayden, A., & Wilson, J. (2017). Beyond „GDP" indicators: Changing the economic narrative for a post-consumerist society? In M. J. Cohen, H. S. Brown, & P. Vergragt (Eds.), *Social change and the coming of post-consumer society: Theoretical advances and policy implications*. Routledge, 170–191.

Helfrich, S., & Bollier, D. (2019). *Frei, fair und lebendig – Die Macht der Commons*. transcript.

Jackson, T. (2017). *Wohlstand ohne Wachstum – das Update: Grundlagen für eine zukunftsfähige Wirtschaft*. oekom.

Jessop, B., Brenner, N., & Jones, M. (2008). Theorizing sociospatial relations. *Environment and Planning D: Society and Space*, 26(3), 389–401.

Johanisova, N., & Fraňková, E. (2017). Eco social enterprises. In C.L. Spash (Ed.), *Routledge Handbook of ecological economics: Nature and societ*. Routledge, 507–516.

Jones, J. P., Woodward, K., & Marston, S. A. (2007). Situating flatness. *Transactions of the Institute of British Geographers*, 32(2), 264–276.

Joutsenvirta, M. (2016). A practice approach to the institutionalization of economic degrowth. *Ecological Economics*, 128, 23–32.

Kallis, G. (2019). *Limits: Why Malthus was wrong and why environmentalists should care*. Stanford University Press.

Kenis, A., & Lievens, M. (2015). *The Limits of the Green Economy. From reinventing capitalism to repoliticising the present*. Routledge.

Koepp, R., Schunke, F., Köhler, C., Liebig, S., & Schröder, S. (2015). *Arbeit in der Postwachstumsgesellschaft. Diagnosen, Prognosen und Ge-genentwürfe*.

Working Paper 6/2015 der DFG-KollegforscherInnengruppe Postwachstumsgesellschaften, Jena.

Kothari, A., Salleh, A., Escobar, A., Demaria, F., & Acosta, A. (2019). *Pluriverse: A post-development dictionary*. Columbia University Press.

Latouche, S. (2009). *Farewell to growth*. Polity Press.

Leyshon, A., Lee, R., & Williams, C. C. (2003). Alternative economic spaces. *Economic Geography*, 81(4), 437–438.

Loick, D. (2017). *Anarchismus zur Einführung*. Junius.

Longhurst, N. (2015). Towards an 'alternative' geography of innovation: Alternative milieu, socio-cognitive protection and sustainability experimentation. *Environmental Innovation and Societal Transitions*, 17, 183–198.

Marston, S. A., Jones, J. P., & Woodward, K. (2005). Human geography without scale. *Transactions of the Institute of British Geographers*, 30(4), 416–432.

Martínez-Alier, J., Pascual, U., Vivien, F. D., & Zaccai, E. (2010). Sustainable degrowth: Mapping the context, criticisms and future prospects of an emergent paradigm. *Ecological Economics*, 69(9), 1741–1747.

Mason, P. (2016). *Postcapitalism. A guide to our future*. Penguin Books.

Massey, D. (2008). *World city*, (Reprint). Polity Press.

Meadows, D. H., Randers, J., & Meadows, D. L. (2004). Limits to growth: The 30-year update. 1st edition. Routledge.

Meretz, S. (2014). Keimform und gesellschaftliche Transformation. *Streifzüge*, 60, 7–9.

Metzger, J. (2017). Soziale Wohnungswirtschaft zwischen Gebrauchs- und Tauschwert. Ein Beitrag zur Debatte um die Neue Wohnungsgemeinnützigkeit. In M. Hawel, & Herausgeber_innenkollektiv (Eds.), *Work in progress. Work on progress*. VSA, 232–244.

Moore, A. (2008). Rethinking scale as a geographical category: From analysis to practice. *Progress in Human Geography*, 32(2), 203–225.

North, P., & Cato, M. S. (2017). *Towards just and sustainable economies: The social and solidarity economy North and South*. Policy Press.

Paech, N. (2013). Economic Growth and Sustainable Development. In M. Angrick, A. Burger, & H. Lehmann (2015), *Factor X: Re-source - designing the recycling society (Eco-efficiency in industry and science (30))*. 2013th edition. Springer.

Painter, J. (2010). Rethinking territory. *Antipode*, 42(5), 1090–1118.

Patel, R., & Moore, J. W. (2018). *A history of the world in seven cheap things: A guide to capitalism, nature, and the future of the planet*. Verso Books.

Purser, R. E. (2019). *McMindfulness: How mindfulness became the new capitalist spirituality*. Repeater Books.

Raven, R., Schot, J., & Berkhout, F. (2012). Space and scale in socio-technical transitions. *Environmental Innovation and Societal Transitions*, 4, 63–78.

Rockström, J., Steffen, W., Noone, K., Persson, Å., Chapin, F. S. I. I. I., Lambin, E., Lenton, T. M., Scheffer, M., Folke, C., Schellnhuber, H. J., Nykvist, B., de Wit, C. A., Hughes, T., van der Leeuw, S., Rodhe, H., Sörlin, S., Snyder, P. K., Costanza, R., Svedin, U., Falkenmark, M., Karlber, L., Corell, R. W., Fabry, V. J., Hansen, J., Walker, B., Liverman, D., Richardson, K., Crutzen, P., & Foley, J. (2009). Planetary boundaries: Exploring the safe operating space for humanity. *Ecology and Society*, 14(2), 32.

Rosa, H. (2016). *Resonanz: Eine Soziologie der Weltbeziehung*. 1st edition. Suhrkamp.

Rosa, H., Dörre, K., & Lessenich, S. (2017). Appropriation, activation and acceleration: The escalatory logics of capitalist modernity and the crises of dynamic stabilization. *Theory, Culture & Society*, 34(1), 53–73.

Rosa, H., & Henning, C. (2018). *The good life beyond growth: New perspectives*. Routledge.

Rosol, M. (2018). Alternative Ernährungsnetzwerke als Alternative Ökonomien. *Zeitschrift für Wirtschaftsgeographie*, 62(3-4), 174–186.

Schatzki, T. R. (2016a). Keeping track of large phenomena. *Geographische Zeitschrift*, 104(1), 4–24.

Schatzki, T. R. (2016b). Praxistheorie als flache Ontologie. In H. Schäfer (Ed.), *Praxistheorie. Ein soziologisches Forschungsprogramm*. transcript, 29–44.

Schmelzer, M., & Vetter, A. (2019). *Degrowth/Postwachstum zur Einführung*. Junius.

Schmid, B. (2019). Degrowth and postcapitalism: Transformative geographies beyond accumulation and growth. *Geography Compass*, 13(11), 1–15.

Schmid, B., Reda, J., Kraehnke, L., & Schwegmann, R. (2019). The site of the spatial. Eine praktikentheoretische Erschließung geographischer Raumkonzepte. In J. Everts, & S. Schäfer (Eds.), *Handbuch Praktiken und Raum. Humangeographie nach dem Practice Turn*. transcript, 93–136.

Schmid, B., & Smith, T. S. J. (2020). Social transformation and postcapitalist possibility: Emerging dialogues between practice theory and diverse economies. *Progress in Human Geography*, 030913252090564.

Smith, A., Voß, J.-P., & Grin, J. (2010). Innovation studies and sustainability transitions: The allure of the multi-level perspective and its challenges. *Research Policy, 39*(4), 435–448.

Smith, T. S. J. (2019). 'Stand back and watch us': Post-capitalist practices in the maker movement. *Environment and Planning A: Economy and Space, 52*(3), 593–610.

Späth, P., & Rohracher, H. (2012). Local demonstrations for global transitions—Dynamics across governance levels fostering socio-technical regime change towards sustainability. *European Planning Studies, 20*(3), 461–479.

Springer, S. (2014). Human geography without hierarchy. *Progress in Human Geography, 38*(3), 402–419.

Srnicek, N., & Williams, A. (2016). *Inventing the future: Postcapitalism and a world without work*. Revisited & updated edition. Verso Books.

Tsing, A. (2015). *The mushroom at the end of the world: On the possibility of life in capitalist ruins*. Princeton University Press.

van den Bergh, J. C. J. M. (2011). Environment versus growth — A criticism of "degrowth" and a plea for "a-growth". *Ecological Economics, 70*(5), 881–890.

Vandeventer, J. S., Cattaneo, C., & Zografos, C. (2019). A degrowth transition: Pathways for the degrowth niche to replace the capitalist-growth regime. *Ecological Economics, 156*, 272–286.

Wright, E. O. (2010). *Envisioning real utopias*. Verso Books.

Reducing working hours in small enterprises as a post-growth practice?

Hubert Eichmann

In 2018 the online marketing company 'eMagnetix' in Upper Austria switched to a 30-hour week, while continuing to pay its 22 employees the same full-time wage. The CEO, Klaus Hochreiner, justifies the reduction of working hours by citing advantages for three parties. Thanks to the increased free time, the employees are more even-tempered, more satisfied and more productive. Output is improved, which then benefits the employer and, especially, the customers (Hausensteiner 2019). The entrepreneur Lasse Rheingans has gone a step further with his IT agency in Bielefeld, Germany. In 2017, he and his 15 employees introduced a five-hour day, or 25-hour week, while continuing with full-pay, initially as an experiment. They claim to be the first company in Germany to take such a step (Hausensteiner 2019).[1]

How do the increasing number of enterprises that are reducing working hours without reducing pay fit into post-growth or degrowth discourses calling for the abandonment of economic growth (e.g. Kallis/Kalush/Flynn et al. 2013; Knight/Rosa/Schor 2013; Nässén/Larsson 2015)? Are concrete examples of reduced working hours evidence that post-growth positions are not just theoretical, largely macro-economic models, but are rather increasingly disseminated in the realities of the business world (Gebauer 2018; Schmid 2018)? Or is it only justified to speak of post-growth in this context if there is a move away from commercial objectives like profit, productivity or size (volume of employment) – and correspondingly from growth? Does it even make sense to apply post-growth concepts to the business level? Or is this a pointless undertaking? Even given the need for economic shrinkage on the

---

1 Also see: https://www.zeit.de/zeit-spezial/2018/01/25-stunden-woche-lasse-rheingans-agentur-bielefeld/komplettansicht (28.01.2020)

macro-scale, in future not all businesses will need to be persuaded to shrink no matter what their field of activities or structural organisation. On the contrary, from a post-growth perspective, it may be better to promote businesses that excel in terms of conserving resources or focusing on the common good (Sommer 2018; Wiefek/Heinitz 2018), as far as possible in combination with employee-friendly or even democratically constituted working conditions. In brief: does it make sense to speak of post-growth on the meso-level of the enterprise or would it be more appropriate to restrict attention to concepts like the 'transformative company' (Pfriem/Antoni-Komar/Lautermann 2015; Antoni-Komar/Kropp/Paech et al. 2019), because this approach is more conceptually open to diverse desirable paths?[2]

One of those arguing in favour of the latter approach is Bernd Sommer, who wishes to avoid misunderstandings by emphasising that the transition to a society which is not dependent on growth does not require every company to shrink or not to grow: 'On the contrary, in the context of such structural transformation it can be the case that certain industries and enterprises grow or multiply while others disappear. What is crucial is just that in the long-term the continued existence of individual enterprises and the stability of societies overall do not depend on endlessly sustained growth' (Sommer 2018: 20).

Representative of relevant findings are those of a research project on growth-neutral enterprises and post-growth pioneers by Jana Gebauer and Julian Sagebiel, in the course of which a broad survey of about ca. 700 SME in Germany was also carried out. The enterprises were asked about their growth orientation and it emerged that the majority, circa 60 %, had either no (34 %) or only limited (25 %) growth ambitions (Gebauer/Sagebiel 2015; Gebauer 2019). This will not surprise people who are themselves active in or research the world of small and micro enterprises and thereby tend to encounter growth aversion rather than growth ambitions. The criticism of business management principles like maximisation of profits, productivity and turnover is misguided, at least when it is applied generally without taking into consideration the fact that large companies usually (can or must) act quite differently from small ones. On the other hand, just because small

---

2   With 'impact dimensions' like self-empowerment, collaborative empowerment, self-sufficiency, economic self-limitation, deceleration, regionalisation/localisation, renaturation (Pfriem/Antoni-Komar/Lautermann 2015).

companies are not focused on growth does not mean that it is possible to assume a transformation is at work.

Reductions in working hours of one-person enterprises (OPEs) with or without a transformative agenda

This paper draws on material gathered in qualitative interviews in small and micro enterprises from the creative industry in Vienna, especially from the graphics and internet business. The image of freelancers working long and unlimited hours around the clock automatically springs to mind. However, this notion needs to be overhauled, if only because the lack of supervisory instances means that autonomous working rhythms are more heterogeneous (see Bührmann/Hansen 2012; Muckenhuber 2014). Furthermore, individual strategies can or must be adapted more quickly, e.g. because the self-employed are not subject to working time regulations or because adaptation is necessary when there is a drop in orders. Examples of reduced or shorter working hours (in relation to daily, weekly, seasonal or other rhythms) include part-time self-employment, for instance because of childcare duties;[3] a reduction in the time invested due to increases in efficiency (or, on the other hand, a lack of orders); and e.g. the realisation of a long-cherished wish to slow down after many years of professional life. Socio-ecological goals or collectively managed constellations with distinct company democracy also often correspond to preferences for reducing working hours.

Nonetheless, organisations that reduce working hours as the result of an explicitly transformative approach, for instance as part of an overall strategy to conserve resources or a democratic charter, probably remain something of a niche phenomenon. On the other hand, it is argued here that many one-person enterprises or micro enterprises follow a risk-averse 'no growth' path or tend to strive to reduce their own input, e.g. measured in working hours. This occurs, however, in diverse ways, without an ecological imperative of action or the motivation of a post-growth principle. Rather, in the middle of their professional lives (when many career goals and advancement ambitions have been realised or abandoned), actors socialised in micro enterprises rec-

---

3 20 % of male and 45 % of female OPEs and 8 % of male and 18 % of female 'employers' (i.e. entrepreneurs with employees) work part-time in Austria (Statistik Austria 2016: 91 ff.)

ognise that (further) growth would involve a great deal of effort. They therefore focus on stabilising their economic prospects, for instance aiming to work less but without a reduction in income.

The following sections use empirical cases drawn from two research projects as a basis for discussion of working time practices that involve fewer working hours than the full-time jobs of non-self-employed persons. The first section presents no-growth paths that lead to a reduction in working hours where the actors involved do not suggest that their course of action is motivated by socio-ecological or other related factors. The examples are drawn from interview-based research conducted in 2016 with 14 self-employed persons. Working hours were a side issue here and interviewees were therefore not selected according to the number of hours they worked. It is nonetheless interesting that about half of those interviewed categorised themselves as working less than full time (four women, three men; a total of seven men and seven women were interviewed). The subsequent section presents the results of a company case study from 2019 which was conducted in the course of an investigation into alternative business models. This example demonstrates a transformative approach where a group of people with a history of working as OPEs formed an occupational association aimed at professionalising and reducing their hours of paid work.

Redcing working hours without a transformative agenda

Of the 14 self-employed persons from the design and internet verticals who were interviewed in 2016, only two are employers in a literal sense, i.e. they employ staff in their own businesses. The others are legally 'independent self-employed' and most do not define themselves as having an explicit focus on expansion. Becoming an employer is thought to be extremely risky because of the associated costs. Nevertheless, it is usually important for freelancers to avoid a go-it-alone existence, because this means that only a very small range of services can be offered and also, for instance, makes it difficult to bridge long absences resulting from illness or holidays. The *modus operandi* for those who do not work in a joint company with a partner (thus for almost all of those interviewed) is therefore a sustainable network of colleagues active in the same professional field, or at least in complementary lines of business. Little seems to remain of grand artistic ambitions after a professional career in the project world, or only in the form of subsidiary projects that are not intended for the market. Such ambitions are outweighed by an eye for the necessities: providing professional services, sustaining cost-income ratios, ensuring capacity utilisation and maintaining market reputation – all while preserving a balance between creative work and (the moderately popular) commercial management.

The survey analysis revealed the heterogeneous nature of working time strategies among self-employed individuals from the Viennese creative industry. Looking first at those who estimated that they worked more than an average of 40 hours a week (about half of those interviewed), few proved to be true 'workhorses'. Long working hours were explained by particularly intensive phases of work, e.g. filming sessions for filmmakers which often include idle periods, but also by artistic lifestyles with some of the creatives rejecting the notion of a divide between the spheres of paid and unpaid work. The interviewees who suggested that they did not work more than 40 hours a week on average over the year can be divided into two groups. Firstly, successful and somewhat older self-employed individuals, who are now slowing down and improving their quality of life after a work-intensive past of mixed success. The motto here is that professional success is no longer everything, the next generation should rather be the ones to hold the front line.

For example, after the bankruptcy of his company in the financial crisis of 2008/2009, the owner of an internet agency changed his field of business and today works as a self-employed photographer. The bankruptcy did not leave him untouched: as well as losing his assets he now has a significantly lower income. At the same time, he recognises advantages in his present professional situation as he suffers from much less stress than when he managed his company with 20 employees.

'I: If you now sum up, the years 2005 and 2015: income, working hours and satisfaction with what you do …
M: Less, less, exorbitantly more.
I: So in terms of expenditure of time sort of reasonable?
M: It is reasonable. Naturally, there are phases where a lot is going on.' (Photographer, aged 50)

Somewhat different reasons for restricting working hours to not more than 40 hours are given by the second group of younger self-employed persons who have many years of working life in front of them but nonetheless do not want to dedicate their lives just to paid work. Their argument for working shorter hours is based largely on the fact that they began their working lives as employees and only entered self-employment later. The professional socialisation of this group occurred through providing more or less creative services in the world of advertising agencies. In many sequences of dialogue, such biographies serve as an apparent paradox to desired working hours and practices: several of the interviewees chose to switch to self-employment because they realised that they did not want to end up as workaholics in the agency rat race. They hoped that being self-employed would allow them more sovereignty over daily and weekly working hours. At the same time, starting with a job as an employee provided experience about standard working hours and their meaningfulness. In contrast, limiting working hours is often of minor importance for those who start their working lives in self-employment and do not know anything else.

Rather than unlimited self-exploitation, in the course of gathering professional experience many people become concerned not with maximising output but rather with achieving a sustainable balance between external demands and their own resources. A frequently mentioned objective is to achieve as stable an income as possible while continuing to establish a market position with limited inputs of work(ing time). In some cases, restricting the working hours invested in profane creative services is also intended to free resources for their own artistic interests. It should be noted that those interviewed from the younger group (i.e. aged +/- 40) with shorter working hours tend not to be among the low earners in this sample, on the contrary a number of them are commercially well established.

One example of this is an entrepreneur who for five years has filmed advertising slots for the PR department of a large company, for instance for jubilees or regular quarterly reports. This major customer is profitable enough for the commercial filmmaker to earn a good income – while not working more than an annual average of 15 to 20 hours a week. He seems to spend the time thus gained on his own interests. For instance, in the year before the interview he used the network that he had developed in his previous job with a film production company to gain an assistant's job on the Austrian location of an international blockbuster action film. Being part of this high-end production was a great learning experience for him. He realises that he would have to reorganise his whole strategy if he lost his major customer.

> 'I: If you average it all out, working very intensively for a few weeks a year and then often less: approximately how many working hours a week do you have?
> L: Well, perhaps 20 hours, if you spread it all out and add everything in. I mean, other things always come up too... In the last year I've really worked a lot. If I now look at the hours again... actually, I would rather say 15 hours a week, so on average. If I leave out the last year.' (Commercial filmmaker, aged 42)

In comparison we consider a graphic designer who set up her own company with a colleague about five years before the interview, after working for years in a large advertising agency. The young company was able to quickly gain a good reputation despite the difficult market – in part through ex-colleagues who had moved to the PR departments of advertising purchasers. Now that her partner has left the business, the interviewee works as an OPE and coordinates a considerable network of freelancers with whom she can tackle relatively large projects. As the acquisition and care of customers has become her core competence, she maintains a central position in the network and earns correspondingly well. She has reduced the amount of creative work she undertakes in favour of project management and outsources a great deal to the freelancers.

> 'I: Do you actually plan to expand?
> Z: No, it's better to do less and demand more for it. So generally I always want to do less than I'm doing. And I think that after ten years you can say, yes, people come to me for a certain reason. Because they think it's good...
> [...]
> I: How about your working times, overall, if you count hours in the week: more or less than 40 hours?
> Z: Well certainly not more, I can't imagine that. [...] No, the aim is simple: better paid hours.
> I: Yes, okay. But better paid hours may mean that I work the same amount and earn more or I earn the same amount and then have less work.
> Z: No, I work less because I ... because it's so well paid, I can much better afford someone else to do the work ... so that I can have it pretty cushy.' (Graphic designer, aged 38)

Founding an association and reducing working hours as a transformative approach

So, what is different about certain organisations that justifies labelling them 'transformative'? I analyse this using the example of a company that is also in the internet industry, which facilitates comparison. This case is part of a series of case studies scrutinising diverse 'alternative' organisational models, ranging from co-operatives to fab labs to the peer-to-peer economy and barter exchanges.

The company in question is a fusion of (so far) five one-person enterprises (three men and two women aged between 35 and 60). The individuals concerned have known each other for a long time through various networks and project constellations but only decided a year ago to legally amalgamate as a joint graphics agency, not in the usual legal form of a limited company but as a co-operative. In addition to fulfilling their desire for greater interaction and community, the decision to form an association was motivated, firstly, by the fact that this allows the entrepreneurs to hold employment contracts (with unemployment insurance benefits). None of the five founding members escapes the need to find customers, but the revenue is now generated in the name of the co-operative, is administered by the co-operative and is then paid to the members according to their employment contracts or working hours. In the initial years, profits are reinvested, e.g. in office infrastructure. It should be mentioned that the five members of this co-operative do not all contribute their entire turnover to the new association, several continue to serve some of their existing customers on a self-employed basis. The association approach is clearly intended to reduce individual business risk. Furthermore, personal liability is limited to a reasonable sum, namely double the amount of the individual investment of circa 2000 euros. As entrepreneurs but simultaneously also neo-employees, there is also the option of drawing unemployment benefit if necessary.

Secondly, the foundation of the co-operative was motivated by a wish for solidarity. For instance, those involved hoped for more democracy than is generally found in a joint-stock company, because in the articles of association it was agreed that each member should have one vote rather than the number of votes being governed by the amount of an individual's investment. There is undoubtedly a transformative aspect to this resolution, which should also help to encourage moderate corporate growth. Contrary to post-growth or shrinkage paradigms, the co-operative is interested in recruiting new members, up to 10-12 in the medium term, in order to extend and safeguard the portfolio. Self-employed acquaintances with complementary competences are therefore offered an opportunity to join the association and thus a chance of escaping the typical insecurity of freelancers.

> 'I: Why a co-operative actually?
> G: Actually it is, for me at least, the greater amount of solidarity. And a different focus now, not so much profit optimisation, which is of course rather the case in a limited company. [...] Till now, we've had a year, it has gone very well. Also we went into this affair on an equal footing, that's already a different understanding.' (Graphic designer, aged 49)

Thirdly, during the interviews several members of the co-operative made clear that they were particularly concerned with restricting their working hours, initially through professional cooperation or project organisation. The desire for more (working-time) efficiency in everyday procedures is naturally not in itself a transformative approach, for instance in socio-ecological terms. However, the additional reasons given are of interest. The focus is not primarily on reducing the number of weekly working hours – for instance, by introducing a binding 30-hour week or something similar, like in other enterprises. That would apparently be relatively difficult for those interviewed during this case study. After the years they have spent organising their own working rhythms, it requires a great deal of effort to even discover how many hours a week they work on average (strictly speaking vs. broadly speaking, etc.). The desire to reduce working hours seems more connected to two specific objectives.

Firstly, the aim is to have more time for creative work, volunteering or alternative pursuits other than their primary professional activities. Four of the five interviewees mentioned diverse non-commercial activities that require a relevant amount of time (1x artistic activity, 2x volunteer work, 1x academic thesis). Those involved do not want to give up such pursuits. Indeed, the intention is that the association should facilitate their non-professional interests by stabilising business operations and the understanding that professional commitments should generally not exceed a 40-hour week.

Secondly, the topic of reducing working hours reflects a desire to take longer breaks but with a right to return to work ensured by membership of the association. As 'habitualised' self-employed service providers, several of the interviewees are all too aware of the problem of being absent for a longer period of time without running the risk of losing customers (e.g. longer holidays abroad), not to mention extended periods of recuperation from illness or burnout conditions. Hence there was a desire to leave the self-employment-past behind and finally enjoy the chance of a break – safeguarded by the vehicle of participation in the co-operative.

> 'B: And the next thing is that there is also a wish to be replaceable. That it is positive if you are replaceable, because then you get breaks for other business and generally.
> I: Have I understood it properly: I can finally be away for longer and then have no problem coming back?
> B: That is a really strong argument for me, namely also that the culture is that it is not just okay but rather that it is even to a degree welcomed. I know that from other organisations, that it is often extremely problematic if people want to back off even just a bit, take leave or educational leave or do voluntary work or something like that.' (Graphic designer, aged 44)

Conclusion

In discourses on post-growth economies, arguments focus on whether and to what extent entire economies can be brought to pursue a no-growth path, particularly for ecological reasons. Discussion considers the policy agendas that should be established – and why it is difficult to identify significant transformation movements on the enterprise level, apart from pioneers in rather narrowly defined sustainability niches or in diverse non-profit worlds. In contrast, this paper argues that a significant proportion of one-person enterprises already implicitly follow a no-growth path and thus actually want to reduce their input, e.g. measured in working hours, rather than expand. This manifests itself in diverse ways and is likely to be far removed from post-growth imperatives.

Using interviews with self-employed creatives in Vienna, it has been demonstrated that many actors develop aspirations that result in the stabilisation of their own output. Their working hours then vary with peaks and troughs in capacity utilisation but average less than 40 hours a week. Many actors perceive the limits of their own resources by the time they are in the middle third of their professional biographies. In light of these limits, it is then about achieving a reasonable balance between input and output. In line with this aim, many entrepreneurs tend to proactively restrict and reduce their working hours. And of course, there are numerous pioneering companies from which much can be learnt.

Cited literature

Antoni-Komar, I., Kropp, C., Peach, N., & Pfriem, R. (2019). *Transformative Unternehmen und die Wende in der Ernährungswirtschaft.* Metropolis Verlag.

Bührmann, A. D., & Hansen, K. (2012). Plädoyer für eine Diversifizierung des unternehmerischen Leitbildes in Forschung und Beratung. *Arbeit,* 21(4), 291–305.

Gebauer, J. (2018). Towards growth-independent and post-growth-oriented entrepreneurship in the SME sector. *Management Revue, 29*(3), 230–256.

Gebauer, J. (2019). Transformatives Unternehmertum aus der Postwachstumsperspektive. In M. Christ, B. Sommer, & K. Stumpf (Eds.), *Transformationsgesellschaften. Zum Wandel gesellschaftlicher Naturverhältnisse.* Metropolis Verlag, 184–204.

Gebauer, J., & Sagiebel, J. (2015). *Wie wichtig ist Wachstum für KMU? Ergebnisse einer Befragung von kleinen und mittleren Unternehmen.* IÖW publication series 208/15.

Hausensteiner, H. (2019, December 17). Weniger ist mehr. *KOMPETENZ-Online.* https://kompetenz-online.at/2019/12/17/weniger-ist-mehr/

Kallis, G., Kalush, M., Flynn H. O., Rossiter, J., & Ashford, N. (2013). "Friday off": reducing working hours in Europe. *Sustainability, 5*(4), 1545–1567.

Knight, K. W., Rosa, E. A., & Schor, J. B. (2013). Could working less reduce pressures on the environment? A cross-national panel analysis of OECD countries, 1970-2007. *Global Environmental Change, 23,* 691–700.

Muckenhuber, J. (2014). *Arbeit ohne Ende? Zur Arbeitsrealität der „neuen" Selbständigen.* Herbert von Halem Verlag.

Nässén, J., & Larsson, J. (2015). Would shorter working time reduce greenhouse gas emissions? An analysis of time use and consumption in Swedish households. *Environment and Planning C: Government and Policy, 33*(4), 726–745.

Pfriem, R., Antoni-Komar, I., & Lautermann, C. (2015). Transformative Unternehmen. *Ökologisches Wirtschaften – Fachzeitschrift, 30*(3), 18.

Schmid, B. (2018). Structured diversity: A practice theory approach to postgrowth organisations. *Management Revue, 29*(3), 281–310.

Sommer, B. (2018). Postkapitalistische Organisationen als Keimzellen einer Postwachstumsgesellschaft. Working Papers der DFG-Kollegforscher_innengruppe „Postwachstumsgesellschaften".

Statistik Austria (2016). *Arbeitsorganisation und Arbeitszeitgestaltung. Modul der Arbeitskräfteerhebung 2015.* Verlag Österreich GmbH.

Wiefek, J., & Heinitz, K. (2018). Common good-oriented companies: Exploring corporate values, characteristics and practices that could support a development towards degrowth. *Management Revue, 29*(3), 311–331.

Lessons from Practice

The emancipatory project of degrowth

An interview with Andrea Vetter and Matthias Schmelzer, conducted by Meret Batke, Mai Anh Ha and Bastian Lange

Andrea Vetter writes, researches, talks and organises for socio-ecological change; primarily for the *'Haus des Wandels'* ('House of Transformation') in eastern Brandenburg, for the *'Konzeptwerk Neue Ökonomie'* ('Laboratory for new economic ideas') in Leipzig and for the journal *'Oya: enkeltauglich leben'* ('Oya: grandchildren-compatible living'). She teaches 'Transformation Design' at University of Fine Arts in Braunschweig.

Matthias Schmelzer works with *'Konzeptwerk Neue Ökonomie'* on social utopias, alternative economics and degrowth and is a research assistant at the University of Jena. He is actively involved in the climate justice movement.

In debates on post-growth and degrowth, how do you dissociate yourselves from right-wing spatial semantics?

Matthias Schmelzer: One of the main thrusts of the postgrowth or degrowth discussion – in our German book on this concept we use both terms almost synonymously – is to confront the neoliberal, authoritarian and fossil globalisation with a vision of a more small-scale economic system that focuses on needs and care. This has certain superficial similarities with right-wing spatial semantics or imaginings, so that those on the right have at times taken up 'post-growth' as a keyword. In particular, the far-right faction of the AfD [*Alternative für Deutschland* – Alternative for Germany] expresses views that refer to a small-scale approach, and several years ago they used the term 'post-growth economy'.

From an emancipatory, left-wing perspective, the possibility of appropriation is of course problematic for critical debate and for a vision of a regionalised and de-globalised economy. That's why in our view the basic motivation and focus for emancipatory post-growth and degrowth policies should always be the prospect of global justice, which goes hand in hand with a call for open borders. Open primarily in relation to the free movement of people, not necessarily also of goods, services and capital – it may very well be reasonable to discuss certain restrictions there. For instance, implementing a post-growth economy in a globalised world economy will certainly involve controlling flows of capital in the transition period.

In discussing alternatives to borders, the degrowth debate uses the term 'open re-localisation' to clearly distinguish this from culturally closed 'bioregions'. A central part of degrowth practices, and one that is still insufficiently implemented, is for instance practical solidarity with refugees who have been deprived of their rights to freedom of movement.

Is that a kind of internal decolonisation or de-imperialisation that every individual should practise?

Matthias Schmelzer: In the degrowth debate the focus is on economic categories such as GDP that we have internalised and on questioning our Western vision of what makes a good life. Serge Latouche, one of the early pioneers of degrowth, proposed terming this a 'decolonisation of the imaginary', but there is also criticism of the use of this notion. In essence this criticism says that 'colonisation' and 'decolonisation' are terms that were coined to apply to very specific historical and social contexts and today their main function is to address racism and the consequences of colonisation. When these terms are transferred to another field such as economics, then their critical potential is taken and appropriated for something else. Nonetheless, the fundamental idea of questioning and freeing ourselves from entrenched imaginaries about hierarchical society and capitalist economies is central to the degrowth discussion.

Are there practical examples for this fundamental idea of degrowth?

Andrea Vetter: A change of perspective is needed to learn to really see the world in which I live. One example is the omnipresent smartphone. If I look closely at the phone in my pocket, what materials it is made of, which factory it was manufactured in, what infrastructures are necessary for it to work, then I learn to see what relationships are concealed beneath its shiny black surface – namely exploitative relationships that spread around the whole globe. All the global, growth-driven, exploitative relations are contained in the materiality of the quite everyday things that we surround ourselves with – whether in the concrete of our houses, in the plastic and microelectronics of our devices or in the fossil fuels that transport us and keep us warm. Sharpening this view of the world helps me to discern the world in which I find myself and then to engage collectively with others to change these exploitative relationships.

Do processes like the planned phase-out of coal represent an opportunity?

Andrea Vetter: Yes, that could really be the case – for instance in the Lausitz region, a big lignite mining area in East Germany, there's a plan to invest 17 billion euros in the so-called structural transformation by the 2030s. This money could be used to initiate a socio-ecological model region, if there was a lot more cooperation with local civil society actors. Instead though, the road network is being upgraded and tax breaks are offered in an attempt to attract industry. I think it's fatal to try to move forward into the next 20 years with yesterday's concepts – with the same imperial ways of life and economic approaches that have led to ecological and social destruction. After 1990 and the end of the GDR, people in the Lausitz region already experienced one structural transformation, a brutal process. Now they deserve better than the foul promises of the same 'blossoming landscapes' that have not come true in the last 30 years.

What are the core topics and core processes of an emancipatory degrowth economy, also in relation to spatial references used by the political right?

Matthias Schmelzer: The right-wing and racist approach to space involves strengthening closed, bio-ethnic regions. Degrowth is about the opposite, namely global justice, for the sake of which globalisation processes must be driven back in several fields – like so-called free trade. This somewhat complicated line of argument means that it is not always easy for the degrowth discussion to gain a foothold in left-wing emancipatory debates. There's a lot of scepticism because historically speaking, most concepts that focused on regionalisation and criticism of industrialism were reactionary or against global justice.

It is especially important to talk about socio-ecological transformation, to stop people being afraid of the future and of changes. This needs to occur on a very concrete basis, which is why socio-political demands play such a great role in the degrowth discussion. Ecological and social issues must be very closely linked together.

In nearly all proposals of the degrowth and post-growth debate, demands for a radical redistribution of income and wealth are central – concepts that focus on a universal basic income or concepts involving radical cuts in average working hours and periods of employment. These are suggestions that could actually be tried out experimentally in model regions like the Lausitz, where transformations to phase out coal dependency are necessary. In these experimental regions, society as a whole must take on responsibility and ensure funding to make this sort of approach possible. Current politics, however, is not moving in the direction of transformations or a fundamental rethinking of economic and social priorities.

Is it understandable that people, for instance in the Lausitz region, are afraid of a third – ecological – transformation?

Matthias Schmelzer: The so-called 'reforms' or 'transformations' of recent decades have not improved the lives of most people. Fears or concerns are therefore understandable, as transformations usually bring something bad for people. But it is difficult to sympathise with an attitude that scapegoats people who are discriminated against, have fewer resources and less access to power. That is what is happening at the moment, because in the widest sense migrants and people of colour are being made the scapegoats. There are numerous investigations that show that there is no obvious rational connection between problems in the rural areas of eastern Germany and the immigration policy of recent decades. Nonetheless, many people believe this is the case and see concepts like homeland (*Heimat*) and right-wing nationalist politics as a solution. It is important to set clear boundaries against such racist attitudes. And it is important to make clear that the economic policy of the AfD is not one that will benefit 'ordinary people' – on the contrary. Nonetheless, in the current political situation it is an important challenge to convincingly convey the message that the pending socio-ecological transformation is one that really does provide a good life for all.

Andrea Vetter: I think it's also important here not to take a universalising approach and pretend all the rural regions of eastern Germany are the same. If you really go to a specific village and talk to the people you see that the conditions are different in each village. One village faces demolition to make way for a lignite mine – of course the residents there are pleased if coal is phased out quickly and their village is saved. In another village nearby some of the men work in mining and are worried about losing their jobs. In a third village the residents are resigned because the solar-panel factory there closed several years ago, due to renewable energy legislation that destroyed large parts of renewables industry in East Germany, which by the way had a similar number of employees to the lignite industry.

The difference is though that one industry has a powerful lobby behind it and the other doesn't. This means that media and politics tend to exaggerate phenomena and discourses that actually have little to do with the real life and perceptions of local people.

What do manifestations of right-wing spatial semantics look like in transformation regions in East Germany?

Andrea Vetter: In many East German municipalities a lot of people over the age of 60 actually tend to vote for the left, for historical reasons. In the election in Thuringia for example, it was primarily people between 30 and 45 who voted for right-wing parties like the AfD. This has its roots in the political vacuum of the 1990s when GDR state institutions suddenly disappeared and with them a lot of local cultural institutions where young people were socialised. Right-wing extremists from West Germany deliberately targeted the East at this time, doing 'missionary work' there. So it was not simply the case that 'the people' in the countryside suddenly discovered their racism, but rather that this was targeted and promoted by right-wing extremists and activists.

But it is also important to look specifically at good examples and options. There are many engaged actors locally who have for decades countered right-wing narratives with youth work and education, and especially in the so-called structurally disadvantaged regions there are also many spatial pioneers who are experimenting with creative, emancipatory and ecological lifestyles. I think there are certainly links to post-growth discussions in rural post-socialist areas – with these new actors who enter into abandoned spaces but also with the experiences and knowledge of the older generations, whose everyday lives still include subsistence production, repairing things and being frugal with resources. It is indeed possible to link this local subsistence orientation with sustainable, feminist and anti-racist contexts instead of letting the right-wing propagandists do their work. But this needs political long-term work on a local level.

Matthias Schmelzer: Realistically speaking, it is also understandable that degrowth concepts strike more of a note in urban contexts, as degrowth is also about the depriveleging of people who profit particularly strongly from the imperial mode of living. Those who live in cities are also those who participate most strongly in the imperial mode of living, who fly most and who consume more than average, as high incomes strongly correlate with ecological footprints. That is also why it is important to set the discourse straight. The main problems of the imperial mode of living, of externalisation societies and for the climate catastrophe are not the car drivers in rural East Germany, and not the miners, but rather the growth-oriented, profit-driven economic system that primarily benefits an urban, globally oriented elite.

Is it possible to learn to live a post-growth life?

Matthias Schmelzer: The pending transformation process is an unbelievably multifaceted, complex and long-term project. If we work for an ecological, social and democratic economy, then it's important to understand how various transformation strategies complement each other. We need spaces where alternatives can be tried out on a small scale and new post-growth practices and imaginaries can be learned. In the same way we also need far-reaching reforms in institutions and infrastructures. And we need strong social movements that fight for counter-hegemony. That is especially important because what the present-day political parties propose in their party programmes is, in our view, completely insufficient for a future-proof society and economy. That's why we start with strengthening social movements, driving civil society discourse and so shifting the space of what is imaginable and possible.

Andrea Vetter: For years, the '*Konzeptwerk Neue Ökonomie*' has been involved in organising many conferences, but we also deliberately take the degrowth summer schools out to places, e.g. as climate camps. Temporary places like climate camps are heterotopias where new routines can be established and counter-hegemonic solidaric modes of living can be tested out. For one week, these heterotopias create a strong resonance between hundreds or thousands of people who practise energy sufficiency and democratic self-organisation – be it in using and caring for compost toilets, building solar turbines or organising shared childcare.

Experiences in workshops, camps, conferences or practical workcamps like this are an important part of transformative learning. Our target groups are often mostly young, highly educated people who haven't decided yet what work they want to do or where they want to live. If, early on in their professional careers, a lot of these people get impulses encouraging them to approach their lifepaths quite differently and not to seek the well-trodden paths, then that makes a big difference. If people decide to work for a socio-ecological transformation there are a lot of jobs to do: establishing new institutions, networks and cooperatives, as well as changing existing institutions from the inside. As a social anthropologist and transformation designer, I've witnessed over and over again the importance of such temporary heterotopias for making a profound change in people's lives.

What transformation strategies are required to work towards a post-growth society?

Andrea Vetter: The 'Laboratory for New Economic Ideas' works together with various social movements that have different target groups, e.g. with the network 'Care Revolution', which includes 80 smaller groups based in German-speaking countries concerned with the topic of care work –both paid and unpaid care-givers like nurses, parents or sex workers, and also care-receivers, who for instance employ assistants.

The idea is to deepen a discourse in wider society around care work. The people who are involved in 'Care Revolution' recognise the need for a society beyond growth but argue from a different perspective than the ecological one. We emphasise the links between the social and ecological crises and believe it is important to tackle both together. This means including the ecological question in the question of care work and the transformation of the economy and also the other way round – if from an ecological perspective we need a very different economy then we must put care work at the heart of this different economy. We work with actors who are starting from different places and we draw up and support strategies about how the various issues can be more closely interlinked.

What challenges emerge?

Andrea Vetter: We need institutional, fundamental reforms that extend the scope of action for existing nowtopias and movements. Every time a nowtopia project starts in a concrete location, it becomes obvious that the existing laws, subsidies and legal forms are generally aimed at profit-oriented and large actors and work against socio-ecological pioneers. We need fundamental institutional reforms to change the parameters of the economic system – top-down, if you like – and simultaneously bottom-up strategies to create local ways of living characterised by more solidarity; they inspire and learn from one another. To achieve this, we need a counter-hegemony that involves interventions in the public sphere of the media and education, but also includes practices like civil disobedience and forms of radical protest. This is all happening at once and requires appreciation and respect for one another. No individual can tackle all the fields of social change at the same time, but together we can take further steps.

Degrowth
A kind of pragmatic utopian thinking, re-politicising humanistic debates

An interview with Dr Helen Jarvis, conducted by Christian Schulz

Helen Jarvis is Professor in Social Geography at Newcastle University, UK. Helen's research focuses, among other things, on the compatibility of family and work, on the significance of public spaces and on the 'social architecture' of new collaborative living arrangements. She is also concerned with the role of civic engagement in sustainable urban development.
https://www.ncl.ac.uk/gps/staff/profile/helenjarvis.html#background

What do degrowth approaches mean for your own research?

Helen Jarvis: I very much embrace degrowth thinking as a social geographer, so for me it is all about the relevance of geography as a scholar-activist. I probably don't think of myself as employing a fully-fledged participatory action research. My degrowth understanding is closely aligned with a kind of pragmatic utopian thinking. So, my collaboration with external partners and a broad based alliance of community organisations, really of bottom-up civil society is probably messier and more about agitating action than it is participatory action research. Indeed, a lot of what I'm doing is not really research at all, it's more about working within civil society. But going back to what I understand as the relevance of degrowth for geography and myself as a social geographer: for me it's about re-politicising humanistic debates concerning where and how we live with each other on the earth. It starts with questions that geography has always worked with in terms of urban development, urban planning, liveability, but it is saying that the question 'where and how we live' is not adequately managed through the current lens of urban planning. We must completely reimagine those relationships.

What can we contribute to 'spatialise' the degrowth debate?

Helen Jarvis: For me, the spatial geography of degrowth is about the scale of living and the scale of civil society alliance and activism. So degrowth is not just an economic concept and the counter-hegemonic narrative that degrowth contributes to, it is more about opening a scale of action both in scholarship, a scale of action that is much more about activism and social change and transformation, but also a scale of activism. My focus, geographically, is on that meso-scale, so it's not about the individual consumer citizen, the individual making choices about how and where they live, but rather the meso-scale of thinking and acting differently. I think re-politicising the urban politics and spatial justice debates allows for – it's not really using the language of degrowth, but I see it as entirely compatible – this idea of conviviality, the political sense of conviviality. What is public space for? It's for this renewed idea of a civil society. There's also a sense of a space that's free from private interests and market interests and the state and is reworking conditions of possibility. It's socio-spatial.

To what extent are our textbook models and theoretical and conceptual underpinnings challenged by degrowth thinking?

Helen Jarvis: I think that social geography has a similar problem, perhaps, to economic geography, certainly in the textbooks, in that there is a tendency I think to slip between this preoccupation with identity politics and the individual and a cultural social geography of identity and a sense of 'where is the radical critique?'. Maybe that's not really the way to express it, I suppose I don't see a lot of the degrowth discourse or degrowth as a counter-hegemonic narrative entering social geography. And I also have always been a little bit frustrated by this disconnect between, for instance, issues around the housing crisis and the social justice side of that, and precarious employment and the corrosion of working life and the social justice implications of that, and bigger debates around nature and environmental sustainability. So, degrowth discourse, for me, as many advocates talk about it, this kind of missile concept, this bombshell, a symbolic term, it's an opportunity to say there isn't a kind of meta-theory that's going to make solutions between social and economic justice align together. But this bombshell concept does allow us to recognise the interdependence, the mosaic of things like housing, employment, and social everyday realities, such as feelings of isolation or inclusion and the conventional hyper-privatised neighbourhood.

This goes back, in terms of my journey, to the work I did years ago now, 2001–2005. I was working closely around work-life balance, I wrote the book *Work/Life City Limits* in 2005, and I didn't use the word degrowth, but looking back it was entirely about engaging with the ideas of degrowth. I talked about practical limits to growth, and it was bound up in this meso-scale of home-work family nexus, and I felt it was critically important to revive this idea of human-environment connections but not in the way that actor-network theory was more than representational: it was instead about everyday pragmatism. Where are the limits to the possibilities for people to act intentionally, to consciously follow the grain of a moral limits to growth, to do what they feel is right for their ethic of care? In current parlance this would be in the context of climate emergency. So, as far as the early inspiration of degrowth, I was motivated by the work of Anders Hayden: he wrote this book called 'Sharing the work, sparing the planet', and he was talking there about working hours reduction – as one part of a virtuous circle of reducing over- and excessive consumption and waste. And what was useful about this was that it offered a simple way into degrowth, but what I also liked was that it very easily linked that nexus of 'where and how we live' in relation to housing, transport and commuting, the everyday decisions of getting children to and from school, whether we walk and cycle, whether we can walk or cycle, the relationship of space and time. He conceptualised, in a compelling way, all that most vicious or virtuous connectedness that either locks us into a very unsustainable and exploitative relationship with others and the planet or allows us to step out of that lock-in effect.

So, the notion of scale seems to play a major role in your work?

Helen Jarvis: I wouldn't want you to take away from this discussion that I privilege the local. Obviously, the work I do around collaborative housing and cohousing is about a scale of belonging and intentional practice. This scale is necessarily limited in size. Cohousing schemes tend to view this optimal scale as around 25 households while the intentional 'we thinking' practised in an eco-village would be around 150 people. Both examples describe an intimate scale of belonging and collaboration. At the same time, it would be wrong to extract these intentional scales from their wider ecology. This multi-scale thinking resonates with what Ivan Illich conjured up really nicely in the notion of a 'commune of communes' whereby you could say that the scale of belonging is nested within multiple scales that are 'scaled out' rather than 'scaled up': not one large scale of region, but a region made up of scaled-out intimate scales of belonging. A good example of that would be the current social movements of lasting change around the school climate change strike (I was at one on Friday), and Extinction Rebellion. These all operate through a process of social affinity groups. The language of an affinity group, or the scale of an affinity group, is aligned with face-to-face alliances whereby people can build relationships of trust and seek common ground. For example, I'm involved with Citizens UK which is broad-based community organising, a bit like the Barrack Obama model of community organising, and this is on a person to person scale of listening to what the problems are and then acting collectively on achievable, meaningful change. This way it's helpful to think of scale rather than territory because these are spatial scales that are necessarily interpersonal and context dependent, so the local isn't just a scale of belonging, it's of the earth, or the terroir. Slow-food and slow-cities movements also show this, as well as Extinction Rebellion. When it works with an indigenous local knowledge, it's about what gives meaning and purpose to environmental action, in and of, a place. So, I don't want to sound like I'm wanting the best of all worlds here, but I don't think it should be a debate of 'is the local or is the region the most relevant geographic spatial lens?'. For me, as a social geographer, it's about the interpersonal and the empowered ability to act as changemaker.

How do you convey the notion of degrowth in your teaching?

Helen Jarvis: Well, I think there is a problem with language, and in my undergraduate teaching, I tend not to use the term degrowth. It's not very easily understood. It doesn't translate very well; it becomes quite abstract. Again, I tend to draw upon the language of civic activism, and on alliances and co-operation and on the ability to unlock the capacity to act. I draw a distinction between individuals acting on their own lifestyle habits as being quite disadvantaged, and I demonstrate alternative forms of groupwork and group dynamics. To help overcome the language barriers, I introduce scenarios and examples of inspirational degrowth activists and scholars into my teaching. I have a set of cards that tell the stories of urban food growers and people who have organised local sharing economies. These provide a real name, a face and a story, to offer a joined-up belief in degrowth practice. It is difficult for students to relate to degrowth when it is presented in a theoretical and abstract way and that has caused quite a lot of misunderstanding. Degrowth theory is widely considered either to be very fuzzy or very ideological, so to cut through that I go to the level of introducing my own perspective. I say 'I'm a single parent, it's crazy how I have to manage a house and all aspects of a private life, and working full-time', and all these things 'I'm one person', and then I say 'when I've gone to stay in Christiania, or a cohousing project, it has been possible to live collaboratively, in a more tribal way, with others, to raise children together and to organise our housing solutions and work collectively'. So, I introduce a lot of myself as a practical way of cutting through that fuzzy, ideological understanding of degrowth. And that says that I acknowledge having reached a point in my life as a parent, and I'm thinking here of the climate emergency, where I must act – we must act. In that respect the methods of teaching are about hope and the real potential we must harness to make a difference collectively, rather than as individual consumers.

I'm taking a group of students in the spring to Copenhagen, for an annual field trip. I usually take them to a housing cooperative or cohousing scheme, as well as to the former squatters' settlement of Christiania, where I've done some research before. But I'm also going to be meeting up with some anthropology scholars at Copenhagen University who have been making comparisons between the kind of environmental sensibility and mindset that most Copenhageners are encouraged to practice, recycling in their households, and travelling by bicycle etc., versus more intentional ways of reducing energy use through sharing, in cohousing but also in eco-communities. This is interesting because it shows us what we can achieve collectively that we can't manage individually. And it's not just about the scale, it's about the social learning that takes place, we retain privacy but when we live a little more consciously with others and make decisions that have a bigger impact on others, I think it pushes us to degrow, to step off the treadmill of work and consumption.

If you were given an unconditional degrowth research grant allowing you to hire a postdoc for two years, what would be the topical focus of your project?

Helen Jarvis: I am very interested – and this is going to sound more esoteric, when you are given the opportunity to reflect and research in more depth, it does come down to more a burning curiosity – I'm very interested in this sense of intentionality: we are all torn between contradictions to do the right thing but also to live in the now, and I think there's something about working in a group, collaboratively, which is incredibly difficult. I know this from all the endless committee meetings I sit on to try and make change happen. So, I am motivated to explore this socio-cultural but also psychological and socio-technical infrastructure of intentionality: what really will facilitate and unlock collaboration? How do we scale out a new 'normal' of being intentional in a way that stimulates this virtuous cycle of being intentional for people and the planet? It could be that I would explore this through a movement such as Extinction Rebellion, because within that movement, there's been a real tension between anarchy, where people pursue their own action, the example here was that there was some direct action of jumping on trains and public transport which seemed to completely contradict the idea that public transport is a good thing for the environment. So, my ideal research would harness the power of groups and collaboration, allowing that to go in myriad different directions. I'm interested in this tension between harnessing the power of collaboration and citizen action, civic action, but also this idea of what soft infrastructure would propel 'we-thinking' and intentional behaviour, intentional practice, to reach beneficial results for the planet, for the people of the planet.

I have a longer-term goal to write a book, and there's a suggested working title: 'Being intentional for people and planet'. It would be an anthology of my work on various apparently quite radical eco-communities in different places. What do we learn from them about different capacities to change and to work collaboratively?

II. Spaces of Possibility

'We need places for experimentation where the new options provided by post-growth societies become tangible.'

Uwe Schneidewind

Growth independence through social innovations? An analysis of potential growth effects of social innovations in a Swiss mountain region

Pascal Tschumi, Andrea Winiger, Samuel Wirth, Heike Mayer, Irmi Seidl

Social innovations are being increasingly discussed as solutions to the diverse challenges faced by rural, peripheral areas. However, the economic growth effects of social innovations are unclear. One of the open questions is whether social innovations trigger new growth in regions or contribute to growth independence. This paper seeks to fill this research gap. To this end, an inventory of social innovations in the Swiss mountain region of the Bernese Oberland has been compiled and the potential growth effects (economic growth stimulation and economic growth independence) of the social innovations were investigated using specially developed indicators. Ideal types of social innovations with particularly marked potential growth effects are presented as the results of the investigation.

The analysis of social innovations and their growth effects is undertaken in the context of the social, economic and ecological challenges facing Swiss mountain regions. Out-migration is quite high in Swiss Alpine regions, amounting to about 11% of the population between 1981 and 2010 (Bundesamt für Raumentwicklung, 2012). The consequence is an aging population. In the course of the Euro crisis that began in 2010 the Swiss franc increased in value so that revenue from European visitors sank noticeably (Müller-Jentsch, 2017). Furthermore, scarcity of building land for new infrastructure and buildings is increasing (Bundesamt für Raumentwicklung, 2017). In addition, the maintenance of basic services is threatened, especially in the health sector (Cerny/Rosemann/Tandjung et al., 2016). Last but not least, the mountain regions are particularly strongly affected by the numerous consequences of climate change (Schmucki/Marty/Fierz et al., 2017).

Swiss regional policy aims to promote entrepreneurship and innovation with the help of regionally initiated projects and thus to counter the economic challenges (Staatssekretariat für Wirtschaft, 2017). This policy takes an export-based approach, assuming that economic growth in a region is triggered by key sectors that serve external demand. However, this growth-oriented approach has its limitations. Not every region has a leading export sector or the potential to develop one, not least because Swiss mountain regions are socio-economically heterogeneous (Mayer/Rime/Meili et al., 2018). Furthermore, the probability of the revenue generated circulating in these regions sinks as the mobility of people and goods in the Alpine area increases (Segessemann/Crevoisier, 2016). The Swiss regional policy of the late 2010s accordingly lacked 'situationally adaptable (also non-economic) perspectives' (Peter/Rink/Forster et al., 2016: 6, translated from German).

This is the background against which social innovations are recommended as a solution to problems in peripheral and rural areas. Firstly, social innovations are proposed by representatives of EU organisations as a means of increasing economic growth in such areas (European Commission, 2017; Nicholls/Edmiston, 2018). Secondly, researchers like Dax and Fischer (2018: 297) and Dewald and Rother (2019) argue that future regional development approaches should extend beyond strategies that target growth to address local participation and social innovation. Social innovations could help regions to solve their problems (Bock, 2016; Neumeier, 2012), for instance by successfully implementing knowledge from outside the region (Noack/Federwisch, 2019). Post-growth authors emphasis the potential of social innovation initiatives to contribute to a (more) growth-independent society and economy and thus to (more) growth-independent regions (Elsen, 2014; Seidl/Zahrnt, 2022). Much discussed examples include local currencies, community housing projects or repair initiatives (Burkhart/Schmelzer/Treu, 2020; Habermann, 2009).

This brief insight into the academic discourses shows that social innovations are attributed with various impacts on regional growth. However, research on these impacts is not particularly advanced (Pelka/Terstriep, 2016: 13; Secco/Pisani/Da Re et al., 2019: 10) and the extent to which social innovations can stimulate regional growth or contribute towards growth independence remains unclear. This is the point which this chapter seeks to address. The research question on which it is based is: What are the potential economic growth effects of social innovations in the Bernese Oberland?

The Bernese Oberland is a mountainous area that lies north of the Swiss high Alpine region and has about 200,000 inhabitants in an area of circa 2,900 km². With around four million overnight stays a year, the tourism industry accounts for over 35% of gross domestic product (GDP) for many places (Rütter/Rütter-Fischbacher, 2016). International tourism has a long tradition here and has always followed a growth-oriented strategy (Ebneter/Liechti, 2019; von Rütte, 2007). The economic structure, the culture and public and private stakeholders are correspondingly influenced by the dominant role of tourism (Haisch, 2017: 221 f.). Developments within the region are by no means homogeneous. Tourist centres like the Jungfrau region and the municipalities of Grindelwald and Lauterbrunnen and their surroundings are characterised by high and slightly growing volumes of overnight stays (with annual overnight stays amounting to almost one million) (Bundesamt für Statistik, 2018a). In Grindelwald the population is also growing slowly (2010 to 2016). This contrasts with the far east of the region where the number of overnight stays in the municipalities Meiringen and Hasliberg fell from 2013 to 2018 (Bundesamt für Statistik, 2018a). With the exception of the central municipality Meiringen, the population in the far east is declining (Bundesamt für Statistik, 2018b).

Social innovations and growth (in)dependence

Social innovations are the goal of many political programmes (Grimm/Fox/Baines et al., 2013) and the focus of newly founded research centres (e.g. Stanford Center for Social Innovation or Young Foundation). However, the definitions and understandings of social innovations in the literature are most diverse. This may be because the various disciplines – transformation research, sociology, regional sciences or economics – conduct research on social innovations using their own definitions (Edwards-Schachter/Wallace, 2017). Meta-analyses of social innovations confirm the different research streams (Ayob/Teasdale/Fagan, 2016; Edwards-Schachter/Wallace, 2017; van der Have/Rubalcaba, 2016). One important strand of research expects social innovations to have positive effects on society. In particular authors who focus on local development are well-known for this research, especially Moulaert and Mulgan. They view social innovations as solutions for social problems and as impulses for empowerment and for changes in social relations (Moulaert/MacCallum/Hiller, 2013; Mulgan/Tucker/Ali et al., 2007). Another strand of research revolves around the work of Franz, Hochgerner and Howaldt (2012) and adopts a sociological and more neutral perspective to the effects of social innovations, focusing primarily on changed social practices and relations. Mumford (2002) sees social innovations as providing new ideas about how social relations and social organisation could be structured to achieve a common goal. The creative process of generating and implementing innovation is the focus here, also within businesses. Overall, it can be noted that some definitions focus more on the innovation process while others concentrate on the results or effects of the innovation. This paper uses a definition that integrates the different orientations and draws on the bibliometric analysis by Ayob, Teasdale and Fagan (2016). The definition is as follows:

A social innovation consists of new forms of cooperation of individuals or organisations that lead to new ideas, of which the implementation is at least considered. In regional development, such innovations can have a positive impact on society, improve the quality of life and/or change social or power relations.

This definition allows for a rather broad understanding of social innovations and an open approach to the phenomenon under investigation. It is suitable for application to the Swiss mountain region with its multifaceted socio-economic structures, as social innovations do not only emerge in connection with the problems or challenges of this rural area but are also developed in response to economic growth opportunities.

The basic precondition for our definition of a social innovation – a new form of cooperation – is based on a sociological understanding that conceives of 'new' as extraordinary for the geographical area of investigation. For a social innovation, it is crucial that this new cooperation leads to a new idea, the implementation of which is at least considered (Ayob/Teasdale/Fagan, 2016). Furthermore, the definition includes two characteristics that describe the effect of a social innovation: first, a positive effect for society; second, the transformation of social relations and power relations.

In order to examine the link between social innovations and growth, relevant concepts of growth are clarified in the following. Enterprise growth refers to both growth in volumes of sales, production and orders and also growth in the financial profitability of an enterprise (turnover, profit, cashflow, return on investment). We understand enterprises as organisations that pursue business practices, i.e. they create and exploit 'deliverables to cover third-party requirements with due regard to economic efficiency' (Lück, 1990, translated from German). This includes 'classical' companies but also associations, foundations and cooperatives. Regional growth primarily refers to the growth of regional gross domestic product, i.e. the total of regional value added. Growth independence is not understood as the opposite of growth, namely shrinking. We rather adopt the meaning established in the post-growth literature (see Schmelzer/Vetter, 2019: 158 f.; 171): the ability of a society including its economy and its institutions to continue to fulfil its functions but no longer to be existentially dependent on economic growth (Seidl/Zahrnt, 2010; Seidl/Zahrnt, 2022). Basic social and economic functions include safeguarding livelihoods, participation in society for all, basic infrastructure and healthcare.

Methodology

There is currently no comprehensive overview of social innovations in mountain regions and existing inventories (for the Alpine region) are neither systematic nor do they extend beyond case studies (see SIMRA, 2018). Our comprehensive inventory of social innovations in the Bernese Oberland helps to close this gap. It utilises a database of innovative projects, organisations, offerings or initiatives that were planned or carried out in the Bernese Oberland between 1997 and 2018. To compile the inventory[1], various databases from regional development programmes[2] and innovation prizes[3] were identified and merged. An online survey of the municipal secretaries (the senior administrative officers) of all 76 municipalities of the Bernese Oberland was also conducted in order to identify other local projects and initiatives.[4] In addition, a systematic online search and newspaper review[5] was conducted

---

1 The inventory is publicly accessible on the website www.sozinno.unibe.ch
2 New Regional Policy (*Neue Regionalpolitik*, NRP); Innovation, Cooperation and Knowledge Development in Tourism (*Innovation, Zusammenarbeit und Wissensaufbau im Tourismus*, Innotour); Regional Conference East Oberland (*Regionalkonferenz Oberland-Ost*, RKOO); Social Innovation in Marginalised Rural Areas (SIMRA); the association 'vorwärtsbeo'.
3 Milestone, Prix Montagna, Swiss Mountain Award, Bernese Innovation Prize, PrixWINtutti
4 The survey was able to identify 26 potential social innovations.
5 Five regional newspapers were examined.

between January and June 2019. Overall, it was possible to identify 979 potential social innovations.

With the help of an analysis matrix consisting of 23 evaluation criteria[6], we identified the social innovations that corresponded to the definition above. The goal of the social innovation was assessed in order to determine if it fulfilled the two additional characteristics. A total of 68 social innovations were identified, 32 of which aim to achieve positive effects for society and six of which aim to change social relations and/or power relations. To identify the social innovations, all projects and initiatives in the database were independently evaluated by two researchers. The intercoder reliability of the analysis is 90%.

In a subsequent step, the social innovations that had been identified were assessed in terms of their potential growth effects using theory-based indicators. The set of indicators that we developed for this analysis is based on the literature on drivers of enterprise growth (Gebauer/Lange/Posse, 2017; Mewes/Gebauer, 2015; Posse, 2015; Richters/Siemoneit, 2019) and on strategies of non-growing enterprises (Liesen/Dietsche/Gebauer, 2013; Posse, 2015). The aim was to derive indicators from these business strategies that could be applied to the region and to economic actors. This involved identifying the mechanisms of the growth or non-growth strategies of enterprises. From these mechanisms, it was possible to derive 39 indicators which point to growth stimulating or growth independence effects. Hence, the indicators capture two different growth effects: first, the effects that stimulate economic growth in regions or enterprises (henceforth called growth stimulation effects); second, effects that make these regions or enterprises more growth independent (henceforth called growth independence effects). In order to analyse the potential effects of the 68 social innovations in our inventory, we assessed which indicators could potentially apply to which social innovation. To this end we gathered additional information on the emergence, implementation or goal of the social innovations through online research. The evaluation was independently carried out by two researchers with an intercoder reliability of 88%.

---

6 The analysis was based on criteria for the following categories: Cooperation / Novelty / Idea / Bernese Oberland / Improvements in quality of life / Changes in social relations / Changes in power relations.

Growth effects

The following table displays the indicators and their growth effects as developed from the literature analysis.

Table 1: Indicators of growth independence and growth effects / Sources: primarily Gebauer/Lange/Posse, 2017; Paech, 2012a; Posse, 2015

No.	Indicator	Growth effects
U1	Regional sales structures	Less price competition; some degree of guaranteed market; adaptation to consumer needs; promotion of small businesses (U8)
U2	Regional procurement structures	Less price competition; guaranteed market for manufactured products; promotion of small businesses (U8)
U3	Economic actors in close contact	Reduced price competition; adaptation to consumer needs; some degree of guaranteed market; building of trust with at best favourable financing and reduced pressure to generate returns
U4	De-commercialisation of production	Absence of the growth dynamic of capitalist market relations; greater self-sufficiency
U5	Reduction in hours of paid work	Decline in consumption and reduction of capitalist market dynamics
U6	Low debt capital and interest	Less pressure to generate returns to pay interest/dividends; less outside control by external investors
U7	Low capital intensity in production	Less pressure to generate returns to pay interest/dividends; less outside control by external investors
U8	Small or medium-sized enterprise	Less striving for growth, no negative scale effects (administrative costs etc.), improved crisis resistance and less dependence on market dynamics
U9	Communication in favour of limiting consumption and production	Limiting growth in line with consumer demand
U10	Communication of social and ecological indicators	Focus on entrepreneurial success through various enterprise goals

No.	Indicator	Growth effects
U11	Niche markets	Less price competition; some degree of guaranteed market
U12	Long useful life	Limiting growth caused by consumer demand
U13	Craft skills for maintenance and repair	Limiting growth through consumer demand; de-commercialisation (U4)
U14	Prosumers	Adaptation to consumer needs; limiting growth through consumer demand; niche markets (U11); de-commercialisation (U4)
U15	Self-managed enterprise	Broader understanding of entrepreneurial success than just growth; small and medium-sized businesses (U8)
U16	Substitution of products by services	Less economies of scale in providing services than products, i.e. less growth dynamics
U17	Product sales (fair prices, purchase guarantees, no bulk discounts)	Less price competition; reduced cost pressure, reduced incentives for economies of scale
U18	Low advertising expenditure	Limit on growth caused by consumer demand
U19	Short value chain	Limit on the number of enterprises involved that are striving for growth; production volume aligned with demand
U20	Regional value chain	Less price competition; involvement of smaller enterprises; guaranteed demand; production volume aligned with demand; possibly favourable external financing.

Table 2: Indicators of growth stimulation and growth effects / Sources: primarily Gebauer/Lange/Posse, 2017; Paech, 2012a; Posse, 2015

No.	Indicator	Growth effects
S1	Bulk discounts when purchasing	Incentives for more consumption or production
S2	Remuneration of management according to growth figures and market value	Strategic and operative growth focus
S3	Higher proportion of fixed costs in production	Incentive to increase production to realise economies of scale
S4	Higher leverage	Great pressure to generate returns to pay interest/dividends; more outside control by external investors
S5	Planned obsolescence	Increase in consumer demand
S6	Increasing consumption (psychological obsolescence, symbolic, emotional brand communication)	Increase in consumer demand
S7	Innovation (process, product, technology)	Increased production due to increased productivity of innovations; new demands due to new products (features)
S8	Volatile capacity expansion	Increased need for outside investment; long-term pressure to grow
S9	High capital requirement (for research and development)	Great pressure to generate returns to pay interest/dividends; development of products with scaling potential; high levels of outside control by external investors
S10	High capital intensity of production	Great pressure to generate returns to pay interest/dividends; maximisation of economies of scale; high levels of outside control by external investors

No.	Indicator	Growth effects
S11	Focus on communication of financial operating figures	Focus on the growth goals of enterprises
S12	Continuous development of new/differentiated products and services	Promotion of product sales by enterprises increased demand and consumption
S13	Legal form public limited company	Great pressure to generate returns to pay dividends/improve the share price; heteronomy by external investors
S14	Economic actors with loose contacts	Limited adaptation of products to consumer needs and therefore more consumption; price competition; marketing strategies like planned obsolescence and measures to promote consumption
S15	Entrepreneurial goal of economic growth and profit maximisation	Focus on the growth goals of the enterprise
S16	High advertising expenditure	Promotion of growth dynamics through consumer demand (needs); maximisation of economies of scale
S17	Spatially dispersed value chain (high spatial distance / increase in spatial distance)	Enterprises focused uniformly on growth and profit; increased competition; exploitation of economies of scale and extension of markets; little adaptation of production volumes to demand (potential for overproduction)
S18	Long value chains	Numerous companies involved with a drive for growth; increased competition; exploitation of economies of scale and extension of markets; production volumes not adapted to demand (potential for overproduction); low levels of trust between actors and thus increased need for capital and interest due to more insecure loans
S19	Great competitive pressure	Growth strategies like price and quantity competition; maximisation of economies of scale; strategies to increase productivity; active marketing

The following section presents by way of example the mechanisms that lead to growth independence and from which – amongst others – the two ideal types of social innovation can be derived. A low level of debt capital (U6) means there is less pressure to make profits in order to pay interest (Binswanger, 2009). An absence of outside investors is thus associated with lower profit expectations, better options for control by the management and greater transparency (Posse, 2015). A short value chain with few actors (U19) means that there are fewer debt financed enterprises involved who need to make profits (Paech, 2012b). Regional value chains have a similar effect (U20) (Gebauer/Lange/Posse, 2017; Gebauer, 2018; Paech, 2012b; Posse, 2015). They make it more likely that a strong bond develops between producers, consumers and investors. Product prices then become less important because consumers have a closer relationship with the producers. The latter therefore experience less pricing pressure (Posse, 2015). The involvement of consumers in production (U14) helps to align the product with consumer needs. This allows production resources to be more efficiently adjusted to actual product needs (Leismann/Schmitt/Rohn et al., 2012). The relations between the actors involved are also strengthened (Bakker/Loske/Sherhorn, 1999; Schor, 2010). Furthermore, guaranteed sales (U17) reduce pricing pressure for producers all along the value chain as a fixed price is agreed in advance (Gebauer, 2018; Gebauer/Lange/Posse, 2017). In addition, low capital intensity of production (U7) reduces dependence on outside investment because less investment in capital (in machinery etc.) is necessary (Paech, 2012b).

The indicators numbered S1 to S19 listed in the Table 2 describe the growth stimulation effects. These effects are, for instance, generated through the creation of consumer needs and emotions in advertising (S16) (Gebauer, 2018; Gebauer/Lange/Posse, 2017). A physically and spatially dispersed value chain (S17) can reduce trust between actors and thus increase the pressure to generate returns (Paech, 2012b). For instance, less trust means that a higher collateral is required for lending transactions; this takes the form of higher interest payments which need to be generated with profits (Paech, 2012b). Furthermore, production innovations are viewed as growth-inducing if the production of ever more new products is linked to capital investments (S7) (Paech, 2012a). Products for status consumption (S6) are primarily developed for saturated markets in order to generate more demand (Paech, 2012b; Posse, 2015).

Social innovations and their potential growth effects

Many different actors participated in the 68 social innovations that were identified. Most frequently involved are enterprises and private individuals (both 20%) and, in addition, state organisations, tourism organisations, associations, research institutes and foundations. One-third of the social innovations are located in the primary and secondary economic sectors, two-thirds in the tertiary sector. Social innovations are present in diverse fields like tourism, mobility, agriculture, health and education. They emerged both in remote shrinking areas and in economically growing central municipalities in the Bernese Oberland.

One aim of this paper is to identify those of the 68 social innovations that are characterised by pronounced potential growth effects. By focusing on these 'extreme types' in terms of growth effects we can identify ideal-typical forms of social innovations. A social innovation was only selected as an 'extreme type' if the number of relevant growth stimulation indicators corresponded to a maximum of 25% of the number of relevant growth independence indicators of the same social innovation (and vice versa, i.e. opposing effects are small). This ensured that clear tendencies can be recognised. In total, eight social innovations were classified as these two 'extreme types'. These innovations fulfilled at most 7 of the 19 growth stimulation indicators and at most 12 of the 20 growth independence indicators. The remaining 60 social innovations in the inventory are not further considered in the following discussion: either they display few growth effects or they have many growth effects in both directions.

The four social innovations with the most indicators pointing to growth independence are a cooperatively organised Alpine dairy and cheese company, a community supported agriculture (CSA) project, a cooperatively organised multi-generational house, and a building group within the framework of a solar energy cooperative in which members construct their solar systems together.

These social innovations have in common that they utilise no, little or interest-free external capital. The planned multi-generational house is partially financed by the interest-free capital of members of the housing association (Zukunft Hasliberg, 2019: 12). Interest-free finance is provided for the CSA in advance by purchasers of the products. A donation enabled the dairy and cheese company to be developed with little external investment.

The solar energy building group is financed by the group members. Those who install a solar system are supported by other members who already have such a system. The working hours invested by others are then worked off by those who already have the new system when they help construct another member's system.

These four social innovations are also characterised by short and regional value chains and close links between the actors involved. The cooperative dairy and cheese company, for instance, only uses milk from the surrounding farms, which leads to a close relationship between the suppliers and the processors of the milk. The same is true for the CSA where consumers purchase the products directly from the farm without an intermediary. The relationship between the producers (farmers) and the consumers is exceptionally close, in part due to direct cooperation in production.

For three of the four social innovations prosumers play an important role. Prosumers are consumers who are also involved in the production of the product or service that they later consume. The CSA is one such model, and in the solar energy cooperative a significant proportion of the solar systems is also built by those who will later use them. These forms of production represent a de-commercialisation of production. The work that prosumers put into producing the service is not remunerated in monetary terms. This is similarly seen in the concept of the 'caring community' that is pursued by the generational house. It states that the 'need for care should not be fulfilled only by professional institutions' but rather by cooperation between non-professional actors like neighbours or volunteers with state and professional partners (Zukunft Hasliberg, 2019: 7).

Furthermore, three of the four social innovations have guaranteed purchasers. For example, the dairy and cheese company can rely on sales to a major Swiss distributor, while the farmers of the CSA have guaranteed purchasers in the form of the prosumers. Three social innovations also have a low level of capital intensity in their production. In the solar energy cooperative, the solar systems are mostly installed by hand using little machinery. In comparison to industrialised cheese production, a great deal is also done by hand in the cooperative cheese company and there is little mechanisation. The same is true in the agricultural project thanks to the involvement of the prosumers.

The four social innovations with pronounced growth stimulation effects are a bad-weather insurance for holidaymakers; a tour package that combines Alpine bus tours with historical hikes; a specially equipped direct train to a skiing destination; and a partnership between five golfclubs with a dedicated membership card.

All four social innovations are commercial tourist ventures that are actively advertised and are characterised by economic growth goals. The weather insurance is intended to bring new visitors and thus increased revenue to the tourist businesses at the destination where the insurance is available. The same objective is pursued by the direct train connection and the hiking package. The golfclub membership card aims to make paying to become a member of a club more attractive and to increase the golfclubs' revenues.

Another characteristic of all four social innovations is that production and consumption of their offerings occur in a (physically) spatially dispersed value chain. In three of four cases this is linked to the more distanced relations between the stakeholders involved. An illustrative example is provided by the weather insurance. It was developed by an established insurance company in a Swiss city outside the mountain region, is sold by a tourism organisation in an Alpine holiday destination and is purchased by tourists from all over the world. The profits go to the insurance company and the tourism organisation. The relationships between the actors are somewhat distanced, both spatially and socially.

Two of these social innovations are active in highly competitive markets. First, the bus/hiking tour which offers historical hikes combined with postbus trips to distinguish itself from other more unspecific hiking offers. Second, the weather insurance, which covers a very specific risk that is not yet catered for by the insurance market.

Two social innovations involve product innovations that are intended primarily for status consumption or are advertised using emotional brand communication. The genuine characteristics of products intended for status consumption serve the purpose of social display and not the direct satisfaction of needs (Reisch/Raab, 2014: 933). The golfclub membership card is an example of status consumption because the costs amount to several 10,000 Swiss francs, which can hardly be fully justified by the actual benefits – playing golf. It is possible to identify emotional brand communication in the case of the bus tours and historical hikes. Advertising draws on the well-loved Swiss tradition of postbuses and aims to trigger emotions and thus win customers.

Discussion and prospects

This paper reflects on the various effects of social innovations in growth terms. Based on an inventory of social innovations in a Swiss mountain region, we analysed the potential growth effects with a set of indicators specifically developed for this purpose. Eight of the 68 social innovations of our inventory can be assigned to two extreme types: social innovations with potential growth independence effects and social innovations with potential growth stimulation effects. Based on the characteristics of these extreme types we devised two ideal types of social innovations, as seen in Table 2.

Table 3: Ideal types / Source: authors

	Social innovation: Growth independence	Social innovation: Growth stimulation
Description of ideal types	A social innovation that promotes growth independence comprises a new form of cooperation, which frequently involves private individuals. The new idea is often an alternative form of production and consumption that focuses on social and ecological goals. Conventional economic goals take a backseat.	A social innovation that stimulates growth comprises a new form of cooperation between actors who primarily pursue economic goals. The new idea that is developed is often a commercial product or service that can be assigned to a specific sector. Non-economic goals take a backseat.
Main characteristics	- No, little or interest-free outside capital - Minimal advertising expenditure - Close ties between producers, consumers, suppliers - Short and regional value chains	- Economic growth goals - Advertising expenditure for commercial products - Spatially dispersed value chains
Other characteristics	- Prosumers - Guaranteed market / fair prices - De-commercialisation of products/services - Low level of capital intensity - Short value chains - Regional value chains - Regional sales structures	- Weak relations to consumers - Active communication of financial indicators - Symbolic consumption / emotional brand communication - High level of competition - Differentiated product innovation

The growth effects of social innovations presented here are potential effects and have not been measured empirically. To gain more robust results, the indicators and their interactions need to be empirically investigated and, to further improve understanding, research should focus on preconditions for the emergence of social innovations in regional contexts. The motivation of the various actors plays an important role, especially with regard to the growth effects. Innovation biographies would be an appropriate tool (Kleverbeck/Terstriep, 2018). In addition, the set of indicators shows that further investigation must include both quantitative and qualitative dimensions.

In light of the diverse challenges facing mountain regions, this paper demonstrates that it can indeed be appropriate for regional policy to focus on social innovations. If regional policy aims to promote growth independence then it should not promote social innovations per se, but must rather target the characteristics of the social innovation projects and initiatives described above. It may therefore be helpful to promote a combination of characteristics in order to initiate sustainable and growth-independent regional development.

It seems necessary to ask whether such developments can advance the transformation to a post-growth society. Undoubtedly the examples identified here are niche projects of very limited economic significance. Nonetheless, they demonstrate what distinguishes social innovations and enterprises that contribute towards growth independence, and what aspects and factors should, for example, be promoted by regional and economic policy in order to expand growth independence. At the same time, the examples serve as role models and strengthen the economic independence and resilience of a region. They also show that the well-being of the population can benefit from economic activities in a post-growth society, compared to a growth-oriented economy. Impulses from peripheral areas are certainly not sufficient to lead to higher-level structural changes in, for instance, welfare and employment systems, as would be necessary for a post-growth society. However, regional-economic restructuring in such regions can reduce local socio-economic problems and improve quality of life.

Cited literature

Ayob, N., Teasdale, S., & Fagan, K. (2016). How social innovation 'Came to be': Tracing the evolution of a contested concept. *Journal of Social Policy*, 45(4), 635–653.

Bakker, E., Loske, R., & Sherhorn, G. (1999). Wirtschaft ohne Wachstumsstreben – Chaos oder Chance? Studien und Berichte der Heinrich-Böll-Stiftung 2, Springer.

Binswanger, H. C. (2009). Nachhaltigkeitsorientierte Umternehmungsverfassungen. In H.-Ch. Binswanger (Ed.), *Vorwärts zur Mässigung : Perspektiven einer nachhaltigen Wirtschaft*. Murmann, 150–160.

Bock, B. B. (2016). Rural marginalisation and the role of social innovation; A turn towards nexogenous development and rural reconnection. *Sociol. Ruralis*, 56, 552–573.

Bundesamt für Raumentwicklung (2012). *Monitoring Ländlicher Raum. Synthesebericht 2012*. Self-published.

Bundesamt für Raumentwicklung (2017). *Bauzonenstatistik Schweiz*. Bern. https://www.are.admin.ch/are/de/home/raumentwicklung-und-raumplanung/grundlagen-und-daten/bauzonenstatistik-schweiz.html (2020, January 29th).

Bundesamt für Statistik (2018a). *Beherbergungsstatistik (HESTA)*. Self-published.

Bundesamt für Statistik (2018b). *Regionalporträts 2018: Gemeinden*, Bern. Self-published.

Burkhart, C., Schmelzer, M., & Treu, N. (2020). *Degrowth in movement(s): Exploring pathways for transformation*. John Hunt Publishing.

Cerny, T., Rosemann, T., Tandjung, R., & Chmiel, C. (2016). Ursachen des Hausärztemangels – ein Vergleich zwischen Frankreich und der Schweiz. *Praxis*, 105(11), 619–636.

Dax, T., & Fischer, M. (2018). An alternative policy approach to rural development in regions facing population decline. *European Planning Studies*, 26(2), 297–315.

Dewald, U., & Rother, J. (2019). Wirtschaft fördern und fordern: Die Gemeinwohl-Ökonomie als Impuls für nachhaltige Wirtschaftsförderung. In J. Stember, M. Vogelgesang, P. Pongratz, & A. Fin (Eds.), *Handbuch Innovative Wirtschaftsförderung: Moderne Konzepte kommunaler Struktur- und Entwicklungspolitik*. Springer, 1–22.

Ebneter, L., & Liechti, K. (2019). Einblicke – Ausblicke. In F. Achtenhagen, & F. Gogolin (Eds.), *Bildung und Erziehung in Übergangsgesellschaften*. Springer, 41–47.

Edwards-Schachter, M., & Wallace, M. L. (2017). "Shaken, but not stirred': Sixty years of defining social innovation. *Technological Forecasting and Social Change, 119*, 64–79.

Elsen, S. (2014). Soziale Innovation, ökosoziale Ökonomien und Community Development. In S. Elsen, & W. Lorenz (Eds.), *Social innovation, participation and the development of society. Soziale Innovation, Partizipation und die Entwicklung der Gesellschaft*. Bozen-Bolzano University Press, 231–263.

European Commission (2017). ISIB-03-2015 – Unlocking the growth potential of rural areas through enhanced governance and social innovation. Self-published.

Franz, H.-W., Hochgerner, J., & Howaldt, J. (2012). Challenge social innovation: An introduction. In H.-W. Franz, J. Hochgerner, & J. Howaldt (Eds.), *Challenge social innovation*. Springer, 1–16.

Gebauer, J. (2018). Towards growth-independent and post-growth-oriented entrepreneurship in the SME sector. *Management Revue, 29*(3), 230–256.

Gebauer, J., Lange, S., & Posse, D. (2017). Wirtschaftspolitik für Postwachstum auf Unternehmensebene: Drei Ansätze zur Gestaltung. In F. Adler, & U. Schachtschneider (Eds.), *Postwachstumspolitiken: Wege zur wachstumsunabhängigen Gesellschaft*. oekom, 239–251.

Grimm, R., Fox, C., Baines, S., & Albertson, K. (2013). Social innovation, an answer to contemporary societal challenges? Locating the concept in theory and practice. *Innovation: The European Journal of Social Science Research, 26*(4), 436–455.

Habermann, F. (2009). *Halbinseln gegen den Strom: anders leben und wirtschaften im Alltag*. Ulrike Helmer Verlag.

Haisch, T. (2017). Interplay between ecological and economic resilience and sustainability and the role of institutions: evidence from two resource-based communities in the Swiss Alps. *Resilience, 6*(3), 215–229.

Kleverbeck, M., & Terstriep, J. (2018). Analysing social innovation through the lens of poverty reduction: five key factors. *European Public and Social Innovation. Review, 2*(2), 15–29.

Leismann, K., Schmitt, M., Rohn, H., & Baedeker, C. (2012). Nutzen statt Besitzen – Auf dem Weg zu einer ressourcenschonenden Konsumkultur. In Heinrich Böll Stiftung (Ed.), *Schriften zur Ökologie. Band 27*.

Liesen, A., Dietsche, C., & Gebauer, J. (2013). *Wachstumsneutrale Unternehmen.* IÖW publication series 205/13.

Lück, W. (1990). *Lexikon der Betriebswirtschaftslehre, 6. edition.* Moderne Industrie. kiehl.

Mayer, H., Rime, D., Meili, R., & Bürgin, R. (2018). *Experteninput für das Postulat Brand. Vorschläge für einen territorial differenzierten Ansatz der NRP zur gezielten Förderung der Schweizer Berggebiete.* Self-published.

Mewes, H., & Gebauer, J. (2015). Transformative Potenziale von Unternehmen, die nicht wachsen wollen. *Ökologisches Wirtschaften, 30*(3), 27.

Moulaert, F., MacCallum, D., & Hiller, J. (2013). Social innovation: intuition, precept, concept, theory and practice. In F. Moulaert, D. MacCallum, & A. Mehmood (Eds.), *The International Handbook on Social Innovation, Collective Action, Social Learning and Transdisciplinary Research.* Edward Elgar Publishing Ltd, 13–24.

Mulgan, G., Tucker, S., Ali, R., & Sanders, B. (2007). *Social innovation: What it is, why it matters and how it can be accelerated.* Skoll Centre for Social Entrepreneurship. Oxford University Press.

Müller-Jentsch, D. (2017). *Strukturwandel im Schweizer Berggebiet: Strategien zur Erschliessung neuer Wertschöpfungsquellen.*

Mumford, M. D. (2002). Social innovation: Ten cases from Benjamin Franklin. *Creativity Research Journal, 14*(2), 253–266.

Neumeier, S. (2012). Why do social innovations in rural development matter and should they be considered more seriously in rural development research? – Proposal for a stronger focus on social innovations in rural development research. *Sociologia Ruralis, 52*(1), 48–69.

Nicholls, A., & Edmiston, D. (2018). Social innovation policy in the European Union. In R. Heiskala, & J. Aro (Eds.), *Policy Design in the European Union.* Springer, 161–190.

Noack, A., & Federwisch, T. (2019). Social innovation in rural regions: Urban impulses and cross-border constellations of actors. *Sociologia Ruralis, 59*(1), 92–112.

Paech, N. (2012a). *Nachhaltiges Wirtschaften jenseits von Innovationsorientierung und Wachstum.* metropolis.

Paech, N. (2012b). *Liberation from ExcessThe road to a post-growth economy.* oekom.

Pelka, B., & Terstriep, J. (2016). Mapping social innovation maps; The state of research practice across europe. *European Public und Social Innovation Review*, 1(1), 3–15.

Peter, C., Rink, D., Forster, S., Hömke, M., Kopp, M., & Messerli, P. (2016). Entwicklung in ländlichen Räumen und Bergregionen ohne Wachstumsperspektiven. ICAS-Kolloquium Bern, 2016, January 15.

Posse, D. (2015). *Zukunftsfähige Unternehmen in einer Postwachstumsgesellschaft*. Springer.

Reisch, L. A., & Raab, G. (2014). Konsum, symbolischer. In M. A. Wirtz, (Ed.), *Dorsch – Lexikon der Psychologie*. Hogrefe, 933.

Richters, O., & Siemoneit, A. (2019). *Marktwirtschaft reparieren*. oekom.

Rütter, H., & Rütter-Fischbacher, U. (2016). *Wertschöpfungs- und Beschäftigungswirkung im ländlichen und alpinen Tourismus*. Rüschlikon.

Schmelzer, M., & Vetter, A. (2019). *Degrowth/Postwachstum zur Einführung*. Junius.

Schmucki, E., Marty, C., Fierz, C., Weingartner, R., & Lehning, M. (2017). Impact of climate change in Switzerland on socioeconomic snow indices. *Theoretical and Applied Climatology*, 127(3-4), 875–889.

Schor, J. B. (2010). *Plenitude. The New Economics of True Wealth*. Tantor Media Inc.

Secco, L., Pisani, E., Da Re, R., Rogelja, T., Burlando, C., Vicentini, K., Pettenella, D., Masiero, M., Miller, D., & Nijnjk, M. (2019). Towards a method of evaluating social innovation in forest-dependent rural communities: First suggestions from a science-stakeholder collaboration. *Forest Policy and Economics*, 104, 9–22.

Segessemann, A., & Crevoisier, O. (2016). Beyond economic base theory: The role of the residential economy in attracting income to swiss regions. *Regional Studies* 50(8), 1388–1403.

Seidl, I., & Zahrnt, A. (2010). Anliegen des Buches und Übersicht. In I. Seidl, & A. Zahrnt (Ed.), *Postwachstumsgesellschaft: Konzepte für die Zukunft*. Metropolis, 17–22.

Seidl, I., & Zahrnt, A. (2022). *Post-Growth Work: Employment and Meaningful Activities within Planetary Boundaries*. Routledge.

SIMRA – Social Innovation in Marginalised Rural Areas (2018). *Collection of examples of social innovation in Mountain Areas*. Self-published.

Staatssekretariat für Wirtschaft SECO (2017). *Die Neue Regionalpolitik des Bundes*. Self-published.

van der Have, R. P., & Rubalcaba, L. (2016). Social innovation research: An emerging area of innovation studies? *Research Policy, 45*(9), 1923–1935.

von Rütte, H. (2007). Geschichte – Vom Hirtenland zum Erlebnispark. In A. Wallner, E. Bäschlin, M. Grosjean, T. Labhart, U. Schüpbach, & U. Wiesmann (Eds.), *Welt der Alpen – Erbe der Welt*. Yearbook of the Geographischen Gesellschaft Bern 62/2007.

Zukunft Hasliberg (2019). *Generationenhaus Hasliberg. Projektbeschreibung und Konzept*. Self-published.

Criteria for post-growth residential development: The example of the city of Zurich

Olivia Wohlgemuth, Marco Pütz

1. Introduction

In most large cities in Switzerland, population and economic growth combined with changed lifestyle habits and a demand for more living space have led to a shortage of land as a resource. Revised spatial planning legislation, which came into force in 2014, puts an end to continued urban sprawl and requires that future development be located in existing building zones (LaRES 2014). The creation of additional housing presents some difficulties as 95% of the building zones in Zurich have already been developed, which means that the focus is now primarily on densification (Wüest Partner 2018: 73). Numerous innovative housing projects demonstrate how inner urban development can be successfully realised and that densification can create value for the entire population.

Growth independence concepts are attracting increased attention from spatial sciences. The post-growth debate could therefore provide an approach that allows urban development to focus on ensuring future growth is more sustainable, quality-oriented and goes beyond the purely quantitative economic growth paradigm. The strategy for sustainable spatial development in the canton of Zurich (LaRES 2014) and other guiding principles for good building already include requirements for ecological and social housing, so approaches from the post-growth debate are also being addressed. These include, firstly, innovations in building techniques and, secondly, housing concepts that reduce individual land consumption and counter social individualisation through flexible uses and shared areas.

This paper is based on a Master's thesis that investigated the city of Zurich as a case study, exploring the extent to which post-growth can be a guiding principle for residential development and examining which preconditions are required for post-growth housing (Wohlgemuth 2019). The paper aims to develop criteria for post-growth housing projects. To this end the following sub-questions are analysed:

- What are the criteria for future-oriented residential development and what is required for these criteria to be fulfilled?
- To what extent are existing requirements for sustainable, ecological and social housing already post-growth oriented?

The paper is structured in five sections. Section 2 presents the theoretical and conceptual framework. Subsequently Section 3 gives an overview of the methodological approach. The findings are presented and discussed in Section 4 and Section 5 provides conclusions.

2. Urban development, housing and post-growth

The topic of urban housing offers much scope for realising post-growth economies or a post-growth society. It is obvious that urban development, urban planning and an appropriately organised housing industry could make post-growth housing possible. Thanks to cooperatives or other non-profit developers, housing is traditionally a topic that is very close to post-growth ideas. However, even though numerous current housing projects have a great deal to do with post-growth, the theme has been subject to little conceptual research and is comparatively new. In the volume *Housing for degrowth – Principles, models, challenges and opportunities*, Nelson and Schneider (2019) provide one of the few up-to-date overviews of the challenges and unfavourable developments that characterise the property industry and discuss how post-growth approaches could offer a response. However, the volume primarily presents examples from practice, ranging from squats to collective forms of living to architectural innovations. The focus is not on a theoretical-conceptual categorisation.

In order to demonstrate the conceptual relations between housing and post-growth, in the following we first outline the most important challenges faced by housing in the future and then formulate three central post-growth approaches for housing/residential development.

2.1 Challenges for housing in the future

The challenges for housing in the future that are discussed in the scientific and grey literature generally include both ecological and social aspects. To describe the specific situation in Zurich, in this section we draw primarily on planning documents and literature with a clear link to the city of Zurich:

- *Impulse zur Innovation im Wohnungsbau* (Impulses for innovation in housing) (Birrer and Glaser 2017)
- *Auszeichnung für gute Bauten der Stadt Zürich* (Award for good building of the city of Zurich) (Hochbaudepartement Stadt Zürich 2019)
- *Leitfaden und Checklisten zur nachhaltigen Arealentwicklung für Städte und Gemeinden* (Guidelines and checklists for sustainable site development for cities and municipalities) (Hugentobler and Wiener 2016)
- *Langfristige Raumentwicklungsstrategie Kanton Zürich* (Long-term spatial development strategies canton of Zurich) (LaRES 2014)
- *Leitfaden – Erfolgsfaktoren sozial nachhaltiger Sanierungen und Ersatzneubaten* (Guidelines – Success factors of socially sustainable redevelopments and replacement new builds) (Martinovits/Diethelm/Durisch et al. 2015)
- *Raumplanungsbericht* (Spatial planning report) (Kanton Zürich 2018)
- *Akzeptanz städtischer Dichte: Erwartungen und Prioritäten zum Wohnen in der Stadt Zürich* (Acceptance of urban density: Expectations and priorities for housing in the city of Zurich) (Zimmerli 2018)

On the basis of the current planning documentation and literature we identified eight challenges for housing in the future:

1. Resource and energy efficiency: Housing projects should be as resource-conserving as possible and consider energies from renewable sources. They should also contribute towards achieving the objectives of a '2000-watt society'. Buildings should retain their value in the long term and have long useful lifetimes, they should thus be as adaptable and flexible as possible.

2. Green spaces and open spaces: Sufficient green spaces are important for a good urban climate and biodiversity. In addition, high-quality outside spaces are needed where residents can spend quality time. Concepts for sharing, swapping and building communities need suitable settings and spaces that can be collectively used.
3. Planning procedures: Information and transparency are important aspects of planning procedures and increase acceptance of changes. Good dialogue between the authorities, developers and the people affected is also indispensable. Furthermore, the public should participate in planning and thus improve projects.
4. Densification: Inner urban development is an overall objective. A high density of uses and efficient land use are crucial. The densities applied should be specific to the locality and in keeping with the surrounding area. Occupancy densities must be increased so as to keep per capita consumption of residential space to a minimum.
5. Society: Buildings must support the development of socially and functionally mixed neighbourhoods. Furthermore, community life, cohesion and belonging should be strengthened, which leads to lively settlements with collectively used spaces. Buildings must contribute towards a city for all.
6. Housing forms: Buildings must be constructed for flexible use and residential space must offer qualities for various lifestyles. This includes new forms of dwelling and an attractive mix of housing with diverse dwelling typologies. Ground floors should also be diversely utilised.
7. Quality of life and sustainability: Buildings should provide a framework for sustainable ways of life and dwelling. Furthermore, sustainably conceived housing projects can strengthen awareness of sustainability issues. In general, a project should improve the quality of life of residents.
8. Fair prices and affordable rents: Low-cost and affordable housing should always be the objective of residential construction. The post-growth debate proposes the idea that the pursuit of profit and speculation must be renounced.

2.2 Post-growth approaches for housing

In the well-known and seminal works of the post-growth debate, the topics of housing and urban development play a rather minor role. Thus the works of Victor (2008), Latouche (2009) and Jackson (2016), all important in the international debate, focus primarily on critiques of growth and capitalism, providing introductions and overviews. The key publications of the German-language post-growth literature also mainly provide orientation and cover the most important terms, concepts and backgrounds of the interdisciplinary debate (e.g. Seidl/Zahrnt 2010, Paech 2012, Schmelzer/Vetter 2019). These fundamental works and also many other publications, often with an applied approach, mention numerous projects and initiatives that are planned and implemented in cities. However, the link to the city tends to remain implicit. Cities or urban neighbourhoods are usually just locations for, e.g., transition towns or urban gardening initiatives. Urbanity, city milieus and the role of urban development and planning receive very little attention. Xue (2019: 185 f.) clarifies that it is necessary to explicitly view the city and post-growth together:

> 'Degrowth depicts a desirable future society that is ecologically sustainable, enhances quality of life and achieves social justice. This means achieving social welfare and social justice while shrinking our levels of production and consumption due to the existence of ecological limits. Both research and social practices need to bridge the domains of welfare and environmental sustainability. For urban planners, the integration of both domains raises a question: What is required to make a sustainable city socially just, or, to make welfare societies ecologically sustainable in the urban context?'

Post-growth is not yet used as a guiding principle for urban development. It is equally rare for housing and post-growth to be considered together in the literature. When, however, post-growth is discussed as an approach for housing, it is possible to identify three general thematic fields: sufficiency, the good life and housing justice.

Sufficiency: Sufficiency on the individual level means requiring fewer material resources and changing lifestyles and consumption habits. Sufficiency 'aims for people to change their behaviour without compulsion and to limit or replace practices that overuse resources. It strives for the sufficient, environmentally friendly consumption of energy and materials through low demand for resource-intensive goods and services' (Stengel 2011: 140). It is important to note here that a sufficiency strategy does not demand that people do without what is necessary but rather assumes that an understanding of what is necessary will lead people to voluntarily do without (Stengel 2011: 140).

Good life: In a broad sense, post-growth is about striving for a good life for all. This is not about understandings of prosperity based on material consumption, but about different understandings that rather 'include the complexity of people as relationship beings, overcome the division between production and reproduction and give more space to needs that are not focused on growth and optimisation – like time prosperity, stable and intensive relationships or meaningfulness' (Schmelzer/Vetter 2019:169).

Housing justice / a right to housing: The current debates on rising property prices and housing shortages trigger questions about who owns the land and how cities should develop in the future (Schulz 2017: 13). In particular, population groups with low incomes find it increasingly difficult to rent housing in cities. Post-growth views housing as a human right and a basic need, which means that a dwelling should be neither a financial investment nor a status symbol (Schneider 2019: 16).

In addition to these three topics there are numerous other post-growth oriented approaches that could play a role in urban development (Schulz 2017: 11 ff.): solidarity economies (e.g. neighbourhood shops, swap shops, local currencies), alternative energy concepts (e.g. energy cooperatives operating for the common good), community food production (urban gardening, urban farming), shared offices (e.g. co-working spaces) or shared forms of use (e.g. spaces and infrastructures for the sharing economy). As these approaches are not directly related to housing they are not further pursued here.

3. Methodology

Methodologically speaking, this investigation is based on a qualitative, interpretative research design. The data were gathered for three case studies in a total of 17 guided, semi-standardised expert interviews. The interviews were transcribed and evaluated using a structured and summarising form of content analysis.

The case studies were selected from housing projects that had won prizes in the 'Competition for good buildings' (*'Wettbewerb für gute Bauten'*) of the city of Zurich. Every five years building projects are chosen and presented with awards by an expert jury consisting of architects, town planners, other specialists and representatives of the city council and administration. These projects act as role models for high-quality building and make an important contribution to the quality of the city of Zurich (Amt für Städtebau Zürich, 2016). As the current competition cycle has not yet been finalised, the last prizes awarded for buildings constructed between 2011 and 2015 were considered as possible case studies. Of these, residential buildings were filtered out and three case studies were chosen, all of which were developed by cooperatives. Overall, three or four people from the board of the cooperatives or the team of architects of each project were interviewed. In addition, the interviews covered a fourth group of experts from consultancy, the urban administration and research.

Table 1: Overview of case studies / source: Amt für Städtebau Zürich, 2016 and data from the interviews

Grünmatt development Zurich-Friesenberg	Hunziker-Areal Zurich-Oerlikon	Apartment complex Klee Zurich-Affoltern

		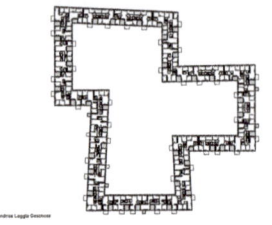
Developer Family Home Cooperative Zurich (*Familienheim Genossenschaft Zürich, FGZ*)	**Developer** Building cooperative 'more than housing' (*'mehr als wohnen'*)	**Developer** Non-profit Building and Rental Cooperative Zurich (*Gemeinnützige Bau- und Mietergenossenschaft Zürich*) and Building Cooperative Hagenbrünneli (*Baugenossenschaft Hagenbrünneli*)
Description The first replacement new build of the FGZ. A contemporary garden city with low rows of buildings and small, private front gardens was created.	**Description** A car-free development with 13 different residential buildings, high density and a mixed community with strong social cohesion.	**Description** Clover-shaped building with a shared park by two cooperatives with different philosophies.
Special feature A hybrid type of construction was chosen for the new build. Today 490 people live in Grünmatt, where previously only 200 people lived in single-family homes on the same site (+145%). Land consumption is very low, 33 m² per person. The previously large private gardens have given way to a shared exterior space.	**Special feature** The Areal was developed as a jubilee project for the 100th anniversary of the Zurich housing cooperatives and serves as a platform for innovation and learning. The entire Areal is based on a community concept with community rooms and meeting zones. There is a large social mix of inhabitants, reflecting the population of the canton of Zurich.	**Special feature** The shape of development provides a large interior courtyard, a high-quality and exciting outside space. Architectural interest is provided by the two-storey loggias that are staggered across the floors, while the treetops divide up the façade. This avoids the impression of a six-storey building.

4. Results

Based on current planning documents and literature, Section 2.1 identified eight challenges for housing of the future. These challenges were empirically assessed in the interviews, allowing the requirements for future-oriented housing development to be documented. These requirements have been linked to the post-growth debate and further developed to create a catalogue of criteria (Table 2).

Table 2: Catalogue of criteria for post-growth housing / Source: the authors

Inner urban development   Create compact structures
Land consumption   Limit individual living space
User density   Strive for high social density
High density of interaction   Promote high levels of interaction through architectural and organisational measures
Mixed land uses   Interlink housing, work, retail and recreation to guarantee short distances
Diversity   Mixed population (lifecycle, lifestyle, income, profession, etc.)
Energy sufficiency/ saving resources   Reduce energy consumption and use energy from renewal sources; save resources in construction and utilisation
Green spaces   Extend and protect green spaces for a good microclimate
Appropriation areas   Ensure areas are available that can be freely designed and managed
Participation   Involve those who are affected in the planning process and in design
Price   Affordable housing for all population strata

5. Inner urban development

Inner urban development and densification are central elements of spatial development. This enables as many people as possible to live in the city and protects open spaces. The focus here is on building density, i.e. the built fabric, the ratio of the volume of built structures to the surface area of the plot (Wüest Partner 2018: 12). A high building density is equivalent to a high volume of built structures per hectare of the built-up zone.

The dark side of urban sprawl is the loss of natural areas and the increase in traffic. However, densification is also criticised as it is often seen as negative and constricting. Densification therefore needs to always be linked to quality of life – denser is not fundamentally better or worse.

Land consumption

In order to realise inner urban development and densification, limiting personal living space is crucial. Equally, it is important that the city is accessible as a place of residence for all. Better exploitation of space means there is room for more people in a building or city. This can, first, be achieved by improving the housing, for instance through well-designed floorplans that omit as unnecessary additional square metres of living space that do not create higher quality. A second option is to limit individual living space with occupancy regulations. A third possibility is provided by collectively used areas like guest rooms or offices that can be shared by a number of people if required.

> 'Housing is something very existential, it needs great care. If you say that you must give up a family dwelling because the children have moved out, I think that's right. You have to do it like that, because otherwise the concept doesn't work, that you say that you do without living space but have instead high-quality and low-priced living space and would like to again make that available then perhaps a generation later to new people. The security of housing, that nobody needs to be afraid of ever being without suitable housing, must be there.' (Interview 15)

User density

User density refers to the number of people who spend time in a place and is seen as a prerequisite for people meeting one another (Kretz/Kueng 2016: 55). User density can also be understood as population density or social density and should not be seen as equivalent to built density. A high built density does not in itself mean that more people spend time in a place. If space requirements per person increase and built density remains the same, then the user density sinks. With inner urban development it is important to ensure that the use of land is sufficiently great rather than simply building more concrete.

High density of interaction

A high user density does not guarantee that people meet and exchange experiences. Loneliness is said to be a problem of modern societies as people feel alone even though urban densities are relatively high. To counter this, housing constructions must allow interaction between residents. Architectural and organisational measures should thus promote rather than hinder community life and exchange between the residents of a building. The design of exterior spaces and the management of semi-public areas has a great influence on whether a building can be collectively used or not. In addition to architectural measures, such as the design of stairways and entrances, shared rooms and infrastructures, e.g. workshops, are important for creating a collective living environment. Among the organisational measures are neighbourhood events or the decentralisation of specific administrative tasks and the organisation of leisure commissions, which include cultural and leisure committees.

To protect the private sphere, it is necessary to find a balance between community and options for withdrawing. An additional difficulty is that such measures are strongly dependent on the residents. Nobody can be forced to communicate with other people. Nonetheless, a framework should be created that promotes and supports such exchanges, should they be desired.

Mixed land uses

Ground-floor uses create more lively neighbourhoods with more diverse functions so that the direct surroundings are not just a place of residence but also a place where leisure time can be spent. As well as retail options and leisure facilities in the neighbourhood, co-working spaces can increase the mix of uses. In a 'city of short distances' with a compact structure and mixed land uses, the daily trips to work, the shops and for leisure activities can be undertaken on foot or by bicycle (Beckmann/Gies/Thiemann-Linden et al. 2011: 64). Concentrating retail facilities in shopping centres or pronounced mobility hinder the development of a city of short distances. This leads to an acceptance of longer trips for sport and leisure activities (Beckmann/Gies/Thiemann-Linden et al. 2011: 61). Nonetheless, mixed uses are necessary to create an attractive residential environment and 'short distances create the possibility of doing without motorised transport so that less resources need to be used. Short distances are also building blocks of a lifestyle and consumption profile that leaves a smaller ecological footprint' (Beckmann/Gies/Thiemann-Linden et al. 2011: 50).

Diversity

According to Kretz and Kueng (2016: 50), diversity means 'that different uses, user groups, social milieus and spatial manifestations are present in one space'. In relation to residential development, diversity means that different population groups should be represented in a housing project. A mix of ages, incomes and lifestyles improves the quality of an area and counters segregation. Social mixing of this sort can be achieved in an apartment building by providing different types of dwelling units that attract different people. Such mixing hinders the emergence of disadvantaged neighbourhoods. Furthermore, a high level of diversity can also prevent the development of luxury neighbourhoods for population groups with high incomes. There are, nevertheless, arguments in favour of segregation. The spatial concentration of people in similar situations and with similar interests facilitates the development of specific facilities and infrastructures (Häussermann/Siebel 2001: 73).

Saving resources and energy sufficiency

The ecological footprint of the building industry is enormous: worldwide, the industry uses 40% of global resources (Emprechtinger 2019). In order not to exceed the ecological viability of the planet and due to increasing shortages of building materials like gravel and sand, future building must be as resource efficient as possible. In addition to an economical use of resources for building construction, renewable energies must be used for power in the finished building. No reliance should be placed on technological advances, as while energy efficiency can be continuously improved, sufficiency strategies are nonetheless required:

> '(...) If I want to approach something in a sufficient way then first I ask myself whether I need it at all. If I just make it more efficient then I quickly reach the conclusion: now it's more efficient, now I can have more of it. Which need not lead to using less resources at all, but just that you've optimised something.' (Interview 12)

Furthermore, the height, orientation and colour of façades affect the climate. Varied building heights are better for wind effects, and paler colours reflect more light so that the buildings heat up less.

Green spaces

As well as protecting the landscape, the treatment of green spaces inside the city is crucial. A compromise must be found between green space and inner urban development. Green spaces can make a decisive contribution towards adaptation to climate change and provide protection from overheating. In addition, consideration must be given to the greening of facades, species conservation and biodiversity. Thus native plants should be utilised and not all areas be built with basements so that large trees are able to develop deep roots. Green spaces also increase the attractiveness of the residential environment and housing quality.

Appropriation areas

By appropriating open space around dwellings, it becomes possible for people to influence their own living environments. Areas must therefore be planned that have no defined use and that can be managed by the urban residents themselves. Appropriation areas of this sort help a neighbourhood to develop its own distinct character and allow residents to identify with their surroundings. Appropriation is only possible if there is a low level of regulation and a high degree of flexibility in utilisation so that people are as free to act as possible (Kretz/Kueng 2016: 72).

Participation

The idea of a participative procedure is that development can occur with the public and their thoughts and ideas can be included in the planning process. Furthermore, pursuing collaboration and co-design with the public means that changes are more readily accepted and the quality of the project benefits.

> 'There is also a certain capital that is brought in. People invest their time, that is their free time, and there are certainly also good and justified idea.' (Interview 16)

It is, however, always important to define precisely who can participate and what the goal of participation is.

Price

The provision of affordable housing for all strata of the population enables the foundations for a good life to be laid. Housing is a basic need and is existential, which is why urban housing must be affordable for everyone no matter which income bracket they are in.

> 'I don't like anything about this profit-oriented housing, which isn't sustainable, because people say that they just want to get money out of it now, with overpriced rents.' (Interview 1)

As there are different income structures there are also different notions of affordability. It is therefore important that in the future all price segments should be represented in the city. This is the only way to enable diversity. Similarly, there should be different price structures on the project level, which can be achieved with different types of dwellings.

6. Conclusion

The paper shows that much of the housing that is described as future-oriented or sustainable is already in the spirit of the post-growth debate. Post-growth can be a future-proof guiding principle for residential development in cities and supplement existing principles (inner urban development, quality of life, '2000-watt society'). Post-growth approaches to urban development have to date seldom been analysed in relation to classical housing projects and estate developments, and instead have usually emerged as alternative approaches parallel to the housing market. Although the link to such projects is important, an approach with majority appeal is required, one that is also supported by developers on the classical housing market. The paper demonstrates that post-growth in housing can indeed be generalisable and need not be limited to alternative concepts like transition towns.

Cooperatives play a key role as their form of organisation gives residents a voice and allows their participation in the design of the residential environment. In addition, cooperatives are well known for their experimentation with new ideas and alternative paths. Non-profit developers remove land and real estate from speculation and provide dwellings according to the cost-rent principle, the housing is affordable for most population strata and is usually cheaper than on the classical housing market. The goal of non-profit developers is to provide environmentally and socially sustainable housing. They are often also pioneers in the transformation of existing forms of housing. Cooperatives are therefore suitable partners for post-growth housing projects.

As well as the non-profit developers as an innovative, post-growth oriented form of organisation, innovations are needed on the technical side and in infrastructure and architecture. With their manifesto for future-proof architecture and structural engineering, architects, engineers and urban planners have demonstrated that they too can act as pioneers of change and can assume responsibility for transformation (DAI 2009). Urban development stakeholders involved in housing development have, firstly, responsibility for ensuring that enough dwellings are available for all at a reasonable price. Secondly, housing developers need to ensure that the right housing is planned and built, i.e. dwellings that meet the needs of residents with their different lifestyles and that respond to changes in society.

If post-growth is recognised as a guiding principle for future-oriented housing development, the 'Competition for Good Building' in the city of Zurich could in the future become a competition for post-growth housing. The award-winning projects are already post-growth oriented. A change of terminology for this competition would lead to the post-growth concept becoming better known and could allow the ideas behind it to be more broadly disseminated. Although post-growth is familiar to many academics, a focus on the planning and practice level would further strengthen awareness.

The award-winning projects that were used as a basis for selecting the interview partners, can be viewed as showpieces because they fulfil many of the criteria for post-growth housing. A distinguishing feature of the Hunziker-Areal is that functional neighbourhood infrastructures have been developed in the exterior to create more than just a residential estate. The entire Hunziker-Areal is conceived in terms of community with numerous collective areas and meeting zones. There are over 40 neighbourhood groups active in various fields. Furthermore, the residents of the development reflect the population mix of the canton of Zurich. The whole development experiments with different forms of dwelling and architectural measures. A post-growth perspective suggests, however, that the Hunziker-Areal requires more green spaces. It would be possible to have less sealed surfaces, even though commerce needs a delivery zone for trucks. Green spaces would ensure that the development remains cooler in the summer and would provide inviting places to spend time in, especially as there are very few green spaces in the surrounding area.

The apartment complex Klee in Zurich-Affoltern is an attractive housing development with 340 dwelling units for just under 1000 residents, located on the edge of the city. The social density is high, but the skilful architecture provides many open spaces that can be used by residents. The fact that two cooperatives with different philosophies collaborated on this project made it possible to attract different people. A stricter implementation of all the post-growth criteria could achieve a better mix of uses. Although Affoltern is somewhat remote, a focus on public uses in additional spaces on the ground floor would bring life to the area throughout the day.

The Grünmatt project shows how a neighbourhood of single-family homes can be redeveloped to provide attractive dwelling space for more people than before. There are now almost 500 people living in the development where 200 people previously lived. The new build resembles a modern garden city with numerous shared exterior spaces and rooms. Individual consumption of space is thus low, just 33 m² per person. Another important point is the intelligent heating concept of the Family Home Cooperative (*Familienheim Genossenschaft*), which recovers waste heat from large companies in the city, stores it in three boreholes and uses it for heating. From a post-growth perspective, efforts should be made to attract a broader mix of residents. The development is very attractive for families and draws many families with small children, but a greater mix of residents would increase quality of life.

In this paper, post-growth has been examined as a guiding principle for housing in the city of Zurich. It would be interesting to apply the same approach to the municipalities of the agglomeration, which is where most land take is currently occurring. This would also allow investigation of whether criteria that are relevant for future-oriented housing projects in the city are also applicable to the municipalities of the agglomeration. As the topic of housing cannot be considered in isolation, future research should also focus on urban development as a whole. This would allow consideration of topics like mobility and the construction of offices and commercial buildings.

Cited literature

Amt für Städtebau Zürich (2016). „*Auszeichnung für gute Bauten*" *der Stadt Zürich 2011–2015*. Self-published.

Beckmann, K. J., Gies, J., Thiemann-Linden, J., & Preuss, T. (2011). *Leitkonzept – Stadt und Region der kurzen Wege. Gutachten im Kontext der Biodiversitätsstrategie*. Umweltbundesamt Verlag. UBA Texte 48/2011.

Birrer, A., & Glaser, M. (2017). Impulse zur Innovation im Wohnungsbau. *Im Fokus*, 2017(02).

DAI – Verband Deutscher Architekten und Ingenieurvereine (2009). *Klima-Manifest der Architekten, Ingenieure und Stadtplaner.* http://www.klima-manifest.de/praeambel.html.

Emprechtinger, F. (2019). *LEAD Innovation Management. Bau 2019: Diese 4 Trends bewegen die Baubranche.* https://www.lead-innovation.com/blog/bau-2019-trends-baubranche.

Häussermann, H., & Siebel, W. (2001). Integration und Segregation – Überlegungen zu einer alten Debatte. *Deutsche Zeitschrift für Kommunalwissenschaften (DfK)*, 40(2001-1), 68–79.

Hochbaudepartement Stadt Zürich (2019). *„Auszeichnung für gute Bauten" der Stadt Zürich.* www.stadt-zuerich.ch/gute-bauten.

Hugentobler, M., & Wiener, D. (2016). *ANANAS – Leitfaden und Checklisten zur nachhaltigen Arealentwicklung für Städte und Gemeinden.* vdf.

Jackson, T. (2016). *Prosperity without Growth. Foundations for the Economy of Tomorrow.* Routledge.

Kanton Zürich (2018). *Raumplanungsbericht 2017. RRB Nr. 630/2018, Vorlage 5470.* Self-published.

Kretz, S., & Kueng, L. (2016). *Urbane Qualitäten. Ein Handbuch am Beispiel der Metropolitanregion.* Hochparterre.

LaRES – Langfristige Raumentwicklungsstrategie Kanton Zürich (2014). *Schlussbericht 2014.* Self-published.

Latouche, S. (2009). *Farewell to growth.* Polity Press.

Martinovits, A., Diethelm, E., Durisch, C., Kessler, B., Nigsch, S., & Noger, P. (2015). *Leitfaden – Erfolgsfaktoren sozial nachhaltiger Sanierungen und Ersatzneubaten. Stadtentwicklung Zürich.* City of Zürich Press.

Nelson, A., & Schneider, F. (2019). *Housing for degrowth. Principles, models challenges and opportunities.* Routledge.

Paech, N. (2012). *Befreiung vom Überfluss. Auf dem Weg in die Postwachstumsökonomie.* oekom.

Schmelzer, M., & Vetter, A. (2019). *Degrowth/Postwachstum zur Einführung.* Junius.

Schneider, F. (2019). Housing for degrowth narratives. In A. Nelson, & F. Schneider (2019), *Housing for degrowth. Principles, models, challenges and opportunities.* Routledge, 14–30.

Schulz, C. (2017). Postwachstum in den Raumwissenschaften. *Nachrichten der ARL*, 47(4/2017), 11–14.

Seidl, I., & Zahrnt, A. (2010). *Postwachstumsgesellschaft. Konzepte für die Zukunft.* metropolis.

Stengel, O. (2011). *Suffizienz. Die Konsumgesellschaft in der ökologischen Krise.* oekom. Wuppertaler Schriften zur Forschung für eine nachhaltige Entwicklung 1.

Victor, P. A. (2008). *Managing without growth. Slower by design, not disaster.* Edward Elgar Publishing.

Wohlgemuth, O. (2019). *Wohnen im Postwachstum. Ein Leitbild für eine zukunftsorientierte Wohnraumentwicklung in der Stadt Zürich.* Unpublished Master's thesis.

Wüest Partner (2018). *Siedlungsentwicklung nach innen in den Städten. Studie im Auftrag des Schweizerischen Städteverbandes.* Self-published.

Xue, J. (2019). Housing for degrowth. Space, planning and distribution. In A. Nelson, & F. Schneider (2019), *Housing for degrowth. Principles, models, challenges and opportunities.* Routledge, 185–196.

Zimmerli, J. (2018). *Akzeptanz städtischer Dichte: Erwartungen und Prioritäten zum Wohnen in der Stadt Zürich. Vorstellungen von öffentlichem Raum und grossen Überbauungen.* Raum + Gesellschaft Press.

Makerspaces
Third places for a sustainable (post-growth) society?

Matti Kurzeja, Katja Thiele, Britta Klagge

1. Introduction

For several years there has been discussion of the significance of so-called 'third places' for a sustainable and future-oriented society. The currently much-discussed open workshops or makerspaces are third places of this kind (e.g. Lange 2017). Although a theoretical debate on the importance of third spaces and third places has been ongoing for decades in social sciences, makerspaces are a relatively new phenomenon. Such cooperation between people in collectively used places is particularly interesting and is discussed in the post-growth debate as a hopeful symbol of urgently needed social transformation towards sustainability (e.g. Simons/Petschow/Peuckert 2016, Smith/Light 2017).

By questioning the classical relationship between production and consumption, makerspaces provide important stimuli in all three dimensions of sustainable development and are thus considered as a positive vision of a new industrial DIY/DIT revolution (DIY – Do-it-yourself, DIT – Do-it-together) (Gershenfeld 2005). Taking the transformative potentials of third places as a starting point, we argue that makerspaces are catalysts for more sustainability, especially with regard to their social functions. This is because they (can) contribute towards consolidating a culture of making and thus to implementing a post-growth society. We begin the discussion by considering what third places actually are and how they contribute towards a sustainability transformation. Attention then turns to the specific phenomenon of makerspaces, considering their potentials as third places in the post-growth context. The article closes with a conclusion and prospects for further research.

2. Third places and sustainable development

The terms 'third space' and 'third place' can be traced back to debates in and on cultural and social theory. Important authors are Ray Oldenburg (1989), Homi K. Bhabha (1994) and Edward W. Soja ([1996] 2007). Third spaces and places have received much attention within post-colonial studies (Struve 2017: 227) and have also been discussed in geographical research. This article draws on the various concepts and then applies them to makerspaces in the context of post-growth.

2.1 From 'third space' to 'third place' – theoretical approaches

Third space is concerned with the interaction of culture, identity, space and power relations. Drawing on postmodern definitions of space as the articulation of social power relations (Massey 1994: 120), Bhabha proposes reading spatial identities and individuals' movements in space as the result of history, hybridity and hierarchy. Bhabha conceptualizes third space at the interface between the representation of space and representational space, which is where change emerges (Elmborg 2011: 342 ff.). In terms of the transformational power of cultural difference, 'third space is the space of potentially meaningful contact between cultures and people' (ibid.: 344) and thus a kind of space of possibilities that emerge from cultural exchange between people (Struve 2017: 226). Edward W. Soja ([1996] 2007) refers further to the difference between third space as opposed to first space and second space. While first space is understood as a 'real' space, limited by the built environment, and second space is the space that is perceived and negotiated in discourse, third space refers to the combination of the two (Soja [1996] 2007: 56f.). This understanding views third space as being characterised primarily by hybridity and openness (Austen 2014: 49).

The spatial theory conceptions of Bhabha and Soja are characterised by a high degree of abstraction (Struve 2017: 228) and do not provide a tangible basis for the analysis of concrete places and their potentials. However, since the late 1980s numerous authors have tackled the issue of transferring these concepts and applied third place concepts to everyday places like cafes, kiosks, neighbourhood centres or libraries (e.g. Elmborg 2011, Peterson 2019). One of the first who conceived of third place as a public place was the urban sociologist Ray Oldenburg (1989: 20 ff.) . From his perspective, transformation can only emerge in a public place that is outside the home (first place) and place of work (second place), as encounters between strangers on neutral ground can only occur in a place to which nobody has personal ties (ibid.: 26). There must also be low thresholds for participating in interaction processes. People's social status should not play a role, or at least plays much less of a role than in other places. The precondition for encounters between different people is that the place is open and freely accessible (Sleeman 2012: 37). This includes ensuring that the atmosphere is inviting and fulfils the needs of users, but standards should nonetheless be simple (function before appearance). In addition to openness towards new participants, communication is seen as decisive for setting things in motion and managing change. The design of third places therefore needs to focus on community and enable collaborative work. The conversational atmosphere should not be tense but needs to be playful and conspirative, giving the individual a feeling of warmth and belonging to the group. This can be further underlined by regular joint activities and events (ibid.). Before our attention turns to how these conditions are fulfilled in makerspaces, we discuss the extent to which third places are relevant from the perspective of sustainability.

2.2 Third places and their role in sustainability transition

Since at least the 1970s, critiques of growth have been an established part of scientific debate. At the beginning of the 2020s, these critiques are often thought of under the heading of 'sustainability', a term which is used extremely vaguely and is linked to numerous different concepts (Pufé 2018: 93). Drawing on the concept of the sustainability triangle (ibid.: 112 f.), we do not consider the three dimensions of sustainability (ecological, social and economic dimensions) as pillars standing next to one another but as an integrative 'common whole' (ibid.: 113, translated from German). This approach to sustainable development can also be applied to third places.

If we consider the global sustainability goals (SDGs) developed by the United Nations (UN 2015) and the sustainability principles as summarised by Pufé (2018: 116), it can be seen that third places offer a whole series of starting points for a sustainability transformation. As meeting places they enable encounters and networking between people of different age groups (principle of intergenerational justice) and between those of different origin, gender, religion and social status (principle of intragenerational justice) (ibid.). As they are generally intended as long-term structures, they support the creation of inclusive and resilient social and cultural infrastructures in towns and cities (SDG 11) – also in line with the sustainability principle 'think global, act local' (Pufé 2018: 116). Thanks to the opening up and pooling of cultural offerings, education and encounters, third places are 'anchor points for cultural diversity and a cultural contribution towards strengthening social cohesion, creating equivalent living conditions and strengthening identity' (MKW NRW 2019, translated from German). In the long run, they contribute to the promotion of psychosocial well-being (SDG 3) and lifelong learning (SDG 4) and support the transformation of processes of production and consumption from a growth-based economy towards a socio-ecological economy focused on the common good (SDG 8).

Third places are primarily relevant for meeting social sustainability goals, although there are complex interactions with other dimensions (Bauriedl 2008: 33). In the following, the example of makerspaces is used to explore how third places function and contribute towards a social transformation to (more) sustainability.

3. Makerspaces as third places of the post-growth society

In order to understand why makerspaces can be understood as third places, they are initially described in brief. Subsequently, their potential as infrastructure for a sustainability transformation is critically discussed in the context of post-growth discourses.

3.1 High-tech workshops for everyone: Development, organisation and examples

Debates held in the 1980s and 1990s about the predicted end of mass production and the increasing flexibilisation of industrial production (Piore/Sabel 1985) have been spurred on since the turn of the millennium by radically new digital and networked production and additive manufacturing technologies. This is the context in which authors like Gershenfeld (2005, 2012) and Anderson (2012) developed a positive vision of a new industrial DIY/DIT revolution, in which the relationship between production and consumption is renegotiated through cooperation between people using shared production facilities.

Figure 1: Map of makerspaces in Germany

Source: the authors (data research: Matti Kurzeja; graphics: Irene Johannsen)

In the international literature, makerspaces are variously referred to, for instance as 'community-based fabrication workshops' (Hielscher/Smith 2014). In German-speaking countries the term *Makerspace* describes open workshops with digital infrastructure that are dedicated to 'collaborative (digital) production in publicly accessible spaces' (Simons/Petschow/Peuckert 2016: 29, translated from German). It thus acts as an umbrella term for various manifestations of workshops (Smith 2017: 6) that make available tools and technologies which were originally confined to the sphere of industrial production (Gershenfeld 2012: 44). Makerspaces are a global phenomenon and are growing in number: in 2006 there were only a few dozen, by 2016 almost 1400 (Browder/Aldrich/Bradley 2019: 461). In Germany alone there are now over 200 makerspaces spread across the whole country, although primarily in the larger cities (Figure 1).

The origins of today's maker movement (Anderson 2012, Hatch 2013) can be traced back to the hacker community of the late twentieth century, who worked collaboratively on software and hardware in so-called hackerspaces (Cavalcanti 2013a). Indeed, some makerspaces call themselves hackerspaces, drawing on the hacker movement, although this is not an established term, unlike that of fab labs (fabrication laboratories), a concept initiated in 2001 by Neil Gershenfeld from MIT which also had considerable influence on the maker movement and serves as a point of reference for many makerspaces (Gershenfeld 2005). The magazine *Make*, in existence since 2005, and 'maker faires', festivals where makers can present their projects and creations, have further encouraged the emergence of places worldwide that are dedicated to collaborative digital production in facilities open to the public (Burke 2014: 11). The maker movement differs from previous open workshop movements, DIY movements and independent work initiatives in two ways. First, the available technologies and open hardware concepts enable participants to develop their own new technologies. Second, social-media platforms allow intensive forms of cooperation over large distances, based on digital collaboration (Smith 2017: 7).

'DingFabrik' Cologne

The *DingFabrik* ('ThingFactory') founded in 2010 in Cologne describes itself as a 'combination of open workshop, hackerspace and fab lab'. It is organised as a non-profit association and run by about 120 association members (as of mid-2019). The DIY principle characterises its offerings, such as workshops and information sessions, and it is a grassroots democratic organisation with regular plenums where all important decisions are discussed. Both the operations and the premises are largely financed by membership fees. The premises house a store for materials and areas for woodwork, metalworking, screen printing, sewing and bicycle repairs, but also facilities for working with hardware and software and computer-based maker tools like a laser cutter, 3-D printer and a CNC milling machine. There are courses to learn how to use specific tools, lectures, working groups and projects that explicitly focus on the sustainable use of resources and offer corresponding 'help to self-help' (e.g. repair cafes). The weekly crafting afternoon is perfect for getting an idea of the place. What happens in the *'DingFabrik'* is just as diverse as the raw materials and tools used: from bicycle repairs to making furniture and musical instruments to the development and construction of complex technical equipment like CNC-milling machines or laser cutters. The *'DingFabrik'* is thus an example of a makerspace initiated and run by civil-society actors.
Further information at: https://dingfabrik.de/

A makerspace at the urban district library of Cologne-Kalk

The library of the urban district Kalk is run by the city of Cologne and was comprehensively renovated in 2018. Since then, it has a making room, with finance provided by a fund for neighbourhoods with special development needs. The library was designed with the aim of creating a non-commercial place for cultural interaction, experimentation, tinkering and participation. The design process included the architects and the library team but also involved the active participation of residents of Kalk. Based on the concept of an 'open library', the premises can be used without staff support during the opening hours of the district town hall. Visitors identify themselves with their library cards at the entry panel and can use the place independently. The makerspace is located on the ground floor and in close vicinity to the library itself with its communal areas to spend time in and a comprehensive collection of media. It provides a 3-D printer, educational robots, laptops, tablets, soldering equipment and corresponding self-help literature. Every week tools and techniques are explained in workshops to anyone interested. In addition to courses for learning to use 3-D printers, there are courses on programming and building electric circuits, on robot control systems and on single-board computers. It is also possible for individuals to hold their own courses in open hours for 'Kalk's makers'. Another part of the Kalk makerspace concept is the 'Maker Mobil', a cargo bike that can be used flexibly for events in the city and promotes the makerspace among the general public. Through its integration in the urban district library, the Kalk makerspace illustrates how state actors, especially public libraries and museums, are embracing the DIY movement and the concept of third places, thus finding ways to embrace digitisation and the resulting social change (Rasmussen 2016: 547, Braybrooke 2018: 41).

Further information at: https://www.stadt-koeln.de/artikel/04943/index.html

Among those running the makerspaces are associations, which have often emerged from local (grassroots) initiatives (see the example in Box 1), but also research institutes, universities, schools, public libraries (see the example in Box 2) and even businesses. The focus and facilities provided by the workshops are correspondingly varied: from spaces for learning to empowering places of DIY production to state-funded 'innovation laboratories'; from voluntary, grassroots democratic organisations to classical enterprise hierarchies. Makerspaces are often financed by membership fees but also by donations, public funds, sponsoring or proceeds from events (Cavalcanti 2013b). Despite these different forms of organisation, makerspaces can be regarded as third places, especially due to the low-threshold access to (digital) production equipment and the particular significance of community, as the two case studies from Cologne illustrate.

3.2 Makerspaces as infrastructure for transformation?

In the context of sustainability and post-growth debates, makerspaces are exciting because they provide spaces and opportunity structures for alternative and potentially transformative economic practices. Even if they lead something of a niche existence within society as a whole, they point to paths towards a sustainable post-growth economy (e.g. Lange 2017: 40). Smith (2017) suggests that activities in makerspaces facilitate participation, openness and community and can generate transformative social innovations. In their capacity as third places, makerspaces are a kind of technical and social infrastructure for a socio-ecological sustainability transformation. By promoting a culture of repairing and upcycling (for instance in repair cafes), they enable digital, decentralised production and can, thanks to extended product lifecycles and closed material cycles, contribute to a reduction of resource consumption and CO_2 emissions (Smith/Light 2017:164).

3.3 Open access to resources as a basis for encounter and interaction

For third places to emerge as places of social participation they must have a low threshold of access. Although practices vary between makerspaces[1], it is this 'open access for the broad public' (Simons/Petschow/Peuckert 2016: 29, translated from German) that defines them as 'community-oriented spaces' (Smith/Hielscher/Dickel et al. 2013: 4). In addition to access to material resources like tools, they provide access to non-material resources, especially knowledge. With the growing importance of access to technology and its use for social participation (Ringwald/Schneider/Cagan 2019), makerspaces carry out groundwork in a rapidly changing technology landscape. There are diverse opportunities for participation ranging from attending workshops to membership to designing your own offerings. As the example of the '*DingFabrik*' in Cologne clearly demonstrates, makerspaces are in many cases established and run by their users. Makerspaces in public institutions, like in the urban district library of Cologne-Kalk, are more closely managed

---

1 In line with their settings, there are periods for selectively public processes in most makerspaces (e.g. for members, university students, school students, etc.), which temporarily limit access.

but here users are also increasingly involved in the design of premises and offerings (Rasmussen 2016: 547).

Access to resources often involves collective forms of property. Due to the collaborative organisation of production, several authors discuss makerspaces as a version of 'commons-based peer production' (Kostakis/Niaros/Giotitsas 2015). However, there are examples of makerspaces with a commercial, hierarchical form of organisation (e.g. the business TUM MakerSpace GmbH near Munich), and even in non-commercial, association-based makerspaces the process of communalisation can be limited, for instance when working with consumable materials (Seravalli 2014). At the same time, however, the production practices based on open-source software and hardware make it possible to avoid many of the exclusions that are characteristic of classical concepts of property. Furthermore, the vast majority of makerspaces in Germany are run as associations or public corporations and do not have a direct profit orientation.

3.4 Lifelong learning through and with community

Makerspaces offer their users 'neutral ground' where they can realise individual and collaborative projects within a community. Surveys reveal that community is a decisive factor here: in addition to the production of objects and software-hacking, social aspects and learning have been identified as central reasons for participation (e.g. Moilanen 2012). There is continuous interaction between collaboration, mutual teaching, learning by making and the finished products. Makerspaces in general – not just the ones in public libraries – thus become places of informal education and demonstrate the strong link between social capital and lifelong learning (Ferguson 2012: 26). While the concrete culture of community is shaped in diverse ways, important principles are captured by the headings of the 'Maker Movement Manifest' by Hatch (2013): 'make', 'share', 'give', 'learn', 'tool up', 'play', 'participate', 'support' and 'change'.

A particularly important aspect of the community in makerspaces is its playful and conspirative character: 'Play, fun, and interest are at the heart of making' (Martin 2015: 35). The movement is characterised by a positive culture of failure which understands experimentation and tinkering as new impulses for learning, so that in the end skills are acquired and goals reached (ibid.). As informal places of education, makerspaces offer their users an opportunity structure for empowered, voluntary and informal (adult) learning processes (Schön/Ebner/Grandl 2019). There is furthermore potential for their use in formal educational institutions like schools and universities (Barrett/Pizzico/Levy et al. 2015, Martin 2015), as is already the case in Cologne-Kalk, where the Maker Mobil is used for school events (see Box 2). In any case, in and through makerspaces, users are becoming prosumers; they can acquire and share knowledge, and develop and experiment with sustainability innovations at a local level. They thus provide ideas and approaches for a post-growth society.

3.5 Critical reflection on the post-growth potential of makerspaces

Use of the term 'makerspaces', like that of 'third places', has become almost inflationary and tends to be applied to a diffuse space of possibility. Peterson (2019: 35) argues nonetheless that it is important not to abstract encounters in such places from their historical, political and geographical contexts. Rather, they do not exist outside of social power relations, which are materialised in such places and impact on the individuals involved (Berlant 2016: 395). It is therefore necessary to investigate concrete examples to establish the extent to which makerspaces in practice fulfil expectations and which exclusions they (re)produce.

In terms of the ecological effects of makerspaces, Hielscher and Smith (2014: 44), for instance, emphasise that positive ecological evaluations of 'grassroot digital fabrication' remain speculative because the relevant effects depend on which materials are used for production. It is rather the case that a whole range of conditions must be met if the decentralised and individualised production in makerspaces is to be described as ecologically sustainable (Petschow/Ferdinand/Dickel et al. 2014, Olson 2013). Similarly, not all makerspaces are characterised by the radical break with capitalist growth logics that post-growth approaches demand (Schmid 2019: 3). Indeed, there are diverse and increasing interactions between makerspaces and processes of capitalist exploitation (Morozov 2014). For example, in the RepRap project the idea of a freely available and easily replicable 3-D printer ended up as a commercial and very profitable product (Söderberg 2013). This example indicates the problems caused by commercial and political actors (for instance state institutions in China and the USA) who support 'making' as a way to promote economic growth and innovations (Morozov 2014). At this point, logics of commercial exploitation and growth collide and compete with the self-image of many makerspaces as collective economic spaces for independent making and as alternatives to a consumer and throwaway society. The claim that makerspaces are places of low-threshold access should also be critically examined. The costs for machines, premises, insurance, etc. can be considerable (Cavalcanti 2013b), which, for instance, means that members of the '*DingFabrik*' pay a minimum monthly fee of 23 euros (17 euros for low-income groups). Many makerspaces have voluntary or progressive (solidarity) fees, demonstrating the efforts made to promote inclusivity and broad social participation, but in practice people with low incomes are unlikely to feel addressed by the initiatives in the first place. Finally, in a number of cases the ongoing commercialisation of makerspaces runs counter to any logic of inclusion (Hielscher/Smith 2014: 49).

The divergence between aspiration and reality is revealed by a glance at the users of makerspaces, who are not representative of society as a whole, but are more often than average white, male and well-educated (Make 2012). Several initiatives have attempted to tackle this problem by focusing on traditionally underrepresented groups. In this vein, special makerspaces offer socially marginalised groups like people of colour ('Liberating Ourselves Locally' in Oakland) or people with disabilities ('Selfmade' in Dortmund) access to the making culture in a protected space. However, such places, and explicitly feminist makerspaces (e.g. the 'Mz* Baltazar's Lab' in Vienna), do not follow the concept of an openly accessible third place but rather the concept of a safe space 'in which boundaries offer both safety and a platform for political resistance' (Toupin 2014: 7).

4. Conclusion and prospects

The notion that, as third places, makerspaces can provide impetus for sustainable development in the sense of post-growth must be critically assessed, particularly in light of the increasing capitalist exploitation of such spaces. Sustainability, equitable participation, empowerment and a democratisation of production are not necessarily inherent to makerspaces. Nonetheless, as collaboratively used, participative places, they bring people into contact with one another and with technology. They thus offer diverse points of departure for post-growth discourses and relate to all three dimensions of sustainable development (ecological, social, economic). Particularly on the social level, they promote collective learning processes and are important places of encounter where digital participation can be experienced, and they can therefore contribute towards achieving social sustainability goals. Makerspaces are thus starting points for, and the result of, transformation processes, as well as catalysts and opportunity spaces for testing and developing transformative practices.

Nevertheless, makerspaces are embedded in existing social power relations and produce their own exclusions. The growing interest of commercial actors is associated with the threat of commercial appropriation, which constrains the transformative power of makerspaces. Simultaneously, the concept of makerspaces as third places is being increasingly seized upon by municipal actors involved in urban development (policies). From a geographical perspective, it is particularly exciting to observe the extent to which such places (can) challenge hierarchical management styles (Braybrooke 2018: 43) and how their participative structures and processes (can) develop and realise into new governance styles and forms, e.g. in urban development.

Cited literature

Anderson, C. (2012). *Makers: The new industrial revolution*. Crown Business.
Austen, M. (2014). *Dritte Räume als Gesellschaftsmodell. Eine epistemologische Untersuchung des Thirdspace*. Studies from the Münchener Institut for ethnology 8.
Bauriedl, S. (2008). Die „Nachhaltige Stadt": Ein Patchwork unterschiedlicher Nachhaltigkeitsdimensionen. In S. Bauriedl, D. Schindler, & M. Winkler (Eds.), *Stadtzukünfte denken. Nachhaltigkeit in europäischen Stadtregionen*. oekom, 28–54.
Barrett, T., Pizzico, M., Levy, B., Nagel, R. L., Linsey, J. S., Talley, K. G., Forest, C. R., & Newstetter, W. C. (2015). *A review of university maker spaces*. Georgia Institute of Technology.
Berlant, L. (2016). The commons: Infrastructures for troubling times. *Environment and Planning D: Society and Space, 34*(3), 393–419.
Bhabha, H. K. (1994). *The location of culture*. Routledge.

Braybrooke, K. (2018). Hacking the museum? Practices and power geometries at collections makerspaces in London. *Journal of Peer Production*, 12(2), 40–59.

Browder, R. E., Aldrich, H. E., & Bradley, S. W. (2019). The emergence of the maker movement: Implications for entrepreneurship research. *Journal of Business Venturing, 34*(3), 459–476.

Burke, J. J. (2014). *Makerspaces: a practical guide for librarians* (Vol. 8). Rowman & Littlefield.

Cavalcanti, G. (2013a). Is it a hackerspace, makerspace, techshop, or fablab. *Makezine.* https://makezine.com/2013/05/22/the-difference-between-hackerspaces-makerspaces-techshops-and-fablabs/ (01.04.2021).

Cavalcanti, G. (2013b). Making makerspaces: creating a business model. *Makezine.* https://makezine.com/2013/06/04/making-makerspaces-creating-a-business-model/ (01.04.2021).

Elmborg, J. (2011). Libraries as the spaces between us: Recognizing and valuing the third space. *Reference & User Services Quarterly, 50*(4), 338–350.

Ferguson, S. (2012). Are public libraries developers of social capital? A review of their contribution and attempts to demonstrate it. *The Australian Library Journal, 61*(1), 22–33.

Gershenfeld, N. A. (2005). *Fab: the coming revolution on your desktop – from personal computers to personal fabrication.* Basic Books.

Gershenfeld, N. A. (2012). How to make almost anything: The digital fabrication revolution. *Foreign Affairs, 91*(6), 43–57.

Hatch, M. (2013). *The maker movement manifesto: Rules for innovation in the new world of crafters, hackers, and tinkerers.* McGraw Hill.

Hielscher, S., & Smith, A. (2014). *Community-based digital fabrication workshops: A review of the research literature.* Working Paper Series SWPS 2014-08. http://sro.sussex.ac.uk/id/eprint/49214/1/2014-08_SWPS_Hielscher_Smith.pdf (01.04.2021).

Kostakis, V., Niaros, V., & Giotitsas, C. (2015). Production and governance in hackerspaces: A manifestation of commons-based peer production in the physical realm? *International Journal of Cultural Studies, 18*(5), 555–573.

Lange, B. (2017). Offene Werkstätten und Postwachstumsökonomien: kollaborative Orte als Wegbereiter transformativer Wirtschaftsentwicklungen? *Zeitschrift für Wirtschaftsgeographie, 61*(1), 38–55.

Make (2012). *Maker market survey: An in-depth profile of makers at the forefront of hardware innovation*. http://cdn.makezine.com/make/bootstrap/img/etc/Maker-Market-Study.pdf (01.04.2021).

Massey, D. (1994). *Space, Place and Gender*. Polity Press.

Martin, L. (2015). The Promise of the Maker Movement for Education. *Journal of Pre-College Engineering Education Research (J-PEER)*, 5(1), 30–39.

MKW NRW – Ministerium für Kultur und Wissenschaft des Landes Nordrhein-Westfalen (2019). *Dritte Orte*. https://www.mkw.nrw/kultur/arbeitsfelder/dritte-orte (01.04.2021).

Moilanen J. (2012). Emerging hackerspaces – peer-production generation. In I. Hammouda, B. Lundell, T. Mikkonen, & W. Scacchi (Eds.), *Open source systems: Long-term sustainability. OSS 2012. IFIP Advances in Information and Communication Technology 378*. Springer, 94–111.

Morozov, E. (2014). A critic at large: making it. *The New Yorker*. https://www.newyorker.com/magazine/2014/01/13/making-it-2 (01.04.2021).

Oldenburg, R. (1989). *The great good place. Cafés, coffee shops, bookstores, bars, hair salons, and other hangouts at the heart community*. Paragon House.

Olson, R. (2013). 3-D printing: A boon or a bane? *The Environmental Forum*. https://fabfoundation.org/resource-folder/pdfs/OLSON_FORUM_NOV-DEC_2013-1.pdf (01.04.2021).

Peterson, M. (2019). *Meeting spaces: Everyday spaces of multicultural encounter*. Self-published. http://theses.gla.ac.uk/41179/7/2019PetersonPhD.pdf (01.04.2021).

Petschow, U., Ferdinand, J.-P., Dickel, S., Flämig, H., Steinfeldt, M., & Worobei, A. (2014). *Dezentrale Produktion, 3D-Druck und Nachhaltigkeit – Trajektorien und Potenziale innovativer Wertschöpfungsmuster zwischen Maker-Bewegung und Industrie 4.0*. IÖW publication series 206/14.

Piore, M. J., & Sabel, C. F. (1985). *Das Ende der Massenproduktion: Studie über die Requalifizierung der Arbeit und die Rückkehr der Ökonomie in die Gesellschaft*. Wagenbach.

Pufé, I. (2018). *Nachhaltigkeit*. Bundeszentrale für politische Bildung.

Rasmussen, C. H. (2016). The participatory public library: the Nordic experience. *New Library World*, 117(9/10), 546–556.

Ringwald, R., Schneider, T., & Cagan, T.-P. (2019). *Smart Cities gestalten. Daseinsvorsorge und digitale Teilhabe sichern*. Self-published.

Schmid, B. (2019). Degrowth and postcapitalism: Transformative geographies beyond accumulation and growth. *Geography Compass*, 13(11), 59.

Schön, S., Ebner, M., & Grandl, M. (2019). Makerspaces als Kreativ-und Lernräume. Werkstätten mit digitalen Werkzeugen aus Perspektive der Erwachsenenbildung. *Magazin Erwachsenenbildung.at, 13*(35-36), 2–12.

Seravalli, A. (2014). While waiting for the third industrial revolution: Attempts at commoning production. In P. Ehn, E. Nilsson, & R. Topgaard (Eds.), *Making futures: Marginal notes on innovation, design, and democracy*. MIT Press, 99–116.

Simons, A., Petschow, U., & Peuckert, J. (2016). *Offene Werkstätten – nachhaltig innovativ?* IÖW publication series 212/16.

Sleeman, M. (2012). There's No Home Like Place? In P. Myers (Ed.), *Going home: Essays, articles, and stories in honour of the Andersons*. Oak Hill College, 33–40.

Smith, A., Hielscher, S., Dickel, S., Soderberg, J., & van Oost, E. (2013). *Grassroots digital fabrication and makerspaces: Reconfiguring, relocating and recalibrating innovation?* SPRU Working Paper SWPS 2.

Smith, A. (2017). *Social innovation, democracy and makerspaces*. SPRU Working Paper SWPS 10.

Smith, A., & Light, A. (2017). Cultivating sustainable developments with makerspaces. *Liinc em revista, 13*(1), 162–174.

Soja, E. W. ([1996] 2007). *Thirdspace: Journeys to Los Angeles and other real-and-imagined places*. Blackwell.

Söderberg, J. (2013). Automating amateurs in the 3D printing community: Connecting the dots between 'deskilling' and 'user-friendliness'. *Work Organisation, Labour and Globalisation, 7*(1), 124–139.

Struve, K. (2017). Third Space. In D. Göttsche, A. Dunker, & G. Dürbeck, (Eds.), *Handbuch Postkolonialismus und Literatur*. Springer, 226–228.

Toupin, S. (2014). Feminist hackerspaces: The synthesis of feminist and hacker cultures. *Journal of Peer Production, 5*, 1–11.

UN – United Nations (2015). *Transforming our world: The 2030 Agenda for sustainable development*. https://sustainabledevelopment.un.org/content/documents/21252030%20Agenda%20for%20Sustainable%20Development%20web.pdf (01.04.2021).

Performing gaps
The relationship between alternative economies and urban planning in Dortmund

Le-Lina Kettner, Samuel Mössner

1. Introduction: Alternative economies in urban planning processes

In light of the urgent global crises, both science and practice alike emphasise the necessity of a 'progressive, emancipatory, socio-ecological transformation' (Acosta/Brand 2018: 17, translated from German). Key actors of the transformation process are so-called alternative initiatives, whose approaches aim to establish local resources and regional economic cycles in the context of critiques of the traditional growth paradigm. Alternative initiatives are often located in urban areas characterised by dynamic and high concentrations of exchange and diversity that encourage spaces of opportunity for the emergence and testing of alternative economic approaches (Krueger/Schulz/Gibbs 2017). These spaces are often fiercely contested (Kipp 2018: 212). They are locations of political negotiation, as practices of transformative innovation and alternative action are associated with a questioning and criticism of the hegemonial settings and patriarchal power relations linked to traditional economic understandings.

At the heart of the critique is an understanding of success and growth that focuses primarily on quantifiable variables. Numerous initiatives and social movements therefore try to counter these traditional economic forms with *other* ways of assessing value that use alternative and non-quantifiable factors. Such approaches include practices of solidarity, civil society self-organisation, sufficiency and all notions that focus on social well-being, health and social justice. Particularly prominent in the literature are discussions of 'transition town movements' (Hopkins 2008), revived debates about urban commons (Helferich 2012; Nikolaeva/Adey/Cresswell et al. 2018), economies for the common good and cooperative approaches. All of these approaches are characterised by their criticism of conventional patterns of consumption, production methods, top-down forms of organisation and competitive market economy behaviour (Schmelzer 2018; Schmid 2018; Müller 2018; Lange 2017). Both science and practice therefore see such approaches as playing a significant role in driving the transformation of society.

While resistance as protest can indeed function outside of social structures, this article argues that it is not only resistant activities outside of social norms and fields that are of great importance. In order to establish and perpetuate alternative approaches and initiatives, ultimately an interface with the societal mainstream is required. For alternative initiatives this interface primarily involves cooperation with municipal administrations, planning and politics. Alternative initiatives are frequently dependent on spaces and areas in the city which urban planning authorities allow them to use (sometimes temporarily). Urban administrations and policies enable the emergence of these niche spaces, protect them from market forces (even if often only temporarily) and, ideally, provide the necessary infrastructure.

At the same time many of the focuses of the heterogeneous post-growth initiatives mentioned above coincide with the original tasks of urban planning. Beyond a neoliberal 'public management' approach (Peck/Theodore/Brenner 2013; Fuller/Geddes 2008), urban planning continues to be viewed as the guardian of urban processes (Klaer 2008: 203) and is tasked with creating opportunities for social action and managing them within the framework of political guidance. Urban planning should focus on the objective of creating good living conditions for all parts of society (Wiezorek 2017: 53).

Urban planning administrations are thus less rejecting of alternative approaches than the classical neoliberal critique implies. Nonetheless, in the context of well-rehearsed and routine administrative practice, the initiatives are often (benevolently) marginalised, which hinders the development of cooperative, equal relations between alternative initiatives and urban planning. The literature contains research on the emergence of alternative economies, sub-cultural initiatives and growth-critical innovations in local areas and their diffusion on different spatial scales (Gibson-Graham 2008; Roelvink 2011; Fuller/Jonas 2003; Schulz/Affolderbach 2015). However, the nexus between alternative initiatives and the bodies of urban administrations and planning has received comparatively little attention to date.

In light of the lack of research into the potential of interactions between initiatives and urban planning, the empirical study on which this article is based attempts to identify theoretical, abstract and explanatory approaches from the empirical field (Strauss/Glaser 1967). Using the case of the city of Dortmund, the empirical research focused on the requirements and support needed by the initiatives to enable better urban integration beyond neoliberal appropriation. To this end, interviews were held with representatives of various initiatives and the urban administration and participant observation was conducted in the period from February to May 2019.

It quickly became clear that there were significant gaps in the interaction and cooperation between urban planning and initiatives, as we briefly outline in Section 2. A possible explanation for such gaps is provided in Section 3, drawing on the social theory of Judith Butler (1991; 1995). On a conceptual level, we argue that it is important to recognise the gap between the externally defined, hegemonic characterisation of what alternative initiatives should be, on the one hand, and the self-performance and lived-out position of the initiatives, on the other hand. This gap is responsible for the speechlessness alternative initiatives and urban planning mutually experience and for potential misunderstandings between them. We want to demonstrate here that Judith Butler's notions of performativity and processes of subjectification, which were originally related to social constructions of gender identities, can also be applied in research of economic dualism (mainstream – alternative) and have particular potential for providing explanations of the lack of effectiveness of alternative initiatives in urban contexts.

2. The marginalisation of alternative economies in urban planning

The growing number of alternative approaches in the fields of supply, consumption or sufficiency and mobility indicates not only the great potential here for urban development and planning but also the increasing spatial relevance of these activities. However, despite numerous proposals for sustainable, democratic and participative urban planning (Elsen/Reifer/Oberleiter et al. 2015; Klaer 2008), post-growth initiatives and approaches have so far been largely marginalised in urban planning processes.

Although in theory towns and cities are called upon to apply post-growth initiatives, in practical terms this does not occur. However, on the level of federal state politics in, for instance, North-Rhine Westphalia, such initiatives are given considerably more attention (WIKUE). The consumer advice centres and other organisations that are concerned with the networking of so-called 'spaces of possibilities' (Kerekes 2015, translated from German) also refer to the significance of these initiatives and their contribution towards the transformation of society. A similar position is adopted by planning sciences. The (urban) policy side occasionally recognises individual potentials but seldom specifies ways of fully exploiting these potentials. Accordingly, in many cities – including Dortmund – there are strong networks between individual initiatives, but for questionable reasons they tend to be reluctant to involve urban planning and administration.

In Dortmund, for example, structural change resulting from the steel crisis that started in the 1970s enabled the early establishment of a broad landscape of alternative initiatives and approaches. Dortmund is characterised by a comparatively high number of still unutilised brownfield sites, and in recent years there has been a strong focus on promoting the cultural and creative economic fields. The city particularly favours a policy that promotes a creative economic milieu true to neoliberal maxims (Florida 2005). This involves, firstly, a creative approach being taken to the brownfield sites. Secondly, it recognises an innovative strength in niche economies and creative initiatives that can successfully overcome the effects of deindustrialisation (Wascher/Hebel/Schrot et al. 2018: 4). The policy is flanked by a focus on the university as a locational advantage and the embedding of the city in the 'Spatial Strategy for the Ruhr 2035+' ('*Raumstrategien Ruhr 2035+*'), which inter alia aims to attract and retain businesses (Wagner/Hegmanns 2017: 91 ff.).

A creative scene has developed in the shadow of this classical neoliberal economic policy, giving rise to many initiatives based on alternative economic approaches. These initiatives benefit from the availability of the old brownfields and comparatively low-price housing and commercial sites. However, they also profit from the political promotion of creative and small-scale innovation, the creative milieu surrounding the colleges and university and a supra-regional planning strategy that supports such approaches.

Nonetheless, there are barriers to the development of alternative initiatives, but – in the general opinion of the various actors – they could be overcome with the use of cooperative approaches by the urban administration and planning.

In Dortmund, however, this kind of cooperation is extremely rare in practice. In our research interviews, representatives of alternative initiatives repeatedly referred to a lack of flexibility and openness and insufficient trust and goodwill on the part of urban planning. The wish was expressed that there should be more courageous support of approaches that the city does not view as contributing significantly to traditional economic growth. In this context, reference was made to the need for better support and the development of growth-independent criteria for urban planning (Lamker/ Schulze Dieckhoff 2019).

A central role is played by the interpretation and application of (legal) regulations, statutes and ordinances, which – in the opinion of the initiatives – could sometimes be more creative, even within the framework of the existing provisions. Due to their low degree of institutionalization, the alternative initiatives often have great difficulty fulfilling or complying with rules and regulations. From the point of view of the alternative initiatives, the urban administration's self-conception of themselves as the 'guardian of laws and regulations' and their associated notion that 'all [rules] are enacted for a good reason' (Interview 6 2019) is not conducive to flexibly supporting the concerns and projects of the initiatives. Especially for initiatives that are active at the borders of regulation conformity or that move outside the provisions, urban planning needs to apply small-scale, cautious and situationally specific efforts to transfer them into formal structures. However, this is only possible if the initiatives' activities are recognised as valuable in the first place. Moreover, it is often unclear which regulations apply to new or different ideas, which can then lead to misunderstandings and later to rejection. In addition to the problem of adherence to a largely inflexible set of regulations, the initiatives also criticised the inertia and anxiety of urban planning vis-à-vis innovations and change and in this context 'wished [...] that then the plans of thirty years ago were not dug out but that people would really look at the current situation and really determine the true needs' (Interview 2 2019). Many initiatives were discouraged by the fast and direct rejection of their ideas. There was a wish for more dialogue about the reasons for the rejection so that it would perhaps be possible to together identify a different way in which the individual projects could be implemented (Interview 1, 2, 5 2019). Lastly, attention was drawn to the discrepancy between bureaucratic processes and procedures and the temporal and spatial routines and rhythms practised by the representatives of the initiatives. This is a classic problem of cooperation between alternative initiatives and urban administrations and is much discussed in the literature (Cramer 2013; Selle/Wachten 2011; Selle 1997).

Private-sector planning offices (Interview 6 2019) also support this impression of a lack of flexibility and exercising of individual discretion. This similarly confirms the need to allow experimental trial-and-error to be part of planning and to 'first let things just go their own way a bit' (ibid.). This is, however, only possible under cooperative conditions when there is no shying away from conflict.

These and other statements seem to contradict the self-definition and self-perception of urban planning within the urban administration. Those responsible for planning suggest that informal instruments help them to be particularly agile and react flexibly to different claims and types of use. The urban administration furthermore emphasises that urban planning processes are extremely 'people-oriented' (Stadt Dortmund o. J., translated from German). Interviews with representatives of the urban administration also clearly show that seeking individual solutions and especially compromises is indeed a major concern of planning. Here reference was made to the way in which the requirements of alternative initiatives had been accommodated by making generous use of the scope for weighing up interests (Interview 5 2019): 'They are colleagues with whom you can consider how you can manage something like that and how you can do that. And a great deal is possible there'. The urban administration demonstrates openness towards projects with an uncertain or risky outcome (ibid.) and explicitly states in this context that funding does not depend on success or on agreements about objectives. Projects that planning representatives predict will fail even right at the beginning are particularly difficult to fund, but plausible reasons are nonetheless put on the table: 'Why should I fund a project that I think from the outset will fail? [...] Well, basically I just fund the learning process. How many euros is a learning process worth in comparison to a project that you can see will work?' (ibid.).

In summary, the empirical insights show that alternative initiatives and projects are fundamentally possible in Dortmund but they have to be based primarily on *established* visions, values and understandings of the meaning and success of urban planning. In addition to the focus on traditional ideas, the empirical findings also suggest there is mutual misunderstanding and that this results in a lack of support. The mutual misunderstanding is not caused only by inertia within the urban administration. The flexibility often displayed by the urban administration frequently goes unrecognised by the initiatives. The relationship between the urban administration and the alternative initiatives is characterised by different perceptions, contrary expectations and conflicting ideas which lead to a general speechlessness with one another.

The selection of empirical approaches discussed above demonstrates that alternatives to established, conservative and traditional structures and values are not always understood by the urban administration as criticism. They are rather viewed as open spaces and innovative experiments and are acknowledged by the dominant system of urban planning. The relationship between urban planning – which represents the dominant hegemonial system – and alternative initiatives – which understand themselves as counterprojects to existing capitalist routines – is characterised by power asymmetries (Healy 2009). The initiatives coexisting in economic and planning niches are therefore denied the ability to effectively represent a justified counterproposal to capitalist economic forms. Even with well-intended funding and support they are basically assessed as trivial and incapable of entering into *real* competition with capitalism (North 2007: 22). They may be viewed as interesting and promising exotics but are nonetheless degraded and marginalised within the existing system.

Closer observation reveals, however, that this marginalisation, as already implied above, does not take the form of one-sided exclusion or simple repression. Rather, a complex coexistence between dominance (urban administration) and alternative (initiatives) emerges in which the marginalised alternative as a 'constructed other' develops into an indivisible part of the identity of the whole (Hillebrand/Zademach 2013: 11). The marginalisation is thus part of a complex and mutual dependency between the hegemony and the marginalised. As Healy (2009) puts it, marginalised initiatives are indivisibly linked to the acknowledgement of dominance. He describes this interaction as binarity (ibid.: 6).

While this view of marginalisation is, on the one hand, helpful for further consideration of the interface between urban planning and alternative economies, on the other hand it carries the risk of misunderstanding the ambivalence of the alternative within the hegemonial system. Alternative initiatives can only exist within the dominant system (Linnemann 2017: 8 f.) but they nonetheless still attempt to subvert and reformulate existing power relations (Müller 2018: 218 f.). It would therefore be fatal to write off alternative initiatives as integrated elements of the dominant system and thus to accept their marginalisation as a matter of course.

In Section 3 we take a theory-oriented look at the interface between dominance and alternative and, starting from the marginalisation of alternative initiatives, shed more light on this complex coexistence. The aim is to conceptually grasp the mutual speechlessness outlined above, which contributes to the underpinning of the dominant and the alternative. This should increase understanding of what hinders the development of a cooperative coexistence of initiatives and urban planning. Our focus is therefore on *what* and *how* the positions of the alternative initiatives and urban administration are constituted. Here we draw on Judith Butler's understanding of performativity as this allows a conceptual approach that helps to render the incomprehension of those involved explicable and tangible by revealing so-called performing gaps.

3. 'Performing gaps': on the difference between the performativity and self-perception of alternative initiatives in urban planning

With her work in the social sciences, the US philosopher Judith Butler has made a significant contribution to understanding individual and social differences as the result of a process of social construction. At the heart of Butler's proposition is the idea that existing power relations are fed by ritualised speech acts which emanate from specific performative constructions. Such constructions are the result of hegemonial attributions, practices, values and ideas in society, which are stabilised by the performativity of the social environment (Healy 2009: 4). Butler understands performativity as the result of specific, cultural constituted performances (Fischer-Lichte 2013: 41). For Butler these performances manifest themselves, for instance, in the social perpetuation of binary gender identities, or for Healy in the dominance of neoliberalism (Butler 1991; Healy 2009). Everything that exists outside of these settings appears (inter alia) as economically vulnerable and temporary or, for instance, as scientifically or socially irrelevant and becomes marginalised (Callon 1998; Healy 2009: 4).

The discursive constitution of otherness and difference and the resulting marginalisation does not always or only occur via language and speech acts (Austin 1962), but is also expressed via symbolic actions (Fischer-Lichte 2013: 41 ff.). The 'speechlessness' with which urban planning and alternative initiatives encounter one another (as described in Section 2), and their mutual inability to recognise the potential of the other, can be understood as the difference between externally ascribed and self-perceived positions. In theoretical-conceptual terms, we argue here that this represents the gap between alternative initiatives and urban planning that must be overcome – it results from different performativities, that is, from different constructions of the *self* in relation to an *other*.

The social marginalisation of alternative initiatives occurs primarily through a distancing from capitalist structures. Their marginality becomes apparent through the lack of an accurate fit with the established and institutionalised rules and ideas of growth-oriented planning. However, the positioning of alternative initiatives occurs not only through attributions from the outside – for instance on the part of the urban administration, planning or traditional business ventures. The initiatives themselves understand their lack of fit, difference and marginalisation vis-à-vis the mainstream as the core of their own identity (see Section 2). They use strong symbolics and speech acts related to their marginalised position to articulate their *otherness* and, for instance, more *sustainable* nature as alternatives. Terms like solidarity, cooperation, market independence, sustainability and nature conservation and, on the other hand, terms from which they consciously and decidedly distance themselves – growth, market and competition, resource exploitation – become powerful attributes with which the initiatives reproduce their own subordination.

The initiatives thus actually strengthen the boundaries of the discourse. Their self-attribution reinforces these boundaries instead of weakening them and this in fact undermines the actual intention of the initiatives. Their existence is made possible by their own reproduction of the discourse but at the same time limited by it. What alternative initiatives have to be, how they have to design themselves, what positions they should criticise, and what institutions and forms of the economy they should address – all this is defined from the outside. Paradoxically, this limits their ability to act to precisely the sphere in which they are also visible to the outside under the discursive hegemonial conditions (Butler 1991). Alternative initiatives are only perceived as long as they appear as utopian, largely ineffective activities that do not fit into existing structures and routines, that disregard rules and that even dare to criticise. Outside of these boundaries they are irrelevant for urban planning.

Here the performing gap between the expectations placed on alternative initiatives from the outside and their own self-positioning becomes clear. They have potential as actors of urban development where they fulfil the expectations of the system: as urban gardening projects that enhance the inner city in terms of design, participation and attractiveness; as open bicycle repair shops that contribute nicely to social integration in the neighbourhoods; or as activists who self-organise to utilise an old-industrial space for creative and artistic projects, at a low cost to the administration. Here they comply with common ideas of volunteering and civil society engagement, enriched in their case by an exotic unconventionality. Outside of this perception of the exotic alternative, initiatives often go unnoticed, for instance as innovators of a holistic and more sustainable urban food supply who also address aspects of formal planning. Or as supporters of the mobility transition, which must also be integrated into current and future transport planning. Or as evidence that the existing regulations and legislation (such as the Federal Building Code) are long outdated and inappropriate.

While these boundaries of the discourse are initially accepted by alternative initiatives and are even underpinned by their self-positioning as 'alternative', they themselves see their strength primarily in the outwards shifting of this boundary. They wish to be integrated in planning as a serious partner capable of making a coherent and important contribution to planning change. The performing gap can be explained by drawing on the well-known tales of Till Eulenspiegel: as long as the court jester wore his jester's cap and amused people, he was accepted even when his stories and antics contained serious criticism of the ruling system. But he was never accepted as an advisor to the court, although he perhaps considered himself to be precisely that.

This perspective offers a possible explanation for the inhibited interaction and the speechlessness between the initiatives and urban planning described above. Clearly the societal definition of alternative economies is much narrower than their self-definition and self-perception. Urban planning (as the dominant system) exclusively adopts the prevailing discourse on alternative economies, so its scope for action is similarly limited to the socially recognised space or discourse. It remains unrecognised that the identity formation of the initiatives deviates in parts from the categories of the socially hegemonic discourse about alternative economies. In the constructed niche of their own marginalisation, alternative initiatives can act and prevail. If they emerge from the marginalisation and position themselves as something beyond the expectations attributed from outside, then they are no longer perceived. It is therefore impossible for alternative initiatives to stimulate substantial and fundamental change. The key finding is that this performing gap is constructed with recourse to hegemonial discourse from outside (for instance from the urban administration and planning) but is also constituted by the initiatives themselves through their self-attribution as alternative and marginalised. The gap between the external definition and inner performativity thus represents the space of their own failure. Their ability to act increases the more they confirm the hegemonial discourse with their self-definition.

4. Conclusion

It seems that the present understanding of planning faces a dilemma. On the one hand, the intentions of urban planning to improve the quality of urban life correspond with the motivations of the initiatives. On the other hand, urban planning is subject to a striving for growth while the initiatives have a no-profit orientation and act outside the existing regulatory framework. This means that serious interaction between the two makes little sense.

The results of our article suggest that the balance of power between alternative economies and urban planning is not only subject to structural, legal or formal restrictions. Rather the cooperation is also influenced by mutual spoken contradictions and contextual factors. Differences in perception about what urban planning and alternative initiatives should achieve play a role in the lack of interest in mutual interaction.

External hurdles also make the existence of the initiatives more difficult. Their willingness to cooperate with urban planning is generally limited, particularly due to an avoidance of dependencies. The structures of the dominant economic system prove particularly decisive for the conditions of interaction. Judith Butler recognises the failure of performative acts as providing potential for change and the emergence of subversive spaces (Wucherpfennig/Strüver 2015: 111). Political discursive strategies can create spaces of possibility for difference and promote a broader social definition of 'alternative' and of 'urban planning'. Butler speaks here of interventionist practices that make local contradiction possible (ibid.: 115). In this way performative reinterpretations allow space for change to develop as emerging confusions lead to new ways of thinking. This should lead not only to diverse thinking about economies but equally to discussion about a more diverse understanding of urban planning. The debate about post-growth planning offers opportunities for precisely this, such as the reinterpretation of planning instruments, more creative and daring processes and a radical rethinking of the fundamentals of urban planning (Grotefels/Mössner in Lamker/Schulze-Dieckhoff 2018: 6). The alternative initiatives are part of and an expression of dynamic developments that live new rules of the game and can develop social impact. Their potential to generate discursive effects should therefore not be underestimated and confined to a marginalised space.

Cited literature

Acosta, A., & Brand, U. (2018). *Radikale Alternativen: Warum man den Kapitalismus nur mit vereinten Kräften überwinden kann.* oekom.
Austin, J. L. (1962). *How to say things with words.* Clarendon Press.
Butler, J. (1991). *Das Unbehagen der Geschlechter.* 21st edition. Suhrkamp.
Butler, J. (1995). *Körper von Gewicht. Die diskursiven Grenzen des Geschlechts.* Suhrkamp.
Callon, M. (1998). *The laws of the markets.* John Wiley & Sons.
Cramer, J. (2013). Architektur: Stadtplanung und Städtebau. In H. A. Wieg, & C. Heyl (Eds.), *Stadt: Ein interdisziplinäres Handbuch.* J. B. Metzer, 1–45.
Elsen, S., Reifer, G., Oberleiter, E., & Wild, W. (2015). *Die Kunst des Wandels: Ansätze für die ökosoziale Transformation.* oekom.
Florida, R. L (2005). *Cities and the creative class.* Routledge.
Fuller, C. & Geddes, M. (2008). Urban governance under neoliberalism: New labour and the restructuring of state-space. *Antipode*, 40(2), 252–282.

Fuller, D., & Jonas, A. E. G. (2003). Alternative financial spaces. In A. Leyshon, R. Lee, & C. C. Williams (Eds.), *Alternative economic spaces*. Sage Publishing, 55–73.

Gibson-Graham, J. K. (2008). Diverse economies: Performative practices for 'other worlds'. *Progress in Human Geography, 32*(5), 613–632.

Glaser, B., & Strauss, A. (1967). *The discovery of grounded theory: Strategies for qualitative research*. Aldine Transaction.

Healy, S. (2009). Alternative economies. In R. Kitchin, & N. Thrift (Eds.), *The International Encyclopedia of Human Geography*. Elsevir, 338–344.

Helferich, S., & Heinrich-Böll-Stiftung (2012). *Commons – Für eine neue Politik jenseits von Markt und Staat*. transcript.

Hillebrand, S., & Zademach, H.-M. (2013). Alternative economies and spaces: Introductory remarks. In H.-M. Zademach, & S. Hillebrand (Eds.), *Alternative economies and spaces*. transcript, 9–22.

Hopkins, R. (2008). *The Transition Handbook*. Chelsea Green Publishing.

Kerekes, T. (2015). *Möglichkeitsräume – Der urbane Raum als Keimzelle des Wandels*. Grüne Bildungswerkstatt.

Kipp, M. (2018). Commons. In B. Belinda, M. Naumann, & A. Strüver (Eds.), *Handbuch Kritische Stadtforschung*. 3rd edition. Westfälisches Dampfboot, 212–217.

Klaer, E. (2008). Partnerschaften zwischen Städten/Regionen und der Solidarischen Ökonomie. In S. Giegold, & D. Embshoff (Eds.), *Solidarische Ökonomie im globalisierten Kapitalismus*. VSA.

Krueger, R., Schulz, C., & Gibbs, D. C. (2017). Institutionalizing alternative economic spaces? An interpretivist perspective on diverse economies. *Progress in Human Geography, 42*(4), 569–589.

Lamker, C., & Schulze Dieckhoff, V. (2018). Mit oder gegen den Strom? Postwachstumsplanung in der Fishbowl. *Planung neu denken online*, (2), 1–7. http://www.planung-neu-denken.de/images/stories/pnd/dokumente/1_2019/lamker-etal.pdf (2019, November 5).

Lange, B. (2017). Offene Werkstätten und Postwachstumsökonomien: Kollaborative Orte als Wegbereiter transformativer Wirtschaftsentwicklungen? *Zeitschrift für Wirtschaftsgeographie, 61*(1), 38–55.

Linnemann, K. (2017). Die Gouvernementalität widerständiger Alltagspraktiken: eine konzeptionelle Annäherung an Postwachstum, Subjektivierung und alltägliches Gegen-Führen. *Zeitschrift für Wirtschaftsgeographie, 62*(3-4), 1–14.

Müller, C. (2018). Alternatives Wirtschaften. In B. Belina, M. Naumann, & A. Strüver (Eds.), *Handbuch Kritische Stadtforschung*. 3rd edition. Westfälisches Dampfboot, 217–223.

Nikolaeva, A., Adey, P., Cresswell, T., Lee, J. Y., Nóvoa, A., & Temenos, C. (2018). Commoning mobility: Towards a new politics of mobility transitions. *Trans Inst Br Geogr*, 44(2), 346–360.

North, P. (2007). *Money and liberation: The micropolitics of alternative currency movements*. University of Minnesota Press.

Peck, J., Theodore, N. M., & Brenner, N. (2013). Neoliberal urbanism redux? *International Journal of Urban and Regional Research*, 37(3), 1091–1099.

Roelvink, G., St. Martin, K., & Gibson-Graham, J. K. (2015). *Making other worlds possible: Performing diverse economies*. University of Minnesota Press.

Schmelzer, M. (2018). Degrowth und Postwachstum. *PERIPHERIE*, (150-151), 336–339.

Schmid, B. (2018). Repair's diverse transformative geographies – lessons from a maker community in Stuttgart. *Theory and Politics in Organization*, 19(2), 229–251.

Schulz, C., & Affolderbach, J. (2015). Grünes Wachstum und alternative Wirtschaftsformen. *Geographische Rundschau*, 65(5), 4–9.

Selle, K. (1997). Kooperationen im intermediären Bereich – Planung zwischen "Commodifizierung" und "zivilgesellschaftlicher Transformation". In K. M. Schmahls, & H. Heinelt (Eds.), *Zivile Gesellschaft. Entwicklung, Defizite, Potentiale*. Leske + Budrich, 2–58.

Selle, K., & Wachten, K. (2011). Instrumente der Stadtplanung. Ein Überblick über die Möglichkeiten kommunaler Akteure an der Stadtentwicklung mitzuwirken. In K. Selle, K. Wachten, U. Berding, & G. Schmitt (Eds.), *Was ist Stadtentwicklung? Lehrbausteine Stadt, Landschaft, Planung. Baustein Instrumente*. Self-published, 1–12.

Stadt Dortmund (o. J.). *Stadtentwicklung*. https://www.dortmund.de/de/leben_in_dortmund/planen_bauen_wohnen/stadtplanungs_und_bauordnungsamt/stadtplanung/stadtentwicklung/index.html (2019, November 11).

Wagner, A., Hegmanns, T., & Knudsen, M. (2017). Flächen bedarfsgerecht entwickeln – Raumbezüge der Wirtschaft. In J. Polivka, C. Reicher, & C. Zöpel (Eds.), *Raumstrategien Ruhr 2035+: Konzepte zur Entwicklung der Agglomeration Ruhr*. Kettler, 91–105.

Wascher, E., Hebel, F., Schrot, K., & Schultze, J. (2018). *Labore sozialer Innovation. Ausgangspunkt für sozial innovative Initiativen*. kosi-lab. Self-published.

Wiezorek, E. (2017). Mythos Kooperation. Über kooperatives Handeln in der Stadtentwicklung. In A. Besecke, J. Meier, R. Pätzold, S. Thomaier (Eds.), *Stadtökonomie – Blickwinkel und Perspektiven*. Universitätsverlag der TU Berlin, 53–55.

WIKUE – Wuppertal Institut für Klima, Umwelt und Energie gGmbH (2017). *Analyse von Ansätzen der Alternativen Ökonomie: Nachhaltigkeitswirkungen und Handlungsbedarf für die Landespolitik NRW – Explorative Analyse*. Self-published.

Wucherpfennig, C., & Strüver, A. (2014). "Es ist ja nur ein Spiel." – Zur Performativität geschlechtlich codierter Körper, Identitäten und Räume. *Geographische Zeitschrift*, 102(3), 175–189.

Town and countryside in flux
The significance of urban functions for the vitality of rural areas and the importance of individual and systemic solutions for the realisation of a growth-critical way of life

Anna Szumelda

Rural life can be described in many different ways depending on who is talking, thinking or writing about precisely which rural areas. Descriptions of rural areas often view them in relation to urban centres and distinguish between rural areas that are close to cities and those on the periphery. What is the importance of cities for people who live in rural areas far away from urban centres? How important is physical distance from areas of economic growth for the everyday life and work of these people? What individual and systemic solutions are there and could there be that would make a growth-critical way of life possible? This is the subject of this article. The discussion is based on the example of statements, observations and experiences of people who live in rural areas, some of which are remotely located. Firstly, examples are drawn from qualitative interviews that I conducted as part of an empirical investigation in two different rural areas in east and south-east Poland. Secondly, the findings are based on my own observations of everyday life and work in a small village located far from urban centres in north-west Poland (see Figure 1 for the location of the case-study regions).

Figure 1: Location of the districts of Szczecinek (north-west), Lubartów (east) and Krosno (south-east), where the case studies described below originate. The map also shows the distribution of town and cities (grey), the spheres of influence of urban centres (red-orange-yellow) and the distribution of peripheral areas (green) in Poland.

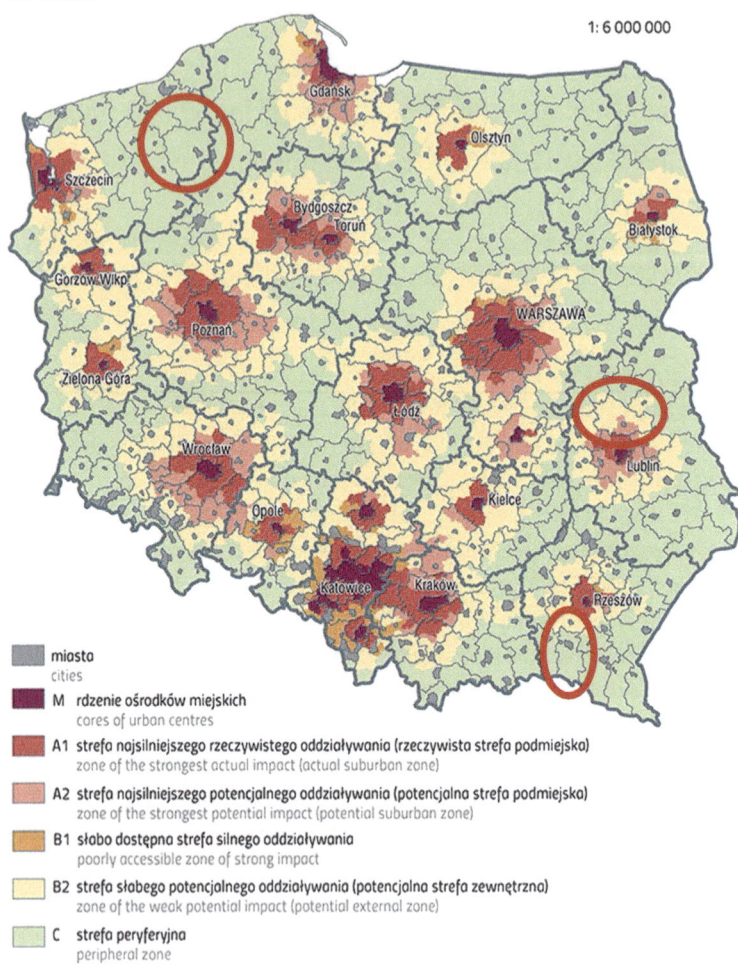

Source: author based on Bański/Czapiewski (2009)

In order to gain a better understanding of the context of the case studies discussed below, I first present some general characteristics of rural areas in

Poland. In addition, I briefly describe how a number of political documents view the relationship between rural and urban areas in Poland. In some measure, rural areas in Poland are conversely defined as non-urban, as 'districts beyond the administrative boundaries of cities, thus as rural municipalities or as rural parts of urban-rural municipalities' (MRiRW 2014: 75). Whether municipalities are regarded as urban or rural depends on the population density. This categorisation classifies 93.1% of Poland's territory as rural and suggests that 39.2% of the Polish population live in rural areas (see MRiRW 2014: 8). However, even if definitions of rural areas distinguish them from urban, elsewhere the two spatial categories are described as being interrelated. Strategic and conceptual documents like, e. g., the 'Strategy for the sustainable development of rural areas, agriculture and fishing 2012–2020'[1] and the 'National spatial planning concept'[2] describe both the diversity of rural and urban areas – their diverse socio-economic constellations and associated functions, problems and development opportunities – and also the mutual relations between rural areas and cities. When examined more closely, however, these documents are concerned with the relationship between rural areas and *a specific type* of urban area: the economically prosperous, infrastructurally well-equipped and culturally attractive urban centres. The focus is thus on the relationship between rural areas and urban areas characterised by economic growth and its consequences – desirable and undesirable. Rural areas account for by far the largest share of the territory of Poland. While the network of towns and cities is spread quite evenly across the country it is not as dense as, e. g., in Germany, which is of similar size. This means that in Poland a fairly high proportion of rural areas are located comparatively far away from urban centres and 'growth areas' (see Figure 1).

Of interest here is the importance for rural dwellers not only of the potential accessibility of the administrative entity 'city' but also of the actual availability of specific functions associated with (economically prosperous) cities. This will be demonstrated in the following using examples from the everyday

---

1 Original title of the document: '*Strategia zrównoważonego rozwoju wsi, rolnictwa i rybactwa na lata 2012–2020. Załącznik do uchwały nr 163 Rady Ministrów z dnia 25 kwietnia 2012 r. (poz. 839).*' (MP 2012 poz. 839)

2 Original title of the document: '*Koncepcja przestrzennego zagospodarowania kraju 2030. Załącznik do uchwały nr 239 Rady Ministrów z dnia 13 grudnia 2011 r. (poz. 252).*' (MP 2012 poz. 252)

life of people who live in rural areas, in some cases in peripheral locations. The examples are related to the topics of mobility, agriculture and securing a living, and lifestyle preferences. They reflect many socially and ecologically problematic phenomena, the causes and increase of which are linked to economic processes of growth and concentration and solutions for which are sought in the growth-critical sustainability discussion.

Mobility

Mobility makes it possible to reach an urban centre from a rural area in the first place. A great deal can only be dealt with in the city – purchases beyond what can be bought in the village shop, attending school and cultural events, visits to (specialist) doctors and the authorities, and not least gainful employment. Access to this social infrastructure is necessary. In order to access it despite the lack of or marginal nature of public transport links from villages to the nearest urban centres, individual motorised mobility has been increasing for years. This is also the case in the rural areas which are the focus of this article. The effects of this individual mobility on the volume of traffic and the way in which the relationship between urban and rural areas has been changed by the accessibility thus created is impressively demonstrated by the following quote:

> 'My husband and I live with our two grown-up children in the countryside. Two years ago, we moved to a house in a village. It's wonderful and we never want to go back to the city. But we can only say that because four cars are parked in our backyard. In the mornings each of us takes one of them and drives off in a different direction. Ten years ago, we would never have moved to a village because if you lived in a village then there was simply no chance of getting away from it.' (WSPGOA)[3]

---

[3] The quotes come from interviews that were carried out for the empirical investigation described above, and from private conversations. Both the interviews and the private conversations were conducted in Polish. The abbreviations at the end of the quotes (e. g. WSPGOA) provide information about the origin of the interviewee or interlocutor, but remain encoded here to ensure data protection.

The quote shows how the solution to problems on the one hand can have consequences on the other hand. Individual mobility has made cities and important social infrastructure accessible to the residents of rural areas. The decision of the woman speaking and her family in favour of a lifestyle oriented towards 'less' has consequences in the form of a simultaneous 'more'. 'Less' here refers to the slower or generally more restricted availability and utilisation of goods and services found in the city, as called for in the growth-critical debate with demands for a sufficient lifestyle (see Linz/Bartelmus/Hennicke et al. 2002; Mölders/Szumelda/Winterfeld 2014; Paech 2012; Sachs 1993; Stengel 2011). However, ultimately this 'less' is not necessarily sufficiency oriented and the 'less' with regards to urban noise and built-up space is associated with a 'more' in terms of the traffic volumes, noise and emissions pollution, congested streets, higher resource consumption etc. that are linked to individual motorised mobility. The tone of the quote cited above suggests that the speaker is conscious of the ambivalence of increasing individual mobility. However, for the family decision, the scales tipped in favour of the desired life in the countryside (which they did not necessarily view as growth critical), as the availability of individual mobility meant that they did not have to give up links to the city.

Such decisions, and the wish of rural residents to be connected to urban infrastructure, are understandable. To counter the consequences associated with increased individual mobility, it is therefore worth considering a policy-based or entrepreneurial approach to creating or maintaining connectivity between rural areas and cities. In the rural district of Szczecinek in northwest Poland, there are examples of both. A private bus company from the area has taken on the task of providing bus connections between a number of surrounding villages and the city of Szczecinek. The service is comparatively frequent, which makes it an attractive alternative to the car, providing good mobility in particular for older people from the villages and school students. Since September 2019, the city of Szczecinek has also offered a free bus service. These free bus routes are restricted to the urban area – buses travelling beyond the urban area to the nearest villages must still be paid for, although options are being explored for making at least some of them free of charge in the future, as was once the case for a limited period of time. The motivation for the free buses is not necessarily to be found in the town council's ecological or growth-critical convictions, but rather in the need to fulfil election promises made at the last municipal election. It is possible for the municipality to finance the venture thanks to business taxes received from a large and prosperous company located in the urban area – income that is not available to every municipality. However, despite all reservations concerning motivation and finance, ultimately the free urban service makes a notable contribution to reducing car traffic in the city.

Agriculture and securing a living

The rural regions where the examples used in this article are located, are on the opposite geographical sides of Poland (see red circles in Figure 1). The differences between the regions in east and south-east Poland and the region in the north-west in terms of agricultural structures could hardly be greater. Even in the socialist era there were scarcely any large state agricultural enterprises in east and south-east Poland and today agricultural structures continue to be characterised by small-scale family farms, while the northwest was dominated by large state farms until 1989 and today still displays a large-scale agricultural structure. Thus, for instance, in 2019 the average size of farms in the south-eastern voivodeship of Podkarpackie was 4.90 hectares, while in the north-western voivodeship of Zachodniopomorskie it was 31.44 hectares (ARiMR 2019). The social upheavals and challenges associated with the regionally specific, structural transformation of agriculture are nonetheless quite similar in both regions. Agriculture has lost significance as a source of income since the 1990s. Particularly in the south-east, the majority of the agricultural holdings are simply too small to generate a sufficient and satisfactory income (see Szumelda 2019). In the north-west, the closure of the state farms after 1989 put almost all the employees out of their jobs without enough alternative sources of income having developed outside of agriculture.

Being able to make a living is essential to rural dwellers. Both in the east and south-east with their small-scale agricultural structures and in the north-west with its large-scale structures, there are fewer and fewer opportunities to do so within agriculture, which has left more people dependent on sources of income from elsewhere – usually in cities. Farmers from the small-scale agricultural structures of east and south-east Poland who I spoke to in the course of the empirical investigation, repeatedly reported on the migration of their adult children to the nearby (or in some cases, more distant) cities, because the children did not see any chance of earning their livings with jobs in the countryside. In light of the limited profitability of the small agricultural enterprises in particular, a number of farmers actually explicitly advise their children not to remain in farming but to focus rather on a different profession, as the following statement from a farmer makes clear:

> 'I already told my sons and my daughter in the past, you can live in the country but work in the city. Because this farm doesn't bring in any income. I won't persuade any of my children to stay here in the village and take over the farm when we are no longer here. There's no point, just turning over the field. But they can live here.' (WLPLAK)

If no employment is available in a nearby city then several of the farmers do not see any way in which they could leave farming and pursue another professional occupation. They remain in agriculture due to a lack of alternatives and assess their work in farming with corresponding diffidence:

> 'Maybe I like it, maybe not, you get used to it so and just keep doing it. And also where would you find another job here?' (WPPKOA).

These examples also highlight the ambivalence of a number of (supposedly) growth-critical lifestyles and the problematic phenomena associated with them, particularly social aspects. On the one hand, in many respects there is extremely justifiable criticism of the intensive, industrial and very growth-oriented production methods that are often associated with large-scale agricultural structures. However, on the other hand, it is not possible to draw the reverse conclusion that 'small-scale' agricultural structures are per se and unreservedly compatible with (growth-critical) sustainability concepts simply because they seem to fulfil demands formulated in the growth-critical debate for sufficient and subsistent lifestyles. As the examples presented above demonstrate, from the point of view of those who run the small farms and have to independently earn their livings from them, 'small' is sometimes 'too small'. If they are unable to extend their farms and hence their incomes, then this can result in the inadequate securing of their livelihoods and in poverty. And if the farmers only remain in agriculture because they lack alternatives and not because of a freely made decision, then this can lead to great dissatisfaction with the situation or to a resigned attitude, as illustrated by the farmer's statement above. Both phenomena – the inadequate securing of a livelihood and dissatisfaction with a way of life that was not chosen voluntarily – are incompatible with (growth-critical) sustainability considerations, especially in social terms.

However, the talks with farmers in east and south-east Poland showed that there are ways of earning an adequate income and securing a satisfactory living even with a small farm. Some farmers recognise and make use of options within farming. For instance, they come together to form producer organisations, specialise their farms, make optimal use of the natural conditions and enter into various formal and informal collaborations. In this way they are able to earn an adequate and satisfactory income with their small farms. The farmers express satisfaction with their professional situation, their income and general living conditions. An example from the rural region in north-east Poland furthermore shows that it is not only small-scale agricultural structures that are potentially compatible with a growth-critical lifestyle. The large biodynamic farm where I work is located in this area and covers about 2000 hectares. Given the size of the farm it is tempting to apply growth-related criticism but, especially in agriculture, it is not only the size of structures that is important but also the kind of agricultural methods in use. The biodynamic approach is growth critical in that it consciously renounces quick, short-term and large financial profits and has many ecological advantages. In social terms, the large structure is also advantageous because having many workers means that each individual can take holiday and days off and also find cover for illness – something that farmers working on their own often struggle with, especially those in animal husbandry.

The EU's common agricultural policy with its pronounced spatial impact has a particular role to play in enabling the systematic take up of individual or entrepreneurial solutions of this kind. In order to avoid only supporting agriculture that is based on the growth of farms and production, funding should be directed particularly towards producer organisations and sustainable farming methods, which often require a greater number of labourers (and are thus more cost-intensive) and therefore are not currently used by the majority of farms.

Lifestyle preferences

In the relationship between urban and rural, many people are attracted not least by the urban lifestyle. Naturally tastes differ and different people come to different conclusions about what it is like to live in the city or in the countryside. For instance, a number of rural dwellers particularly value things that are often linked to rural areas – the quiet, the few people, being surrounded by nature. A farmer in east Poland told me:

> 'I like to fish. Then I sit by the river and the frogs croak. Sometimes in the evening, if it's warm, my wife and I sit on the steps and listen to the frogs croaking from the meadows. Anyone who hasn't experienced that will probably ask themselves, what does he see in these frogs? But they should just come and listen. It's really wonderful when you sit there at night and the nightingale sings. Those are things that you don't pay attention to in everyday life because nobody has time for them, but if you have a moment and attend to it, then it's very lovely. Sometimes my wife asks me why are you going there, to the river? Why don't you sleep in? [...] But when I sit there, even if I'm not sleeping, I rest.' (WLPLOK)

For another farmer from south-east Poland I spoke to, it cannot be deserted enough, even in a sparsely populated area:

> 'There are more and more people here, everything's being built up. There are still a few villages in the area but everything's being bought up. You can't find peace and quiet anywhere now. I'm thinking of emigrating to Ukraine...' (WPPKIB)

But it is not like that for everyone and not everyone finds themselves in the countryside by choice, as the statement by one farmer shows:

> 'I love cities, I like marketplaces best. I love them. I can't see enough of the old buildings. [...] Here in the village it's pitch-black, except when the moon shines at night, then it's lovely. I love it when the moon shines, that's beautiful, but only then. [...] I love it when it's light, I don't like the dark, not at all. And then it's also so quiet here, a deathly silence. [...] In the countryside it's quiet, yes, but you also get bored with this quiet.' (WPPKZK)

Opportunities for children and young people to venture beyond a particular radius around the village where they live also contributes to their education and self-confidence. The head of a village in south-east Poland who is particularly committed to children and young people from her village, talks about the great experience it was for them to take part in sporting events and thus to have the opportunity to travel as they had never before '*got beyond D*.' (WPPKAW). She explained that the self-confidence of the children and young people benefited enormously, afterwards they behaved quite differently in school and also generally.

These examples are related more to the cultural than the material level of the everyday life of rural dwellers, but they too highlight the field of tension between the sufficiency lifestyles called for by growth critics and the consequences that arise from a rejection of these (not always freely chosen) lifestyles. Lifestyle preferences are an individual decision. It is difficult to imagine being allowed to prescribe whether someone should live in the city or in the countryside. Someone who feels more comfortable and fulfilled with an urban way of life or who seeks the proximity of a centre of economic growth for simple 'reasons of survival' (securing a livelihood) cannot be blamed for this. Nonetheless migration to (prospering) cities, that is, to centres of economic growth, causes problematic phenomena like urbanisation, high population density, rising rents, overloaded communication and supply infrastructures, etc., while the rural areas face difficulties associated with the thinning of the population (depopulation).

It is thus even more important to consider the examples presented above that illustrate how individual lifestyle preferences can be taken into account on a systemic level without causing problematic phenomena – accompanied by the decoupling of cities from rural areas, or centres of economic growth from areas with too little growth. The examples show the importance of the anchor functions that cities have in the countryside surrounding them. For rural dwellers it is important not just that cities are accessible. Rather, above all, certain cultural and material urban functions must be maintained so residents can pursue their lifestyle preferences without necessarily having to leave the rural areas where they live. The Polish network of cities is spread fairly evenly across the country, which provides good potential for establishing anchors of this sort throughout the country. However, especially the smaller urban centres with less than 50,000 inhabitants face challenges in maintaining their urban functions. Many of these centres are just as affected by outwards migration as the rural areas. The closure of businesses and the downsizing of the administration and supply structures has meant that they can provide fewer and fewer gainful employment opportunities and are therefore increasingly unattractive, especially for younger people. In contrast, in Poland businesses and people alike are particularly attracted by the so-called Big Five, the metropolitan regions of Warsaw, Krakow, Poznan and Wroclaw and the region of Gdansk, each of which has over a million residents. Economic growth and population increase are concentrated in these metropolitan regions. Businesses and people decide to move to these metropolitan regions rather than to smaller urban centres, which leads to the smaller cities becoming progressively smaller until at some point they are 'too small' to fulfil their urban functions and thus their anchor functions for the urban population and for the residents of the surrounding rural areas, as Przemysław Śleszyński, Professor at the Institute of Geography and Spatial Organisation of the Polish Academy of Sciences,[4] explained in an interview with the newspaper Gazeta Prawna (2018). This presents regional planning research and policy with the task and challenge of developing instruments that can counter this pull effect and the problematic phenomena associated with it on many levels, both in the metropolitan regions and in the areas located beyond them.

Resumé

This article has discussed examples from the everyday lives of people who live in rural areas, some of which are located far from urban centres. It has illustrated the great importance of the accessibility of cities and the maintenance of urban functions, especially in smaller urban centres. This ensures the vitality of the surrounding rural areas and facilitates sufficiency-oriented lifestyles. The examples referred to the topics of mobility, agriculture and securing a living, and lifestyle preferences. They highlight some of the consequences of the concentration of excessive economic growth in a few regions and the simultaneous absence or at least severe restriction of growth processes in other regions. The case studies show the effects that the unequal distribution of economic growth processes has on the every-

---

[4] Polish name of the institute: *Instytut Geografii i Przestrzennego Zagospodarowania PAN*

day life of people dwelling in rural regions, some of which are far from the centres of economic growth. The strong concentration and thus unequal distribution of economic growth processes can be countered on individual, entrepreneurial and systemic levels. The examples discussed show that the local (municipal), national (regional planning) and international (agricultural policy) political levels can be effective here. From a growth-critical and sustainability-oriented perspective, it is valuable to consider cities and rural areas in their functional interconnections. Especially instruments of spatial planning and agricultural policy should target this functional connection much more strongly than has been the case to date. It is important to work towards maintaining the urban functions of (small) towns in order to strengthen their anchor function for the rural areas surrounding them, promote regional economic cycles and counteract the emergence of social, economic and ecological imbalances between regions.

Cited literature

ARiMR – Agencja Restrukturyzacji i Modernizacji Rolnictwa (2019). *Ogłoszenie nr. 1 prezesa agencji restrukturyzacji i modernizacji.* https://www.arimr.gov.pl/pomoc-krajowa/srednia-powierzchnia-gospodarstwa.html (2020, January 22).

Bański, J., & Czapiewski, K. (2009). Typologia gmin według zasięgów oddziaływania dużych miast. In J. Bański (Ed.), *Atlas obszarów wiejskich w Polsce. Rozdział 6: Funkcje gospodarcze.* IGiPZ PAN. https://www.igipz.pan.pl/atlas-obszarow-wiejskich-rozdzial6.html (2020, January 22).

Gazeta Prawna (2018). *Śmierć małych miast. Odnowione centra to nie wszystko, potrzebna jest praca. Wywiad.* https://biznes.gazetaprawna.pl/artykuly/1182717,przemyslaw-sleszynski-smierc-malych-miast-w-polsce.html (2020, January 22).

Linz, M., Bartelmus, P., Hennicke, P., Jungkeit, R., Sachs, W., Scherhorn, G., Wilke, G., & Winterfeld, U. von (Eds.) (2002). *Von nichts zu viel. Suffizienz gehört zur Zukunftsfähigkeit.* Wuppertal papers 125.

Mölders, T., Szumelda, A., & Winterfeld, U. von (2014). Sufficiency and subsistence – on two important concepts for sustainable development. *Problems of Sustainable Development*, 9(1), 21–27.

MP (2012) poz. 252/ Monitor Polski poz. 252. *Koncepcja przestrzennego zagospodarowania kraju 2030. Załącznik do uchwały nr 239 Rady Ministrów z dnia 13 grudnia 2011 r. (poz. 252).*

MP (2012) poz. 839/ Monitor Polski poz. 839. *Strategia zrównoważonego rozwoju wsi, rolnictwa i rybactwa na lata 2012–2020. Załącznik do uchwały nr 163 Rady Ministrów z dnia 25 kwietnia 2012 r. (poz. 839).*

MRiRW – Ministerstwo Rolnictwa i Rozwoju Wsi (2014). *Program Rozwoju Obszarów Wiejskich na lata 2014–2020 (PROW 2014–2020). Skrócona wersja programu.*

Paech, N. (2012). *Liberation from excess. The road to a post-growth economy.* oekom.

Sachs, W. (1993). Die vier Es. Merkposten für einen maß-vollen Wirtschaftsstil. *Politische Ökologie*,11(33), 69–72.

Stengel, O. (2011). *Suffizienz. Die Konsumgesellschaft in der ökologischen Krise.* oekom.

Szumelda, A. (2019). *Der Beitrag kleiner landwirtschaftlicher Betriebe zur nachhaltigen Entwicklung ländlicher Räume. Eine Untersuchung in ausgewählten Regionen Polens.* PhD thesis, Leuphana University Lüneburg

Lessons from Practice

The role of interstitial spaces in the growing urban region of Hamburg

An interview with Michael Ziehl, conducted by Mai Anh Ha, Meret Batke and Bastian Lange

'Urban upcycling' is involved in various projects that contribute towards the sustainable transformation of cities. Such projects include the promotion of social innovations, new forms of cooperation and implementation processes. They are user-driven and therefore suitable for contributing to the common good. www.urban-upcycling.de

What does urban upcycling mean to you?

Michael Ziehl: For me, urban upcycling is a practice in which I focus primarily on two resources: first, on the built fabric where instead of demolition and new builds it is more about the conversion and repurposing of existing buildings; second, on locally embedded networks in the neighbourhood and communities of users, for instance, artists, makers and activists. In many cases, these networks need to be developed or at least strengthened. Overall, I guide and support such user-driven project development for existing buildings.

What is special about the activation of brownfields or interstitial spaces?

Michael Ziehl: From a spatial theory perspective, this is not about space as a container but rather about social processes. I act primarily as an advisor and intermediary between the various actors that are relevant for user-driven development processes. These actors normally include the users themselves but also political and administrative stakeholders, investors and residents.

Would you describe yourself as a kind of initiator of such developments?

Michael Ziehl: When I first started working in this field, then I initiated these sorts of developments myself. In the meanwhile my activities have shifted somewhat. These days, I initiate fewer concrete projects but focus rather on platforms or agencies like 'urban upcycling' that support user-driven developments.

How do agencies and initiatives of this sort operate?

Michael Ziehl: Every project's different of course, but there are still parallels between them. Normally a relatively loosely knit network or fixed group of people have a specific place in mind where they want to implement something.

What sort of places are these?

Michael Ziehl: Often they're buildings that are empty and are meant to be developed. My clients feel the need to have at least some input into these developments or to develop the entire property in line with their own ideas. This means that guidance is needed in many areas.

What does the advisory or intermediary service of the agencies and initiatives consist of?

Michael Ziehl: What is important here is the self-organisation, how a group can get organised so that it is able to act and how it maintains that ability. Often, the group lacks a legal form, or existing structures need to be professionalised. As urban development also always involves conflict about access to and the use of space, it may be important for such groups to gain a better negotiating position vis-à-vis other stakeholders. Later on, guidance about dealing with buildings and the authorities is required, especially in connection to building permits and use permits. Financing these projects is also a challenge. Public funding often plays a key role, but foundations and private investors who are concerned about sustainable urban development are also important. In many cases they're not seeking maximum returns but of course they don't wish to lose money either.

Can you name a concrete example here, also with regard to Hamburg?

Michael Ziehl: A good example is the *'Zählerwerk'* ['Meter Works'] on the site of the former power station Bille in Hamburg-Hammerbrook. This is an on-going project that is just coming into being. The users first approached me because of construction and licensing issues regarding the utilisation of the *'Schaltzentrale'* ['Control Centre']. Then an idea emerged about combining community-oriented uses with new forms of work in the much larger *'Zählerwerk'* which is directly next door. At the moment, I'm working with the initiators on a development concept of this kind and on the specific objectives that they wish to achieve with it. In many cases, formulating a concrete strategy for implementation is one of my tasks. We're currently holding talks with political representatives, the city administration, the owners and the neighbours so that these stakeholders are involved at an early stage.

Who else is involved and contributes other expertise to the projects?

Michael Ziehl: For *'Zählerwerk'* the Heritage Office is also important. For instance, they contribute technical expertise when it comes to types of renovation or conservation. As a rule, architects also play a central role, especially in planning and construction processes. During construction work, all sorts of building firms are naturally also involved. In addition, numerous authorities contribute their expertise. For my work, the urban development authorities are also relevant because the focus is often on areas in transition, urban development areas. I often also work with the *'Hamburg Kreativ Gesellschaft'* ['Hamburg Creative Company']. They're owned by the city and have experience in supervising real estate projects. Even though they're primarily interested in promoting the creative economy, they can be an important intermediary between users and relevant stakeholders in politics and administration.

How does the practice of repurposing match to the context of the city of Hamburg, where the focus is on growth and expansion?

Michael Ziehl: The projects I'm involved in are of course always in the context of the growing city. I understand many of them as alternatives to an urban development that's largely dependent on growth, because they attempt to find an alternative way of approaching urban growth and its consequences. At the heart of many of the user-driven projects is that the protagonists want to mitigate socially negative effects on the neighbourhood level, by creating public spaces with rather low rents and by trying not to encourage gentrification processes.

How can processes of urban upcycling contribute to a post-growth society?

Michael Ziehl: To become a post-growth society, in my opinion we actually also need growing economic sectors and areas of society. Areas must grow that are really sustainable and that contribute to the resilience of cities. In relation to urban development, what should not be promoted are rather practices that rely on demolition and new builds. So I think that user-driven projects in existing properties can contribute to realising alternatives to growth-focused and profit-oriented project development. Their impact on growth-oriented urban development is hard to evaluate, but I often observe that users who say, 'We want to do that ourselves, we want to take on more responsibility in urban development,' are motivated by exactly that, even if they wouldn't express it like that.

Is there an example in Hamburg where it was possible to conserve structures of this sort?

Michael Ziehl: It's not primarily about conservation but about development paths that offer an alternative to the logic of growth. Many contradictions arise here. That can be seen in the example of the *'Alte Bahnmeisterei'* ['Old Railway Depot']. The building is in the *'Kreativquartier Oberhafen'* ['Creative Quarter of Oberhafen'] and is part of the Hafencity [waterfront urban development area]. It's been repurposed and ateliers, collective workshops, a co-working space and a large club have been developed, all as interim uses. Of course, this creative quarter is part of the growing city of Hamburg and is intended to make it more attractive for creative talents from elsewhere, who often appreciate a tolerant environment. It's thus also a positive location factor for internationally active companies looking to locate in Hamburg. At the same time, the *'Alte Bahnmeisterei'* is a place with low rents where people can risk experimenting – in this concrete case, for instance, by putting a great deal of voluntary commitment into running a club there, which is seen by many as a rare creative space in Hamburg.

What contribution do projects like the creative quarter of Oberhafen make to Hamburg?

Michael Ziehl: I think that an important aspect is that these spaces are used to negotiate what kind of future urban development we want to have. In Oberhafen there have been, for instance, conflicts about how exclusive and expensive it should be allowed to become there. Should it be more of a productive place or primarily an event location? From my point of view, the users of the 'Alte Bahnmeisterei' make their presence felt positively in these debates. Whether they can actually be successful with their aims is another question.

Are there other challenges?

Michael Ziehl: Especially areas that are in transition often only make temporary contributions to urban development: interim uses that are then often displaced by more expensive, economically more conventional projects. Especially because of this, an important aspect of my work is to get away from just interim uses to projects that have long-term security and development prospects for users, e.g. through leasehold contracts or the purchase of property.

Are there successful examples of that in Hamburg?

Michael Ziehl: I view the area of Gängeviertel with its recently adopted 75 year leasehold contract as a very successful example. Another example is the Viktoria barracks which the users bought as the fux-cooperative and are now developing for the long term. In the immediate proximity of the 'Schaltzentrale' mentioned above, there is the flood basin area where the development process was initiated and managed by the 'Hamburg Kreativ Gesellschaft'. There at least it was possible to get 20-year contracts of use.

What opportunities do you see in these niches, abandoned or precarious spaces in relation to safeguarding urban space?

Michael Ziehl: The niches provide opportunities to try out models of alternative project development, which then must not remain restricted to the niche. Upscaling and outscaling definitely have to occur. Especially with the Gängeviertel there's a hard fight going on to ensure that it doesn't remain a one-off exception but is the opposite: a model project. The stakeholders involved in the *'Zählerwerk'* also have this aim. My concern is to further develop the diverse user approaches to models that support other user-driven projects. That doesn't in any way mean that it should all be like, e.g. the Gängeviertel, because people's needs vary greatly. Fundamentally, for me it is about working with people locally and with the material potentials of places to circumspectly develop our cities. In my view, thinking about urban and neighbourhood development in this way is an important key for a post-growth society.

'Hobbyhimmel' – an open workshop in the context of post-growth

An interview with Martin Langlinderer, founder of 'Hobbyhimmel' ('Hobby Heaven'), Stuttgart's first and largest open workshop, which opened its doors to the public in 2015.

Post-growth played a central role in the project from the very beginning. Through sharing tools and machines, people are given the opportunity to produce and repair things themselves and in doing so to (re)learn old and new skills and relationships to materials and objects.
The collective use of the workshop means that tools and knowledge are shared. This not only ensures efficient use of the 'tools' as a resource but also enables mutual learning and collective doing.
In addition, the workshop allows organisations with a sustainability or social focus to use the fully equipped premises, in some cases in return for a donation, in some cases free of charge, and in this way supports the organisations' activities.
More than 40 volunteers support 'Hobbyhimmel', which is independently financed and receives no subsidies.
Interview conducted by Benedikt Schmid

Could you briefly describe for the readers what 'Hobbyhimmel' is and how the project works?

Martin Langlinderer: *'Hobbyhimmel'* is the first open workshop in Stuttgart. You can imagine it as follows: a large factory hall of over 300 m² with lots of materials, machines, tools and equipment, which we make available to the public, especially to private individuals. In the hall there are different areas for manual work with wood, metal or textiles, and also areas for electronics, bicycle repairs and modern production technologies – a fab lab [fabrication laboratory] with laser cutters, 3-D printers and a large CNC milling machine.

So, we offer equipment from all possible trades and crafts, and the idea is primarily that people who otherwise have no access to tools or machines or who rarely need them, use the workshop collectively. We are open seven days a week for everyone, especially in the evenings and on weekends. The workshop is only run by volunteers. We have between 40 to 50 volunteers who look after the project and run the place in their free time – opening the workshop, invoicing, being available to provide information, giving instructions and offering courses.

A particularly important point is that we are completely self-financed. That means we don't have any external funding to work with, but rather in the meanwhile – 2019 is the fourth year – the project finances itself completely independently and is also profitable.

The user groups of the workshop are very diversified. The main part is made up of private people who simply have no way of doing handicrafts at home – usually in their apartment they can't make noise, they can't get things dirty, they don't have the necessary tools and it's usually not reasonable to buy them if the tools are only used occasionally. But of course there are also other user groups. As well as the private users there are the commercial users who manufacture products or produce prototypes in the workshop. We also have training courses from private colleges or other educational providers who use the workshop, especially during the day. In addition, we have team events for companies, not forgetting the many non-profit organisations that use the workshop for their projects.

'Hobbyhimmel' is a project of the *Verein zur Verbreitung Offener Werkstätten* [Association for the Distribution of Open Workshops], which has dedicated itself to the goal of increasing broad social awareness of the topic of open workshops.

Can you briefly tell us what role the project plays for a post-growth economy or how 'Hobbyhimmel' can be described from a post-growth perspective?

Martin Langlinderer: For me, post-growth is the opposite of what most people currently believe: that we can produce more and more, sell more and more, consume more and more and do that at the expense of the global resources available to us. The post-growth economy is basically the antithesis, which says that we don't need constant growth. We must use resources much more efficiently and focus more on sufficiency, which will also make us more independent of external factors.

In our practical example it is firstly about people preferring to collectively use good, long-lasting tools rather than everyone buying their own cheap tools. With us, apart from tools people also share knowledge. If a number of people meet in one place and share their know-how then everyone can benefit from one another.

An important point apart from sharing is, secondly, the topic of repairing, so with a little effort keeping things that already exist running for longer. Repairing has become increasingly difficult in recent decades – due to poor supplies of replacement parts, planned obsolescence and other obstructions. Especially with our regular repair cafes we want to make it as easy as possible for people to get access to special tools and the necessary knowledge.

And thirdly, the topic of do-it-yourself. I have a different relationship to things I've made myself and I tend to use them longer because I know how much work I put into them and how to fix them.

In addition to private users, we also support local initiatives that deal with sustainability issues. They can use the workshop very cheaply, usually for free, and this makes it easier for them to implement their projects and activities, which are also moving towards a post-growth economy.

'Hobbyhimmel' has been supported by the 'Association for the Distribution of Open Workshops' for some time. Can you explain a bit what that's about?

Martin Langlinderer: From the very beginning the basic idea of the workshop was: one workshop is good, a lot of workshops are much better. But opening and running many workshops involves a lot of effort. Our approach is to organise this as simply as possible. This has led to the development of a social-franchise concept. That means that we make all the know-how that we have gained – all the documentation, the processes – available to other people free of cost and on an open-source basis. We also provide on-site advice so that new workshops don't have to learn everything from scratch.

That's why we founded the association, which is dedicated to the goal of helping other workshops to set up and to get established, and we provide them with anything we can give. We also collect tools through donations from private people, firms and e.g. school closures that we can pass on to new projects. If a number of workshops all operate according to the same principle, then the founding of each additional workshop will get easier.

And the aim is that in every urban neighbourhood low-threshold working space should be available to people, with very short distances on foot or close connections to an open workshop and very easy accessibility. That's why being open seven days a week is a cornerstone for us. In terms of price our workshop is also very accessible, which contributes towards acceptance and ultimately also the broad offerings and the diverse range of tools. We have tools and equipment in all possible fields. It's a holistic, low-threshold approach that we pursue here. Those are the components with which we try to really increase the reach and the impact of the topic of open workshops.

If you imagine that people from urban planning and local politics came to you and would like to support you in your project. What would you like those people to do?

Martin Langlinderer: Of course. I would be delighted if these people would approach us. Then we could say that we want free premises or start-up funding. Basically, I think that it's important that cities and municipalities see open workshops as important social components and start to establish them or at least promote their future development.

For me open workshops have a similar status to youth centres, swimming pools or libraries. These are all establishments that are open to everybody and are financed with public money. These establishments are an important component for society: for social cohesion, for personal development, for exchange of knowledge and so on.

They're all important establishments but they too are always only used by part of the population. And that's where I see open workshops, they're also used by certain people and like a library – to stick with this example – they contribute a great deal to knowledge generation and knowledge dissemination. Perhaps not necessarily on an intellectual basis but in the field of practical knowledge: old knowledge about handicrafts but also new technical competences. The mutual exchange is an extremely important element because otherwise, to put it bluntly, we all degenerate to simple consumers who just believe what people tell them: it's not possible to repair that, the only option is persistent gluing, there are no replacement parts, you need to throw that away and buy a new one, the fabric can only be washed three times. As a consumer, you become increasingly dumb if you're not knowledgeable about these things and then you can't make any active, conscious decisions in terms of a post-growth economy, which is about long-lasting, resource-saving products and processes. In relation to open workshops, politics and planning should use the principle of libraries as a role model: in every urban district there's a local library and open workshop and perhaps there's a large central library and a large central open workshop where there are more and specialised tools and machines. And the urban planners can then think: 'In both, important resources are shared, in one case books, in the other case machines, but in both cases knowledge' – there are so many parallels that you can draw. So, if you ask what tip I have for urban planning, then I would try to tighten this connection in their minds so that they can't forget it.

How do you imagine a transformation beyond the topic of open workshops?

Martin Langlinderer: My approach is one of small steps and setting an example. Every time I try to think consciously about what I buy and where I go. I certainly don't always get it right, in that I don't always make the most ecological, most efficient decision that favours sufficiency. For me it's also important that I no longer just use my labour in the regular economy but mainly invest it in other topics that I believe are more socially relevant. This means that I have significantly less money than I used to have but more fun and more freedom.

I sure think you can inspire people to think about things, to take small steps. But it's a long and small-scale process that's apparently not going to occur top-down. That's why we need a solid grassroots basis. There's probably not going to be much change from politics so for me it's a bottom-up process.

Many thanks for the interesting discussion.

Neighbourhood farms as new places for participation and grow-your-own

An interview with Heike Brückner and Jan Zimmermann, conducted by Mai Anh Ha, Meret Batke and Dr Bastian Lange

The neighbourhood farm (Quartierhof) project was developed with the 'Urban Farm Dessau' in the Dessau neighbourhood 'Am Leipziger Tor'. The idea behind the project is to test strategies for creating local food supplies and grow-your-own approaches for healthy food and renewable energies. The aim is to create an urban farm that also serves as an innovative place of learning where economic value creation is linked to education and social work.
www.urbane-farm.de
Heike Brückner is a landscape planner who focuses on post-industrial cultural landscapes and productive urban landscapes. Since 2010 she has been researching post-fossil urban and regional development and initiated the 'Urban Farm Dessau' project. Among other things, she brings knowledge on permaculture to the project.
Jan Zimmermann is a qualified horticultural engineer and owner of a company offering ecological garden services in Dessau. Since the beginning of the project he has been involved as a leader, gardener and visionary.

What is the 'Urban Farm Dessau'?

Jan Zimmermann: In Dessau we have green areas that we're trying to make usable. There are various options here, e. g. food production or the production of renewable energies. A most important point with the Urban Farm is education, which plays a role because of course we're not doing it just for us but also for interested people and children who want to learn something and need education.

What is characteristic of the project?

Jan Zimmermann: The area's directly surrounded by five-storey prefabricated buildings. We're on open meadowland in-between. The project grows a little every year as the area is enlarged a bit every year. As to what grows there, for example vegetables, herbs or potatoes.

Heike Brückner: We like to talk about our project as a 'neighbourhood farm' – a kind of urban farm that is collectively worked by neighbours and people from the neighbourhood. We ask ourselves what we actually need to supply ourselves with food or renewable energies in the city. So how, e. g., a cycle of soil improvement can be organised or how a waste management cycle can be created. We tried out the latter with children in an educational project by fermenting leftover food in a mini biogas plant. We use the gas to boil water for tea and the leftovers from this mini biogas plant are used to fertilise the beds – a simple way to celebrate and demonstrate such circular approaches.

What is the spatial extent of the neighbourhood farm?

Jan Zimmermann: There are a number of separate segments that together make up a cultivated area of about 500 to 600 square metres.

Heike Brückner: I would describe it as a decentralised farm, one that's not necessarily traditional with a farmhouse in the middle from which beds and fields are then cultivated in rays or rings. But rather according to the principle that wherever a stakeholder starts to cooperate with us, like for instance the adjacent *Volkssolidarität* [People's Solidarity] or the women's centre, something's created – for example, a raised bed, an orchard or the potato field.

How does the network of the neighbourhood farm work?

Jan Zimmermann: From the very beginning we organised a gardening meeting that's held for two or three hours every Wednesday afternoon. One of us is present and various, very different people come – ranging from retired people to children who drop by on their way to and from school. Participants are people from the neighbourhood but also some from the suburbs. They join in because they think that the project's exciting and want to be part of it.

Heike Brückner: Between about 3 and 13 people participate. In winter there are somewhat less but then in summer there are sometimes about 15 to 20 people.

Do you own the area?

Jan Zimmermann: We use it in consultation with the owner without a complicated set of contracts.

Heike Brückner: The advantage for the owner is that the area is cared for.

Is the project based on the idea of a commons?

Heike Brückner: Yes, we focus on the principle of a commons in terms of a collectively farmed area. Decisions about what's farmed where or, e. g., where the soil should be improved are made collectively. Which projects do we want to support together? Should animals be included and who will look after them? We discuss all these and other questions collectively.

Jan Zimmermann: An association was founded to bear responsibility for the project. But also primarily so that it's not a loose network and to make it possible to apply for public and private finance.

What effect does the regional context of Dessau have on the project? What is the spatial context that the project refers to?

Jan Zimmermann: In Dessau we have the phenomenon that there's been a great deal of demolition and that means that a lot of brownfield sites have emerged without anyone knowing what should be done with them. Especially where neighbourhoods still exist, the demolition of houses led to open areas that then became overgrown, which was not really to the liking of the residents. That's how we developed the idea of making use of these brownfields. Then with the implementation the question of what is actually possible emerges. The idea of making a vegetable garden is simple but then really implementing this on a brownfield of this sort is something completely different. That's what I would describe as the specific Dessau context, that we have a lot of areas available and that demolition has led to the emergence of new open areas.

What is the background against which the project developed and what resources does Dessau provide?

Heike Brückner: The background consists of the themes of shrinkage, shrinking cities, and how you can plan and manage cities with no growth. Between 2002 and 2010 the Bauhaus Dessau tackled this issue, focusing especially on what instruments were required. In the course of the 2010 *Internationale Bauausstellung (IBA), Stadtumbau* [International Building Exhibition Urban Redevelopment], we developed an instrument to encourage people to cultivate vacant areas. With reference to the gold-mining times in bygone America, we named these areas 'claims'. People could adopt 400 square metres of open space for an interim use or in the form of a concession agreement. That was fairly successful. The urban farm can be understood as a further development of the claims project. Then, of course, there are the big social issues. For instance, that sourcing organic food from far away is outrageous when Dessau has the potential to produce it locally. Or when, on the one hand, young people don't know what they want to do professionally in the future and, on the other hand, we see what a desperate need there is for a new generation of gardeners who can work with ecological cycles. These are the wider social contexts that also motivate us here.

What is the relationship between the region and your neighbourhood farm?

Heike Brückner: We notice that a structure like the neighbourhood farm is relevant when you think about transformation strategies for working towards a sustainable, post-fossil society. What we are testing here is also relevant for cities that are in economic growth. Our experiences are also transferable to other contexts like that. Every neighbourhood, every municipality needs a neighbourhood farm of this sort. A neighbourhood farm as an infrastructure that allows people to participate, to learn a future profession and to practise ecological cycles. Gaining the know-how and the practical experience that we need for the future.

Are you transferring this project approach to other regions?

Jan Zimmermann: The topic of urban farming, local supplies and grow-your-own is definitely relevant in many areas. Whether in Berlin, Leipzig or Hamburg, everywhere there are people who are interested in producing their own food in a different way. Often there isn't enough space, which means that the implementation varies. But no matter whether in a vegetable crate, a potato sack or on the balcony... the idea that there are alternatives to the supermarket offerings of conventionally produced food that's been transported over great distances, that idea is there already. Lots of people come to us who want to see how we've done it, who are inspired by it and who then create their own development path.

What connections are there between your project in Dessau and projects in other cities?

Heike Brückner: A special feature in Dessau is that we understand the project as a structuring element in a spatial reorganisation of the entire city. We have adopted the image of an 'urban garden realm' here, a landscape with islands of urban development.

Nuclei for local supply and grow-your-own initiatives of this sort are developing in many places, for instance the *Stadtgärtnerei Annalinde* [Urban Gardens Annalinde] in Leipzig or the various initiatives of the *Solidarische Landwirtschaft* [Community Supported Agriculture (CSA)]. The link is creating small urban units and productively using the landscape in between so that cycles of local supply and grow-your-own can develop.

What is the relationship of the neighbourhood farm to the historical idea of the 'Gartenreich' ['Garden Realm']?

Heike Brückner: The link can be found in the idea of productivity. The *Dessau-Wörlitzer Gartenreich* has the guiding principle of combining utility and beauty. But people often forget that behind this aesthetic landscape was an economy. Decentralised farms were scattered throughout the countryside, cultivated the landscape and made it useful.

Is there a specific link between the individual projects?

Heike Brückner: I think that overall this allows a negotiable space to emerge, a new commons. If people can relate to how their food is produced, then an understanding develops of how a cycle is organised etc. That's certainly the connecting factor between the various projects in the different places.

Is the project being copied in the region?

Heike Brückner: This effect, that we trigger a kind of activating impulse, that is occurring. But we haven't yet got the potential to fully duplicate the project. You always need people who can then implement the idea.

Jan Zimmermann: A student project has been founded and has led to a garden being developed, one that's collectively used. At the university there's also a demand for raised beds which will be used for growing food. Or in childcare facilities. We already have quite a presence in Dessau. In talks with a range of people we discover that they know and appreciate what we do. That's an interesting observation, but of course you never know what influences have led to any specific idea.

III. Spaces of Conflict

'The need [for post-growth] arises from sustainability issues, social injustice and international interactions which growth logics fail to acknowledge, define as problematic or view as necessary.'

Kim C. von Schönfeld

Provincialising degrowth
Alternatives to development and the Global South

Antje Bruns

1. Introduction

The exploitation of people, raw materials and nature is leading to an intensification of socio-ecological crises on a planetary scale, with links between environmental change and inequality becoming increasingly clearly defined. At the same time, these links reveal the international division of labour. The Global North consumes, produces and emits. The environmental risks and impacts are externalised – especially at the expense of societies in the Global South.[1] A fundamental transformation of the resource-intensive patterns of production and consumption in the Global North is thus necessary in order to make a socially and environmentally just life possible for everyone, including those in the Global South. Degrowth is a transformative approach that calls for fundamental changes to the economic and social model in the Global North (Brand/Krams 2018). It draws on a tradition of thought that reaches back to the concept of 'décroissance', which should be read as a criticism of the hegemonial idea of development. Development, as a Western invention, is indivisibly connected to economic growth and builds upon inequalities between North and South (Latouche 2006).

---

1 Global North and Global South are not geographical concepts although the majority of the rich human population live in the northern hemisphere and a large share of the poor population live in countries in the south. 'North' and 'South' are rather metaphors for the social, economic and ecological inequality which is caused by capitalism and colonialism on a global scale.

Degrowth focuses on the need for transformation in the Global North. This highly necessary search for alternatives must not lose sight of the global interactions and long-distance impacts of 'our' transformation. The socio-ecological systems in the North and South are so closely interconnected that socio-ecological transformation processes in the Global North can reproduce new geographies of inequality in the Global South. Precisely because we are trying to achieve a good life for all, it is important to bear these relational patterns in mind, as we are primarily the ones who are living 'not beyond our means but beyond the means of others' – as Stephan Lessenich expresses it, referring to global socio-ecological inequalities and non-contemporaneity (Lessenich 2018: 203, translated from German). These inequalities, with winners and the privileged on the one hand and losers and the marginalised on the other hand, are deeply inscribed in (neo-)colonial and capitalist economic and social systems (Latouche 2006). The historical roots reach far back, dividing the world into colonised and colonisers. In the world order thus created, the project of European Modernity became hegemonic (Mignolo 2007; Quijano 2000), which is why any search for alternatives to the capitalist system must tackle its dark side – colonialism. Historical amnesia would disregard the lines connecting the colonially established system of resource exploitation to the Eurocentric world order and knowledge system.

Despite the critical voices heard from sustainability and transformation studies, ways of thinking and approaches from the Global South seldom influence theory building, the development of concepts or policy strategies. Elsewhere, attention has been drawn to gaps in the fields of climate policy (Bauriedl 2015) and urban development (Bruns/Gerend 2018). It is thus right to ask who actually speaks for the future of the Earth (Lövbrand/Beck/Chilvers et al. 2015) and who is absent or rendered absent from this discourse (Escobar 2016). The marginalisation of voices constrains discourses and is associated with a dominance and standardisation of knowledge – a process that has been described as epistemic violence (Spivak 1988). Often epistemic violence takes the form of subtle concealment, as is the case, for instance, when we speak of a global world society. This supposedly integrative planetary perspective conceals unequal relations, disguising discrepancies between this representation and the agency of those people who have scarcely contributed to the socio-ecological crisis but are particularly affected by it.

In this article, inequalities between North and South and their historical development are used as an analytical lens through which to focus on different settings and narrative strands of the socio-ecological crisis and transformation discourse. This highlights colonial continuities in the discourse of the Anthropocene and further emphasises that decolonial options must be included in the degrowth debate. The narrative adopted by earth system sciences targets the planetary scale and draws a veil of ignorance over the geographies of inequality. In contrast, it is precisely the inequality caused by colonial practices and mentalities that is the focus and starting point of theories and approaches from the Global South. As epistemic disobedience (Mignolo 2011), such approaches offer decolonial alternatives to Eurocentric thinking, knowledge and action and are therefore – and this is the central argument of the article – indispensable for the degrowth debate.

The involvement of epistemologies from the South (Escobar 2016) is necessarily a reflexive process that is associated with a calling into question of Western knowledge production and orders. It enables the recognition and acceptance of critical and alternative ways of thinking from the South – such as post-development and environmental justice – acknowledging them as productive questioning of Western theories. In this way it becomes possible to decentralise and provincialise the Eurocentric perspective on the socio-ecological crisis in the Anthropocene (Chakrabarty 2008).

2. The socio-ecological crisis in the Anthropocene...

Discussion about the necessity of transformation is – especially in the German-language spatial sciences debate – strongly linked to the Anthropocene discourse. This implies that colonial continuities are produced or revealed, as is demonstrated below. There is namely no single narrative about the Anthropocene. It is rather the case that there are different understandings about what characterises the crisis in the Anthropocene and which imperatives of action should be derived.

3. ... from the perspective of earth system sciences

This reading of the Anthropocene suggests that human beings influence processes relevant to the earth system on a global scale, and that this development accelerated with industrialisation and the associated growth in the use of fossil fuels (Steffen/Crutzen/McNeill 2007). Urbanisation and globalisation have contributed to the 'great acceleration', culminating in the geological era known as the Anthropocene. Geological eras are commonly determined by the discipline of geology which uses a 'golden spike' in sediments and rocks to declare a new stratigraphical era.

The characteristics and also the drivers of planetary transformation are the extensive and widespread exploitation, sealing and degradation of land and natural ecosystems and the emissions caused by the use of fossil fuels. These processes, which indicate the interwovenness of social and natural processes, result in global climate change, the loss of biodiversity and the accumulation of plastic in water bodies, soil and animals (Zalasiewicz/Williams/Smith et al. 2008). The speed and dimensions of this transformation are so great that there is increasing evidence of exceeding the tipping point and crossing planetary limits (Steffen/Richardson/Rockström et al. 2020). It is assumed that within certain social and biophysical boundaries, the earth's system is dynamic and variable and can deliver central functions. If, on the other hand, tipping points are exceeded, then the socio-ecological system behaves non-linearly and is beyond regulation. To prevent the socio-ecological collapse of the earth's system, there is a need for political intervention. On the international scale, Sustainable Development Goals (SDGs) are viewed as a promising instrument. They are now also implemented on national and subnational levels to promote and support a sustainable and just future by combining state action, economic measures and civil society activities. Although the SDGs are not legally binding, the resonant optimism about governance that they embody can hardly be ignored. In this ideal, global sustainability and justice are negotiated as feasibility issues to be tackled by techno-managerial governance. The combating of poverty continues to be linked to economic growth, with an emphasis on the role of private business (BMZ 2016). There is still an assumption that technological solutions and economic modernisation in the context of a 'policy of controls' can suffice (Adloff/Neckel 2019, translated from German). However, this model of transformation does not focus on reducing structural, political or economic inequality as part of a profound change of path.

Furthermore, this narrative of planetary transformation in the Anthropocene is problematic due to its 'universalised interpretations of causes' (Bauriedl 2015: 16, translated from German). These interpretations conceal the fact that not all people are equally responsible for the increased energy consumption or ecological footprints related, for instance, to tourism, but rather just the few who have the necessary socio-economic status and passports. This concealment is associated with the depoliticisation of the Anthropocene discourse, which is significant in that it fosters neo-Malthusian arguments and racism. For instance, it is argued that unbridled population growth (in the Global South) and the demand for resources that results from it are responsible for the crisis (Gottschlich/Schultz 2019). It is a small step from such arguments to controlling population in the name of climate protection. Furthermore, attention is deflected from issues of justice and distribution and the necessity of changes in patterns of production and consumption in the Global North.

4. ... from the perspective of critical geography

In contrast, narratives about the socio-ecological crisis in the Anthropocene told from the perspective of critical geography focus on deeper causes and contradictions and highlight inequalities in the architecture of responsibility between North and South. The socio-ecological crises are not the responsibility of 'humanity' but are products of an unequal colonial and capitalist world order in which there are a few winners and many losers (Brand/Wissen 2011). In the colonial past, geologists contributed to this world order by mapping raw materials and precious metals. Once the position and distribution of the deposits were known, they began to be mined so as to feed industrial development and wealth in the Global North. The colonial powers were interested in raw materials such as gold or colonial goods – e. g. cocoa. Today's Ghana even used to be called the 'Gold Coast' after the coveted metal, and was colloquially known as 'the mine', making the matter even clearer (Yusoff 2018). The many slave castles along the 'Gold Coast' tell the story of another aspect of colonial exploitation in which people became a commodified good. Kathryn Yusoff, Professor for Inhuman Geography, explains how closely the emergence of the Anthropocene is interlinked with this inhuman system, which transformed (black) people into a means of production. Yusoff shows that the connection between geological knowledge and the development of political power constitutes the Anthropocene (Yusoff 2016).

The question of when the Anthropocene began is thus not an innocent one. Investigation into its origins reveals the historical continuities in the way in which the processes of extraction and the appropriation and exploitation of nature are associated with processes of wealth accumulation and the development of the capitalist world system (Yusoff 2018). This asymmetry is characteristic of the Anthropocene, which, viewed in this way, began long before industrialisation. On the other hand, if the search for the 'golden spike' is reduced to finding evidence of certain markers in sediments, not only is the question of the Anthropocene's origins depoliticised but the suffering and deaths of black enslaved people are erased from global history. This creates an absence which is sustained into the present time and is important for the spaces of thought and action which make the future.

5. Inequalities and externalisation

The discussion above has shown that 'business-as usual' is not only or primarily precluded by the danger of crossing a biophysical or social tipping point in the future. A profound change of path is also urgently required by historically rooted socio-ecological inequalities and injustices, which are actually worsening at the present time.

5.1 Inequality

Inequality is primarily understood and measured as economic inequality. This makes it even more astounding that up to just a few years ago, there was no sound data analysis from which reliable conclusions about the development of worldwide inequality could be drawn. It seems unnecessary to say that this is not viewed as a coincidence but rather as the result of the furthering and protection of particular interests (Ernst/Losada/María 2010).

Thomas Piketty's book *Le Capital au XXIe siècle* drew attention to the lack of inequality research. Piketty analysed historical data going back to industrialisation and showed how wealth concentration has increased since the middle of the twentieth century. This growth in inequality is the result of political decisions which promised that economic growth, technological advances and increased private investment – e. g. in infrastructure – was to the benefit of all. Instead, prioritising the economy over social and/or ecological needs led to an increase in inequality that substantially threatens democratic and social development (Piketty 2015).

Increasing inequality, whether between countries or within societies, runs counter to the goals of transformation, particularly as there is a widening divide between private and public capital. In many rich countries, public capital has been declining since 1980 while private capital has increased (Alvaredo/Chancel/Piketty et al. 2018), a trend due in part to privatisation policies. This restricts the scope for public action and management intended to achieve socio-ecological change – a dramatic development in light of the challenges. In Germany, as in many other countries, the public sector is responsible for services of general interest and for providing social and technical infrastructure and pursues the goal of creating equivalent living conditions in all areas of the country. De facto, however, the public sector is increasingly unable to provide basic services for the benefit of all. Various studies of recent years have shown that in Germany and in other countries, the divide between poor and rich, and between prosperous and declining regions, is growing ever larger and limits the future viability of regions (Slupina/Dähner/Reibstein et al. 2019).

Future viability begins with imaginings about the future that cognitively structure action. Local urban and regional research (on the knowledge level) and urban and regional planning (as policy practice) are still steeped in a way of thinking that follows the dictates of growth, modernity and development. They thus reproduce colonial mentalities (Bruns/Gerend 2018). This is revealed, for instance, by the elevation of the European city to the very definition of a developed, modern city. A contrast is provided by the Oriental (and hence underdeveloped) city which is devalued by this process of comparison. Such an understanding of the underdeveloped Oriental city is recorded as 'knowledge' in the textbooks of urban research. It is then transferred and given substance when neighbourhoods with a higher proportion of residents with a migrant background are automatically termed 'problem neighbourhoods' (Ha 2014). A critical review of these derogatory attributions is necessary not only in light of the increasing diversity of society. The 'reproduction of racism as a colonial legacy in the city' (ibid.: 42, translated from German) must be countered as a matter of principle.

The term 'development' (and 'underdevelopment') and the idea of 'modernity' are central elements of the Eurocentric world view and are reflected in notions of the 'city'. In cities like Accra (Ghana), where many people live without secure access to water, water provision is only thought of in terms of the central, networked water infrastructures which are required by structural adjustment support programmes and funded by World Bank investments. This is in line with Western imaginations of the modern city. Such reforms and investments have failed to reduce socio-ecological inequality[2] in terms of access to drinking water, but they have proved a lucrative source of income for Western investors. And it seems that this is precisely the reason that a decentralised, heterogeneous system of water infrastructure consisting of water sellers, tankers, wells and waterpipes, is inconceivable (Bruns/Gerend 2018). Or, to put it another way: alternative infrastructure solutions that are adapted to everyday practices and lifeworlds would challenge the Western hegemony.

Contributions from the South promote ontological and epistemological options that allow thinking to embrace a pluriverse (instead of a universe): 'the understanding of the world is much broader than the western understanding of the world. This means that the transformation of the world, and the transitions to the pluriverse or the civilizations transitions adumbrated by many indigenous, peasant, and Afrodescendant activists, might happen (indeed, are happening) along pathways that might be unthinkable from the perspective of Eurocentric theories' (Escobar 2016: 16). A transformative change of path that manifests epistemological openness and thus reflexively includes decolonial options inevitably questions power and dominance relations.

The geopolitical dimensions of development and transformation can be demonstrated using current discussions about energy policies. While decarbonisation of the fossil energy system combined with a drastic drop in energy use is of key significance for successful, socio-ecologically just transformation in the Global North, it is not sufficient to address inequali-

---

2 Socio-ecological inequality research – as a still comparatively young and fairly undifferentiated research field – can draw on still less data (Dietz 2014).

ties between North and South. Even the International Energy Agency clearly identifies such contradictions in the world energy outlook on their webpage:

> The gap between the promise of energy for all and the fact that almost one billion people still do not have access to electricity. The gap between the latest scientific evidence highlighting the need for evermore-rapid cuts in global greenhouse gas emissions and the data showing that energy-related emissions hit another historic high in 2018. The gap between expectations of fast, renewables-driven energy transitions and the reality of today's energy systems in which reliance on fossil fuels remains stubbornly high. And the gap between the calm in wellsupplied oil markets and the lingering unease over geopolitical tensions and uncertainties. (IEA 2020).

The sense of calm in the face of the disparities is shocking. By way of comparison: energy use per capita in Germany is circa 164 gigajoules per annum (BP 2019) and in Ghana is circa 1.5 gigajoules per annum (Energy Commission Ghana 2018). It speaks volumes that the figures for Ghana are not even itemised in the annual energy report by BP but are simply included in the 'rest of Africa'.

European energy policy is not just about energy security (especially not in the Global South), but is about safeguarding the existing geopolitical order, as the European Commission's Green Deal demonstrates. In January 2020, the President of the Commission Ursula von der Leyen presented the new strategy for the EU's foreign trade policy, which includes ambitious emissions goals for 2030 and aims for the EU to be completely climate neutral by 2050. To this end, European Union policy, especially growth policy, is to be redirected to pursue the overriding objective of 'combating climate change'. The reorientation of growth policy is embedded in geopolitical notions concerning the position of Europe in light of global political changes (weakening of the USA and an up-and-coming China). This calls for a united Europe, which requires disparities between the European countries to be reduced. Even if the financial package is entitled 'Just Transition Fonds', the 'just' refers only to disparities within Europe – between old coal mining districts and abandoned industrial areas on the one hand and the economically prosperous regions on the other (Europäische Kommission 2020). The energy transformation in Europe thus continues to be based on a concept of growth (even if it has been green-washed), and this growth in Europe requires an exterior space that uses less resources than it provides.

5.2   Externalisation

Unlimited growth is impossible and will only be made possible by drawing boundaries between spaces, income segments, ethnicities or other markers of difference. Growth as an element of 'capitalism cannot sustain itself from itself. It lives from the existence of an "exterior" [...].' (Lessenich 2018: 42, translated from German) This unequal order of global resources (Altvater 1992) is deeply inscribed in people's lifestyles and everyday practices, in the form of an 'imperial way of life', as Ulrich Brand and Markus Wissen describe it. 'The way of life of the Global North is imperial in that it requires fundamentally unlimited – politically, legally and/or forcibly secured – access to resources, space, labour capacity and sinks elsewhere' (Brand/Wissen 2011: 82, translated from German). Externalisation is thus a constituting element of the asymmetrical relationship between North and South. It is related both to the extraction of resources and the outsourcing of environmental impacts, risks or sinks (Gerber/Raina 2018; Foster 2011), and the impacts of the latter are at least as drastic as the extraction of resources.

Climate policy is one of the newer externalisation trends. For instance, the expansion of biodiesel in Europe has enormous effects on local land use and thus on the livelihoods of many people in the Global South. The emissions trading system used to implement the Kyoto protocol also follows imperial logic because industries in the Global North can buy their way out of obligations to reduce emissions – at the cost of development opportunities in the Global South. This system is therefore correctly described as 'carbon colonialism' (Bauriedl 2015: 16, translated from German) in that it reproduces existing inequalities and consolidates power relations. Countries of the Global South that – like Ghana – are characterised by a consumption of energy and resources that is far below average are left with hardly any scope for development.

The inequality of lifestyles and development options is conceptualised and evaluated differently in degrowth and post-development approaches:

> It is clear that many countries in the South with very low per capita incomes cannot afford *degrowth* but could use a kind of *sustainable development*,

directed at real needs such as access to water, food, health care, education, etc. This requires a radical shift in social structure away from the relations of production of capitalism/imperialism (Foster 2011: 7).

Social movements in countries such as Ecuador or Bolivia are testing alternatives as part of this 'shift'. The matrix of objectives here is not built around profit but around social needs. However, Foster's choice of the term 'sustainable development' is misleading, as development is understood as the opposite of underdevelopment and is therefore rejected as (culturally) imperial. Therefore, the term 'post-development' was thus coined, not to refer to alternative developments but rather to convey a notion of alternatives to the ideal of development that involve local and plural knowledges (Escobar 1995; Ziai 2012).

6. Alternative spaces for thought and action – Provincialising degrowth

Although degrowth, with its fundamental criticism of the imperial lifestyle, has indisputable parallels to approaches like 'post-development', a number of authors argue that degrowth lacks links to the needs and knowledge of people in the Global South. This disconnectedness is seen as the reason why degrowth has no significant position in social or scientific debate in the Global South (Rodríguez-Labajos/Yánez/Bond et al. 2019). Escobar, for instance, suggests that there is no natural alliance between the different concepts and approaches in the transformation discourse, but that a pact could be produced in a productive process of mutual encounter, learning and unlearning (Escobar 2015).

Learning can be drawn from the social movements and the indigenous groups that have come together in South America to demand and live an alternative to the threats of overexploiting nature and resources. *'Buen Vivir'* ('Good Life') is an alternative, post-extractivist model intended to overcome the multiple capitalist crisis. It embraces plural imaginings of the world and the future and is therefore understood as an epistemological paradigm change (Gann 2013: 84). The participative and emancipatory character of the constitutions in Ecuador and Bolivia is emphasised, as is the resulting relativisation of Western modernity. The opening up of the concept of work is central here, as this allows different social configurations and a good life. Buen Vivir can thus be understood as a concrete utopia with which to overcome colonial continuities.

In comparison, degrowth seems to be a relatively narrowly defined movement that could profit from greater reflection on North-South relations on the one hand and the plural epistemologies of the South on the other. In this sense degrowth requires provincialisation to expose Eurocentric perspectives in a reflexive process, so that ultimately the European context can be transcended and new epistemologies accepted. This is important for critical spatial and transformation sciences, but equally so for spatial planning. Political practice makes local and regional decisions that affect development trajectories and result in resource needs, governing far into the lifeworlds of people in the Global South.

Cited Literature

Adloff, F., & Neckel, S. (2019). Modernisierung, Transformation oder Kontrolle? In K. Dörre, H. Rosa, K. Becker, S. Bose, & B. Seyd (Eds.), *Große Transformation? Zur Zukunft moderner Gesellschaften.* Springer, 167–180.

Altvater, E. (1992). *Der Preis des Wohlstands: Oder Umweltplünderung und neue Welt(un)ordnung.* Verlag Westfälisches Dampfboot.

Alvaredo, F., Chancel, L., Piketty, T., Saez, E., & Zucman, G. (2018). *World inequality report 2018.* World Inequality Lab.

Bauriedl, S. (2015). Eurozentrische Weltbürgerbewegung. Zum WBGU-Sondergutachten Klimaschutz als Weltbürgerbewegung. *GAIA - Ecological Perspectives for Science and Society, 24*(1), 13–16.

BMZ – Bundesministerium für wirtschaftliche Zusammenarbeit und Entwicklung (2016), *Wirtschaft – Chancen für nachhaltige Entwicklung. Privatwirtschaft als Partner in der Entwicklungszusammenarbeit.* oekom Verlag.

BP (2019). *Full report – BP statistical review of world energy* 2019. Self-published.

Brand, U., & Krams, M. (2018). Zehn Jahre Degrowth als radikale politische Perspektive: Potenziale und Hürden. *Forschungsjournal Soziale Bewegungen, 31*, 18–26.

Brand, U., & Wissen, M. (2011). Sozial-ökologische Krise und imperiale Lebensweise. Zu Krise und Kontinuität kapitalistischer Naturverhältnisse.

In A. Demirovic, J. Dück, F. Becker, & P. Bader (Eds.), *VielfachKrise im finanzdominierten Kapitalismus*. VSA Verlag, 78–93.

Bruns, A., & Gerend, J. (2018). In search of a decolonial urban transformation. *GAIA – Ecological Perspectives for Science and Society, 27*, 293–297.

Chakrabarty, D. (2008). *Provincializing Europe: Postcolonial thought and historical difference*. Princeton University Press.

Dietz, K. (2014). *Researching inequalities from a socio-ecological perspective*. desiguALdades.net working paper series 74.

Energy Commission Ghana (2018). *2018 Energy (supply and demand) outlook for Ghana*.

Ernst, T., & Isidoro Losada, A. M. (2010). Nord-Süd-Beziehungen: Globale Ungleichheit im Wandel. *Aus Politik und Zeitgeschichte (APuZ), 10/2020*, 10–15.

Escobar, A. (1995). *Encountering development: The making and unmaking of the Third World*. Princeton University Press.

Escobar, A. (2015). Degrowth, postdevelopment, and transitions: a preliminary conversation. *Sustainability Science, 10*, 451–462.

Escobar, A. (2016). Thinking-feeling with the Earth: Territorial struggles and the ontological dimension of the epistemologies of the South. *AIBR, Revista de Antropología Iberoamericana, 11*, 11–32.

European Commission (2020). *Regulation of the European Parliament and of the council establishing the Just Transition Fund*. COM(2020) 22 final. EN.

Foster, J. B. (2011). Capitalism and degrowth: An impossibility theorem. *Monthly Review, 62*, 26.

Gann, A.-L. (2013). Das Konzept des Buen Vivir in der ecuadorianischen Verfassung aus feministischer Perspektive. *Femina Politica – Zeitschrift für feministische Politikwissenschaft, 22*, 81–93.

Gerber, J.-F., & Raina, R. S. (2018). Post-growth in the Global South? Some reflections from India and Bhutan. *Ecological Economics, 150*, 353–358.

Gottschlich, D., & Schultz, S. (2019). Weniger Klimawandel durch weniger Menschen? Feministische Kritik am neomalthusianischen Revival. In Fachstelle Radikalisierungsprävention und Engagement im Naturschutz (Eds.), *Aspekte Gruppenbezogener Menschenfeindlichkeit im Natur- und Umweltschutz – eine Debatte*. FARN, 24–29.

Ha, N. (2014). Perspektiven urbaner Dekolonisierung: Die europäische Stadt als ‚Contact Zone'. *sub\urban. zeitschrift für kritische stadtforschung, 2*, 27–48.

IEA – International Energy Agency (2020). *World energy outlook 2019*.
Latouche, S. (2006). *Le pari de la décroissance*. Fayard.
Lessenich, St. (2018). *Neben uns die Sintflut. Wie wir auf Kosten anderer leben*. Piper Verlag.
Lövbrand, E., Beck, S., Chilvers, J., Forsyth, T., Hedrén, J., Hulme, M., Lidskog, R., & Vasileiadou, E. (2015). Who speaks for the future of Earth? How critical social science can extend the conversation on the Anthropocene. *Global Environmental Change, 32*, 211–218.
Mignolo, W. D. (2007). DELINKING. *Cultural Studies, 21*, 449–514.
Mignolo, W. D. (2011). Epistemic disobedience and the decolonial option: A manifesto. *Transmodernity, 1*, 3–23.
Otto, I. M., Donges, J. F., Cremades, R., Bhowmik, A., Hewitt, R. J., Lucht, W., Rockström, J., Allerberger, F., McCaffrey, M., Doe, S. S. P., Lenferna, A., Morán, N., van Vuuren, D. P., & Schellnhuber, H. J. (2020). Social tipping dynamics for stabilizing Earth's climate by 2050. *PNAS – Proceedings of the National Academy of Sciences of the United States of America, 2020*, February 4, 117(5), 2354–2365.
Piketty, T. (2015). About capital in the twenty-first century. *American Economic Review, 105*, 48–53.
Quijano, A. (2000). Coloniality of power and Eurocentrism in Latin America. *International Sociology, 15*, 533–580.
Rodríguez-Labajos, B., Yánez, I., Bond, P., Greyl, L., Munguti, S., Ojo, G. U., & Overbeek, W. (2019). Not so natural an alliance? Degrowth and environmental justice movements in the Global South. *Ecological Economics, 157*, 175–184.
Slupina, M., Dähner, S., Reibstein, L., Amberger, J., Sixtus, F., Grunwald, J., & Klingholz, R. (2019). *Die demografische Lage der Nation. Wie zukunftsfähig Deutschlands Regionen sind*. Springer.
Spivak, G. C., & Morris, R. C. (1988). *Can the subaltern speak?* Columbia University Press.
Steffen, W., Crutzen, P. J., & McNeill, J. R. (2007). The Anthropocene: Are humans now overwhelming the great forces of nature. *AMBIO: A Journal of the Human Environment, 36*, 614–621.
Steffen, W., Richardson, K., Rockström, J., Cornell, S. E., Fetzer, I., Bennett, E. M., Biggs, R., Carpenter, St. R., Vries, W. de, & Wit, C. A. de (2015). Planetary boundaries: Guiding human development on a changing planet. *Science, 347*(6223), 1259855.

Yusoff, K. (2016). Anthropogenesis: Origins and endings in the Anthropocene. *Theory, Culture & Society, 33*, 3–28.

Yusoff, K. (2018). *A billion black Anthropocenes or none*. University of Minnesota Press.

Zalasiewicz, J., Williams, M., Smith, A., Barry, T. L., Coe, A. L., Bown, P. R., Brenchley, P., Cantrill, D., Gale, A., Gibbard, Ph., Gregory, F. J., Hounslow, M. W., Kerr, A. C., Pearson, P., Knox, R., Powell, J., Waters, C., Marshall, J., Oates, M., Rawson, P., & Stone, Ph. (2008). Are we now living in the Anthropocene? *GSA Today, 18*(2), 4-8.

Ziai, A. (2012). Post-Development: Fundamentalkritik der „Entwicklung". *Geographica Helvetica, 67*, 133–138.

Financing post-growth?
Green financial products for changed logics of production

Sabine Dörry, Christian Schulz

1. Introduction

Current debates on 'green finance' and 'sustainable investments' are shaped by the search for alternative ways of investing large volumes of capital to provide economic returns while abiding by certain social and ecological standards. The large institutional investors pursuing such goals include pension funds, insurance companies and foundations – as well as sovereign wealth funds. At the same time, many of the international financial centres (IFCs) where 'green' financial products are 'produced' are attempting not only to rebrand their core activities, but also to create new conditions for 'green' (and sustainable) investments. These new conditions comprise, e. g., regulations and standards, new trading platforms, new degree programmes at universities and marketing techniques. Despite such dynamic developments there is currently no indication that the financial sector is reassessing or questioning the growth-based principles, mechanisms and motives of a financialised global economy. In contrast, the real economy is increasingly turning to alternative approaches, especially in regional contexts, such as the circular economy and enterprises with a common good orientation, some of which are funded by civil society or are semi-public, e. g. the social and solidarity economy, citizens' cooperatives, etc. Due to their specific focus, orientation and, not least, size, many of these activities are of negligible relevance for the large investors mentioned above. There is an obvious discrepancy in granularity here with large investments primarily targeting large, international climate protection projects; however, there is also a conflict of institutional logics and motivations. This article attempts to explore this field of tension and illustrates possible post-growth approaches within the financial economy.

Post-growth debates and research have paid intensive and increasingly differentiated attention to topics like production, consumption, models of working hours, land ownership and infrastructure (Weiss/Cattaneo 2017; Demaria/Kallis/Bakker 2019) but has to date displayed little concern with the financial sector. Although work on alternative or parallel currencies, the renaissance of cooperative banks or ethical forms of investment has fairly explicit links to post-growth, more fundamental and critical consideration of the established financial system has only been undertaken on a more general level. This includes, for instance, neo-Marxist critiques of financialisation and civil-society debates about the social and ecological dimensions of the global financial economy (e. g. *Finance Watch*).

When postulating a post-growth reorientation of the economy, two perspectives on the financial sector seem particularly interesting. First, what is the role of finance in the transition to more sustainable economic approaches (for initial findings on the energy transition see, e. g., Zademach/Dichtl 2016)? Second, to what extent do the business models and practices of the financial economy remain entrenched in growth logics or indeed themselves create continued pressure for growth (for instance for corporations and banks) through the prevailing loan and interest system? Socio-economic and socio-ecological transformation is not possible without the credible participation of the financial institutes. However, 'profit-seeking, risk management and regulation' have made a political-moral problem into an economic one where 'the much-maligned capital markets... play a central role', as the news magazine *Der Spiegel* recently commented (translated from German)[1]. The discussion in the article concerned carbon emissions trading, the EU's 'key tool for reducing greenhouse gas emissions cost-effectively'[2] and large infrastructural projects in the energy field. Such projects result from one-off decisions in favour of solar energy or other sustainable energy sources

---

1 https://www.spiegel.de/wirtschaft/soziales/kann-uns-der-kapitalismus-noch-retten-a-f70ee45b-fab3-4740-9a06-60678b5b1dcf?sara_ecid=soci_upd_wbMbjhOSvViIS-jc8RPU89NcCvtlFc] (20.01.2020)

2 https://ec.europa.eu/clima/policies/ets_en (09.01.2020)

and then define long-term, transregional or even transnational development paths.

Against this background, it seems particularly important to consider more closely the current dynamic development of a financial sector that increasingly portrays itself as be(com)ing 'green'. This development is driven by the growing pressure for adaptation (climate debate, divestment campaigns, new policies, etc.) faced by the financial industry in light of the new circumstances and requirements of the real economy. Furthermore, the financial industry needs to contain the speculative forces that are currently arising from a horrendous imbalance between too much capital[3] and too few (profitable) investment options. The demands for a more sustainable financial system that were made during the most recent financial crisis in 2008/2009 went largely unheard. Indeed, it is unclear how this restructuring should occur and which direction it should take. A ubiquitous catchphrase that describes one version/vision of the financial system of the future is 'green finance', a term that is not only scintillating but also imprecise (Dörry/Schulz 2018). The emerging decisions that indicate possible directions of development are unfolding on many levels and along diverse fault lines defined by conflicting interests and philosophies. Like in the manufacturing sector, it is possible to make a distinction between advocates of a 'technological fix' and proponents of a more fundamental transformation of the economic system. Those supporting a technological fix focus primarily on tackling symptoms rather than causes. They thus call for a 'business as usual' approach, continuing the growth-oriented economic model of the past (in the sense of 'weak' ecological modernisation; Christoff 1996). This distinguishes them from the proponents of a fundamental restructuring of the economic system.

This dualism is manifested in the financial economy between advocates of the prevalent greening hype and advocates of alternative financial

---

3 Of relevance here is the significance of speculatively driven financial activities, but discussion of this aspect is beyond the scope of the paper. Further, massive private wealth is a continually growing part of the financial industry largely based on the legal 'coding' of capital (Pistor 2019), which, together with sophisticated tax regulations, ensures the unrestricted protection of private rents. This represents an enormous field of assets which potentially could productively release immense sums of private capital and thus contribute to more social justice and environmentally friendly investments (although this is illusionary in the current circumstances).

approaches. The latter aim to initiate fundamental change and view financial capitalism as inadequate for the challenges lying ahead. Currently, alternative financial approaches tend to be assessed as marginal and barely scalable. They therefore receive comparatively little political attention – this is also the case against the background of the failure of the Madrid climate summit in December 2019. Nonetheless, new ways of thinking of this sort offer opportunities on the regional level (Zademach/Hillebrand 2014). On the global level, increasing equity gaps are evident, i. e. a funding gap of private capital amounting to billions of euros that must be filled by public sponsors and venture capital finance in order to fund transformation, especially in the areas of social and physical infrastructure (energy, mobility, education, etc.). UNCTAD estimates that funding the ambitious Sustainable Development Goals (SDG) in the long term will require about ca. 5-7 billion US dollars annually (UNEP FI 2018: 3).

Strengthening the role of the public sector also provides opportunities for correcting certain trends in the current financial system. In this respect, by 2050 the EU aims to achieve the ambitious objective of reducing greenhouse gas emissions by 80-95 % in comparison to 1990. A gigantic transformation of this sort requires not only long-term funding but also the restructuring of the financial economy and its governance to create a sustainable system. This is, among other things, a significant driver for the recent development of a *green taxonomy*, which was developed under the leadership of the EU Commission and entered into force on 12 July 2020. In a certain sense, it sets high standards for rethinking the European financial sector. There is a link here to the pending reorientation of the national development banks (e. g. KfW) and their European counterparts (EIB and EIF) to focus on promoting innovation and sustainable business practices by European companies. At present however, sustainability in the financial economy is primarily related to the 'green' domain, which focuses particularly on climate finance.

The two superordinate fields – the sustainable and the 'green' financial economy – in turn harbour numerous nuances and ventures, which cannot be comprehensively addressed here. Due to space limitations, we restrict ourselves rather to broad distinctions and speak, for example, of 'green finance' as an important sub-sector of an emerging 'sustainable' financial industry. The article attempts to systemise the broad lines of argument and to provide an overview of the current state of this complex discussion, followed by succinct consideration of whether and where areas of intersection can be identified and brought together in practice. We believe it is important to include spatial-social dimensions of financial activities (preferably ones that are in transformation) and to outline their effects on regional economies, as these issues are largely ignored by the dominant discourse of the economic mainstream. Hence, this chapter seeks to exploratively outline how and to what extent green financial technologies could contribute to the development of sustainable, post-growth, regional economic cycles. The discussion provides an overview of current scientific approaches and the policy programmes of green finance (Section 2), considers the essential specifics of financing dynamics and logics on different scales (Sections 3 and 4), and concludes by looking ahead and attempting to bring both areas together (Section 5).

2. 'Green finance' – an overview of the current debates and state of research

The research field of green finance is still in the process of emerging. It is also characterised by a somewhat unclear structure, as different disciplines pursue their own research foci and individual institutions bring the interests of strategically important industries and large companies (lignite, automotive industry, etc.) more or less prominently into the discussions. Furthermore, mainstream economists continue to focus on economic growth and, in particular, on elaboration of new rules based on market mechanisms, an uncritical development of financial capitalism that is inherently at odds with sustainable finance. Examples are market-based policy instruments such as emissions trading systems or the attempt to reorder the markets using financial products like green bonds, despite the questionable certification processes related to such bonds (see Section 3 on certification agencies). On the international level, programmes like REDD+ (Reducing Emissions from Deforestation and Forest Degradation) reflect the parallel implementation of economic *and* ecological logics, which – like other programmes – have very different local, subnational and national effects and hinder international harmonisation of green certification for financial products. These individual spatial sensitivities are still hardly considered in the new regulations of the international economic organisations, as we demonstrate in Section 3.

In light of the increase in financial, business and market activities that do not question the growth ideal but are supposed to help solve a multitude of environmental and social problems, it is also important to explore what happens in the transition process when conflicting goals arise from environmental and financial interests. It is necessary to investigate the extent to which an economisation of environmental and development policy leads to processes of rent seeking / rent capture, i. e. to intensified commodification and financialisation – and thus to inequitable access to ubiquities like clean water and clean air, to mention just some examples. The relevance of cross-disciplinary investigation of green finance is thus obvious. But what is meant by 'green finance'? Green finance is part of and not clearly distinct from sustainable finance, which is succinctly defined by the 'Finance Initiative' of the UN Environment Programme (UNEP FI 2018): 'Sustainable finance … seeks alignment with sustainable development targets and policies' (ibid.: 48).

The Sustainable Development Goals (SDGs) are intended to ensure sustainability in economic, social and ecological terms for the foreseeable future. The concept of the Environmental, Social and Governance (ESG) criteria is to set binding standards for sustainable capital, investment and finance, although green finance focuses primarily on environmental investment criteria and climate finance. However, problematic in the long term is that the entire programme of influential international organisations (OECD, UNO, etc.) and multilateral development banks (EIB, ADB, World Bank, etc.) focuses on economic growth, as revealed in the wording of encouragements to private capital investment, for example: '…these could crowd in private investors … as it becomes compellingly clear that the prosperity and well-being of communities is the best way to grow markets and remain competitive' (UNEP FI 2018: 23).

Another issue affecting green finance is insufficient awareness of the importance of context, as reflected in the way in which green finance is assigned different roles in different settings. The investments and financing mainly target the long-term development of non-fossil energy sources and large infrastructure projects (power grids, etc.), which should be accompanied by more social justice and, in particular, long-term returns. In the context of the European and Western industrialised states, green finance is intended to primarily help drive the climate-neutral / climate-friendly transformation of society and the economy. The prevailing line of thought, as seen in the taxonomies, programmes and guidelines for the coming years, is one of a 'technological fix'. However, the aim for the developing and emerging countries is to develop their economies in a climate-friendly and sustainable fashion from the outset, not least to prevent migration and provide growth options for the saturated markets of the Western world. The challenges and parameters therefore differ. In many countries, the implementation and supervision of projects financed (and certified) as 'green' and included in the portfolios of large institutional investors are non-existent or do not comply with Western standards, which then hinders or even prevents urgently needed investment.

In the Western world, large investors and enterprises, reacting among other things to increasing public pressure (Fridays for Future, etc.), have started to reschedule (and redeploy) their investment portfolios (and supply chains). In this way, they are breaking away from the long-dominant, profits-at-all-costs approach dictated by the shareholder-value paradigm and instead pushing for 'impact investments'. While impact investments aim for wealth creation through economic goals, they also want to make positive, measurable (and thus communicable!) social and ecological contributions. A ground-breaking warning was recently issued by Larry Fink, head of the world's largest asset manager BlackRock[4], in which he stressed the rising capital costs and increasing investment risk that would arise if climate and sustainability risks were not adequately addressed. In addition, Fink expects a 'significant reallocation of capital', which is already beginning to manifest itself despite the failed Madrid climate summit. The necessity of decarbonisation is thus driving a shift in the financial and the real economy towards ESG goals (Green and Sustainable Finance Cluster Germany 2018). However, many corporate and bank balance sheets still rely on carbon-based production, and the conversion of large corporate groups to green(er) supply chains is almost unachievable in the short term. The political field in Germany waited too long to introduce binding requirements. But leading industrial enterprises also tend to underestimate the force of the current transition, as demonstrated by the example of Siemens continuing to build new infrastructure for large Australian coal-fired power plants despite pressure from the general (young) public. While it is necessary to give up 'brown energy',

---

4 https://www.blackrock.com/ch/individual/en/larry-fink-ceo-letter?switchLocale=Y (20.01.2020)

it is an extremely risky process in financial terms (G20 2016; Hebb/Hawley/Hoepner et al. 2016; TCFD 2017) as investments made today are tied up in the long-term, often for decades. The pressure to take action means that investors and financiers, as well as political players, are exposed to the danger of choosing the 'wrong' technology paths. Large volumes of disinvestment will therefore also have a significant impact on regional and national economies with primarily CO_2-based energy supplies. This is unchanged by the fact that in the context of quantitative easing (QE) launched in 2012, the ECB under Christine Lagarde declared 'protecting the environment' to be a new core task, promoting green bonds in particular.

These examples clearly demonstrate how important it is to better understand the spatial dimensions of the financial economy – and particularly new financial instruments and financial technologies, in order to address the 'territorial gap' in research and policy related to the implications of particular financial instruments (ESPON 2019). In this context, the literature on financing economic growth has long pointed to both the enormous importance of 'patient capital' and of effective institutions and governments (Commission on Growth and Development 2008) for the productive use and efficient allocation of long-term investments.

These praiseworthy developments are, however, still countered by a certain presumptuousness in the financial industry – to a certain extent underpinned by a lack of corporate resources and knowledge – concerning how the ESG goals should be incorporated in their own portfolios and corporate strategies. This enormous need for new knowledge is being met by many associations and educational/research institutions but their new and evolving offerings in turn require verification and harmonisation. The international financial centres (IFCs), often associated with renowned financial degree programmes at universities, are important localities where this bundled knowledge circulates. However, there is increasing criticism of such one-sided assertions of knowledge sovereignty about green finance, and ever louder calls for the integrative degree programmes of social and environmental sciences to be incorporated in sustainable financial degree programmes.

In face of the complexity of the transition in the financial industry, in 2018 the European Commission adopted the 'Commission Action Plan on Financing Sustainable Growth', advising on which economic activities are ecologically sustainable. This includes reference to the 'Green Taxonomy' of the EU on financing sustainable economic activities, which provides a benchmark for green investments and disclosure of the individual fulfilment of ESG targets. Furthermore, new rankings of 'green' IFCs (UNEP 2017) indicate that their financial ecosystems (including regulators, banks/non-banks[5], rating agencies, law and accounting firms, etc.) have recognised the need for sustainable financing measures and a 'greening' process. Critics also comment on the strong tendency for 'green washing' (Technical Expert Group on Sustainable Finance 2019), not least because sustainable (direct and indirect) finance is primarily undertaken by powerful financial corporations whose activities are closely embedded in the existing logics of financial capitalism.

An important focus in the literature on the relationship between finance and economic development is on the significant shift of global finance and investments away from the banks to private lenders and 'non-banks' who use financial innovations (e. g. social bonds and blended finance, as discussed below) to add 'value' to the portfolios of both private and public investors. This provides the financial industry with an increasing range of new options for the sustainable financing of innovative enterprises and infrastructures (Kaminker/Youngman 2015; UNEP 2011; G20 2016). It also entails a need to better tailor the new financial instruments to the individual financing requirements of regions in order to support their individual capacity building and resilience in the face of future challenges. Little of the progress proclaimed in these progressive visions has so far been implemented or, indeed, can be implemented.

While avoiding 'green washing' is important, so too is preventing so-called 'white washing' where financial institutions only react superficially to the financing needs of social enterprises. This requires a re-evaluation of 'social impact investments' and 'ethical investments'. To this end, the EU has established a Social Impact Accelerator, a public-private finance partnership for impact investments and social entrepreneurship throughout Europe (EIF 2017). Among the leading financial instruments for impact investments are social impact bonds (SIBs), a controversial results-oriented form of impact investment in which state interventions intended to solve social problems are financed with capital from private investors who expect a corresponding return on investment. In connection to this, impact investments known as

---

5 In the jargon of the financial economy, 'non-banks' refers to credit institutions other than banks, e. g. investment funds, venture capital funds and sovereign wealth funds.

development impact bonds (DIBs) and blended finance have emerged, a form of public-private impact investment that is currently important for funding social care and addressing socio-economic inequalities. As with green finance however, taxonomies for 'ethical' and 'social' investments are still in their infancy, have seldom been tested and depend on the development of definitions of a common terminology and on harmonisation with the goals of green (and blue = water-focused) taxonomies.

Furthermore, digitalisation and technologisation provide opportunities to 'disrupt' the established financial system and to promote and accelerate a transition to sustainability. However, few connections have to date been established between sustainable finance and FinTech/digitisation. 'FinTech' is a fairly new term that refers to the convergence of finance and technology, facilitating the creation of digital and online financial products and services. Yet, FinTech also raises questions about systemic risks and appropriate alignment with urban and regional agendas (Dowling 2017; UNEP 2016). The expectation is that in the course of these developments, the IFCs will also have to adapt to shifting roles in the production of sustainable finance. In addition to new growth opportunities, all this also involves new uncertainties about whether existing financial enterprises and industry networks can profit from the new market participants and technologies, for instance when new, alternative forms of finance emerge, such as peer-to-peer lending (crowdfunding) or new kinds of supply chain finance (UNEP 2016; CISL 2017). The 'FinTech Action Plan' (European Commission 2018) aims to promote a more competitive, innovative and stable European financial sector with innovative business models on the EU level; yet again, the action plan is based on growth and has no explicit link to 'sustainable finance' or GreenTech (also see Messner/Schlacke/Fromhold-Eisebith et al. 2019; Technical Expert Group on Sustainable Finance 2019).

3. The logic of green classification systems

New green standards are now used to classify financial products. The following discussion considers the recently developed EU taxonomy for environmentally sustainable economic activities and the role of certification agencies for sustainable financial products and investment strategies, and explains the basic mechanisms of these legitimising green norms. The ecosystem of green standards has already established itself in many financial centres, and this 'engine room' of IFCs is – also for the reasons mentioned above – influenced by powerful interests from industry, politics and society/science.

EU taxonomy[6]

The 'Taxonomy for Sustainable Activities' is part of a series of directed measures within the EU Action Plan on Sustainable Finance. The classification system consists of a list of economic activities with performance criteria that should significantly contribute towards six environmental goals – climate change mitigation, climate change adaptation, protection of water and marine resources, transition to a circular economy, pollution prevention, protection of ecosystems (Technical Expert Group on Sustainable Finance 2019: 3). This is intended to attract capital to achieve the sustainability goals. According to the EU, the 'Green Taxonomy' itself is a 'flexible' and 'dynamic' list of economic activities and criteria relevant for sustainability that 'based on latest scientific and industry experience' (ibid.: 5) can be altered and extended. Ensuring the compliance of the financial strategies and investment portfolios of large institutional investors with these criteria is one of the key challenges for the transition to a more sustainable financial economy. This is audited and communicated by independent certification agencies.

Another closely linked problem that influences the transition to a green financial market is that the taxonomy is a simple binary system: an investment is either green or it is not green. This problem has received scarcely any attention to date; the so-called ESG data shocks (Schumacher/Baek/Nishikizawa 2021) that result can, however, be devastating for investors, halving the market value of enterprises overnight. The principle can be demonstrated with the example of VW's diesel scandal – unrelated to the green taxonomy. An independent study undertaken by the ICCT first officially detected the elevated pollutant levels at VW, rather than the car manufacturer itself or the state supervisory authorities. VW's market value fell substantially after the results were published and the economic and reputational damage for

---

6 The article describes the situation at the beginning of 2020. The EU taxonomy debate has developed considerably since then, as have other phenomena covered/addressed in this chapter.

the corporation were significant. A similar logic would apply in a situation where certification agencies were too generous when certifying green financial products. Independent ex-post audits could then lead to the shares losing their green status. This would not only impact on investors who purchased the shares in good faith for their green investment portfolio but also on the enterprises that had profited from this green investment and now lost their financing and an essential element of their long-term business plan. Such a case is also likely to lead to ruinous damage to the reputation of the certification agencies and thus of the financial centres and financial supervisory authorities that host and supervise the agencies.

Certification agencies

Certification agencies like LuxFlag (Luxembourg) or FNG (Germany) are now a significant element of the ecosystem of IFCs. They are committed to ecological and sustainable principles but primarily use common market and growth logics for implementation and certification. There are large differences between the certification agencies, for instance in terms of transparency in cases when the 'green' standard is awarded. Several testing agencies disclose their questionnaires and the results of their evaluations (at least in part) and thus make their decisions easily comprehensible to the public, but others keep a lower profile, seemingly exploiting this advantage to provide faster certification. If the increasing number of NGOs in the environmental sector and other independent institutes make spot checks of such certifications and reach different conclusions to the testing agencies, this will directly affect the performance of regional and global investment portfolios. Trading in green securities, which then would no longer be 'green', would decline rapidly and thus also directly affect trading on the secondary markets; as a result, many large investors like insurance companies and pension funds would want and need to dump significant bond investments without this green 'label'. At least in the short term, the market would collapse due to a lack of buyers. In short: the market for green finance would suffer considerable and lasting damage. The economic and social consequences of a so-called ESG data shock would be similarly far-reaching: all kinds of projects (e. g. climate and infrastructure projects) that represent large, long-term investments and drive local development would face financing difficulties overnight.

Sections 2 and 3 have broadly outlined the logics of green finance and its classification by certification agencies. Clearly, it is not only the definition of new green standards that is complex and complicated, but also their implementation. For reasons of brevity, we have omitted discussion of the way in which governance structures must change to support the transition of the financial system across very different scales. What should be noted, however, is that the transition to a green financial system at least promises to move away from the short-term focus on shareholder value and to bring long-term ecological and social criteria back to centre stage. The public sector has a major role to play in the form of start-up finance and risk assumption, providing important impulses and incentives for private investment. We believe that this can also open up regional scope for individually linking private sector approaches with sustainable finance. However, this requires that appropriate parameters are created by developing regional institutions and governance to enable the upscaling and equal raison d'être of successful, regional and alternative forms of economic activity and financing. Section 4 discusses a few such examples.

4. Alternative finance instruments and logics

Similar to the situation with the internationally propagated green economy (UNEP 2011) and alternative, post-growth variations (Kenis/Lievens 2015; Bina 2013; Davies 2013; Gibbs/O'Neill 2017; Schulz/Bailey 2014), there are alternatives to the global 'greening' financial sector that are motivated by fundamentally different interests and are generally more public-welfare oriented. By way of example, three increasingly popular instruments are presented here and assessed in terms of their transformative potential: first, complementary currencies and their role in regional value creation; second, forms of the 'collaborative economy' that are supported and co-financed by civil society; and third, the 'renaissance' of cooperative organisations and their investment models.

Complementary currencies

Also known as 'regional currencies', these complementary means of payment have emerged in many places since the 1990s. They are a way to develop and support regional circular economies that – embedded in the logic of alternative economies – successfully break away from over-consumption, speculation with natural 'assets' and land, and economic inflation at the regional level (Thiel 2011; Seyfang 2001). They can promote socially and environmentally sustainable production with short, primarily regional supply chains (Kopatz 2015). *Regiogeld* (regiomoney), as regional currencies are also known in German-speaking countries,

> ... is a type of money privately issued in the form of hard cash and accepted by a number of participants. Its validity is regionally limited, it carries a negative interest rate (or is at least interest-free) and it pursues non-profit objectives (Thiel 2011: 134, translated from German).

Advocates of regional currencies, whose experience goes back to about the 2000s (North 2006, 2007; Lietaer/Dunne 2013), suggest that they bring great regional benefits linked to the explicit promotion of non-profit projects (Gelleri, 2013). In Germany, such currencies include the *'Chiemgauer'* (founded in 2002), the *'Tauber-Franken'* (2005), the *'Landmark'* (2004) and the *'Berliner Regional'* (2005). It is argued that the regions that practise such alternative forms of self-organisation are more stable and effectively crisis-resilient than open regional economic systems that are closely integrated in global value creation and speculation systems (Kopatz, 2015: 105). Such stability is supported by the constant circulation of the regional currency, driven by its interest-free character and stringent devaluation, which often involves 'statutory depreciation days' (Thiel 2011, translated from German). Furthermore, local identity and the social cohesion of inhabitants is strengthened through voluntary work, exchange, cooperation and other social innovations. Seyfang (2001) notes that in the 1990s, the goals of many regional currencies were extended to include broader social and political objectives in addition to ecological aims, especially targeting the formation of community spirit through reciprocity and local participation. In the German debate, increasing attention is being paid to questions concerning the institutionalisation of complementary currencies in market-based economic systems (Degen 2016; Doerr 2019).

Current debates about regional currencies are usually conceptually anchored in or inspired by much earlier and more fundamental attempts to develop complementary currencies. The pioneer of such approaches and probably the most successful project to date was the Swiss 'WIR-Bank', which has existed since 1934. Based on Silvio Gesell's 'free economy' ideas, the *'Wirtschaftsring'* ('Swiss Economic Circle') was founded as an alternative network which today comprises over 50,000 small and medium-sized enterprises. With a turnover of more than 5.5 billion Swiss francs (in 2019), the *Wirtschaftsring* is considerably larger in terms of volume and geographical reach than the aforementioned regional currencies (Stodder/Lietaer 2015). The *'WIR-francs'*, like a growing number of other regional currencies, today often use electronic methods of payment (cash cards, smartphone apps). There is hope that such developments will improve public acceptance of such currencies thanks to their low threshold use.

Collaborative economies and financing models

The example of the community supported agriculture (CSA) is used to demonstrate how civil-society initiatives and idealistic, financial and operational commitment can maintain and further develop sustainable economies. 'CSA' initiatives have emerged not only in urban hinterlands but also in more rural regions and represent a particular form of social engagement working to preserve and develop farming and agriculture in line with sustainability goals. Members of the public can become financially involved (see below) but can also play an active role on the farm. As prosumers who develop an emotional link to the food they purchase, they thus contribute towards the farm's survival (on the role of alternative food networks see Rosol 2018 for more detail). There are various diverse 'CSA' funding models, ranging from formal participation (shares, participation certificates, cooperative shares, partial land ownership) to specific subscription models[7] and concepts based on the commons. In order to gain the basic finance necessary for an operating year,

---

7 In comparison to commercial subscriptions (such as 'vegetable boxes'), they are often more tied to the subscriber's personal contribution/shares and are more dependent on the harvest.

the commons approach, for example, holds so-called 'bidding rounds'. After a budgeting plan and a minimum budget have been presented, all members are asked to voluntarily submit bids to finance some part of the operations in line with their individual capacities. These bidding rounds are repeated as often as necessary to secure the target annual budget. In contrast to models based on participation certificates or subscriptions, this approach decouples the 'giving' and 'taking'. Silke Helfrich sees a 'general pattern of social transformation' in this abandonment of 'the principle of equivalent exchange' (Helfrich 2015: 47, translated from German). A similar decoupling, i. e. financial commitment with no expectation of an absolutely equivalent return, can also be observed in the increasingly popular (internet-based) crowdfunding.

Cooperative banks and investments for the common good

Growing criticism of the financialised world economy, the decoupling of the business models of the financial economy from the financial needs of the real economy, and, not least, issues linked to ecological sustainability and social justice have led to louder calls for finance to focus more strongly on the common good. In addition to the established cooperative banks (e. g. Volks- und Raiffeisen-Banken, GLS-Bank) and public financial institutions (e. g. Sparkassen), a number of civil society initiatives have led to the establishment of more 'citizens banks'. These banks tend to offer their members ESG-compliant savings and deposits options and specific financing concepts. The spectrum of organisations ranges from small local cooperative banks to regional players (e. g. Caisse Solidaire Nord-Pas-de-Calais/Lille) to nationwide and even cross-border models (e. g. Triodos Belgium/Netherlands, Alternative Bank Switzerland, etika Luxembourg) (also see Dörry/Schulz 2018).

Alongside the establishment of alternative banks, voices from civil society are also demanding that the goals and business practices of public institutions should be more closely aligned with the common good. In Belgium, for example, where the state rescue of the Belgian branch of the DEXIA bank in 2012 led to the creation of a new public bank (Belfius), the movement *'Belfius est à nous'* ('Belfius belongs to us') is vehemently demanding more transparency and co-determination. And in Germany, increasing complaints can be heard about the void left by the 'Bank für Gemeinwirtschaft' (BfG), primarily in the context of current debates on affordable housing, public housing construction and municipal real estate holdings. The real estate sector provides another interesting example. Not only are the business practices of this increasingly financialised industry being critically questioned, but alternatives with a common-good orientation are being tested and established with new forms of housing and associated financing and planning models (e. g. joint building ventures ['*Baugruppen*'], new housing cooperatives, independently organised apartment building projects ['*Mietshäuser Syndikate*']).

5. Conclusion and discussion

The above examples show that fundamental changes in production and consumption are, and will increasingly be, dependent on a transformation in the finance sector. These adaptations will need to extend beyond consideration of ethical, social and ecological minimum standards in established products and investment strategies. The finance sector is rather called upon to question conventional business models and their one-sided growth fixation and to focus on the common good. The challenges associated with this are immense – not only in light of the enormous sums of finance that need to be administered and relocated but also in terms of inert systemic constraints. Systemic constraints can be found both in the financial sector itself (new standards, business practices, self-conceptions, value systems, training focuses, etc.) and at a higher level (tax, interest and depreciation policies, economic and research funding, financial market regulation).

If a possible post-growth transition is understood as a democratic process involving the redefinition of societal goals, then it is clear that the reorientation of the financial economy will be part of this process of negotiation. This is obviously easiest where, for example, new public-interest banks are founded (see above), but it can also occur where banks are already publicly or cooperatively owned and, for instance, municipal decision-makers have a right to be heard. Greater proximity to the local dynamics of the real economy and to changing financial needs and investment strategies may favour more fundamental transformations here. At the same time this could offer a new perspective for banks, which are increasingly deprived of their traditional commercial basis in these times of low interest rates, digitalisation and (re-)regulation. It remains to be seen whether this pressure to adapt also similarly impacts non-banks which are practically exempt from banking regulation despite their similar business models. Generally, however, there is also increasing pressure to adapt in the non-banking sector. And it can be assumed that the shift to technology-based fields only postpones the more fundamental need for solutions. The forces of inertia are complex, systemic and integrative, as revealed, for instance, in the daily provision of global liquidity via (largely unregulated) interbank trading and the great dependency of our social security systems on the global financial industry, for instance via the banks, pension funds, life insurance companies and, not least, the functionality of important financial market infrastructures such as SWIFT, Clearstream and Euroclear.

In view of current debates on global climate protection, distributive justice and taxation justice, it seems probable that a central role will be played by the international financial centres with their knowledge bases, innovation potentials and geostrategic positions. It is not yet possible to predict the extent to which the current 'greening efforts' of IFCs favour or facilitate the fundamental transformation of the sector or whether the 'business as usual' policy that they imply actually hinders such a transformation. It is, however, beyond doubt that a significant reorientation of the sector towards post-growth goals will not be able to develop from within the financial sector alone. Rather, strong political, regulatory and scientific support for the process is needed – ideally based on a broad social consensus on the necessity and desirability of transition.

Cited literature

Bina, O. (2013). The green economy and sustainable development: an uneasy balance? *Environment and Planning C: Government and Policy, 31*(6), 1023–1047.

Christoff, P. (1996). Ecological modernisation, ecological modernities. *Environmental Politics, 5*(3), 476–500.

CISL – University of Cambridge Institute for Sustainability Leadership (2017). *Rewiring the economy. Ten tasks, ten years*. Cambridge.

Commission on Growth and Development (2008). *The growth report. Strategies for sustained growth and inclusive development*. World Bank Group Publications.

Davies, A. R. (2013). Cleantech clusters: Transformational assemblages for a just, green economy or just business as usual? *Global Environmental Change, 23*(5), 1285–1295.

Degen, P. (2016). Anderes Geld - Anderes Wirtschaften? Unternehmen und Regiogeld. *Neue Soziale Bewegungen, 29*(3), 98–109.

Demaria, F., Kallis, G., & Bakker, K. (2019). Geographies of degrowth: Nowtopias, resurgences and the decolonization of imaginaries and places. *Environment and Planning E: Nature and Space, 2*(3), 431–450.

Doerr, J.-T. (2019). *Grassroots initiatives and rural development. 40 years of associative democracy in Beckerich and the Canton Réiden.* University of Luxembourg (unpublished).

Dörry, S., & Schulz, C. (2018). Green financing, interrupted. Potential directions for sustainable finance in Luxembourg. *Local Environment, 23*(7), 717–733.

Dowling, E. (2017). In the wake of austerity: social impact bonds and the financialisation of the welfare state in Britain. *New Political Economy, 22*(3), 294–310.

EIF – European Investment Fund (2017). *EFSI Equity social impact investment instruments.*

ESPON (2019). *Financial Instruments and Territorial Cohesion.*

European Commission (2018). *FinTech Action plan: For a more competitive and innovative European financial sector.* COM (2018) 109/2.

G20 (2016). *G20 Green Finance Synthesis Report.*

Gibbs, D., & O'Neill, K. (2017). Future green economies and regional development: a research agenda. *Regional Studies, 51*(1), 161–173.

Green and Sustainable Finance Cluster Germany (2018). *Shaping the future – green and sustainable finance in Germany.* GSFC.

Hebb, T., Hawley, J. P., Hoepner, A. G., Neher, A. L., & Wood, D. (2016). *The Routledge Handbook of Responsible Investment.* Routledge.

Helfrich, S. (2015). Muster gemeinsamen Handelns. Wie wir zu einer Sprache des Commoning kommen. In S. Helfrich, D. Bollier, & Heinrich-Böll-Stiftung (Eds.), *Die Welt der Commons. Muster Gemeinsamen Handelns.* transcript, 36–54.

Kaminker, C., & Youngman, R. (2015). *Sustainable energy infrastructure, finance and institutional investors.* http://m.oecdobserver.org/news/fullstory.php/aid/5228/Sustainable_energy_infrastructure,_finance_and_institutional_investors.html (2020, February 24).

Kenis, A., & Lievens, M. (2015). *The limits of the green economy: From re-inventing capitalism to re-politicising the present.* Routledge.

Kopatz, M. (2015). Wirtschaftsförderung 4.0 - Kooperative Wirtschaftsformen in Kommunen. *Politische Ökologie 142*, 104–110.

Lietaer, B., & Dunne, J. (2013). *Rethinking money: How new currencies turn scarcity into prosperity.* Berrett-Koehler Publishers.

Messner, D., Schlacke, S., Fromhold-Eisebith, M., Grote, U., Matthies, E., Pittel, K., Schellnhuber, H. J., Schieferdecker, I., & Schneidewind, U. (2019). *Digital momentum for the UN Sustainability Agenda in the 21st century.* Berlin. Policy Paper 10.

North, P. (2006). *Alternative currency movements as a challenge to globalisation?* Routledge.

North, P. (2007). *Money and liberation: The micropolitics of alternative currency movements.* University of Minnesota Press.

Pistor, K. (2019). *The code of capital: How the law creates wealth and inequality.* Princeton University Press.

Rosol, M. (2018). Alternative Ernährungsnetzwerke als Alternative Ökonomien. *Zeitschrift für Wirtschaftsgeographie, 62*(3-4), 174–186.

Schulz, C., & Bailey, I. (2014). The green economy and post-growth regimes: Opportunities and challenges for economic geography. *Geografiska Annaler, 96*(3), 277–291.

Schumacher, K., Baek, Y. J., & Nishikizawa, S. (2021). The impact of endogenous firm-level sustainability data on ESG scores and ratings. *Tokyo Institute of Technology Working Paper – G0007.*

Seyfang, G. (2001). Community currencies: Small change for a green economy. *Environment and Planning, 33*(6), 975–996.

Stodder, J., & Lietaer, B. (2015). WIR – Eine Währung, die den Tausch neu erfindet. In S. Helfrich, D. Bollier, & Heinrich-Böll-Stiftung (Eds.), *Die Welt der Commons. Muster Gemeinsamen Handelns.* transcript, 196–198.

TCFD – Task Force on Climate-related Financial Disclosures (2017). *Final report: Recommendations of the task force on climate-related financial disclosures.*

Technical Expert Group on Sustainable Finance (2019). *Using the taxonomy. Supplementary report.*

Thiel, C. (2011). *Das „bessere" Geld. Eine ethnographische Studie über Regionalwährungen.* VS Verlag.

UNEP – United Nations Environment Programme (2011). *Towards a green economy. Pathways to sustainable development and poverty eradication. A synthesis for policy makers.* https://sustainabledevelopment.un.org/content/documents/126GER_synthesis_en.pdf (2020, February 25).

UNEP – United Nations Environment Programme (2016). *Fintech and sustainable development. Assessing the implications.* http://unepinquiry.org/wp-content/uploads/2016/12/Fintech_and_Sustainable_Development_Assessing_the_Implications.pdf (2020, February 25).

UNEP – United Nations Environment Programme (2017). *Accelerating financial centre action on sustainable development.* http://unepinquiry.org/wp-content/uploads/2017/12/Accelerating_Financial_Centre_Action_on_Sustainable_Development.pdf (2020, February 25).

UNEP FI – United Nations Environment Programme Finance Initiative (2018). *Rethinking Impact to finance the SDGs.* https://www.unepfi.org/wordpress/wp-content/uploads/2018/11/Rethinking-Impact-to-Finance-the-SDGs.pdf (2020, February 25).

Weiss, M., & Cattaneo, C. (2017). Degrowth – Taking stock and reviewing an emerging academic paradigm. *Ecological Economics,* 137, 220–230.

Zademach, H.-M., & Dichtl, J. (2016). Greening finance and financing the green: Considerations and observations on the role of finance in energy transitions. In A. Jones, P. Ström, B. Hermelin, & G. Rusten (Eds), *Services and the green economy.* Palgrave Macmillan, 153–174.

Zademach, H.-M., & Hillebrand, S. (2014). *Alternative Economies and Spaces, New Perspectives for a Sustainable Economy.* transcript.

'Status quo avant-gardists' and 'prevention innovators'
Food for thought for the geographical post-growth debate

Bastian Lange, Hans-Joachim Bürkner

1. Polarised discourses and antagonistic reactions to transformations

Political and media discourses in Germany about climate change, energy efficiency, ecological transformation, urban transition and a renunciation of economic growth principles are currently characterised by all the signs of moral polarisation. It is apparently once again about the eternal fight between good and evil, right and wrong. In contrast to many other political controversies, in these discourses the opponents cannot be easily divided into the powerful and the dominated. Rather, new asymmetrical coalitions can be observed – most recently in the compromise reached for phasing out coal at the end of 2019. Here the government and its previous critics come together in rarely seen agreement to commit to the future good and renounce past evil. In contrast, the majority of the population remains largely silent.

Although socio-economic polarisation is progressing, there are only a few, sporadic examples of 'deep drilling' (Bude/Medicus/Willisch 2011) research into geographical milieus that bring differentiation to the coarse-grained debate. Even investigations of environmental awareness in specific milieus often fail to be particularly differentiated, especially if they are loosely based on the well-known Sinus milieus drawn up by the Sinus Institute (Barth/Flaig/Schäuble et al. 2018; cf. www.sinus-institute.de). Such research tends to point out the general relevance of 'young distanced', 'marginal' and 'traditional' milieus (Bundesministerium für Umwelt 2019: 14, 75-78), groups that are said to have little interest in possible solutions to ecological and environmental change. To date, the spatiality of such milieus is still unclear. The only findings about their spatial distribution or the spatially differentiated self-understandings of actors suggest – if at all – a vague urban-rural division (ibid.).

All other milieus, i.e. the so-called established milieu, the critical-creative milieu, the idealistic milieu and also parts of the bourgeois milieu (Bundesministerium für Umwelt 2019: 15), can be lumped together as one side. These groups react to the pressing ecological and economic crises by deriving imperatives to change capitalist economic models, consumption patterns and lifestyles. On the other side are those who do not want to submit to these imperatives, or at least not yet (the 'marginal', 'young distanced' and 'traditional' milieus). In the broad public discourse, they are often indiscriminately represented by their adversaries as opposing modernisation, denying ecological reason and rejecting dialogue.[1] Furthermore, they are also geographically localised and regionalised: the progressive forces are seen as being located in the urban centres, primarily in West Germany, in contrast the reactionary forces are found in rural areas and in the 'left-behind' peripheries, especially in East Germany.[2]

The terms formulated in the title of this paper, 'status quo avant-gardists' and 'prevention innovators', are not understood here as political battle cries. Rather, they are viewed as impartially as possible as heuristic and exploratory concepts. They are motivated by a decided analytical interest in the identification of milieu-specific, i.e. situated social innovations (see Bürkner/Lange in this volume). This allows research and policy prospects to be identified, ones that reflectively focus on groups that resist transformative policies, changes in values and recommended change. Such resistance takes various forms – sometimes subversive and quiet, but often in open communication, demonstrating discursive skill, political well-informedness and aesthetic value judgements. Those involved are not usually members of previously

---

1 For example, Chancellor Angela Merkel commented in her speech to the World Economic Forum in Davos on 23.01.2020 that a refusal to engage in dialogue 'should result in sanctions by society' (Gersemann/Zschäpitz 2020).

2 On the same occasion, Chancellor Merkel also reported that these groups need to face different profits and costs in line with their locations: urban dwellers will quickly benefit from the transformation while rural dwellers will bear a large share of the costs (Gersemann/Zschäpitz 2020).

defined Sinus milieus or lifestyle groups, nor are they everyday 'constructors' of social spaces that have already been empirically reconstructed.

Attributable forms of expression and the groups that support them have an enormous socio-political share in the success or failure of transformation efforts. Their performance and impact are usually overlooked in the public discourses, which mostly concentrate on the 'progressive' protagonists of intended change. Significantly, however, their mere presence and public visibility very quickly lead to shifts in the familiar and morally oriented categories of what is supposedly 'good' and 'right' in ecological terms.

Progressive ecological thinking has a counterpart that is often its contrary in terms of worldviews but is not so far apart in subject matter. This cannot simply be described with the popular categorical dichotomy of 'modern versus antimodern'. For instance, the catchwords propagated by members of the party 'Alternative for Germany' (*Alternative für Deutschland*, AfD) and 'right-wing environmentalists' in rural areas promote a backward-looking, exclusively 'German' attachment to the homeland and thus a return to their 'own' native soil (Röpke/Speit 2019). Ironically, there are links here to the basic convictions held by the progressive forces of younger post-growth orientations, even if only to a limited extent. One example of this is found in the emphasis that both political camps put on local communities, milieu-specific autonomy and a return to manual activities or more simple technologies – thus celebrating a paradoxical conservatism, simultaneously reactionary and progressive. At least a certain amount of green and left-wing moralising may well be due to the perplexity caused by this paradox: such actors sense that they cannot muster convincing arguments to defend themselves against right-wing appropriation.

In a search for the forces working to preserve the status quo, it may initially seem that the centre of society is beyond suspicion. Increased public awareness of dramatic global warming and the related signs of crisis mean that the urgent need for a speedy transformation of the economy and society is now being recognised by the political mainstream. Many political calls and positions adopted by science suggest that it is necessary to implement and enforce changes in the behaviour of the wider population in terms of food, mobility and consumption. In addition to the argumentative basis provided in mainstream discourse, pending legal and procedural regulations are intended to achieve this goal. However, by the end of 2019 there was no notable or measurable change to be seen in figures related to passenger flights or to the food habits of the German population, for instance in a reduction in CO_2 emissions. Even when all possible lag effects are taken into consideration, it seems clear that inertia and resistance to change continue to be ubiquitous and are by no means exceptions to the rule.

2. Why think in terms of 'status quo avant-gardists' and 'prevention innovators'?

In this article we argumentatively approach those designated modernisation and transformation opponents, dialogue blockers and deniers of environmental reason as impartially as possible. To this end, we develop a stance that rejects rampant prejudgements in favour of open analysis and thus turn the page in heuristic terms. We call on our readers to enter into thought experiments and accept a deliberate change of perspectives.

We therefore purposely use the terms 'status quo avant-gardists' and 'prevention innovators' to address groups that are often stigmatised. This shall allow for an unprejudiced and precise view of their positioning vis-à-vis issues of ecologically motivated social change. It shall also illuminate the positions they adopt in larger discourses. By employing these terms, we attribute the putative blockers with the fundamental ability to make original innovations relevant to everyday life. We thus conceptionally distance ourselves with this research programme from the public culture of latent or open prejudgement, which can be contagious within an unsettled research landscape. We perceive the unclear contradictions between an apparently institutionalised, rational neoliberalism and more ad hoc, highly emotionalised and shifting political polarisations to be particularly unsettling.

The article also draws attention to the spatial connotations of rapidly increasing political and social polarisations. In contrast to previous time periods when contrary characteristics were attributed to specific groups of the population and 'their spaces', current social antagonisms are not simply the result of slow auto-dynamic processes of social differentiation, such as social mobility and the emergence of lifestyles. Rather, it can be assumed that the contrasts are deliberately co-produced by politics, and further promoted, in some cases with manipulative intent, to the advantage of the political spokespeople concerned.

Existing socio-economic and socio-spatial disparities in West European societies are thus being politically reframed and rhetorically inflated. They are popularly expressed in opposites like modern/antimodern, progressive/reactionary or eco-conscious/environmentally unfriendly. Conceptual pairs of this sort overlap and colour prosaic opposites like rich/poor, prosperous/crisis-ridden or rural/urban, linking them to moral accusations and assignments of political position.

Crude rhetorical simplifications are no longer limited to the linguistic sphere of everyday media (e. g. digital social networks) but have extended into specialist political, planning and social-policy debates, leading to changes in discursively produced compartmentalisations. Previously empathic narratives of undeserved marginalisation have become narratives containing attributions of anti-progress and latent social threats. They now call for dissociation, a withdrawal of solidarity and sanctions. Simultaneously, such narratives often express general unease with the speed of social transformation and the sudden visibility of social differences rather than convinced political will.

It is not only the apparently progressive discourse that can be interpreted as expressing this unease but similarly also the increasing number of people who are turning to political 'alternatives' with their right-wing nationalist and, in some cases, neo-Nazi policies. These latter 'alternatives' signalise clear intentions towards inertia and a preservation of the status quo (however it may be defined), combined with a tendency towards collective opinions which are anti-progressive, counter-enlightenment and reactionary. The social split associated with progressiveness and reactionaryism probably represents only the tip of a proverbial semantic iceberg. It reduces the far-reaching and complex differentiations of the respective perceptions and policy orientations to simplifying catchwords.

In contrast, social-ecological[3] emancipatory research, which is dedicated to the manifold interactions between societies and natural phenomena, should embrace this social upheaval with curiosity and critical reflection.

---

3 We use the attribute 'social-ecological' to refer to the social transformations that are associated with individual and collective engagement with environmental problems. This includes social change that comprises changes in ideas and ideologies, social relations, policy orientations, everyday practices and forms of communication. We are aware that similar notions were established by US urban sociology in the twentieth century. However, since our focus is not primarily on the city, misunderstandings should be rare.

Urgently required pointers about the emergence of new discursive coalitions and divisions can be gained from a detailed and accurate understanding of milieu-specific and regional interpretations of the situation. The task is to explore the varieties of the construction of meaning and entrenched perspectives relevant to ecologically motivated transformation processes. Likewise, it can be expected that such an approach will uncover new potential for social integration and building bridges. Not least, it should also enable the formulation of suitably inclusive language, policy and options for institutionalisation.

From the perspective of social and spatial sciences, it is particularly interesting which constructions of meaning, patterns of interpretation and concepts of self-affirmation characterise the activities of the resistant milieus. Which categories (e. g. safety/threat, stability/upheaval, custom/ unpredictability, transparency/uncertainty) do these apparently extensive social groupings use to interpret their social and spatial surroundings? How is it that subjective statements are made that seem to be 'contrary to better and available ecological knowledge'? How 'skilfully' do these collectives ignore the dominant discursive frames and the claims to facticity embedded therein? What interpretations of their own otherness do they use to counter them? How are their concepts of otherness locally or regionally created? How effective are the corresponding patterns of interpretation in the public discourses?

In order to provide context and specific detail to this somewhat coarse-grained description of otherness, there is an urgent need to shed more light on the connections between the mainstream's disadvantaging, stigmatising and derogatory ascriptions ('modernisation opponents' and 'dialogue blockers') and the discursive processes that promote them. The aim is thus to confront the unspecific and imprecise ascriptions made by social and political opponents, and their representations in the media, with precise, context-sensitive and scientifically 'grounded' observation.

We assume that there are largely invisible but potentially influential practices of the 'status quo avant-gardists' and 'prevention innovators'. The very fact that they give rise to harsh reactions in politics and the media illustrates the impact they have already acquired. Therefore we embark on a journey to uncover the underlying collective motives, logics of action and patterns of interpretation. On the one hand, the aim is to enable a balanced analysis of social transitions that not only considers for the normatively charged drivers of change but also gives adequate space to their social counterparts. On the other hand, it is also about driving back the pejorative rhetoric which has spread like wildfire in both public and scientific descriptions of change-resistant milieus as being supposedly anti-modern and socially 'left-behind'.

The purpose then is to highlight simplifications that contribute to further political polarisation of social change. Under the surface of crude political and medial representations there is often much more hidden than these representations suggest about the nature of social conflicts and insider-outsider relations. When, for instance, 'Fridays for Future' activism is abruptly compared with banal 'counterreactions' under the heading of 'Fridays for Engine Capacity' (*Fridays for Hubraum*)[4], this is seldom a realistic portrayal of direct action and reaction, but rather a sham battle stage-managed by the media. However, a closer look reveals that there is an underlying game with numerous subtle commendations and disparagements. This game is already a fixed element of everyday repertoires of thought; it is extensively played in social practice.

In light of the deficit of research to date, it is necessary to decipher and understand not only the changes in social practice but also the supra-individual process logics and discursive reproduction mechanisms involved. The latter are probably in part responsible for reifying the deniers and 'deviators' from the mainstream. The mainstream may be defined by political elites and the media but mostly this lacks empirical evidence. The terminologies used tend to promise something that preemptive normativity turns into 'facts'. Against this backdrop, the reason for pursuing a focused analytical goal can be encapsulated in one sentence: there has been extremely little investigation of the concrete reasons for the popularity of othering. It must be clarified which functions are fulfilled by images of a persistent clinging to the status quo, both on the part of the practitioners and by the victims of othering. We need to know more about the social functions fulfilled by images, e. g. as perceived threats to a community or triggers of insecurity and wishes for homogeneity. To get an idea of the nature of the social-ecological transition that has just begun, we should also know the extent to which images and concepts of 'others' are constitutive of current social-ecological change, beyond evident discourse rhetoric.

---

4 As was recently done by the daily *Süddeutsche Zeitung*, see https://www.sueddeutsche.de/panorama/fridays-hubraum-facebook-greta-klimakrise-1.4646132 (27.02.2020).

Another objective is therefore the detailed analysis of the milieu-specific interpretations of the denials and alternate values consciously chosen by the change-resistant milieus. This in no way means that the intention is to employ analytical rhetoric to vindicate or even dignify these change-resistant milieus wholesale. The point of departure is rather an intention to comprehensively evaluate the phenomenon of 'preserving the status quo' through an analysis that pays attention to context and detail. This necessitates adopting manifold changes of perspective, as required by the logic of qualitative social research (Glaser/Strauss 2008). Only with such changes of perspective will it be possible to determine why the actors concerned view their interpretations of meaning as 'logical' and 'convincing' even though they may contain paradoxical elements.

3. Change and status quo in social-ecological sustainability research

3.1 Approaches in transition research

To date, a dominant part of transition research has focused primarily on the explanation, assessment and evaluation of various ways of handling ecological dilemmas. Descriptions are given, for instance, of possible routes to sustainable, resource-efficient and energy-saving social practices. Processes of change, alternative regional pathways of development, the divergence of pro-ecological initiatives from the mainstream, institutional restructuring and the new governance arrangements they require have attracted significant interest in economic geography and neighbouring disciplines. Spatial differentiation is usually undertaken in terms of urban-rural contrasts and by localising sectoral clusters. In addition, this research focus adopts a critical attitude towards development indicators of the Global North and South (Geels/Schwanen/Sorrell et al. 2018).

This impacts upon the way in which socio-political opposition is manifested in the extra-parliamentary sphere. The migrant crisis, the climate crisis and the global food crisis have triggered resistance to government policies which is supported by initiatives like Fridays (Scientists, Parents, Mothers, Teachers, Students etc.) for Future, Transition Towns and Extinction Rebellion, and also by globally active NGOs like Greenpeace, Sea Shepherd and diverse climate alliances. In apparent consensus, they refer to scientific knowledge on the finite nature of planetary boundaries, knowledge that has been available and well-accepted for decades, and call on science to use this as a basis to advocate substantial changes in economic systems, consumption and the associated material flows. The investigative focus of researchers lives up this call. Recently, increased attention has been paid to key actors from ecological vanguard milieus, who are promptly addressed as post-growth pioneers, especially in Western Europe and the Global North.

Numerous models and theories on ecologically relevant social and spatial change explain shifts in development and emerging path deviations and processes of change by referring to the actions of such individuals. Heroic actors play a central role here: risk-friendly entrepreneurs from the green economy; post-growth pioneers experimenting with collective sharing, swapping, repairing and making-at-home (Gebauer/Sagebiel 2015); early adopters of new technologies with their particular values, mobility styles, aesthetics and mindsets; and also prosumers who both consume and produce their own products. They usher in new forms of practice and also allow new regional development paths to become recognisable. These individuals seem unusually open to change and have extraordinarily close experience of transformation. They are assigned attributes like 'innovative', 'creative', 'progressive' and 'modern' and are praised as economic innovators. This labelling practice is in line with the tradition of evolutionary economics, where similar designations are given to central players in innovative regions, creative milieus and clusters (Spigel/Harrison 2018).

In contrast, the opposite side is colloquially described using attributes like 'anti-modern', 'against progress' and 'lagging behind' or – in sociologising jargon as 'de-coupled', 'isolated' or 'change resistant'. These are social milieus of unknown size, probably equipped (but not empirically evidenced) with high internal cohesion. Their members obviously strive for settled lives and focus on stable interpretations of meaning. Nonetheless, these milieus are rarely understood as sui generis phenomena, i.e. as legitimate structuring elements of social change that should be taken seriously. Transition research is far more concerned with describing them as relicts of all that needs to be overcome and thus as transitional phenomena. This creates the impression that they might unnecessarily lay the groundwork for inconsistent and erratic actionist policies.

Incidentally, this involves not only the NGOs, independent initiatives and coalitions for action but also the government policies of the mainstream. For instance, during the German federal election in September 2017, the German government was primarily concerned with 'making' the recalcitrant milieus compatible with modest mainstream approaches towards changed lifestyles, mobility and food. This was clearly seen in the case of the planned climate package for CO_2-reduced infrastructure (see the interview in this volume with C. Mohn on the situation in the Lausitz region). The federal government, however, spoke much less about the social costs implied, or the significance of protests and other forms of opposition for successful transformation, never mind actual negotiations with the 'locals' affected.

3.2 Value-action gaps: Explanations for phenomena of transition resistance

The focus of emerging post-growth analyses has seldom been on explaining the development of resistance to modernisation and progress. Worthy of mention are several interpretations of 'resistance despite knowing better', which are based on psychological experiments. It is suggested that three factors play an important role here: diffusion of responsibility, pluralistic ignorance and 'fear of judgment' (Baecker 1999). First, models of diffusion of responsibility suggest that there is usually a sufficient number of individuals in society ready to undertake the practical implementation of any policy project. From the individual point of view, it can thus always be argued that 'the others should do it first' (ibid.). Second, notions of pluralistic ignorance suggest that in unfamiliar situations individuals automatically prefer to base their behaviour on that of others. However, if – to put it briefly – nobody does anything, then nobody can serve as a model of active intervention and possible change. Third, the concept of 'fear of judgment' suggests that acting in a supposedly wrong way leads to the actors concerned being negatively judged by others.

Psychological consumer research and environmental and sustainability studies offer more explanations. They assume that a discrepancy between knowledge and action exists, known as the value-action gap (Kollmuss/ Agyeman 2002). This is said to ensure the retention of familiar and proven patterns of action. In contrast to the similar theory of cognitive dissonance, which holds that resisting change in difficult circumstances is due to people reviewing their motives for past choices (Beckmann 1984), the value-action gap approach does not focus primarily on motivation but rather on actors' knowledge. Particularly during the spread of social innovations, in society as a whole the paradoxical situation arises that, on the one hand, there is sufficient information to demonstrate that certain lifestyles are disadvantageous. On the other hand, the same lifestyles continue to be led unchanged. For example, missing information about the individual and collective costs of changed behaviour can hinder implementation. We draw further on this concept below in the context of a more fundamental discussion of transformation theory.

3.3 Transformation and milieu analyses

The complexity of comparatively change-resistant social milieus has recently been demonstrated by long-term studies in 'left-behind' East German regions such as Wittenberge (Bude/Medicus/Willisch 2011) and similarly by qualitative research undertaken in the prefabricated housing estates of Lütten Klein near Rostock (Mau 2019). The historical dimension of such milieus has received considerable attention, but observations suggest that there are current milieu constellations in eastern Germany which are equally troubled but have been subject to considerably less research. Such milieus are facing a third social-ecological transformation. The first transformation was triggered by the peaceful revolution of 1989/1990 in the GDR, while the second transformation began with the turn of the century during a dynamic surge in globalisation. It too required people to fundamentally reorient their lives. Finally, the federal government's climate pact of 2019 led to the emergence of another transformation decided upon 'on high'. Henceforth support will be directed towards lifestyles characterised by sustainable and resource-saving mobility and energy. In this complex third transformation, digital technologies and the use of digital communication media play a prominent role in intensifying social and spatial inequality.

The current reactions of the milieus affected by the aforementioned upheavals extend far beyond the visible political resistance seen in eastern Germany. The everyday cultural interpretations and positionings adopted by a cross-section of social strata draw on everyday biographies that include collective experiences with the authoritarianism of the GDR, memories of the powerlessness felt during the transformation of the system in the 1990s, and sustained notions of the apparently unavoidable victimhood of 'ordinary people'. This is exacerbated by signals of uncertainty from the political camps, which were newly established after German reunification. Such signals include a declining belief in the self-healing properties of market forces on the part of the liberals, but also the increasing relinquishment of old expectations of equality and participation by the social democrats. These changes are of course also reflected upon and interpreted by the milieus. In such a situation, the popularity of change-resistant mechanisms can be plausibly explained by transformation theory in terms of people's growing fear that they will have to face further demands and losses of their vested rights in the course of new upheavals.

3.4 Paradoxes of the current social transformation

Leaving aside the special case of post-socialist transformation and the subsequent post-transformation, it is possible that the incipient post-growth focus, together with increasingly rigid climate policies, may create a paradoxical situation for society as a whole. On the one hand, specialist and everyday knowledge about the finite nature of resources and planetary boundaries is increasing, with equally significant contributions from public discussions, media reportage and political discourse. On the other hand, there is a decline in robust experiential knowledge about how people can give up habitual consumption and ecologically unfavourable lifestyles. Many individuals are unclear about what adaptations to the new conditions could look like. Willingness to engage with these changes is stagnating in wide sections of the population, in line with the inability to formulate concrete, attractive objectives and increasingly strong visions of sacrifice and demise.

Other explanations counter such suggestions by underlining the potency of stable behavioural routines, e. g. habitual practices of everyday consumption, food, mobility and leisure. This seems a defence strategy enacted by political elites who often suggest that habits pass unchanged from generation to generation and can only be influenced by drastic measures. It follows that ecologically 'unreasonable' behaviour can be defined as a generational problem, while environment-consuming production models and neoliberal policies remain unmentioned. The Fridays generation can be safely celebrated as innovators and receive official government approval for justifiably punishing the generations of their parents, grandparents and great-grandparents. Quite apart from the paternalist understanding of politics thus exposed ('...they are finally coming to their senses'), the corresponding rhetoric fits into another context of interpretation and narrative that addresses the potential danger to the state posed by an underlying tendency to resist change. This includes recent political accusations concerning the revival of right-wing radicalism, as though it has simply hibernated among the population in recent generations and cannot be controlled without intervention from 'on high'. However, the proponents of notions of habitualism fail to shed much light on the concrete forces working to preserve the status quo in the social milieus.

This is similarly true of the narrative hoping for a technicistic solution to the environmental and climate dilemma (Blühdorn/Butzlaff/Deflorian et al. 2018) and the latest EU Green Deals based on CO_2 pricing and climate-friendly economic restructuring (Claeys/Tagliapietra/Zachmann 2019). As paradigmatic technology models, both approaches are intended to replace the current era of production and create a CO_2-neutral good life for everyone on the planet. This too tends to deny the ability of the population to regulate and emancipate itself. Furthermore, it largely ignores that a reliance on policies with a technical focus is somewhat paradoxical. It suggests that the negative consequences of technology should be countered with further technological measures rather than with alternative, everyday conceptual approaches. A utopia is thus propagandised but, against the background of increasing criticism of technology, the issue of its concrete implementation receives little consideration. It is assumed that old habitualisations can be simply replaced with new ones, without more precisely analysing the role played by habits in social communities that are already burdened by past transformations. This seems an irony of history rather than a promising strategic inventory of rational policy approaches. Once before, socialist human-beings were to be created on the ruins of habitualised bourgeois lifestyles.

4. Blank spots on the map of transformation research

Social science and social-ecological analyses of transition scenarios have played a considerable part in ensuring that certain ways of dealing with ecological imperatives have already been canonised, collectively internalised and defined as guiding policy principles. They suggest that environmental destruction and climate change largely preclude political alternatives or policy options. In the public debate, science thus presents itself as a social avantgarde and proves amazingly compatible with a number of parallel political discourses. For instance, recent sustainability studies (Geels/Schwanen/Sorrell et al. 2018) have drawn up normative frameworks intended to provide a basis for future transition. They then focus primarily on issues of planning, consumption, culture or policy linked to the implementation of the 'necessary' transformations, especially in the field of material cycles, mobility resources, fossil fuels and food.

In epistemological terms this normative research orientation has clear consequences. Established imperatives constructed in the political and everyday spheres are used as an implicit yardstick governing investigative logics, even in advance of the research. The research interest is directed towards the practical enactment of new and unquestioned norms, rather than towards constructions of meaning or the specific rationality of incipient social transformation. Numerous best-practice case studies, feasibility studies, impact analyses and efficiency evaluations are therefore employed to develop applied and practicable findings for user-related policy approaches.

Interest is thus directed towards designing the transformation towards more sustainability and future-proofing rather than focusing on exactly what the transformation means for different actors, what unintended side-effects it brings about, and how socially equitable it promises to be (Hargreaves/Hielscher/Seyfang et al. 2013; Wolfram/Frantzeskaki 2016). In this respect sustainability studies conform to urban transition research, as well as much of the post-growth research undertaken by social and spatial sciences. They all share a subcutaneous attitude that involves following imperatives that are viewed as universally applicable, not only by ecological action groups but also by the political establishment. In the following, we use the neologism 'imperativism' to describe such dispositions to act.

This research focus puts the potential actors involved in the pending social transformation at the centre of attention of the spatial and social sciences. As pointed out by the rapidly expanding scholars' debates on post-growth economies (Schulz 2012), much of the research concentrates on supposedly 'new' actors (Lange 2017), e. g. post-growth pioneers, their obvious practices and spatial utilisation patterns (Othengrafen/Romero Renau/Kokkali 2016). If possible, these actors should have already experienced post-growth transformations relevant to their everyday lives and material flows (Baier/Hansing/Müller et al. 2016) or at least be working on their implementation.

So far, so good? Unfortunately not, for two reasons. First, there has to date been no thorough analysis of the continued phenomenon of justified and voluntary resistance to change, i.e. the clinging on to a hard-earned status quo. This refers primarily to the mental dispositions, ways of thinking and forms of habitus of those who do not allow themselves to be convinced by the new imperativism or who at least maintain a certain distance to it. Second, there is scarcely any discussion of the social upheavals that clearly accompany the imperativism.

The deniers discussed above are not simply behaving in an unreasonable way, wanting to keep old habits for reasons of convenience or due to a lack of education or knowledge. On the contrary, they draw their recruits largely from the high-status middle classes, i.e. relatively well-off and better educated groups who are often viewed as the key performers in society. Business elites are also included (Marg/Walter 2015). Nonetheless, they and their views are strangely marginalised in the political discourse, as though real-world power structures were irrelevant for future-oriented ecological debate. After all, these groups command above-average cultural and economic capital. In addition, little is known about the current forms of communitisation developed by these actors, especially about the social relationships inside the social milieus they belong to.

In addition, for problem-oriented social and spatial research, questions arise as to the social preconditions favouring change resistance and the social impacts of such forces. Do those resisting transformation reject all kinds of ecologically motivated changes – including the value-based renunciation of economic growth postulates – or do they actually accept the 'great' imperative while refusing to support the many small changes associated with it? Do they in this case direct their attention rather to regional and sectoral growth, which they continue to view as desirable? In the light of a lack of empirical data it is only possible to speculate here. These issues are also connected to collective imaginaries, narratives and legitimising practices – phenomena that maintain growth moments in the face of the environmental consequences quasi 'despite better available knowledge'.

The resisters and deniers deserve more serious attention than they have hitherto received, whether they are considered as forces braking ecological-political progress or as responsible reflective thinkers or even as innovative reformers divorced from the social-ecological mainstream. Social science research is ill-prepared for such an endeavour. In practical research terms, for instance, disciplinary approaches lack important conceptual building blocks and connective links that would enable them to adapt exogenous knowledge.

The perspectives of other disciplines can be used in a targeted fashion to critically question widely practised normativisms. The initial aim is to examine the situations requiring explanation by using unaccustomed terms and unfamiliar descriptive rhetoric.

5. Discursive dimensions of the resistance

5.1 Discursive framings

As a first step towards filling the research gap discussed above, sociological approaches related to milieu theory and practice theory appear promising. However, important as they are, it might not be sufficient to concentrate on them. In addition to investigating the character of the resisters and their milieus, it is also important to focus on the discourses in which they appear. More precisely, research should target the manifestations, drivers and functions of political positions of resistance in the discourses about social-ecological transformation and post-growth. From the perspective of media theory, the hegemonic framings that drive the marginalisation of resisters, impeders and other non-conformists must first be described. In particular, the localisation of 'deviators' in certain regions and socio-spatial configurations can be a central element of framings of this sort – providing a new research object for basic geographical investigation of socio-spatial disparities. Framing theory of the late 2000s and early 2010s offers a theoretical foundation here (Chong/Druckman 2007; Matthes 2012). It allows the medial and discursive representation of individual population groups and circumstances to be addressed in terms of pre-existing inclusion-exclusion mechanisms and othering processes (Borah 2011).

The concept of othering refers to the practice of attributing 'other' characteristics that deviate from those of one's own group to groups viewed as socially undesirable or inferior (Jensen 2011; Schwalbe 2000). This is closely related to practices of social identity formation and community building.

Therefore, research on othering can easily be combined with milieu theory. Exemplary analyses of 'resistant' milieus and deniers in East Germany may thus reveal othering practices as 'real' social phenomena, i.e. social facts existing beyond the imaginaries implemented in discourse. This makes it possible to explore the external ascriptions and the self-labelling of those affected, both of which transport hegemonic interpretations of otherness. The small shift in perspective towards hegemony and power relations allows othering to be defined as an outcome of social and political co-production. By considering power relations, othering can be defined as an elite project, namely as the process of forming and addressing political opponents. Othering is thus described as a dual phenomenon, as both everyday practice and as a political discursive process.

With a view to East German sensitivities however, it is possible to move even beyond in-depth descriptions of the 'underdogs' of othering. The self-positioning of the resisters in the discourse can also be adequately addressed. In particular, innovative and constructive elements of resistances and their effects can be uncovered. By investigating the winners of previous transformation spurts (e. g. successful entrepreneurs or lifestyle pioneers), it is possible to identify interpretations of the situation that enable those affected to develop proactive attitudes, produce original solutions and take successful strategic action. Simultaneously, the individual and milieu-specific counterforces to such attitudes can be clearly described, especially the tendency to accept victim roles. Such roles may appear to members of the milieu as part of their own concept of action and personality; yet they also see victimhood as a collective fate. Here what requires clarification is the extent to which frustration and resignation are cultivated as milieu-specific attitudes without abandoning the intention to change the circumstances.

This could provide answers to important questions concerning the constitution of 'status quo avant-gardists' in the social, political and media discourses. Similarly, the issue of role assignments and the chances of prevailing in discourse can be addressed. From the perspective of social geography, these ideas are linked to an aspiration to speak as precisely as possible about the emergence of social and spatial inequality among those who do not 'join in' with ongoing processes of social change.

5.2 Hegemonic perspectives on 'status quo avant-gardists' and 'prevention innovators'

In recent German history, transformation discourses have always been hegemonic discourses. In them, their winners usually describe situations of massive change as necessary, compulsory and legitimated by impending dangers. Precisely this hegemonic view is celebrated with startling regularity in debates on the post-socialist transformation of the 1990s and the post-transformation since the millennium. Whether the focus is on the permanent economic crisis following the transfer of West German institutions to the East, or on the dismantling of socialist industries, or on demographic change and population loss in the 'new federal states', or on the eastwards expansion of the EU and revision of the German and European border regime (Bürkner 2020), or on the symbolic geopolitical build-up against the new and old opponent Russia, or on the consequences of the destabilisation of the Middle East and the waves of refugees from European neighbours – deviations from political common sense are repeatedly attributed to the losers of the social transformation of the last 30 years and particularly localised in East Germany.

According to many government statements and media representations, it seems that in East Germany there are large zones characterised by malcontents, modernisation opponents, recalcitrants and even (old and new) enemies of democracy. This is undoubtedly a powerful construction of space that those in power can conveniently use in line with the *divide et impera* ('divide and rule') motto of ancient Rome. Good and evil thereby organise themselves in a quasi-natural spatial division of labour.

What initially appears to be a continuation of Germany's domestic transformation debate – reduced to a crude East-West dichotomy – hides the many nuances and differentiated views on the connection between ecology, the economy and system transformation. Furthermore, this superficial view disguises the internal conditions in the two 'geographical' camps. It is by no means the case that there are no resourceful innovators in the German crisis regions. Innovative start-ups in the high-tech industry in eastern Saxony and environmental sector companies active on the world market with international networks indicate that there are not only losers and deniers in East Germany. It is also not the case that West Germany has no opponents to ecologically motivated modernisation. For example, the West hosts the permanently crisis-ridden Ruhr area and the rural areas of Lower Saxony with their continued ecological disasters (e. g. the factual and literal 'manure pits' of Germany produced by regional industrialised agriculture). However, these maldevelopments have not triggered noteworthy critique of the relevant politics. On the contrary, these regions are examples of mental and political resistance to change where refusers range from local elites to ordinary citizens.

The national policy discourse and the media debates in Germany do not, however, focus on cooperative learning from the political conflicts surrounding social renewal and the possibility of post-growth. Rather, old resentments are used to further everyday political interests, both to increase newspaper circulations and to gain votes.

6. On the emancipation of the 'status quo avant-gardists' in the post-growth debate – an initial résumé

It cannot be overlooked that in interest-driven discourses, views are strategically advanced that decide on the collective ascription of particular characteristics to people and places. The confrontation with resisters, impeders and 'blockers', and even with their apparently natural habitats, is not only argumentative but also emotionally ridden and moralising. It can be easily identified as part of a hegemonic discourse and corresponding framing.

This opens up promising fields of activity for social and spatial sciences concerned with the phenomenon of change resistance. The first step must be to consider the relevant actors, their political positions, social practices and discursive interventions more closely. It can do no harm to apply a little dialectics in order to avoid the suggestive power of polarising figures of thought. We draw on the dialectic concept of the Frankfurt School of sociology (Adorno 2000) which aims for the open-ended reconstruction of social developments with all their contradictions. In social practice, supposedly conservative elements are always associated with progressive elements. Their individual meaningfulness becomes apparent only in relation to their respective counterparts. Accordingly, a clinging to the status quo can only arise from the actors' cognitive, emotional and social engagement with the alternative positions and modes of behaviour – in this case with active change.

In concrete terms, this may mean that the supposed deniers have good reasons for not (or not immediately) affiliating themselves with superficial action postulates and instead favour more fundamental engagement with alternative ideas. These ideas need not necessarily be reactionary or ignorant of the problem. Especially in times of symbolic policymaking and hectic actionism, pronounced obstructors can also be sources of innovative inspiration. These actors often declare their own forms of social practice, everyday experiences and sensibilities as the starting point of a search for practicable solutions – and thus reject abstract, untried or ideologically preformulated blanket solutions (see Marg/Walter 2015 on the mental and strategic orientations of medium-scale entrepreneurs). Social-ecological analysis should focus more closely on precisely these actors and their deliberate positioning in difficult discursive terrain.

Those affected may hope for open debate, but at present their attempts to influence the future development of society with their 'divergent' demands meet with a rather violent rejection of the thinking on which they are based. Ironically, in the current debates on climate and post-growth – with their rhetoric of urgency and a lack of alternatives –, demands for emancipation and open-ended search processes are in constant danger of being marginalised. With the rhetorical figure of illegitimate 'divergence', such demands can easily be stigmatised as politically undesirable by advocates of the supposedly incontrovertible imperative. This can foster a new authoritarianism that is diametrically contrary to the goals of a broadly based ecological transition and the inquisitive testing of post-growth practices.

This tendency can become a marked brake on innovation, namely if the hegemonic ascriptions of others are repeatedly adopted by those affected. From the perspective of social sciences, it is therefore necessary to carefully observe the extent to which milieu-external sovereignties of interpretation paralyse willingness to act and proactive strategies. In the future, the ambivalent situation of those already marginalised in political space or those threatened with marginalisation must be made visible in good time. This ambivalent situation arises from the dilemma of wanting to be socially and economically innovative but being assessed as incapable of innovation.

The inclusion-exclusion problem involved in othering practices and framings of 'divergence' makes clear that the primary concern of the politically marginalised can only be to work towards their own emancipation. Future analyses must therefore aim to uncover the emancipatory elements of the change-resistant perspective and to describe the degree to which the actors concerned are potential or de-facto avant-gardists, rather than treating them as marginalised groups who lack any potential for change or even a claim to power. If such research findings then feed into the ongoing post-growth debate, then it may be possible to shift the emancipatory perspectives, which are still frequently labelled as a minority concern, into the mainstream.

7. Further ideas and consequences for the discipline

The recognition of research deficits immediately triggers further conceptual questions. From the perspective of milieu theory and discourse theory, it is necessary to provide a context-oriented analysis of change resistance and its impacts, focusing on social differentiations. It can be assumed that supposedly isolationist movements – especially if they are perceived as regional phenomena – indicate more general social resistance that should be analysed and discussed on a broader basis.

It should be noted here that social transformation discourses are not only influenced by abstract norms, values and action logics but also by the interests of heterogenous actors and their prospects of prevailing. Actors enter the confrontations with different socio-economic statuses, different amounts of social capital, different concrete (social, economic and symbolic) profit expectations and different ascribed (qua status) and acquired (in discourse) power or ability to assert themselves.

Greater contextualisation of the regionalisation processes of change resistance is also urgently required. These processes should be understood as an expression of individual and temporary assertions of sovereignty, which emanate from regionally anchored milieus. In their particular spatial-temporal manifestations, such regionalisations can overlap with older socio-spatial disparities. For example, transition processes prescribed by policy from 'on high' (the phase-out of coal, the mobility transition, the taxation of fossil fuels) can lead to a weakening of socio-economic positions simply as a result of marginalising actors because of their spatial distribution, especially when they live in peripheral regions or act as commuters at some distance from centres).

Are these change-resistant milieus then really interested in preventing further socio-economic marginalisation and that is the only reason why they cling to apparently obsolete patterns of mobility, lifestyles and consumption? Or are the denial positions adopted rather as a consequence of the marginalisation of these milieus in the public and political discourses, i.e. tendentially independent of concrete experiences of spatial-social disparities? Such research questions indicate the need to consider new geographical fragmentations and processes of social peripheralisation as normal objects of investigation in post-growth research.

Finally, it is time to pursue focused analyses of discourses and framings to gain important indications of paradoxes, hybridisations and ambivalences in the post-growth debate. Social sciences have for some time been aware that these phenomena are central characteristics of postmodernism; however it is nonetheless easy to lose sight of concrete symptoms and indicators. Reflexive processes are found much more frequently in situations of transition than in plateaued phases of social development. This is because dissent, diverging policy objectives and social upheavals are then more apparent than in less conflictive times. Discursive processes of marginalisation and the imposing of public sanctions on 'deniers' have a direct impact on the social positioning and scope of influence of those affected – which often results in what was weak resistance developing into tougher opposition. In such cases, the attribution 'denier' becomes a self-fulfilling prophecy.

Under these conditions, the critical social sciences must urgently reject hegemonic opinions concerning what is 'good' and 'right'. A failure to do so risks the development of a knowledge culture that affirms existing power imbalances. Such developments are hardly compatible with emancipation and calls for debates on equal footing for all.

References

Adorno, T. W. (2000). *Negative Dialektik*. 10th edition. Suhrkamp.
Baecker, D. (1999). *Organisation als System*. Suhrkamp.
Barth, B., Hansing, T., Müller, C., & Werner, K. (2016). *Die Welt reparieren: Open Source und Selbermachen als postkapitalistische Praxis*. transcript.

Barth, B., Flaig, B. B., Schäuble, N., & Tautscher, M. (2018). *Praxis der Sinus-Milieus®: Gegenwart und Zukunft eines modernen Gesellschafts- und Zielgruppenmodells*. Springer.

Beckmann, J. (1984). *Kognitive Dissonanz. Eine handlungstheoretische Perspektive*. Springer.

Blühdorn, I., Butzlaff, F., Deflorian, M., & Hausknost, D. (2018). *Transformation-narratives and responsibility: The social-theoretical gap in transformation-research*. Self-published.

Borah, P. (2011). Conceptual issues in framing theory: A systematic examination of a decade's literature. *Journal of Communication, 67*(2), 246–263.

Bude, H., Medicus, T., & Willisch, A. (2011). *ÜberLeben im Umbruch. Am Beispiel Wittenberge: Ansichten einer fragmentierten Gesellschaft*. Verlag des Hamburger Instituts für Sozialforschung.

Bürkner, H.-J. (2020). Ostdeutsche Grenzregionen. Für eine transnationale Regionalforschung. In: M. Naumann, & S. Becker (Eds.), *Regionalentwicklung in Ostdeutschland – Dynamiken, Perspektiven und der Beitrag der Humangeographie*. Springer, 57–69.

Chong, D., & Druckman, J. N. (2007). Framing theory. *Annual Review of Political Science, 10*, 103–126.

Claeys, G., Tagliapietra, S., & Zachmann, G. (2019). How to make the European Green Deal work. *Policy Contribution 14*.

Gebauer, J., Sagebiel, J. (2015). *Wie wichtig ist Wachstum für KMU? Ergebnisse einer Befragung von kleinen und mittleren Unternehmen*. IÖW publication series 208/15.

Geels, F. W., Schwanen, T., Sorrell, S., Jenkins, K., & Sovacool, B. (2018). Reducing energy demand through low carbon innovation: A sociotechnical transitions perspective and thirteen research debates. *Energy Research & Social Science, 40*, 23–35.

Gersemann, O., & Zschäpitz, H. (2020, February 20). Wenn die Kanzlerin spricht, „fühlt man sich ethisch zu Hause". https://www.welt.de/wirtschaft/article205293177/Angela-Merkel-in-Davos-Bundeskanzlerin-wird-wieder-zur-Klimakanzlerin.html.

Glaser, B. G., & Strauss, A. L. (2008). *The discovery of grounded theory: strategies for qualitative research*. Routledge.

Hargreaves, T., Hielscher, S., Seyfang, G., & Smith, A. (2013). Grassroots innovations in community energy: The role of intermediaries in niche development. *Global Environmental Change, 23*(5), 868–880.

Jensen, S. O. (2011). Othering, identity formation and agency. *Qualitative Studies,* 2(2), 63–78.

Lange, B. (2017). Offene Werkstätten und Postwachstumsökonomien: kollaborative Orte als Wegbereiter transformativer Wirtschaftsentwicklungen? *Zeitschrift für Wirtschaftsgeographie,* 61(1), 38–55.

Marg, St., & Walter, F. (2015). Unternehmer und Gesellschaft. Einleitende Bemerkungen zum Vorgehen und zur Methodik. In St. Marg, & F. Walter, (Eds.), *Sprachlose Elite? Wie Unternehmer Politik und Gesellschaft sehen.* Rowohlt Buchverlag, 9–29.

Matthes, J. (2012). Framing politics: An integrative approach. *American Behavioral Scientist,* 56(3), 247–259.

Mau, St. (2019). *Lütten Klein. Leben in der ostdeutschen Transformationsgesellschaft.* Suhrkamp.

Othengrafen, F., Romero Renau, L., & Kokkali, I. (2016). A new landscape of urban social movements. Reflections on urban unrest in Southern European cities. In J. Knieling, & F. Othengrafen, (Eds.), *Cities in crisis. Socio-spacial impacts of the economic crisis in southern European cities.* Routledge, 139–154.

Röpke, A., & Speit, A. (2019). *Völkische Landnahme. Alte Sippen, junge Siedler, rechte Ökos.* Links Verlag.

Schulz, Ch. (2012). Post-Wachstums-Ökonomien – (k)ein Thema für die Wirtschaftsgeographie? *Zeitschrift für Wirtschaftsgeographie,* 56(4), 264–273.

Schwalbe, M. (2000). The elements of inequality. *Contemporary Sociology,* 29 (6), 775–781.

Spigel, B., & Harrison, R. (2018). Toward a process theory of entrepreneurial ecosystems. *Strategic Entrepreneurship Journal,* 12, 151–168.

Wolfram, M., & Frantzeskaki, N. (2016): Cities and systemic change for sustainability: Prevailing epistemologies and an emerging research agenda. *Sustainability,* 8(2), 144.

The growth fixation of the European Union
A commentary on the draft Green Deal

Christian Schulz

As the introduction to this book describes, in the wake of the so-called 'economic and financial crisis' of 2007/2008, the EU was – along with the OECD and the UN – one of the most powerful and visible actors worldwide to address the growth paradigm. The 2009 publication of 'GDP and beyond. Measuring progress in a changing world' (European Commission 2009) was unusually clear in its description of the inadequacy of conventional measurement methods and indicator systems for assessing economic development and social prosperity and proposed the overdue inclusion of ecological and social indicators. Similarly, the fact that in subsequent years the EU-Parliament addressed post-growth approaches, at times very visibly (see the interview with Tom Bauler in this book), suggests that there may have been a rethinking of the development goals of economic, infrastructure and social policy. Details of the European 'Green Deal'[1] presented by the 'Von der Leyen Commission' at the end of 2019 were therefore eagerly anticipated (European Commission 2019). Even though mid-February 2020 is too early for a systematic evaluation of the Green Deal, which has so far only appeared in broad outline, an initial assessment of this quite remarkable paper is undertaken here. The focus is primarily on the following questions:

1. What understanding of growth does the Green Deal employ? To what extent is it possible to identify reorientations in comparison to previous

---

1 On the general debate about the post-growth compatibility of Green (New) Deals – also including the US approach, the special issue 'Green New Deal' of the journal *politische ökologie* (Fuhrhop 2019) and the report by the European Environmental Bureau (EEB 2019) are recommended.

development principles – e.g. the Europe 2020 Strategy (European Commission 2010)?
2. To what extent is the Green Deal 'space sensitive' both in terms of the inner-European diversity of spatial contexts and conditions (also see the article by Szumelda in this volume), and in terms of global distribution and justice issues (see the article by Bruns in this book)?

I am fully aware that this evaluation may shortly require revision but believe that a consideration of current political activities on the EU level is nonetheless a valuable contribution to this compendium.

Figure 1: Elements of the EU Green Deal / Source: European Commission 2019: 3

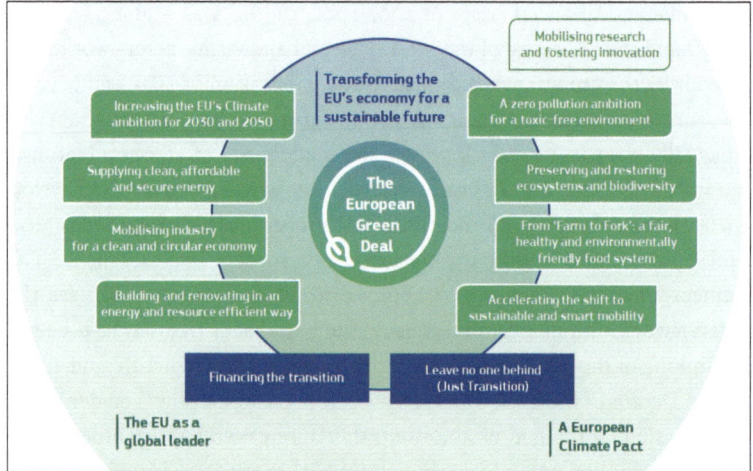

The understanding of growth in the Green Deal

The Green Deal is presented as 'a new growth strategy that aims to transform the EU into a fair and prosperous society, with a modern, resource-efficient and competitive economy where there are no net emissions of greenhouse gases in 2050 and where economic growth is decoupled from resource use' (European Commission 2019: 2). Even just in this preamble, it is possible to discern continued belief in an efficiency-based solution to the resource problem. The subsequent text is dominated by terms such as 'efficiency', 'smart' and 'competitive' and similarly by an evident technology orientation – e.g.

'keep its competitive advantage in clean technologies' (ibid.: 19) or 'leverage the potential of the digital transformation, which is a key enabler for reaching the Green Deal objectives' (ibid.: 7). The term growth itself is not problematised and is used throughout with positive connotations (see Table 1). The terms of 'sufficiency', 'less' and similar concepts do not appear at all.

Table 1: Selected key terms from the Green Deal and frequency of mention

40	Investment/investor[1]
15	Efficiency/efficient
14	Technology/technological
10	Growth[2]
8	Competition/competitiveness/competitive
2	Well-being/welfare
0	Sufficiency/sufficient

Textual basis: European Commission 2019
[1] excluding names like European Investment Bank or InvestEU
[2] with positive connotations throughout

More serious questioning of market-based mechanisms and the resulting patterns of consumption is only undertaken in the section that discusses the upcoming action plan on the circular economy, which includes 'measures to encourage businesses to offer, and to allow consumers to choose, reusable, durable and repairable products. It will analyse the need for a "right to repair", and curb the built-in obsolescence of devices, in particular for electronics. Consumer policy will help to empower consumers to make informed choices and play an active role in the ecological transition. New business models based on renting and sharing goods and services will play a role as long as they are truly sustainable and affordable' (ibid.: 8).

In contrast, other sections reveal a reliance on large-scale technological solutions and the substitution of, e.g., fossil fuels: 'EU industry needs "climate and resource frontrunners" to develop the first commercial applications of breakthrough technologies in key industrial sectors by 2030. Priority areas include clean hydrogen, fuel cells and other alternative fuels, energy storage, and carbon capture, storage and utilisation. As an example, the Commission will support clean steel breakthrough technologies leading to a zero-carbon steel making process by 2030' (ibid.: 10). In the field of renewable energies, the development of offshore wind parks is highlighted as particularly relevant, a very specialised and centralising approach.

The recommendations that are made for the transport sector do not problematise avoidable causes of mobility (e.g. in freight transport or settlement structures). They rather focus exclusively on changes in choices of transport mode (modal split) and, above all, on zero and low emission vehicles and alternative fuels. The investments planned in the building sector, primarily refurbishment intended to improve the energy performance of the existing building stock, focus on thermal insulation and especially on technology-based (smart) approaches. In contrast, there is hardly any mention of new forms of housing, reduced land take, combating high vacancy rates, directing new building activities, etc. (also see Fuhrhop 2019).

Statements made by the Green Deal in the field of agriculture and food production remain extremely vague. The planned 'Farm to Fork' strategy calls for higher product standards and the reduced use of fertilisers and pesticides. However, the inherent structural problems of industrialised agriculture in general and factory farming in particular are not addressed.

The criteria to be applied to sustainable investments (European Commission 2019: 17) will be defined in the EU taxonomy that is currently being developed (see article by Dörry/Schulz in this volume). The taxation reforms announced present the prospect of 'shifting the tax burden from labour to pollution' (European Commission 2019: 17). This refers primarily to CO_2 taxation rather than to the fundamental taxing of resources and materials – as the post-growth movement and the ecological economy have demanded for some time.

Spatial dimensions of the Green Deal

There is no closer consideration of spatial structures or of the role of spatial planning and regional/local conditions for socio-ecological transition processes. Spatial differentiation is only undertaken in the context of structural and social policy measures designed to mitigate new regional inequalities. 'At the same time, this transition must be just and inclusive. It must put people first, and pay attention to the regions, industries and workers who will face the greatest challenges' (ibid.: 2); 'The Just Transition Mechanism will focus on the regions and sectors that are most affected by the transition because they depend on fossil fuels or carbon-intensive processes' (ibid.: 16).

Spatial interdependencies are discussed for the sectoral policies on a global level:

a. In relation to the boundlessness of environmental problems and their causes, e.g. 'The drivers of climate change and biodiversity loss are global and are not limited by national borders' (ibid.: 2);
b. With regard to possible relocations or migration processes ('pollution havens') and the substitution of European products by imported articles from countries with lower environmental standards, e.g. 'there is a risk of carbon leakage, either because production is transferred from the EU to other countries with lower ambition for emission reduction, or because EU products are replaced by more carbon-intensive imports' (ibid.: 6);
c. Referring to the prospect of attractive international markets for 'green' technologies and products, e.g. 'There is significant potential in global markets for low-emission technologies, sustainable products and services' (ibid.: 7).

Part 3 of the Green Deal (European Commission 2019: 20–22) is dedicated to the global role of the EU, primarily in relation to reliance on pioneering (product-) standards, the modernisation of global production chains (environmental and social standards) and the development of trade barriers for products that do not satisfy EU standards. Furthermore, there is favourable mention of global trading of emissions certificates and carbon offsetting measures, direct investment in renewable energies, sustainable everyday practices ('clean cooking') and urban infrastructures in countries of the Global South (especially in African countries). The somewhat utilitarian perspective adopted here is evidently one specific to industrialised countries and includes little serious reflection of global interdependencies or neo-colonial attitudes (see the article by Bruns in this book for more detail).

Conclusion

In comparison with previous strategies, the European Green Deal aims to drive much more ambitious climate policy goals and more determined, cross-sectoral reforms. Nonetheless, the rather uncritical use of the growth concept, coupled with a strong emphasis on competitive technological development, market leadership and export opportunities, suggests strong parallels to other primarily efficiency-based approaches of the green economy (UNEP 2011). However, in contrast, e.g., to the UN Sustainable Development Goals (primarily SDG 8, see the Introduction to this book), this proposal does not use gross domestic product as a parameter for future development or define concrete growth goals. Whether this in itself indicates a move away from GDP and a reorientation towards development goals seems, however, doubtful.

As the article discussed here is only a communication, a proposal by the Commission to the European Parliament and Council, the Green Deal will be the subject of further discussion in the near future. This coincides with the contentious negotiations of the first post-Brexit budget and the budget discussions will also examine the content and objectives of the Green Deal and its funding needs. Initial reactions from the member states (such as France on the topic of agriculture) make it clear that the already moderate ambitions of the paper will be further watered down. There is an opportunity here to use the momentum of current debates on climate policy and growth-critical discussion found in much of society and the economy to take a major step forward. However, the Green Deal finally adopted – if it survives the negotiation process at all – seems very likely to fall far short of its original ambitions. And it will thus have still less in common with a post-growth reorientation than the document discussed here.

Cited literature

EEB – European Environmental Bureau (2019). *Decoupling debunked – Evidence and arguments against green growth as a sole strategy for sustainability.*
European Commission (2009). *GDP and beyond. Measuring progress in a changing world.* Brussels. COM (2009) 433 final. 2009, August 20.

European Commission (2010). *Europe 2020. A strategy for smart, sustainable and inclusive growth.* COM (2010) 2020 final. 2010, March 3.

European Commission (2019). *The European Green Deal.* COM (2019) 640 final. 2019, December 11.

Fuhrhop, D. (2019). Klimafreundliches Bauen und bezahlbares Wohnen. „So ein New Deal ist nicht green" (Interview by Anke Oxenfarth). *politische ökologie,* 37(159), 59–62.

UNEP – United Nations Environment Programme (2011). *Towards a green economy: Pathways to sustainable development and poverty eradication. – A Synthesis for Policy Makers.* www.unep.org/greeneconomy.

Lessons from Practice

We have a responsibility to be a bit more pragmatic

An interview with Dr Yvonne Rydin, conducted by Christian Schulz

Yvonne Rydin is Professor and Chair of Planning, Environment and Public Policy at the Bartlett School of Planning, University College London. In her research on sustainable development, she focuses on planning processes, questions of democratic participation, political power and governance, and the role of civil-society organisations. Her ground-breaking book 'The future of planning: Beyond growth dependence' (2007, Policy Press) critically addresses the growth paradigm of spatial planning.
https://www.ucl.ac.uk/bartlett/planning/prof-yvonne-rydin

What do degrowth approaches mean for your own research?

Yvonne Rydin: My current work is actually focused on planning for low-growth areas. What I'm interested in is looking at areas that seem to be beyond the reach of growth-orientated policies and seeing how they are coping, what their options are. So, the work I'm focusing on at the moment is a comparative study.

In England, this looks at Cambridge and Cambridgeshire. Cambridge is very well known for the Cambridge Phenomenon, a lot of growth both in the hi-tech industry, but also housing and residential development with new urban centres, and I'm setting that in the context of Cambridgeshire, which is very much a county of two halves. In the area to the north and the east, an area we call Fenland and East Cambridgeshire, the settlements are much poorer, with some severe public health problems, severe problems of unemployment, and benefit dependency. It's very, very different to the city of Cambridge, so that makes a good contrast. I'm comparing that with a case in Sweden, in southern Sweden, which is Malmö, also very well known for undergoing a shift from a post-industrial city to a knowledge city. There is also growth along the Malmö-Helsingborg corridor. But in the county of Skåne and in the eastern and northern areas, there is much less economic growth to drive change.

So, what I'm really interested in is looking at the contrasts and identifying what are the options in both cases to the areas to the north and east of the growth centres, beyond simply trying and failing to attract growth. What do you do with the bits that are – and I don't like this language, but people use it – 'left behind areas'? Maybe it's not so much that they are left behind, but that they need something else. For the future, they need a new kind of planning.

I think that planners have very little in the way of tools or visions available for these areas. For instance, in Cambridgeshire I looked at the different districts and their plans; all of them bar one are basically saying 'well, we need more growth' and they just have no idea of how to get that! One district has gone for a more community-based approach, but interestingly they find themselves in conflict with the central government organisation that examines local plans, and that's an interesting story that is still ongoing.

To what extent do these phenomena challenge your textbooks for future planners?

Yvonne Rydin: We have less reliance on textbooks today to be honest, but I think if you look at the syllabuses, even in my own school, and what most of the research is about, it tends to focus on big developments, the big money, the big shifts, urban regeneration, public-private partnerships, mega-projects; it's all very focused on the growth paradigm. I think that's fairly embedded, and I think it does take a bit of rethinking right down at the core; what is the economic model behind this and is it a model that is actually working or not? And I do think this is very much about rethinking the differences between working with big capital and working with small capital, and also working across the economy/society divide. The conventional economic model starts from the differentiation between the household and the firm, two sectors, two sides of the diagram, and I think we need to reconceptualise that relationship as well. So, I've started to play around with ideas of – and I'm sure other people are doing this too – the localised economy, the localised society and localised planning as a way of rethinking how these relationships actually work.

Certainly, what we need is a more hybrid planning system; we need to move away from a one-size-fits-all solution which tends to be the growth solution, and we need hybridity in the planning system, with a recognition that you need to know your context and you need to customise your solution to that context. When you look at context, a localised context, we've got used to looking at the resources of civil society, but I think we're much less used to looking at the resources of endogenous, very small-scale capital. And we need to think about how to work better across the civil society / small-scale capital divide, and consider what capital can do in relation to this. Also we need to work with some of the more localised, embedded, larger scale capital. It might be private sector, it might be public sector, or be on the very fuzzy boundary we now have between the public and the private sector.

I've been reading quite a lot about what happens in the United States; it's very interesting the way that universities and philanthropic foundations very often act as anchor institutions helping to build different kinds of local economy, often with the cooperation of smaller, endogenous, locally owned businesses. They are more accepting of growth coalitions, they are more accepting of urban regimes, and they don't have the same trust in the planning sector that we have, so they are starting from a different place, but there is something here that we can learn from.

Do you see particular methodological implications resulting from this?

Yvonne Rydin: It's much easier, as I tell all my students, to research what's there, and what has happened. And of course, if one is looking, in these lower growth areas, for the options that haven't been tried, that's really, really difficult! You end up in thought experiments, and as academics, you can sort-of look a little silly. You can promote ideas that are not realistic. So, I think there are quite important methodological issues here about how you actually look for what has been missed – the silences, the absences – and then think about how those can be filled, but in a way that makes sense, that isn't just idealism. I think we have a lot of academic papers that do very rigorous research but end with rather idealistic suggestions; we have a responsibility to be a bit more pragmatic in what we actually recommend.

The local scale seems to be of key interest for your work. Why is that?

Yvonne Rydin: In planning, there is a national and even international framework, and we must always take into account that it makes a huge difference: that is, the institutional arrangements that central government puts in place, or state governments in different kinds of political systems. But the question is usually what can you do at a local level – with this site, with this city? So the locality is very much the scale that we want to operate at – to think about what is actually possible at that kind of scale. My hunch or hypothesis is that the kind of knowledge that local planning works with is absolutely central. And the kind of knowledge used – not just data, but also assessments and evaluations – focus the attention in particular kinds of ways. Certainly in the UK system, where I have studied this so far, knowledge is very focused on particular growth dynamics and concerns about releasing land to meet those growth dynamics. I suppose one of the things I am looking for is: what are the alternative knowledge claims, the alternative knowledge sets that we might draw upon to think about doing planning in a different way?

There is a lot of interest in lay and experiential knowledge, and I think that's important where communities are trying to resist the negative effects of growth. But beyond this, I have a feeling that we really need to develop new knowledge, and I suspect some of this is around the knowledge of the local economy, what actually is happening particularly in the SME sector, and what is going on there; generally, we know very little to nothing. And if we don't know about it, how do we harness it, how do we support it? So, my hunch is that I need to look at the different kinds of knowledge claims as a way of thinking about the different kinds of planning that can happen in localities. The interesting picture here is often on the boundary of academic and grey literature and it's about all the little case studies of what's going on all around the world, and trying to pull together all those case studies and learn from them. With conventional methodologies it is difficult to have a rigorous framework for doing that; it's almost detective work, I think.

A lot is written about best practices, in that you have to recontextualise them when you move them to a different space; this is about the knowledge you need about your locality in order to recontextualise well, so that you're not just borrowing things inappropriately. That isn't just about knowing the best practice example, it's also knowing about the context into which you are trying to situate it. So, if you have a training scheme that's a good idea in an American small town, that helped to build the capacities of lower income communities and got them into various kinds of employment, okay, that seems like a good idea. But if we take it to somewhere like Cambridgeshire, then we need to know about the differences between the localities, about how we may retool that idea for this place.

If you were given an unconditional degrowth research grant allowing you to hire a postdoc for two years, what would be the topical focus of your project?

Yvonne Rydin: What I think I would do is I would get somebody and make sure that they are situated in one or a small number of low-growth areas, but get them really embedded in there. Not to do the sort of fly-in fly-out research, which we very often have to do if we are not working in our own backyard. Instead do a quasi-ethnography with local SMEs and smaller businesses and with smaller NGOs, to get to really know this locality and use that to think about how we could work through changes that could actually be put into effect. This would take into account knowledge that is being created elsewhere, but also the barriers that are in place and the institutional arrangements, as in financial or market structures. What I think I would ideally like to do would be to have that embedded kind of research, the opportunity for which I've not had for a very long amount of time now.

This is very demanding and involves a long-term commitment to communities in order to work with them and alongside them. I think it's easier to do that if you do it in your own backyard. I have colleagues who work with communities within London and it works very well; and I can see you have universities in the States, where there is a long distance to the next large place, so academics automatically work on their own town. We in Europe have been pulled away from that a little bit, and have been encouraged to cross boundaries – till now.

We should continue this dialogue with the EU institutions

An interview with Prof Dr Tom Bauler, conducted by Christian Schulz

Tom Bauler is Chair of Environment and Economy at Université Libre de Bruxelles (ULB). In his research on socio-ecological transition he focuses, among other things, on questions of environmental governance, alternative indicators of social welfare and social innovations. In 2018 he was the academic partner and co-organiser of the Post-Growth Conference at the European Parliament.[1]
http://igeat.ulb.ac.be/fr/equipe/details/person/tom-bauler/

How did it come about that the Post-Growth Conference in 2018 was hosted by the European Parliament?

Tom Bauler: There are different layers of explanation as to why we were involved in this. A very personal one is that it was an initial initiative by a Member of Parliament, a Belgian politician called Phillipe Lamberts, who is in 'Ecolo', so part of the Group of the Greens in the European Parliament. I know him a little bit, his parliamentary assistant was a former student of mine and he wrote his Master's thesis under my coordination on material flows in Wallonia and how to re-configure these material flows under a degrowth programme, what would happen with these material flows once you accept that there is some form of degrowth. And Phillipe actually was invited to one of the International Degrowth Conferences, I think it was the one in Budapest.

---

1 https://www.degrowth.info/en/2018/09/impressions-from-the-post-growth-conference-at-the-european-Parliament-in-brussels/ (28.02.2020)

The people around Vincent Liégey and Federico Demaria – involved in the 'degrowth&science network' – started to initiate a reflection on how to create a more formal science-policy interface – a degrowth science, degrowth movements, degrowth activism, policy democracy sort of interface. Their first move was to set up a roundtable session on 'degrowth in parliaments' at this conference. They were looking for keynote participants for the roundtable, and the idea emerged that Phillipe was the MEP to invite. He's a bit atypical as a member of the Green Party, at least for Belgium, because he engages very much with industry and more generally economic activities. As a consequence, he sits also on the more 'hardcore' commissions of the European Parliament, so not the environment or energy, but the industry and the trades and that sort of stuff. He has a very precise idea on what degrowth means for him.

So, it started with that roundtable session and then Phillipe came back from Budapest with quite some enthusiasm, with the consequence that then Olivier came to me in order to request some local academic support for a Brussels EP-conference on de-/post-growth. Olivier reached out to other parties, so there were people from the socialists, from here and there, and they formed a coalition actually, a cross-party group. Phillipe also financed a study on macro-economic modelling exercises, what would it mean, a degrowth trajectory for Europe, in terms of macroeconomic effects. They gave that to colleagues in Barcelona and Italy. When Philippe had that report on his table, Olivier came back to me with more concrete plans. The call came thus actually from two sides, both the degrowth people around Vincent Liégey and Federico Demaria and Giorgos Kallis, and this working group at the European Parliament, and a little bit in between that, ourselves, the local academic partner, and the European Environmental Bureau, which is a federation of environmental NGOs, a lobbying group. We all came together and thought we need to do something and then after a couple of discussions it became quite quickly clear that we had to try to see how far we could enter into a dialogue with the hardcore chief economists of the different European institutions.

So, the event was finally hosted by the Parliament, in their premises?

Tom Bauler: There is a very obvious aspect to this choice. If you want to do something in the European Parliament, you can either be hosted by a Member of Parliament (MEP) or by a group of MEPs. If it's a trans-party group, it achieves more importance in the Parliament itself, you get more attention, and obviously also bigger funding. At one point the leverage was sufficient for Phillipe to try to get the president of the European Parliament (EP) on board. As a consequence, the entire initiative formally became an initiative by the entire Parliament and not just of a bunch of specific MEPs. The line of reasoning was that in 2007 and 2009/10 the EP had organised a series of 'Beyond GDP' conferences, and the present initiative could be linked to that line of debate, ten years later. They understood that that sort of heterodox thinking had already gained access once to the Parliament, and with quite some success as people still speak of it as if the Parliament had had a lead role in that international discussion around the renewal of indicators. So the EP saw a chance to do something like this again, with a post-growth agenda this time.

Was it a one-off event? Or did something happen afterwards in terms of perpetuating this dialogue?

Tom Bauler: Well, the dialogue between the European Parliament and degrowth academia and degrowth movements goes on, in both ways. That relatively loose working group has been extended a little bit at the level of the European Parliament, which has also had to digest the latest elections and the debate around the new Commission. The next move – at the level of the degrowth community – is to organise something at the 'International Degrowth & Ecological Economics Conference' in Manchester this year (2020). So that dynamic goes on.

At the end of the 2018 conference, we had indeed in mind – because we all found the initiative quite productive – that we would continue some of the encounters with the EU officials. The plan was to let the European elections pass, to wait for the new Parliament and the new European Commission, and to then redo a bigger event in Brussels. So if everything goes right we will have a bigger initiative in Brussels again at the level of the institutions. In parallel, meanwhile there is a sort of formalisation of the dialogue, as there have been a series of closed-door events in Brussels. Actually, the call came from the more central orthodox economists at the level of the institutions – to have closed-door events, to discuss more technical issues such as social protection on a degrowth agenda.

In your everyday work as a university teacher and researcher, to what extent can you include degrowth approaches?

Tom Bauler: It is marginal, I would say in my research work, I don't have proper projects that I would say are really on degrowth. I had some activities in the past on alternative economic indicators, which some people say is part of the degrowth agenda, but maybe not. I did something on social innovation. Some of these social innovation issues are also part of a degrowth scenario because of their disruptive nature. Broadly I would say, I don't have a research agenda which focuses on degrowth.

But teaching is very different. My main teaching activities are related to ecological economics, so I teach a form of heterodox economics where macroeconomic issues become very prominent. As a consequence, I quite strongly question growth trajectories being an avenue to bring us to being able to respect climate objectives and adjacent environmental objectives like that. For instance, in my main course I have a whole chapter on degrowth, macroeconomics, macro-ecological economics, which is basically degrowth economics. I also teach a course on environmental consumption and psychology, where I also teach things like frugality and sufficiency which could be seen as being part of a degrowth agenda. The teaching embodies actually quite a lot of links to this literature and its whole mindset.

How do you deal with the fact that most of the textbooks in your field are still rather orthodox?

Tom Bauler: I have a regular textbook which is on environmental economics, I tell my students that that is the technical part of the story, if you want to understand what a market is or what a price is, those sort of technicalities, they should go to that textbook. And then for each chapter, so to speak, for each topic, I have identified a set of more focal readings, which are not textbooks anymore, because textbooks don't exist in all of these fields, it's more a set of papers.

In your research on social innovation, do you face any particular methodological challenges related to the degrowth approach?

Tom Bauler: Yes, I think the biggest challenges are on the methodological side. At the moment we struggle with the fact that all these objects of studies are entangled in very intense dynamics and are changing more rapidly than you can get the data on them. 'Social innovation in the making' is really very challenging in terms of stabilising your object of research and your unit of analysis. It's one of the classical things: it's not so difficult to characterise them, to stay with them one or two years, but to stabilise the object in order to really understand what is happening is really a challenge.

Another challenge that is a little bit more traditional is that there is quite a high demand from a lot of these 'objects' to actually use transdisciplinary or co-creation approaches. For a lot of obvious reasons and for a lot of good reasons, but that methodological avenue is tending to monopolise the method choice a little bit, it's starting to become like a hegemony of method. If you want to study social innovation, you almost are supposed to do it in a co-creational way. I can understand that call in particular, but it gets quite monolithic. I don't like that particularly, I'd prefer more variety, especially when it comes to some of the funding. For Brussels' regional funding for instance, if you want to do research on social innovation, it almost for sure has to be in a co-creational mode. Simultaneously, students, but also PhD candidates or postdocs tend more and more to favour transdisciplinary or co-creation processes. Which is very interesting as such, but it should not be only that.

If you were given an unconditional degrowth research grant allowing you to hire a postdoc for two years, what would be the topical focus of your project?

Tom Bauler: There are two answers to that, the first one is more linked to the current state of affairs in policy design, maybe the transition agenda or something like that. The topic would be defined by a lack of work on the governance of 'exnovation', i. e. trying to understand how to make policies to help society to do the opposite of innovation. Phase out specific socio-technical systems in particular socio-economic sectors. That is one research agenda which is interesting me right now very much; but it would not be a lifetime project. The thing that troubles me at the moment is that I get the impression very selfishly within academia, there is a long way to go to bring us away from the current, present 'bizarreries' which configure our institutions and our activities. In particular the configuration around 'fast science' (fast publications, fast projects, fast solutions ...) which I really find increasingly difficult. I'm not saying everything is bad in the present science business, but I have more and more the impression that academia is a little bit like a headless chicken at the moment, in terms of how my professional life is organised and the activities and lives of those around me.

It's a rich struggle in how to teach, how to research, how to do science actually. What if your projects followed a sort of a degrowth agenda on doing science? That could be very interesting. So one avenue could be to develop some research in a prospective mode on how to understand the future of science, that would be really interesting I guess.

Another thing we are facing over here in Brussels which I am trying to get my head around is to capture the memories of our European institutions. If I look at the very very senior civil servants in the European institutions, I'm surprised by the level of capacity for controversial debates these people have. They are not the typical managers of policy implementation or so; most of them really also see themselves as forging the future of (parts of) humanity; and they come up with deep classical traditional philosophical struggles. Some of them are very conscious about ecological issues, and really pay attention to their own intellectual development because what they are doing is not just implementing policies, designing policies; it's much more important. Being so close to the European institutions really helps to make these observations. A second avenue for future research could be to try to better capture the debates and struggles of ideas which are present in the institutions.

IV. Spaces of Design

POST-GROWTH PLANNING NEEDS...

1. New success criteria as a basis for action
2. Fair & democratic decisions
3. Great transformation through small changes
4. Experimental & creative action
5. Learning to fail
6. All of us to be post-growth planners!

'Post-growth planning is also art and experimentation. Failure is part of it and simultaneously the start of a new experiment aiming at achieving social-ecological transformation.'

Viola Schulze Dieckhoff

Spatial transformations: Process, goal, guideline?

Markus Hesse

This article aims to situate 'transformation' in spatial and planning practice, primarily in the debate about spatial guidelines. This focus arises from the widespread impact that talk of the transformation has now achieved, at least in the German-speaking world. The term 'transformation' has implicit if not explicit guideline character, both in German-speaking countries (WBGU 2011) and internationally, although the focus of 'sustainability transitions' is here somewhat different (Frantzeskaki/Broto/Coenen et al. 2017). Both discourses are increasingly relevant for operationalising paths of post-growth development.

The primary research question addressed by this chapter is: Can spatial transformation be viewed as a guideline and if so, how does this manifest itself specifically in analytical, normative or procedural terms? Does transformation lay claim to being generally applicable or does it have specific focuses – what is the concrete formulation of goals for which level? Or should transformation be understood primarily as a procedural standard, as a metaphor for collective mobilisation towards change, the substance of which tends to remain hidden behind sometimes quite cumbersome participatory processes? Before answers to these questions are explored, the two concepts at the heart of this discussion are briefly considered.

(Great) transformation

The first focus of this discussion is the 'great transformation' (*Große Transformation, GT*) or its semantic sister 'sustainability transitions' (STs), which became extremely popular in research and practice in the 2010s. The use of 'great' in the transformation discourse clearly draws on the work of Karl

Polanyi (1944) as an ideological-historical source, which offers an extremely stimulating synopsis of social, economic and political development. The focus here is on two things: firstly, on experience of the decline of liberal political constitutions under authoritarian regimes and, secondly, on the tension between market liberalism and democracy described by the term 'double movement'. Polanyi viewed this tension as being basically unresolvable as it is unlikely that large-scale political restructuring can be reconciled with democratic principles and practices to any great extent. Part 3 of Polanyi's book then deals with the conditions of freedom in complex societies. Nevertheless, fundamental to Polanyi's thinking is the notion that economic dynamics must be socially 'contained' or re-embedded by an active, interventionist state.

(Great) transformation is related to this tradition of the re-embedding of unfettered technological and economic dynamics in society. This refers to the 'massive, ecological, technological, economic, institutional and cultural process of transition' (Schneidewind 2018, translated from German) facing the world at the beginning of the twenty-first century. It seems that this transition is the only way to solve the many crises of the industrial, natural, economic and social system. Transformation and sustainability transitions thus now represent a kind of mainstream of current environmental, technological and sustainability research (Zolfagharian/Walrave/Raven et al. 2019). As was demonstrated by the choice of topics for the 2019 ARL Congress, which then gave rise to this volume, transformation is now also established in urban and spatial discourse. The heightened sensitivity to evolutionary change found in the transitions debate is particularly inspiring, because at its heart is the search for transitions (!) from situations that really exist to favoured or apparently necessary states. This is linked to questions concerning alternative discourses and how generalisable strategies for sustainability can emerge from niche or pioneer concepts.

The reports by the German Advisory Council on Global Change (*Wissenschaftlicher Beirat der Bundesregierung Globale Umweltveränderungen, WBGU*) contributed tremendously towards popularisation of the great transformation (WBGU 2011, 2016). The WBGU addressed the great transformation in its 2011 report 'World in Transition' (*'Welt im Wandel'*) and emphatically thematised the subject of a 'social contract'. In its 2016 report 'The Relocation of Humanity: The Transformative Power of the Cities' (*'Der Umzug der Menschheit: Die transformative Kraft der Städte'*), transformation was considered in a specific spatial and urban setting for the first time. The report focused on urbanisation processes and cities, linking global, socio-ecological contexts with the question of urbanisation processes. However, the WBGU's arguments are not free of causal fallacies. This is particularly the case for the specific construction of the urban: the fact that the majority of the population is localised in urban areas does not mean that the essence of the problem can be solved in the cities or by the cities or, indeed, that this should be the primary gaol. Angelo and Wachsmuth (2015) criticised this perspective as 'methodological cityism'; the focus on the cities overlooks the crucial role played by the nation states and supranational regulation even in the so-called urban age.

In order to achieve the goals of the great transformation in the urban context, the WBGU report (2016) discusses ambitious normative stipulations. Urban areas – and spatial planning within them – have a key role in the implementation of transformative strategies. 'We need spatial planning!' (translated from German) was the credo proclaimed by Dirk Messner when he presented the report in a keynote lecture at the Dortmund Conference for Spatial and Planning Research in 2018. However, the audience, consisting mostly of representatives of spatially relevant planning and research, were not inclined to automatically accept this dictum – a scepticism that is probably based on a realistic assessment of the status and actual performance of spatial planning. In terms of policy and planning theory, the WBGU's rejection of incremental solutions in favour of one large initiative is somewhat troublesome – especially as the relevant sponsors, strategies and instruments are not identified: 'Within a few years, a paradigm shift must take place in cities: away from incremental approaches, towards transformative changes, in order to preserve the natural foundations of human life and people's quality of life in the long term' (WBGU 2016: 20, translated from German). In contrast, other authors see GT as part of a traditional incremental understanding of planning which uses adaptive strategies to react to increasingly disruptive change (Iwaniec/Cook/Barbosa et al. 2019).

By using the term 'great' (*Große Transformation*), the WBGU report explicitly refers to the political-economic tradition of thought associated with Polanyi. It is therefore all the more surprising that it is in this field that the paper displays its greatest weaknesses: 'It would only be possible to speak of a great transformation in Polanyi's terms if alternatives to the self-regulating market system and market-conform adjustments were sought. If we use this yardstick as a basis, then the half-heartedness of the WBGU's reference to Polanyi becomes clear, as indeed is the case with many other contributions to transformation research' (Thomasberger 2016: 34, translated from German). The WBGU's urbanisation report of 2016 also remains vague about who may be able to tackle the comprehensive task of social transformation in a relatively short time – the global society, pioneers of change, key actors? It contains little of significance about institutions. While general statements are made about land and property, there is a lack of robust proposals on how it might be possible to implement a reorientation of property relations and how the frictions and conflicts inevitably associated with this could be resolved. Schneidewind (2018) is more concrete in his proposals and also reflects on the conditions of the political economy. However, his notions are not necessarily easier to implement: basically, he suggests, all levels and actors of the transformation need only to be properly interconnected with each other.

The redesign of local practices as genuinely *transformative* action can undoubtedly bring new blood to politics, which has clearly manoeuvred itself into dead-ends with its administrative routines, entrenched conflicts of interest and piecemeal solutions. The temptation to overcome such dilemmas with one large initiative is obvious. However, practised transformation has yet, I believe, to prove its effectiveness – and inherent advantages to existing practices. Questions are rightly being asked about the almost inflationary use of real labs: it is at least unclear exactly how existing institutions are to be incorporated into new practices and approaches. And the equally inflationary demand for public participation in whatever transformation may be implemented (although no objections can be raised to participation in principle), triggers the following question: What can be done to avoid the problems of randomness, erraticism and particular interests that are usually found in the 'nightmare of participation' (Miessen 2012, translated from German)?

Guidelines

Guidelines form the second focus of this discussion – against a backdrop that assumes that the great transformation has itself become such a guideline. There seems to be widespread consensus that GT should not be an objective in itself and also that it is not primarily about the process as such, even though this is the impression occasionally made. In its comprehensive approach, GT represents a guideline, a model, a kind of utopian narrative (Giesel 2007; Dahlstrom 2014; Zieschank/Ronzheimer 2017). It offers alternatives to the status quo in what initially appears to be a consistent framework and links general issues (such as the question of growth) with practical and local strategies. In spatial terms, GT builds upon well-known elements of sustainable urban and spatial development, linking them to the narrative of a larger whole. However, the construct of 'transformation' is like its predecessors. They all, de facto, comprise a rather contradictory mixture of control and development goals, of spatial and sectoral focuses, and, finally and decidedly, of procedural elements. In practice, they tend to be somewhat heterogeneous and always extremely abstract, and in this way they achieve a certain hegemony or majority support. Over time such guidelines have proved changeable, occasionally even opportunistic, driven by the *Zeitgeist* (Hesse/Leick 2013). Not only do individuals pursue specific problem interpretations and need to compete for funding, but they are also dependent on temporary fashions, conjunctures and constructs.

This is well-illustrated by the spatial policy discourses of the 2000s and early 2010s, which experienced two major 'turns' and hence changes in focus, at least in the German-speaking and European context. Since the mid-1990s, many European countries have been characterised by a focus on growth instead of the traditional objective of 'spatial balance'; this has been equally true of countries with a decidedly statist planning tradition like Great Britain, the Netherlands and Germany. The focus on growth was associated – not necessarily empirically – with cities or metropolitan regions thanks to their supposed role as drivers of economic development (Aring/Sinz 2006). In the last decade, the multi-layered development processes of urbanised areas (both metropolitan areas and medium sized urban regions) and changed political perceptions have led to a shift in focus to peripheralisation processes and the areas affected by them, especially rural areas, peripheral regions and places with shrinking populations and negative economic development. Attention is now being paid to places that are 'left behind', not least because their populations have increasingly expressed political dissent (Rodríguez-Pose 2018). Most recently, discourses about guidelines and models have begun to include notions of homeland (*Heimat*) and spatial identity, occasionally in a fruitful way, occasionally in association with rather platitudinous attitudes and associations. GT appears here as a unifying superstructure, the really major approach among current narratives on 'green' and 'smart'.

What do these experiences of framings of guidelines for policy and planning strategies teach us for the GT? What should we expect with the 'great' challenges? Are they, as it were, once-in-a-century problems which demand the use of all the big tools the guideline offers and with which practice is correspondingly equipped…? Or are there good reasons for restraint in light of spatial planning's critical self-image (see Lamker/Levin-Keitel 2019 and other papers there)? At first glance, there seems to be much in favour of bringing great narratives into the real world, not least because the problematic situation clearly demands this. At the same time, however, caution is called for: it is important to know what the challenges are and how risks should be dealt with (Blythe/Silver/Evans et al. 2018). It follows that the GT discourse should not only be pluralised but should also be normatively disarmed. It should certainly be possible to describe the extent of the challenge with appropriate precision without losing all humility in the face of the demands made on policy, planning and the shaping of society. If a surplus of normativity leads to positivist traps or promises solutions prematurely, this is also unfavourable for planning.

Critical evaluation

What does all this mean for science and practice? The economist Frank Beckenbach has described the deliberate transition from the transformation of society (or more precisely, from the self-transforming society) to the transformation society as a 'transformation illusion' (Beckenbach 2017). He argues that the term and the concept awaken three types of unrealistic expectations concerning the shaping of society: a *planning* illusion in terms of the predictability and controllability of complex societies; a *regulating* illusion in terms of targeted collaboration between market actors, state actors and civil society actors; and finally an *acceptance* illusion concerning the willingness of society, and not just social niches, to follow such a path. His summary, which he substantiates in scientific (economic) terms, is that the great transformation is unsuitable for use as a guiding principle. The sociologist Armin Nassehi (2019) recently expressed this in more everyday language in an interview with the newspaper *taz* that is well worth reading: 'Anyone can formulate goals' (translated from German), he comments rather sardonically. On the other hand, he argues, formulating robust strategies, implementing those strategies in complex societies and reliably evaluating their effects is much more demanding. This appears to be the real challenge of targeted transformation policies.

This leads to the observation that, at heart, transformation debates still appear to be strongly influenced by the logics and demands of research, as can be seen in the sheer quantity of relevant publications. In comparison, new paths leading to changed practices are greatly underdeveloped. Or, as Koch, Kabisch and Krellenberg (2018: 13) expressed it in their review:

> 'While the normative understanding of urban transformations has gained considerably in importance in urban-related studies and even first steps towards a transformative turn can be identified, this is not reflected in current development processes in cities (...). An implementation gap between the theoretical concept and the empirical cases is clearly visible.'

Furthermore, the literature contains sufficient evidence of implementation problems of the sort that have long confronted normative concepts like sustainable development. Many of the transformation paths that are implemented on a sectoral level are not particularly new and thus do not necessarily enrich the discussion or promise a more effective impact. It seems typical that the corresponding lists fail to actively address past experiences or deal with the barriers to implementation faced by targeted transformation.

This begs the question as to what is genuinely new about transformation – except for greatly increased ambitions concerning social control. I argue that what is new is, *firstly*, the specific relationship between research and practice. Science has assumed an engaged role and adopted a narrative position, problem-oriented rather than fusty, transdisciplinary rather than traditional. Of course, knowledge production and dissemination are fundamental to every transformation, but this development nonetheless triggers questions. With the missionary, almost religious approach of some of the apologists for total transformation, science is, I believe, treading on thin ice – it is making itself dependent on good intentions and interests. Familiarly, this does not always end well. In my opinion, arguments drawn from the philosophy of science speak for more scepticism, perhaps also restraint. I most certainly do not share the view that universities should prioritise their third mission – i.e.

to promote 'transfer' in addition to research and teaching – so it becomes their first mission and should subordinate all practices to this goal (Schneidewind 2018, Section 21). Instrumentalising research in this way would not only fail to make transformation more realistic, it would also damage science. This problem was addressed in detail in a statement on dealing with 'great societal challenges' (translated from German) issued by the German Council of Science and Humanities (Wissenschaftsrat 2015). The great complexity, global dimensions and disciplinary composition of the new types of problems complicate the process of finding the right positioning for science policy and strategy. This has repeatedly led to critical discussion in the 'inner circle' of transformation research (see Grunwald 2015, Strunz/Gawel 2017; Grunwald 2018). Perhaps the interplay of two ideal-types of actors could lead to changed practice: the positioning of research as an 'honest broker' (Grunwald 2018) as postulated by Roger A. Pielke (2007), and the understanding of practice as the action of reflexive practitioners (Schön 1983). This combination could give rise to robust approaches. However, a positioning of this sort demands from both sides 'a high degree of reflexivity and argumentative transparency, the ability to learn not only in analytical-empirical terms but also in normative terms, and a constant questioning of former positions' (Grunwald 2018: 116, translated from German).

What would be new, *secondly*, would be if transformation research considered the implementation of its proposals in more detail, specifically in terms of framework conditions, potentials and barriers (see Dörre/Rosa/ Becker et al. 2019). This has similarly not yet been successfully undertaken by sustainability research. Transformation and sustainability approaches share a common problem in that the extension of the normative timeframe for targets has not automatically led to an increase in their effectiveness. What adjustments should institutions make, how should social security systems be restructured to meet new requirements, what consequences would system transformation have for policymaking, for distributive justice? Which hard cuts can be expected and which gains could compensate for them? In my opinion, a sober view of political realities is required rather than euphemistic talk of a great transformation (see Bettini/Arklay/Head 2017). Valuable stimuli could also be provided by the established political-science field of transformation research, which attracted increased attention in the course of the political transformation of 1989/90 (see Kollmorgen/Merkel/Wagener 2015). Transformation research traditionally investigates the significance of systemic change (political, economic) for institutions, economic systems, practices of political regulation and lifeworlds. Drawing on the overview in Kollmorgen, Merkel and Wagener (2015), there appear to be numerous ideas for further developing the discussion. On the other hand, this most comprehensive presentation has few links to ecological transformation, and even fewer to spatial development. Both discourses deserve more interaction with the other.

Conclusions

Returning to the primary research question, it seems that the charm of 'transformation' may be found in the fact that this term offers an appropriately differentiated notion of evolutionary social change. This represents true progress: this analytical dimension of the term is convincing and should be explored further. On the other hand, it seems unclear whether the concept is sufficient to robustly guide the intended change – does transformation offer more substance than, for instance, sustainable development? Not that this should be understood as opposing the experimental, open and subversive character of transformation per se. However, engaging on the level of the great transformation requires more than just a collection of individual measures and bullet points listing everything that can be thought of or has perhaps been heard around the place, occasionally with a touch of radicalism. I follow Ulrich Brand's (2016) dictum here, that the strategic use of 'transformation' does not necessarily help solve the manifold crises of our times. This is particularly true of the inflationary use of the term – which leads to the specifics of the approach being blurred in a melange of everything and anything, obscuring the potentials of redefining social change dynamics and the corresponding policies not only in terms of terminology but also of content.

If the aim is to credibly, not only metaphorically, engage on the large scale, then concrete ideas for macro-management are required, ones that appropriately influence fundamental determinants of socio-economic development (such as the taxation system, a possible basic income, the recently discussed land question, the role of growth as a driver and constraint …). And there must be some notion of how such ideas can be implemented and what effects and secondary effects their introduction will have, especially in social terms (Blythe/Silver/Evans et al. 2018). If entry into a post-growth era does indeed turn out to be a 'crisis-like and mostly undesirable consequence of structural change' (Wiesenthal 2019: 379, translated from German), then multifaceted frictions are inevitable and we will need to react to them. Only against this background is it possible to consider, experiment with and try out concrete planning tasks. However, this involves a certain dilemma for spatial discourses, which have good reasons for remaining small scale rather than tackling the large scale. As long as the great transformation omits the macro-level (Thomasberger 2016) and aims to provide blueprints for micro-processes instead, then it is nothing more than sustainability in a new guise. This would lead to transformations but not necessarily to the great transformation. Under these conditions, the added value of the grand narrative would be exhausted in 'enchanting' reality, as Tom Sieverts puts it (Sieverts 2015: 19, translated from German). It would not by any means, however, fundamentally change this reality and it is also unclear whether it would in fact be any more suitable than other concepts discussed to date, such as sustainable development. There is therefore a risk that the debate on transformation simply represents a short-lived hype. In the labyrinth of transformations that are really taking place – the desirable, the unintended and the accidental –, it seems that the concept of the (great) transformation has still to prove itself as an effective vision.

Cited literature

Angelo, H., & Wachsmuth, D. (2015). Urbanizing urban political ecology: A critique of methodological cityism. *International Journal of Urban and Regional Research*, 39(1), 16–27.

Aring, J., & Sinz, M. (2006). Neue Leitbilder der Raumentwicklung in Deutschland: Modernisierung der Raumordnungspolitik im Diskurs. *disP-The Planning Review*, 42(165), 43–60.

Beckenbach, F. (2017). Moderne Wirtschaftswissenschaften im Spannungsfeld von Paradigmaentwicklung und Problemlösungserwartungen. Keynote presentation at the IÖW conference „Transformative Wirtschaftswissenschaft im Kontext Nachhaltiger Entwicklung". Berlin, 2017, November 6.

Bettini, Y., Arklay, T., & Head, B. W. (2017). Understanding the policy realities of urban transitions. In N. Frantzeskaki, V. Castán Brotoet, L. Coenen, & D. Loorbach (Eds.), *Urban sustainability transitions*. Routledge, 37–49.

Blythe, J., Silver, J., Evans, L., Armitage, D., Bennett, N. J., Moore, M. L., Morrison, T. H., & Brown, K. (2018). The dark side of transformation: latent risks in contemporary sustainability discourse. *Antipode, 50*(5), 1206–1223.

Brand, U. (2016). "Transformation" as a new critical orthodoxy: The strategic use of the term "transformation" does not prevent multiple crises. *GAIA-Ecological Perspectives for Science and Society, 25*(1), 23–27.

Dahlstrom, M. F. (2014). Using narratives and storytelling to communicate science with nonexpert audiences. *PNAS, 111*(Supplement 4), 3614–3620.

Dörre, K., Rosa, H., Becker, K., Bose, S., & Seyd, B. (Eds.) (2019). *Große Transformation? Zur Zukunft moderner Gesellschaften: Sonderband des Berliner Journals für Soziologie*. Springer.

Frantzeskaki, N, Broto, V. C., Coenen, L., & Loorbach, D. (Eds.) (2017). *Urban sustainability transitions*. Routledge.

Giesel, K. D. (2007). *Leitbilder in den Sozialwissenschaften. Begriffe, Theorien und Forschungskonzepte*. Springer.

Grunwald, A. (2015). Transformative Wissenschaft – eine neue Ordnung im Wissenschaftsbetrieb? *GAIA-Ecological Perspectives for Science and Society, 24*(1), 17–20.

Grunwald, A. (2018). Transformative Wissenschaft als honest broker? Das passt! *GAIA-Ecological Perspectives for Science and Society, 27*(1), 113–116.

Hesse, M., & Leick, A. (2013). Wachstum, Innovation, Metropolregionen. Zur Rekonstruktion des jüngeren Leitbildwandels in der deutschen Raumentwicklungspolitik. *Raumforschung und Raumordnung, 71*(4), 343–359.

Iwaniec, D. M., Cook, E. M., Barbosa, O., & Grimm, N. B. (2019). The framing of urban sustainability transformations. *Sustainability, 11*(3), 573.

Koch, F., Kabisch, S., & Krellenberg, K. (2018). A transformative turn towards sustainability in the context of urban-related studies? a systematic review from 1957 to 2016. *Sustainability, 10*(1), 58.

Kollmorgen, R., Merkel, W., & Wagener, H.-J. (2015). *Handbuch Transformationsforschung*. Springer.

Lamker, C., & Levin-Keitel, M. (2019). Planung im Wandel – von Rollenverständnissen und Selbstbildern. *Raumforschung und Raumordnung, 77*(2), 107–113.

Miessen, M. (2012). *Albtraum Partizipation*. Merve.
Nassehi, A. (2019). „Ziele formulieren kann jeder. Wie kann man die Erderhitzung stoppen? Die einen glauben an Greta, die anderen an den Markt. Der Soziologe Armin Nassehi hat eine bessere Idee". In *taz, die tageszeitung*, 2019, June 17, 20–22.
Pielke, R. A. (2007). *The honest broker. Making sense of science in policy and politics*. Cambridge University Press.
Rodríguez-Pose, A. (2018). The revenge of the places that don't matter (and what to do about it). *Cambridge Journal of Regions, Economy and Society, 11*(1), 189–209.
Schneidewind, U. (2018). *Die Große Transformation: Eine Einführung in die Kunst gesellschaftlichen Wandels*. S. Fischer.
Schön, D. A. (1983). *The reflective practitioner: How professionals think in action*. Basic Books.
Sieverts, T. (2015). Bedingungen der Stadtentwicklung heute: Das Beispiel Karlsruhe. In Stadt Karlsruhe (Eds.), *Auf dem Weg zum räumlichen Leitbild*. KIT Scientific Publishing, 15–19.
Strunz, S., & Gawel, E. (2017). Transformative Wissenschaft: Eine kritische Bestandsaufnahme der Debatte. *GAIA-Ecological Perspectives for Science and Society, 26*(4), 321–325.
Thomasberger, C. (2016). Die Große Transformation und die Marktgesellschaft. *Ökologisches Wirtschaften, 31*(1), 30–34.
WBGU – Wissenschaftlicher Beirat Globale Umweltveränderungen (2011). *Welt im Wandel. Gesellschaftsvertrag für eine große Transformation*.
WBGU – Wissenschaftlicher Beirat Globale Umweltveränderungen (2016). *Der Umzug der Menschheit: Die transformative Kraft der Städte*.
Wiesenthal, H. (2019). Institutionelle Transformationen gestern – und morgen? In K. Dörre, H. Rosa, K. Becker, S. Bose, & B. Seyd, (Ed.), *Große Transformation? Zur Zukunft moderner Gesellschaften: Sonderband des Berliner Journals für Soziologie*. Springer, 367–382.
Wissenschaftsrat (2015). *Zum wissenschaftspolitischen Diskurs über Große gesellschaftliche Herausforderungen*. Position Paper 4594-15.
Zieschank, R., & Ronzheimer M. (2017). *Große Transformation und die Medien – Alternativen zum Wachstum als Leitbild der Kommunikation*. UBA documentations 12/2017.
Zolfagharian, M., Walrave, B., Raven, R., & Romme, A. G. L. (2019). Studying transitions: Past, present, and future. *Research Policy, 48*(9), 103788.

Cornerstones and positions of a precautionary post-growth economy[1]
The end of the growth-based model of prosperity

*Ulrich Petschow, Nils aus dem Moore, David Hofmann,
Eugen Pissarskoi, Steffen Lange*

Environmental crises are increasingly acute. Particularly prominent in the public debate is the climate crisis. The increases in greenhouse gas concentrations in the atmosphere is only one particularly striking anthropogenic intervention in the ecosystems (see Bindoff/Stott/AchutaRao et al. 2013: 869). Humanity has already put other fundamental earth system processes in a critical condition. Thus, for instance, the global volumes of phosphorus and nitrogen entering soils and water bodies have also exceeded critical limits (see Rockström/Steffen/Noon et al. 2009a/b, Steffen/Richardson/Rockström et al. 2015). Less prominent in the public debate is the biodiversity crisis (see IPBES 2019). These developments threaten future generations with drastic and irreversible disadvantages. In contrast to 'traditional' industrial environmental pollution, which can at least to a certain extent be 'filtered out' (and relocated) using add-on technologies, these 'new' challenges are closely linked to our way of life and economic model, which are based on economic growth.

Particularly in the early industrialised countries, this model has undoubtedly contributed towards welfare gains, reflected for instance in greater life expectancy. Globally speaking, in particular the catch-up devel-

---

[1] This article is based on a study undertaken for the German Federal Environmental Agency (*Umweltbundesamt*) (Petschow/aus dem Moore/Pissarskoi et al. 2018), which was conducted by the Institute for Ecological Economic Research (*Institut für ökologische Wirtschaftsforschung*) and the RWI Leibniz Institute for Economic Research (*RWI Institut für Wirtschaftsforschung*). It is available for free download on the Federal Environmental Agency website.

opment of China and the dramatic economic growth associated with it have led to a clear reduction in poverty rates. There is thus little controversy about the positive correlation between economic development and social well-being. However, questions are increasingly being asked about whether and to what extent future generations will ultimately have to pay for these gains.

The early industrialised, prosperous countries are responsible for a disproportionately high share of the impacts on natural systems (in relation to greenhouse gas emissions (GHG-emissions) see Caney 2009: 126). This article therefore focuses on the following questions: What role is played by economic performance and its future development in more prosperous countries like Germany with relation to adhering to planetary boundaries? What (environment) policy implications arise from this? We address these questions by introducing the historical and current growth debates, providing an overview of prominent positions and undertaking a critical analysis that allows us to derive a new proposal: the precautionary post-growth position, which we present for discussion.

Growth and welfare discussions

The discussion about economic growth and growth limits was long neglected in economic discourses, receiving attention mostly from 'outsiders'. Thus, in his essay 'The economics of the coming spaceship earth', Kenneth Boulding (1966) firstly referred to a metaphor popular at the time, that of 'Spaceship Earth', and secondly pointed out the significance of limits (also of the substitutability of factors of production). The first report on 'The limits to growth' by Meadows et al. (1972) led to considerable discussion, even if the possibility of substitution was certainly underestimated in detail. Georgescu-Roegen (1987), and also his pupil Daly (1977), called for other economic models. Consideration of these 'early' warnings underlines that it took the recent changes in the social and media climate at the end of the 2010s to bring sufficient pressure to bear and enable the issue of growth to be addressed again.

Figure 1: Global development of income over time

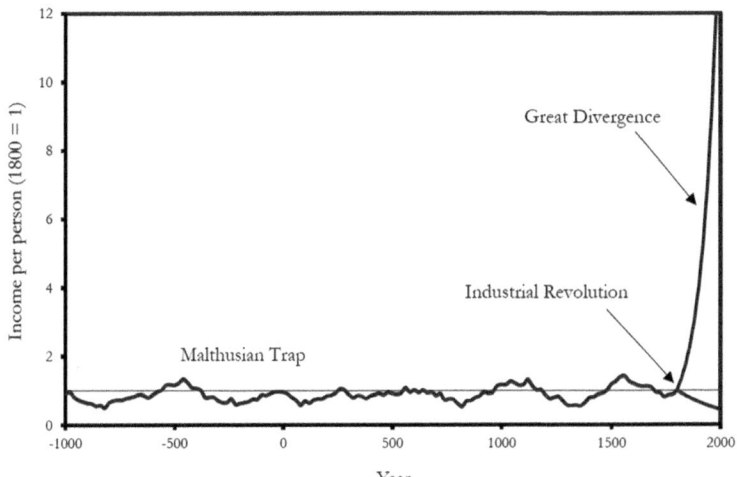

Source: Clark 2007

At least in the long term, economic growth has not in any way been a constant of human development but is rather closely linked to the industrial revolution (Clark 2007). It was the industrial revolution that enabled escape from the 'Malthusian trap'.[2] The special European path emerged not (only) due to the development of technology, but also due to the social conditions that determined whether and how this technology was used.[3] In this vein, Mokyr (2016) highlights the cultural conditions of this social change ("culture of growth") and focuses particularly on fundamental beliefs, suggesting that the transformation of the belief system was primarily linked to perceptions of nature. In combination with the specific contexts in Europe (competition between smaller states or cities) and the emergence of networks (in science and engineering), this transformation was ultimately decisive for the industrial revolution. McCloskey (2016) suggests that it was not the

---

2 Malthus (1803) analysed the relationship between population growth and crop yields. He suggested that population growth occurs in geometric progression while food production increases in arithmetic progression so that there is a natural ceiling due to limits on possible increases in food production. This, according to Malthus, makes economic growth almost impossible (Clark 2007, Fertig/Pfister 2012).

3 As seen in the inventions that were well-known in China but did not lead to similar economic growth.

available energy resources, the innovations of the nineteenth century or the emergence of market institutions that were decisive, as all these factors also existed in other regions. She rather assumes that cultural factors and ideas were key, for instance the emergence of the natural sciences and the 'Republic of Letters' (Mokyr 2016) and thus the development of scientific networks. Denzau and North (1994) also refer to the role played by ideas and institutions in social change. It hence becomes clear that both economic historians and institutional economists see ideas and guiding principles as playing an essential role in economic development. These findings are also relevant for the sustainability discussion, as illustrated by Meyerhoff und Petschow (1996).

The increase in per capita income that occurred as a consequence of the industrial revolution was immense – Figure 1 illustrates the relative development in comparison to the base year of 1800.

This historical growth provided the basis for the emergence of today's dominant growth paradigm and corresponding path dependencies. It was crucially based on the use of fossil and natural resources. The development of income was and is closely correlated with climate gas emissions but also with pressure on various ecosystems. The use of fossil resources has in addition led to other diverse impacts, including profound changes in land use which has had immensely negative consequences for biodiversity. There is a close correlation between the transgression of planetary boundaries and observable economic growth.

Traditionally, gross domestic product (GDP) has been viewed as the key 'well-being indicator' and thus became extremely important for economic policy. But as currently defined, it is not a comprehensive measure of welfare or even economic well-being. It was developed in the context of the economic depression at the end of the 1920s in the USA, largely by Simon Kuznets. As a measure of the value of goods and services produced annually, it was not conceived as a comprehensive indicator of well-being. Nonetheless, even today it continues to exercise immense influence on the actions of national, international and supranational organisations and is deeply embedded in decision-making structures. Criticism of the use of this indicator came to a head in the economic crisis of 2008. A particular milestone was marked by the Stiglitz-Sen-Fitoussi commission (2010), which was convened by the French president Sarkozy to discuss different indicators of economic performance and social progress. This triggered diverse follow-up processes on national and international levels but could do little to limit the pre-eminence of the GDP indicator.

The global challenge of socio-ecological transformation

With the 1.5°C or 2°C objective a central international climate policy goal was stipulated in the Paris agreement. If this goal is taken seriously, then substantial adaptations are required within a period of just a few decades. To date, environmental policy and sustainability policy have not achieved anything close to a sufficiently strong reduction in emissions or ecological damage. Similarly, the world is far from fulfilling the Sustainable Development Goals (SDGs) that lay down 17 objectives for sustainable development in the economic, social and ecological spheres.

Figure 2, cited from O'Neill, Fanning und Lamb et al. (2018), clarifies the global challenge of the necessary transformation, which, on the one hand, requires a massive reduction in resource use and, on the other hand, an increase in well-being (here termed 'social threshold achieved'), particularly in the Global South.

In Figure 2 the y-axis represents the social thresholds that countries reach. The x-axis shows the biophysical boundaries and the transgressing thereof. Early industrialised countries like Germany are shown to have reached a higher standard in terms of the social dimension but clearly transgress the biophysical boundaries. In contrast, other countries, e. g. Sri Lanka, remain largely within the biophysical boundaries but there is considerable room for development in terms of the social dimension.[4]

Central to the line of argument in this article is that ultimately the aim is to adhere to (biophysical) planetary boundaries and, at the same time, to stabilise the social dimension (social well-being) on a high level, or to further develop it to that level. It therefore comes down to 'filling' the empty quadrant on the top left. It is necessary to develop appropriate development paths based on the different starting positions. In the early industrialised countries, there is a dual goal of reducing resource utilisation and maintaining/further developing quality of life (especially for socially disadvantaged citizens).

---

4 In addition, it should be noted that the early industrialised countries can also differ considerably in relation to both biophysical and social boundaries.

Figure 2: Fields of tension: biophysical boundaries and social thresholds

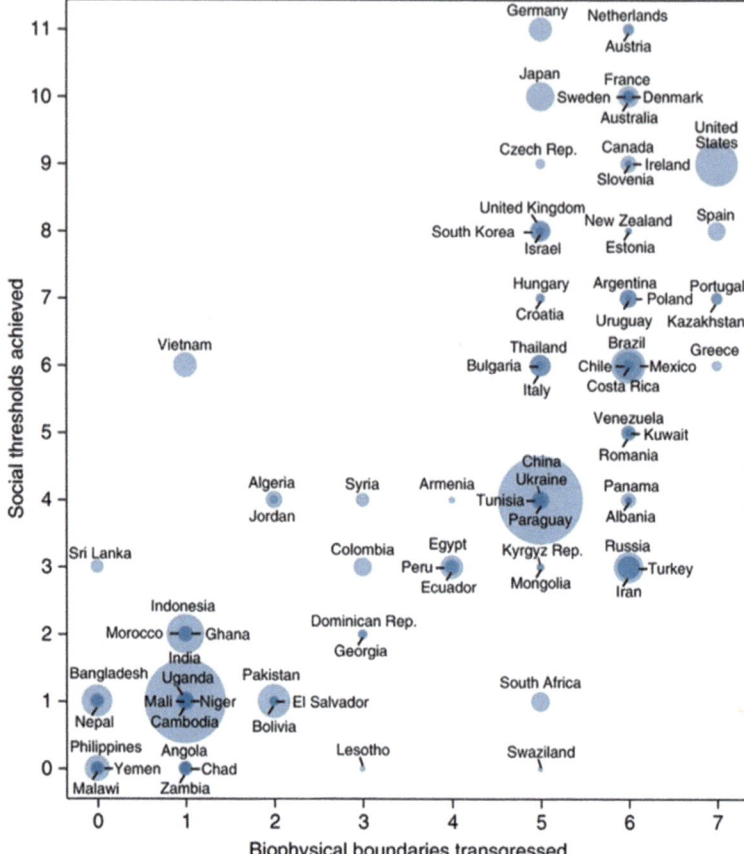

Source: O'Neill/Fanning/Lamb et al. (2018)[5]

---

5 The methodological considerations on which this figure is based are very complex and are therefore not discussed in detail here. Various relevant concepts are combined. Here it should simply be noted that the x-axis comprises the biophysical boundaries transgressed and combines the concepts 'planetary boundaries' (nine boundaries related to critical biophysical processes) and 'ecological footprints' for different types of biophysical resource flows (e. g. CO_2). The resource flows are allocated to the consumers (and thus also include the effects of trade and the imports of products). The y-axis comprises social boundaries/thresholds, drawing on the work of Raworth. Based on Max Neef's human needs approach, Raworth developed a 'safe and just space' (SJS) framework (doughnut approach), which combines the concept of planetary boundaries with the complementary concept of social

In Germany as elsewhere, there is far-reaching consensus in the scientific and political spheres that ecological limits must be adhered to in the long term. How this basically consensual goal is to be achieved is, however, the subject of controversial discussion in both fields.

Two levels can be discerned here. First, there is no agreement about what contribution an individual nation state can and should make to tackling global ecological challenges (see Enquête-Kommission 2013: 477–521). Second, there is key dissent about whether and how the economic system of an early industrialised prosperous country should be changed so as to sufficiently contribute towards an adherence to planetary boundaries without endangering standards of social justice. The relevance of economic development or economic growth for achieving the goals of environmental policy is an especially contentious issue. This is the focus of the rest of this article. We aim to improve understanding of this controversy and derive policy options. To this end, in the next section we develop a systemisation of positions within this social discourse.

Positions in the growth debate

The terms employed in the growth debate – 'green growth' (OECD 2011), 'green economy' (UNEP 2011), 'a-growth' (van den Bergh 2011), 'post-growth' (Zahrnt/Seidl 2010) and 'degrowth' (Demaria/Schneider/Sekulova et al. 2013) – are not always utilised in a distinct and clear-cut fashion. At the same time, it should be noted that in some cases the motivations and discourse contexts behind these terms differ greatly. The discourse surrounding degrowth is fed, inter alia, by feminist positions (a lack of recognition for informal work), anti-capitalist positions (exploitation and self-exploitation), cosmopolitan positions (global inequalities) and of course ecological positions (adherence to planetary boundaries) (see Steffen/Richardson/Rockstrom et al. 2015). The post-growth approach aims to reduce dependence on economic growth in order to overcome ecological challenges and social injustices. For the position 'a-growth', supported particularly by economists, the focus is rather on

---

boundaries. SJS includes 11 social objectives (selected from the documents of 'Rio plus 20' (2012) and the SDGs, which also take into consideration stocks of critical human and social capital (the basic needs requirement).

achieving aims related to quality of life and adhering to planetary boundaries, while the question of growth is of secondary importance as long as the ecological and social goals can be realised (abandoning the one-dimensional indicator GDP). The green-growth position (which does not use one-dimensional GDP as a key performance indicator) assumes that there is no contradiction between growth and respecting planetary boundaries, GDP should rather continue to grow so that environmental objectives can be achieved.

Degrowth versus green growth

Two particularly prominent and clearly antagonistic positions exist within the growth discourse, and their policy consequences clearly contradict one another: degrowth and green growth.

Within the degrowth discourse models, there is much discussion of political measures and instruments that go hand in hand with (or are meant to lead to) a reduction in economic performance. Representatives of the green growth approach instead focus on economic policy measures intended to make it possible to combine further economic growth with enhanced environmental protection. In order to understand where these two positions contradict each other, we have reconstructed their respective (deductively valid) arguments with the help of philosophical argumentation theory. This analysis shows that the degrowth and green growth positions contradict each other in two theses: a descriptive and a normative one. First, they hold differing views on how economic performance would develop in an early industrialised economy (such as Germany) if the country made a sufficiently strong contribution to meeting global environmental goals. Second, they contradict each other in their assessments of the relevance of further economic growth for maintaining quality of life in a society.[6]

---

6 Degrowth and green growth proponents very rarely make explicit which conception of quality of life they hold, i. e. which conception of quality of life should be accepted from their respective perspectives. Mostly, similar abstract terms are used: 'welfare' and 'well-being' (especially in green growth), 'happiness', 'good life' (especially in degrowth). The conceptions of quality of life widely used in philosophical and economic literature are discussed in Petschow et al. 2018, 2020a and 2020b.

Representatives of the degrowth position are committed to the following two propositions (e. g. Kallis 2011, Paech 2012, Demaria et al. 2013 or Latouche 2015a/b):

1. Further economic growth in wealthy countries is not necessary in order for them to maintain their quality of life, which can be preserved or even increased even if aggregate economic output falls.
2. It is reasonably certain that economic output in wealthy countries will decline if they reduce their levels of ecological damage sufficiently.

In contrast, representatives of the green growth movement hold contrary positions (e. g. OECD 2011, World Bank 2012, Jacobs 2013 or Bowen et al. 2014):

1. Further economic growth is still necessary in an early industrialised, prosperous economy in order to maintain or improve quality of life in these societies.
2. It is reasonably certain that with the help of green growth instruments, prosperous countries can sufficiently reduce the ecological damage they cause. Their economic output – albeit in a qualitatively different form – could continue to grow.

We then examined the extent to which these core theses of the two basic positions can be scientifically justified. There are fundamental objections to the degrowth propositions. According to our understandings of quality of life based on the philosophical literature (hedonism, desire fulfilment theory, theories of objective values), the first degrowth thesis does indeed apply. Further economic growth is, in principle, not necessary to maintain the quality of life in a society. However, degrowth representatives do not convincingly explain whether and in particular how this quality of life can be maintained if GDP per capita (very) sharply declines.

The second degrowth proposition claims that it is impossible to sufficiently decouple economic growth from environmental impacts. This is scientifically untenable. Representatives of the degrowth position usually point out how extensive the ecological challenges are, how short the period for reducing ecological burdens is, and how little previous environmental policy efforts have achieved. They also emphasise that a positive correlation between economic growth and the consumption of natural resources and greenhouse gas emissions has been observable since the nineteenth century. The parameters relevant to the success of decoupling – the decarbonisation rates of an economy, development of energy and resource intensities – however, can be influenced politically (e. g. by taxes, incentives, technology promotion, etc.). Thus, forward projections of trends based on a past in which there was no or insufficient political control cannot be used to prove that decoupling cannot or will not succeed in the future.

Whether or not the first proposition of the green growth position is true crucially depends on one's understanding of social quality of life. Some of the views expressed in the philosophical literature on what constitutes a good life or social quality of life do not support the green growth thesis. Conversely, the core thesis of green growth can be justified particularly well if one uses the concept of quality of life supported by welfare economics: quality of life ('welfare' in the language of economics) is then an aggregate of the extent to which individual preferences are met. However, it is not clear why *this* particular understanding of quality of life, as the fulfilment of individual preferences, should guide political action.

Turning to the second green growth proposition, economic-ecological models demonstrate that it is theoretically possible to decouple future economic growth from critical resource consumption and ecological damage. However, model results to date do not demonstrate that this will succeed to a sufficient extent within the available time frame. In addition, the models assume that the technologies required for decoupling will be invented and adopted in good time. It seems hardly possible to make scientifically serious statements on this – at least, such statements must be fraught with great uncertainty; in addition, rebound effects must be considered. Last but not least, there is no robust knowledge about the consequences for future economic performance of reducing all the ecological impacts relevant for compliance with planetary boundaries simultaneously, as opposed to pursuing just one ecological goal, such as the reduction of GHG emissions.

The precautionary post-growth position: a new consensus?

The above discussion demonstrates that degrowth and green growth positions are based on core assumptions that cannot be adequately justified or substantiated scientifically. Neither position can thus claim to serve as the sole strategy for environmental policy action. Based on this criticism, we have developed a third, ideal-typical approach, which we refer to here as the post-growth position. In contrast to degrowth and green growth, post-growth is open and unbiased. It has no strong ex-ante premises regarding either (i) an evaluation of future economic growth or possible future contraction, or (ii) the possibility of sufficient decoupling. According to this position, it is uncertain as to how economic performance will develop if the economies of prosperous countries are fundamentally changed in line with global environmental objectives. There is, however, a serious possibility that economic output will no longer increase or even significantly decrease as a result of this transformation. At the same time, we note that economic performance and the income it generates play an important role because of the current state of the early industrialised, prosperous countries. They are crucial to the functions of fundamental social institutions that provide the components of a good life (e. g. social security systems, expenditure on education, etc.). From this position, we can derive the goal of transforming these social institutions as a precautionary measure, thus ensuring that they can continue to perform their functions independently of economic output. Greater independence from growth would make it possible to maintain a high level of social quality of life even if economic output stagnates or falls. In a society that is more independent of growth in this sense, there would be fewer conflicting goals between economic and environmental targets. Environmental policy measures would thus be less subject to reservations about possible growth impacts.

We chose the term *post-growth* for this ideal-typical position, developed as a third choice between degrowth and green growth. The key political implication of this position – the creation of social institutions that are (more) independent of growth where possible – was, to our knowledge, first emphasised in the volume *Postwachstumsgesellschaft – Konzepte für die Zukunft* (Post-growth society – Concepts for the future) by Angelika Zahrnt and Irmi Seidl (2010). In addition, there are overlaps in content with the position of authors who advocate the concept of 'a-growth' (e. g. van den Bergh

2011) or are close to it content-wise (Jakob and Edenhofer 2014). Moreover, in parallel to the study on which this paper is based, other scientific papers have been presented that have reached similar conclusions, such as van den Bergh (2017) and Scientific Working Group (2018).

We aim to build on these contributions with our precautionary post-growth position. In doing so, we would like to add that the involvement of the public and key stakeholders in deliberative processes is central to a post-growth position. When it comes to developing strategies and instruments, it is in fact dependent on them. Only a deliberative discourse with broad public participation can clarify the level or amount of services that a specific area of society or a specific public institution should provide. In our view, a close iterative exchange between politics, science and the interested public can support such a discourse.

Precautionary post-growth position and societal change

In the growth debate, the green-growth and degrowth positions adopt different perspectives based on central normative considerations and evaluations, some shared, some not.

The commitment to respect planetary boundaries is considered essential by representatives of the positions 'green growth', 'degrowth' and 'post-growth', as well as by the team of authors of the study undertaken on behalf of the Environmental Protection Agency (Petschow/aus dem Moore/Pissarskoi et al. 2018) on which this paper is based.

For example, to be successful green-growth approaches require a decoupling of economic growth and environmental pollution through technological innovations and this to an extent that has not yet been attempted. It also remains unclear whether the necessary decoupling could be achieved quickly enough. Furthermore, the notion that a forceful and far-reaching green-growth strategy (which has not yet been consistently introduced) will not have negative impacts on economic growth in the short and medium term can be disputed.

Regarding the degrowth approach, on the other hand, it is uncertain whether the quality of life in society can be maintained by implementing degrowth measures, and the question of which interpretation of quality of life should be sustained remains normatively controversial.

The societal discourse on environmental policy is characterised by a high degree of segmentation and polarisation, documented most visibly in the dispute on the issue of growth. In this debate, green growth and degrowth mark the opposite ends of a broad and varied spectrum of individual positions. This situation impedes the productive use and combination of important insights from both strands of the debate. Against the backdrop of the antagonistic positions of green growth and degrowth and the need to develop a consistent sustainability policy, it seems highly desirable to explore the potential for mutual understanding in the sustainability debate by trying to identify consensual elements that can be productively applied in policy.

In concrete terms, it should also be noted that the above-mentioned positions still have limited significance for the policy and society. Solution approaches are available but have not been sufficiently taken up. The proponents of a green-growth approach undoubtedly propose suitable instruments from a theoretical perspective, but nevertheless political 'demand' for these instruments and their effective implementation in practice have so far been very limited. Similarly, the ideas and models developed within the ecologically oriented post-growth discourse have so far also had only limited appeal and acceptance.

In view of path dependencies and doubt regarding the directional reliability of the strategies pursued, the precautionary post-growth position aims to initiate a design-oriented search process that focuses on key notions such as the precautionary principle and societal resilience. This participatory, long-term process of societal change can only be controlled to a limited extent. It is intended to open up new options for action and development and must take account of initial social conditions. Compliance with planetary boundaries requires far-reaching societal change. Against the background of our limited knowledge, there is no single concrete transition path or approach that should be pursued in isolation. In our view, instead, action-oriented strategies and corresponding 'policy mixes' must be developed that include combinations of efficiency, consistency and sufficiency.[7] On the one hand, these should draw on appropriate and mutually compatible elements of different strategy approaches and, on the other hand, should connect to 'the here and now'. It will be crucial to promote bottom-up initia-

---

7 On the debate about efficiency, consistency and sufficiency, see for example Huber (1994), current discussion in Schneidewind and Zahrnt (2013) and Loske (2015)

tives and experiments. These can be supported in particular by national and/or international frameworks. For approaches that have been evaluated and assessed by ongoing critical research and thus can provide 'proof' that they achieve what is desirable and intended, the next step is to examine their scalability and whether they can be adopted as top-down policies. Relevant contexts for testing such approaches exist, for example, both in regions undergoing structural change and in the more general challenges of decarbonising energy supplies or promoting the circular economy.

The competing concepts of 'green growth', 'a-growth', 'post-growth' and 'degrowth' differ in their fundamental orientations, in some facets considerably, and are to some extent incompatible with regard to central premises. However, in terms of the recommended instruments, reform approaches and concrete paths for transformation, it is certainly possible to identify considerable overlaps. The precautionary post-growth position draws on these overlaps and is composed of four action strategies which are outlined below (see Petschow/aus dem Moore/Pissarskoi et al. 2018, aus dem Moore and Hofmann 2019, Petschow/aus dem Moore/Pissarskoi et al. 2020a, 2020b).

From the culture of growth to the culture of sustainability

The *first* action strategy promotes cultural change from a 'Culture of Growth' to a 'Culture of Sustainability'. Direct management of this cultural process is only possible to a very limited extent. Nonetheless, it can be seen that social discourses echo the sustainability debate and, currently even more so, the climate and biodiversity discourse. The post-growth/degrowth movement, which is shaped by civil society, is itself an expression of incipient cultural change.

On the question of which factors significantly influence profound processes of social change, there are very different answers in the relevant academic discourses. In discourses on economic history and institutional economics, the thesis is increasingly being advanced that cultural changes can be regarded as the trigger for growth dynamics and the emergence of the growth society. As discussed above, economic growth only became relevant with the start of the industrial revolution and finally began to guide action and policy with the development of the growth indicator GDP.

The hitherto dominant culture of growth is deeply embedded in the formal and informal institutions that 'steer' our societies. If policy approaches are to lead to us living within planetary boundaries, they must therefore go beyond material goals and the instruments directly geared to such goals and must also consider cultural change towards a possible culture of sustainability. A robust process of change towards a sustainable society that enables societal well-being within planetary boundaries will not be possible without a profound transformation (also) of formal and informal institutions (see Williamson 2000, Geels 2011)[8].

Effective design of economic frameworks

The *second* building block of the precautionary post-growth position is adjustment of the economic parameters, in particular through the resolute use of (market-based) instruments to internalise negative environmental externalities and thus ensure effective and systemic coarse-grained management. These instruments include cap-and-trade systems (in emissions trading, for example) or eco-taxes for the cost-effective internalisation of the environmentally harmful effects of production and consumption.

In this respect, there is widespread agreement between the positions in the growth debate. Moreover, most actors putting forward economic arguments consider relative prices to be significant for individual behaviour and the overexploitation of natural resources (such as energy carriers or sinks or the absorption capacity of the atmosphere). Thus, across the board, i. e. among both degrowth and green-growth advocates, changing relative prices is considered an important regulatory element.[9]

Remaining within planetary boundaries, the far-reaching need for change and the necessary economic instruments with which to address this change are all clearly associated with considerable potential for social con-

---

[8] The multi-level perspective (Geels 2011) is currently a widely used heuristic for complex social change processes.

[9] It should be noted that, especially in the degrowth and post-growth discourse, this is rarely made explicit but is rather applied more generally, leading to the development of behavioural orientations which can often have an 'overwhelming' effect on individuals.

flict (for instance with issues of distribution). This must be flanked by additional measures.

Exploration and potential development of new paths of societal development

The *third* approach of the precautionary post-growth position involves exploring and opening up new paths of social development and is complementary to the previously discussed degrowth and green growth approaches. The exploration of more sustainable options for action must be stimulated, accompanied and supported by participatory societal search processes, experimental spaces for new social practices, new innovation policies and research policy approaches.

Inevitably, this means that growth of GDP should no longer be seen as the dominant target of society. Instead, the focus should be increasingly on socially desirable target states (societal well-being, good life, etc.). The social shift towards a culture of sustainability also requires other systems of indicators to guide societal (self-)management.

Innovations will play an important role in these search processes, but relying solely on technological innovations is by no means sufficient (see also Deutscher Bundestag 2013: 477). In the context of defining the 'Grand Challenges' on EU level, prominent calls for more social innovations were heard, i. e. for innovations that focus less on technology and more on new social practices. Since then, the concept of social innovations has been increasingly important in the field of innovation promotion.

These new ways of generating innovations are now also found in the mainstream, with the establishment of real-world laboratories and experimental spaces becoming increasingly ubiquitous ways of generating solutions. At the EU level and also at the national level, consideration is being given to how real labs or experimental spaces can be designed to engender new, sustainable solutions – for example, through the promotion of real-world laboratories in Baden-Württemberg or with a more technical focus like in the German government's energy research programme (BMWi 2018).

Calls for these social innovations come particularly from representatives of the post-growth discourse. The aim is to identify new generalisable solutions that should then be supported by regulation or infrastructural development. Against this background, there is a need to strengthen transformative elements in innovation policy to address socio-technical regimes as a whole, in line with the goals of society. Such an innovation policy would encourage social experimentation and social learning processes so that previously unknown paths to sustainable development become possible.

This is also necessary given the characteristics and path dependencies of the dominant socio-technical 'system', such as current high energy and resource consumption. Representatives of the multi-level perspective believe that economic instruments alone are hardly sufficient to overcome these path dependencies (Kern/Rogge/Howlett 2019). The 'deep transition' approach (Schot/Karger 2018) is linked to this multi-level perspective. Both emphasise the importance of social innovations and do not consider the prevalent focus on technological innovations as sufficient to drive social change processes.

Reduction of growth dependency

Another and therefore *fourth* important path dependency concerns the dependence of important spheres of society and institutions on growth. Consequently, we see a fourth element as constitutive for our proposed precautionary post-growth position: identifying and developing the potential for designing more growth-independent societal institutions and processes. This is, we believe, also essential to increase the resilience of important social systems. Appropriate measures should be implemented if they are shown to be effective and socially acceptable. To this end, appropriate pilot projects should be designed, implemented and evaluated.

If a strategy of increasing growth independence is successful, social acceptance of environmentally motivated policy measures may well increase, despite their potentially negative impact on economic growth. Such policies would suffer less from 'growth proviso' and there would be more scope for an ambitious environmental and sustainability policy.

Existing approaches intended to achieve greater independence from growth are currently proving to be only marginally effective (Petschow/ aus dem Moore/Pissarskoi et al. 2018, Petschow/aus dem Moore/Pissarskoi et al. 2020a, 2020b). Fundamental reform approaches, if any, have to date only been considered for small sections of society and pursued in a series of small experiments. It is therefore hardly possible to draw any conclusions about the generalisability of such approaches or their potential to reduce the existing dependence on growth. However, the prospects of success of the dominant approach so far, the green growth strategy, are uncertain in terms of the chances of decoupling economic growth from negative environmental impacts. It thus seems necessary to continue working on the conception and testing of models that are less dependent on economic growth. We see a considerable need for research in this area.

Conclusion: The precautionary post-growth position as a platform for further discourse

The precautionary post-growth position represents, first, an integrative approach and, second, provides general impetus for further discussion on transformation paths, especially with regard to the economic discourse. The concept of 'growth independence' aims to change prevailing social models and path dependencies and, in this sense, has the potential to bring about far-reaching processes of change.

However, the goal of 'societal well-being within planetary boundaries' must ultimately be specified in processes of societal negotiation, and effective narratives must be developed in a participatory manner. We interpret the precautionary post-growth position, both conceptually and practically, as a relevant and important building block of a yet-to-be-conceived, consistent and global strategy for adhering to planetary boundaries and the SDGs, and for promoting individual quality of life and societal well-being.

From a policy perspective, a post-growth position understood in this way can also be seen as a starting point or essential component of an overarching resilience strategy motivated by responsible ethics. Given the uncertainty about future economic and societal developments, this would enhance the robustness of the transformation process towards a sustainable society within planetary boundaries.

Cited literature

aus dem Moore, N., & Hofmann, D. (2019). Die vorsorgeorientierte Postwachstumsposition. Makronom. https://makronom.de/green-growth-beyond-die-vorsorgeorientierte-postwachstumsposition-34398.

Bindoff, N. L., Stott, P. A., AchutaRao, K. M., Allen, M. R., Gillett, N., Gutzler, D., Hansingo, K., Hegerl, G. C., Hu, Y., Jain, S., Mokhov, I. I., Overland, J., Perlwitz, J., Sebbari, R., & Zhang, X. (2013). Detection and attribution of climate change: from global to regional. In T. F. Stocker, D. Qin, G.-K. Plattner, M. M. B. Tignor, S. K. Allen, J. Boschung, A. Nauels, Y. Xia, V. Bex, & P. M. Midgley (Eds.), *Climate change 2013: The physical science basis. contribution of working group I to the fifth assessment report of the intergovernmental panel on climate change.* Cambridge University Press, 867–952.

BMWi – Bundesministerium für Wirtschaft und Energie (2018). 7th Energy Research Programme of the Federal Government. Innovations for the Energy Transition. Berlin. https://www.bmwi.de/Redaktion/EN/Publikationen/Energie/7th-energy-research-programme-of-the-federal-government.pdf?__blob=publicationFile&v=5 (2021, January 1).

Boulding, K. E. (1966). The economics of the coming spaceship earth. In H. Jarrett (Ed.), *Environmental quality in a growing economy, essays from the sixth RFF forum on environmental quality.* Routledge, 3–14.

Bowen, A., & Hepburn, C. (2014). Green growth: an assessment. *Oxford Review of Economic Policy, 30*(3), 407–422.

Caney, S. (2009). Justice and the distribution of greenhouse gas emissions. *Journal of Global Ethics, 5*(2), 125–146.

Clark, G. (2007). *A farewell to alms. A brief economic history of the world.* Princeton University Press.

Daly, H. E. (1991 [1977]). *Steady-State Economics.* 2nd edition. Island Press.

Demaria, F., Schneider, F., Sekulova, F., & Martinez-Alier, J. (2013). What is degrowth? From an activist slogan to a social movement. *Environmental Values, 22*(2), 191–215.

Denzau, A. T., & North, D. C (1994). Shared mental models. Ideologies and institutions. *Kyklos, 47*(1), 3–31.

Enquête-Kommission (2013, May 5). *Schlussbericht der Enquete-Kommission „Wachstum, Wohlstand, Lebensqualität – Wege zu nachhaltigem Wirtschaften und gesellschaftlichem Fortschritt in der Sozialen Marktwirtschaft".* Deutscher Bundestag Drucksache 17/13300.

Fertig, G., & Pfister, U. (2012). *When did Germany cease to be malthusian? The evolution of the preventive and positive checks, 1730–1870*. Contribution to the 8th BETA-Workshop in Historical Economics. University of Strasbourg, 11–12 May 2012.

Geels, F. W. (2011). The multi-level perspective on sustainability transitions: Responses to seven criticisms. *Environmental Innovation and Societal Transitions*, 1(1), 24–40.

Georgescu-Roegen, N. (1987). *The entropy law and the economic process in retrospect*. IÖW publication series 5/87.

Huber, J. (1994). Nachhaltige Entwicklung durch Suffizienz, Effizienz und Konsistenz. In P. Fritz, J. Huber, & H. W. Levi (Eds.), *Nachhaltigkeit in naturwissenschaftlicher und sozialwissenschaftlicher Perspektive*. S Hirzel Wissenschaftliche Verlagsgesellschaft, 31–46.

IPBES – The Intergovernmental Science-Policy Platform on Biodiversity and Ecosystem Services (2019). Summary for policymakers of the global assessment report on biodiversity and ecosystem services of the Intergovernmental Science-Policy Platform on Biodiversity and Ecosystem Services. S. Díaz, J. Settele, E. S. Brondízio E.S., H. T. Ngo, M. Guèze, J. Agard, A. Arneth, P. Balvanera, K. A. Brauman, S. H. M. Butchart, K. M. A. Chan, L. A. Garibaldi, K. Ichii, J. Liu, S. M. Subramanian, G. F. Midgley, P. Miloslavich, Z. Molnár, D. Obura, A. Pfaff, S. Polasky, A. Purvis, J. Razzaque, B. Reyers, R. Roy Chowdhury, Y. J. Shin, I. J. Visseren-Hamakers, K. J. Willis, & C. N. Zayas (Eds.), Global assessment repot on biodiversity and ecosymstem services IPBES publications. Self-published.

Jacobs, M. (2013). Green growth. In R. Falkner (Ed.), *Handbook of global climate and environmental policy*. Springer.

Kallis, G. (2011). In defence of degrowth. *Ecological Economics*, 70(5), 873–880.

Kern, F., Rogge, K. S., & Howlett, M. (2019). Policy mixes for sustainability transitions: New approaches and insights through bridging innovation and policy studies. *Research Policy*, 48(10), 103832.

Latouche, S. (2015a). Vom Glück zum BIP – und die Alternative des guten Lebens. *Blätter für deutsche und internationale Politik*, 15(12), 83–97.

Latouche, S. (2015b). *Es reicht! Abrechnung mit dem Wachstumswahn*. Deutsche Erstausgabe. oekom.

Loske, R. (2015). *Politik der Zukunftsfähigkeit: Konturen einer Nachhaltigkeitswende*. S. Fischer.

Malthus, T. R. (1803). *An essay on the principle of population; or, a view of its past and present effects on human happiness; with an enquiry into our prospects respecting the future removal or mitigation of the evils which it occasions. Second and much enlarged edition.* Printed for J. Johnson.

McCloskey, D. (2016). *Bourgeois equality. How ideas, not capital or institutions, enriched the world.* University of Chicago Press.

Meadows, D., Meadows, D., Randers, J., & Behrens III, W. W. (1972). *Die Grenzen des Wachstums. Bericht des Club of Rome zur Lage der Menschheit. Aus dem Amerikanischen von Hans-Dieter Heck.* Deutsche Verlags-Anstalt.

Meyerhoff, J., & Petschow, U. (1996). Nachhaltige Entwicklung als langfristiger Wandlungsprozesse. Konsequenzen für die Wirtschafts- und Umweltpolitik. In L. Gerken (Ed.), *Ordnungspolitische Grundfragen einer Politik der Nachhaltigkeit.* Nomos.

Mokyr, J. (2016). *A Culture of growth: The origins of the modern economy.* Princeton University Press.

O'Neill, D. W., Fanning, A. L., Lamb, W. F., & Steinberger, J. K. (2018). A good life for all within planetary boundaries, *Nature Sustainability,* 1, 88–95.

OECD – Organisation for Economic Co-operation and Development (2011). *Towards green growth.* OECD Publishing.

Paech, N. (2012). *Befreiung vom Überfluss auf dem Weg in die Postwachstumsökonomie. 3rd edition.* oekom.

Petschow, U., aus dem Moore, N., Pissarskoi, E., Korfhage, T., Lange, S., Schoofs, A., & Hofmann, D. (2018). *Gesellschaftliches Wohlergehen innerhalb planetarer Grenzen. Der Ansatz einer vorsorgeorientierten Postwachstumsposition.* Texts of UBA 89/2018. https://www.umweltbundesamt.de/publikationen/vorsorgeorientierte-postwachstumsposition.

Petschow, U., aus dem Moore, N., Pissarskoi, E., Bahn-Walkowiak, B., Ott, H. E., Hofmann, D., Lange, S., Korfhage, T., Schoofs, A., Wilts, H., Best, B., Benke, J., Buhl, J., Galinski, L., Lucas, R., Koop, C., Werland, S., & Berg, H. (2020a). *Ansätze zur Ressourcenschonung im Kontext von Postwachstumskonzepten.* Texts of UBA 98/2020. https://www.umweltbundesamt.de/en/publikationen/ansaetze-zur-ressourcenschonung-im-kontext-von.

Petschow, U., aus dem Moore, N., Pissarskoi, E., Korfhage, T., Lange, S., Schoofs, A., & Hofmann, D. (2020b). *Social well-being within planetary boundaries: the precautionary post-growth approach.* Texts of UBA 243/2020.

https://www.umweltbundesamt.de/en/publikationen/social-well-being-within-planetary-boundaries-the.

Rockström, J., Steffen, W., Noone, K., Persson, Å., Chapin III, F. S., Lambin, E., Lenton, T. M., Scheffer, M., Folke, C., Schellnhuber, H., Nykvist, B., de Wit, C. A., Hughes, T., van der Leeuw, S., Rodhe, H., Sörlin, S., Snyder, P. K., Costanza, R., Svedin, U., Falkenmark, M., Karlberg, L., Corell, R. W., Fabry, V. J., Hansen, J., Walker, B., Liverman, D., Richardson, K., Crutzen, P., & Foley, J. A. (2009a). Planetary boundaries: exploring the safe operating space for humanity. *Ecology and Society*, 14(2), art. 32.

Rockström, J., Steffen, W., Noone, K., Persson, A., Chapin, F. S., Lambin, E. F., Lenton, T. M., Scheffer, M., Folke, C., Schellnhuber, H. J., Nykvist, B., de Wit, C. A., Hughes, T., van der Leeuw, S., Rodhe, H., Sorlin, S., Snyder, P. K., Costanza, R., Svedin, U., Falkenmark, M., Karlberg, L., Corell, R. W., Fabry, V. J., Hansen, J., Walker, B., Liverman, D., Richardson, K., Crutzen, P., & Foley, J. A. (2009b). A safe operating space for humanity. *Nature*, 461, 472–475.

Schneidewind, U., & Zahrnt, A. (2013). *Damit gutes Leben einfacher wird: Perspektiven einer Suffizienzpolitik*. oekom.

Schot, J., & Kanger, L. (2018). Deep transitions: Emergence, acceleration, stabilization and directionality. *Research Policy*, 47(6), 1045–1059.

Steffen, W., Richardson, K., Rockstrom, J., Cornell, S. E., Fetzer, I., Bennett; E. M., Biggs, R., Carpenter, S. R., de Vries, W., de Wit, C. A., Folke, C., Gerten, D., Heinke, J., Mace, G. M., Persson, L. M., Ramanathan, V., Reyers, B., & Sörlin, S. (2015). Planetary boundaries: Guiding human development on a changing planet. *Science*, 347(6223), 1259855.

Stiglitz, J., Sen, A., & Fitoussi, J. P. (2010). *Mismeasuring Our Lives*. The New Press.

UNEP – United Nations Environment Programme (2011). *Towards a green economy: Pathways to sustainable development and poverty eradication*. https://sustainabledevelopment.un.org/content/documents/126GER_synthesis_en.pdf.

van den Bergh, J. C. J. M. (2011). Environment versus growth – A criticism of "degrowth" and a plea for "a-growth". *Ecological Economics*, 70(5), 881–890.

van den Bergh, J. C. J. M. (2017). A third option for climate policy within potential limits to growth. *Nature Climate Change*, 7, 107–112.

Weltbank (2012). *Inclusive green growth: The pathway to sustainable development*. World Bank Publications.

Will, S., Richardson, K., Rockström, J., Cornell, S. E., Fetzer, I., Bennett, E. M., Biggs, R., Carpenter, S. R., de Vries, W., de Wit, C. A., Folke, C., Gerten, D., Heinke, J., Mace, G. M., Persson, L. M., Ramanathan, V., Reyers, B., & Sörlin, S. (2015). Planetary boundaries: Guiding human development on a changing planet. *Science, 347*(6223), 1259855.

Williamson, O. E. (2000). The new institutional economics: Taking stock, looking ahead. *Journal of Economic Literature, 38*(3), 595–613.

Wissenschaftliche Arbeitsgruppe für weltkirchliche Aufgaben der Deutschen Bischofskonferenz (2018). *Raus aus der Wachstumsgesellschaft? Eine sozial-ethische Analyse und Bewertung von Postwachstumsstrategien.* Studies of the expert group „Weltwirtschaft und Weltethik" 21.

Zahrnt, A., & Seidl, I. (2010). *Postwachstumsgesellschaft. Konzepte für die Zukunft.* Metropolis.

New roles in collective, growth-independent spatial organisation

Christian Lamker, Viola Schulze Dieckhoff

In the twenty-first century, urban and spatial planning still stands at the fundamental interface between state power, private capital and public interest (Stein 2019: 12). Planners hold a key position for organising the spatial conditions of our society. Responsible spatial development requires all planners to take roles that reflect the great diversity and complexity of society. Collective responsibility must be converted into new ways of thinking and acting by courageously leading processes of collective spatial and institutional design. However, economic growth cannot solve the urgent challenges of spatial transformation encapsulated by keywords like 'sustainability', 'climate change mitigation', 'climate change adaptation' and 'social justice'. Neither can these problems be successfully dealt with as part of a growth-based agenda, for instance through the accelerated designation of building land or technological solutions.

Movements like Fridays for Future and Extinction Rebellion have greatly increased public awareness of long-term catastrophic impacts. Nonetheless, findings concerning the loss of biodiversity, climate change and the negative effects of a focus on growth do not in themselves provide policy options or a clear transformation strategy. The following sections begin by clarifying the significance of the collective organisation of space and responsible planning, situating planners' responsibility within this. The focus then moves to the question: Which roles can planners use to lead a complex sustainable transformation (again)? This chapter adopts a perspective from organisational and system theory to lay the groundwork for a new 'turn to action' (Lamker/Levin-Keitel 2019: 112) and identifies which roles may be promising for growth-independent planning.

Collective organisation of space

In the twenty-first century, there is no absolute shortage of material wealth, housing or resources for people who live in Germany, in Europe and in most other industrialised countries. Nonetheless, familiar ways of thinking and modes of action have been unable to achieve or safeguard a satisfactory distribution of resources within ecological limits. Growth imperatives create socially specific scarcity and continue to be deeply rooted in social, economic and planning institutions, affecting every single individual (Rosa 2016; Savini 2019: 74–76; Schmelzer/Vetter 2019: 42–68; Stein 2019). Correspondingly, urban and spatial planning develops ways in which growth and space can be linked (Bundesministerium für Umwelt, Naturschutz und Reaktorsicherheit 2007; Galland 2012; Rydin 2013; Schulz 2018).

Spatial organisation has always been a matter of concern for all human beings. Our image of urban and spatial planning began to shift as early as the 1970s towards people with their knowledge, interests and opinions. Communication and participation are now established elements of all spatial planning processes. Today's debates on post-growth and transformation particularly emphasise that the organisation and, especially, the fundamental redefinition of space are tasks that everyone can actively pursue (e. g. Schneidewind 2018). Planning is the process by which we continuously organise the design of space over time (van Assche/Buinen/Duineveld 2017: 223; Stein 2019: 13). Terms like 'spatial entrepreneurs', 'change agents' and 'prosumers of space' focus on the fact that each individual acts in space and can deliberately direct this action to further a (socio-ecological) transformation.

In this way, agents of spatial change gain access to diverse and comprehensive resources for engaged action. Planners are relieved of the burden of having to conceive and implement all spatial changes. On the other hand, they acquire the burden of more actively leading transformative processes and their spatial dimensions in complex networks. Following this line of thought, this also means that organising the limited space requires more attention to be paid to commonalities, which can act as a focus and guide for action. Since at least the end of the 1990s, the discussion has focused intensively on improving communication within planning processes and developing instruments that enable broad participation on all levels. The basic approach of urban and spatial planning has changed to favour coordinating, integrating and facilitating activities (Innes/Booher 1999: 11; Lamker 2016:

222). The methodological repertoire has become correspondingly diverse and increasingly elaborate. Managing uncertainty has replaced the search for fixed certainties (Abbott 2005). At least since the Nobel Prize for Economics was awarded to Elinor Ostrom in 2012, spatial planning has increasingly supplemented state and market-based solutions with a reliance on the ability of people to organise themselves for sustainable resource management. At the same time, community control is challenging in itself and a shift to community decision-making processes will not be a sufficient solution alone.

Today we stand at a difficult turning point. On the one hand, participation is anchored at all spatial levels. On the other hand, we face increasing social and spatial differences as well as limits to participation and economic growth (e. g. Hagelüken 2017; Heinrich-Böll-Stiftung 2017). Communicative processes therefore occur in settings where there are absolute limits to development that consensus cannot overcome (e. g. limited building land) or should not overcome (e. g. the destruction of habitats and biodiversity). Every single decision can lead to a proportion of these resources being irrevocably lost. We see the cumulative effects of individual choices – even if many of them are quite well-balanced decisions in themselves.

The collective organisation of space primarily involves finding a just balance between different people in one space and between people in different spaces – right up to an intergenerational and global level. Thinking about post-growth draws particular attention to ecological and planetary boundaries and the interconnectedness of our actions and their effects in global processes (as in Brand/Wissen 2017; Raworth 2018; for planning, the relational approach of planetary urbanisation by Brenner 2014 is comparable). The uncomfortable truth is that without rapid and clear decisions, things often do not work. Complexity and uncertainty are core elements of planning action and cannot be fully or permanently eliminated (Abbott 2005: 238, Lamker 2016: 3–11). Urban and spatial planning are becoming increasingly politicised, analogous to the post-growth discourse (Schmelzer/Vetter 2019: 226). For the collective organisation of space, planners need a basis which they can use to make decisions despite persistent uncertainty, and they require soft as well as hard instruments. There are many decisional situations in which economic growth is incompatible with ecological limits and available resources, particularly if a long-term perspective is taken or the decision at hand is linked to other decisions. This begs the question: What are just decisions under these conditions and how can we imagine just spatial development?

Responsibility of planners

This raises important questions about the responsibility of planners, a responsibility that extends beyond a single delimited space, a short period of time and the people who are alive today. Institutional, collective and individual responsibility are all involved, and the essential rules governing our lives together and our individual courses of actions must thus be adapted. Global change and local action are no longer contradictory. Rio 1992 and many local Agenda-21 processes have installed 'think global, act local' as a new quality of joint action in an unequal world characterised by widely different points of departure. Acknowledging joint responsibility therefore also means including the consequences of actions on individuals and communities that are unknown to the decision-makers (see Gunder/Hillier 2007). In urban research, Brenner (2014) calls for consideration of the negative consequences of urbanisation processes to include the most remote areas on Earth. He uses the term 'planetary urbanization' to refer to the networks of global material flows. Finally, the time horizon of today's decisions extends intergenerationally into foreseeable and potential future generations.

It would be extremely easy to address the responsibility of planners in the narrow context of the planning system: responsible planning within the established system of public urban and spatial planning involves fulfilling rights and duties imposed by formal or informal institutions (similarly here see Needham/Buitelaar/Hartmann 2018: 12; also see Gunder/Hillier 2007: 61). Planners must carry out the tasks and abide by the policy guidelines. The spatial reach of responsibility ends at the boundaries of the administrative jurisdiction or at the boundaries set by mandate. Metaphorically speaking, planners are only an unimportant cog in a machine that fits seamlessly into higher-level processes. A perspective of this sort may be appropriate when working with statutory planning instruments. Defining responsibility so narrowly, however, leaves no room for important post-growth impulses. Change must then come from those who delegate power and responsibility to planners, for instance via political decisions.

Today, social movements like Fridays for Future demand more creativity and more immediate action, especially from established institutions. The call for action is directed not only towards politicians but also explicitly towards all public institutions. There must be situations in which responsibility involves direct action and reacting rapidly to urgent problems. Ever fewer problems stop at administrative boundaries and ever fewer challenges can be tackled within defined jurisdictions.

This discussion extends the concept of responsibility to include the micro- and meso-levels: even the smallest element and/or the smallest movement can change a large system (as also argued by Ekardt 2017; Stein 2019). A small agent may not necessarily be aware of all the effects, but it is very well aware of its own condition and options. This means that the possible ways of changing the system of 'planning' can indeed be conceived within the system of 'planning'. Politicians remain the final level of decision making for urban planning. However, most planning instruments are so complex that it is difficult for politicians to fully understand them, not to mention change them. Planners themselves are thus those who best know their own practice and who can identify and provide immediate starting points for change. In planning situations characterised by undecidability (Gunder/Hillier 2007: 78–82), strength lies in taking responsibility for collective decision-making capacity. Gunder and Hillier (2007: 79–84) emphasise that responsible decisions include the risk of making mistakes. They suggest that planners are responsible for acting as individuals and taking on responsibility that is different to following rules and more than behaving dutifully. Thought of in this way, responsibility is endless, extending across space to the global effects of our actions, across time to potential later generations and across matter to the animate and inanimate environment. This aspect, for example, is highlighted in critiques of a Western, imperial mode of living (Brand/Wissen 2017). Nonetheless, Gunder and Hillier (2007) reduce the burden of responsibility by directing their appeal equally to all planners and by ruling out the possibility of always targeting the correct action in complex contexts.

Role images

At the interface with transformation research, spatial planning is beginning to be reconceptualised, providing integrated, descriptive and explanatory approaches to organise and manage space without growth impulses (Schneidewind 2018; Schulz 2018; Wittmayer et al. 2017: 49–50). Many of these approaches underline that there are possibilities for change, but that courage is required to take the first steps and to encourage others to do the same (Lamker/Schulze Dieckhoff 2019: 8). Debates on planning theory increasingly discuss the fact that planners can accompany, manage or lead, but can never achieve a complete overview – i. e. complete certainty (e. g. Abbott 2005; Lamker 2016). Identifying and assuming individual responsibility requires opportunities to think beyond what is known and to expand the boundaries of possible action – also expanding individual understandings of planners' roles. Tangible roles help planners to increase their own reflexive capacity and to capture new behavioural patterns in comprehensible mental images. They encapsulate the basic attitude of planners, which is increasingly shifting towards actively accompanying transformation processes in pursuit of the abstract goal of greater sustainability (Lamker/Levin-Keitel 2019: 109).

The basis for the understanding of roles employed here is found in organisational and system theory. Roles summarise expectations and thus provide stability in complex systems (Lamker 2016: 93–97). Acting under uncertainty is viewed as normality (Abbott 2005), involving a search for agency despite complex interactions and undecidabilities. Organisational research has little difficulty in recognising action as being fundamentally incomplete and temporary (Schreyögg/Geiger 2015: 13). Clarity about one's own possible roles and the possible roles of others serves to provide temporary stability through coherent behavioural patterns, which are expected to be reciprocal (Lamker 2016: 94). It is fundamentally impossible to completely record, describe or reliably control other systems. Today, a transformation of planners' roles is occurring just as planners who have adopted appropriate roles are also supporting spatial transformation (Wittmayer et al. 2017: 53). Role-reflexivity is especially important in concrete situations where it can offer support and stability in uncertainty (Lamker 2019: 204).

Roles are used here as a tool to further the collective understanding, reflection, support and organisation of transformation in the context of irresolvable uncertainties (Lamker 2019: 201). They serve to reduce complexity within the system of 'planning', i. e. to structure it in comprehensible and manageable elements. As complex behavioural patterns, roles can be applied and adapted, even for roleplay and improvisation in different contexts (also see Innes/Booher 1999: 12; Wittmayer et al. 2017: 50). Instead of fixed actions, planners should have a flexible toolbox of roles with which they can test spatial action, right down to basic assumptions concerning the potentials for change in post-growth approaches. Today's great pace of change means that changing the training of future planners is just as inadequate as relying on the slow diffusion of new ideas. The new roles that are necessary must also be filled by people who want to plan and change in the here and now. Decoupling strict assignments of roles and people creates a bridge between today's reality and possible futures. The decoupling does not force planners to question their own identity. Rather it provides them with an opportunity to better understand their own role in interaction with others and to temporarily 'slip' into other roles in order to improve planning action and increase collective reflexivity and agency with other actors (see Innes/Booher 1999; Lamker 2019). In the following, roles are used to help transfer important behavioural patterns from the post-growth debate to urban and spatial planning. With their focus on agency, they introduce enriching new patterns of behaviour and promote the responsible use of the new paths thus created.

Post-growth impulses

On the one hand, the post-growth discourse looks at institutional norms and structures that often follow an unquestioned growth logic (e. g. Rydin 2013; Stein 2019). On the other hand, it also looks at the possible ways in which individuals can effect change (e. g. Ekardt 2017; Welzer 2013). The interaction of the macro- and micro-levels of decision making and of global and local processes calls for a response by all of us. Investigations and discussion about post-growth are still relatively new and research gaps remain (Schmelzer/Vetter 2019: 232–235). These include the global ecological question of post-growth in relation to social justice and the relationship between post-growth, geopolitics and security policies. However, in the search for arenas of responsibility and transformative roles, urban and spatial planning can draw not only on its own initial post-growth impulses but also on fundamental critiques of existing social and economic models from neighbouring disciplines.

With the work of Piketty (2016), a new basis for understanding the development and meaning of growth has recently been developed in economics, and concludes that growth is leading to extreme national and global inequalities. Growth is not normal. In human history, it rather represents an exceptional situation in the second half of the twentieth century. In addition to analytical approaches, there are alternative economic models such as the post-growth economy (Paech 2012; Jackson 2017), donut economics (Raworth 2018), the common good economy (Felber 2018) and the degrowth movement (Latouche 2010; Konzeptwerk Neue Ökonomie e.V. / DFG-Kolleg Postwachstumsgesellschaften 2017; Kallis 2018). In response to planetary boundaries and the need to improve public welfare, such approaches call for immediate change to our economic practices and lifestyles (for example, with an economic focus in Felber 2018). However, the spatial dimension is still underrepresented (Schmid 2019: 9).

In sociology, critical approaches describe the 'racing standstill' of a society that is in constant acceleration but still fails to achieve a good life (Rosa 2016; Rosa/Henning 2018). However, great change is often also the result of small adaptations in our own behaviour and actions. There are thus also hopeful messages to be found in sociology, focusing on the agency of everyone (Ekardt 2017). Psychology explores the question of why the urge for growth is so deeply anchored in our thought patterns (Fromm 2009; Welzer 2013; Hunecke 2013), even though material possessions only lead to short-term moments of happiness and never to a state of lasting satisfaction. Erich Fromm (2009: 274) accordingly criticises the 'triad of unlimited production, absolute freedom and unrestricted happiness' (translated from German). However, current findings in brain research are encouraging for individuals as well as for cities and regions and suggest that there are possibilities for change, learning and development until the end of life (Hüther 2013; 2018).

There are also links to political activism working within other economic and social models. In 2011, the German Advisory Council on Global Change (*Wissenschaftliche Beirat der Bundesregierung, WBGU*) called for a great transformation (WBGU 2011). In 2013, the Enquête Commission 'Growth, Prosperity, Quality of Life' ('*Wachstum, Wohlstand, Lebensqualität*') also discussed the search for alternatives in its final report (Deutscher Bundestag 2013). In 2014, the first degrowth conference took place in Germany and has since been held annually in other European cities. In 2018, the European Post-Growth Conference, initiated in Brussels by ten MEPs, discussed future-proof policy and a sustainable combination of the environment, human rights and a viable economy.

Finally, in 2018, the Fridays for Future movement was born, becoming a major political force in 2019, right up to the European elections. For the first time, young people around the world are collectively calling on politicians and society to take decisive action and change direction in the face of the climate crisis and planetary boundaries. Since the end of the 2010s, this civil-society 'moral revolution' or 'art of the future' (*'Zukunftskunst'*) (Schneidewind 2018: 476–479) has triggered reflection in many professions about individual political responsibility and possibilities and may be a starting point for political-institutional, technological and economic change. Nevertheless, in Germany it has not led to fundamental policy changes.

There is an increasing amount of work in urban and rural planning that is critical of the deeply rooted (economic) growth orientation of the profession (Janssen-Jansen et al. 2012; Rydin 2013; Hahne 2017; Schulz 2018; Savini 2019; Stein 2019). The growth paradigm pervades planning instruments, institutions and norms and prevents planning from focusing on the common good. A critical view from a post-growth perspective can be valuable here: first, it helps to identify this growth focus on various levels; second, it provides incentives, arguments and visions for a post-growth culture; and third, it offers motivation to productively use the critical pluralism of opinion. In Germany, the Academy for Spatial Research and Planning (*Akademie für Raumforschung und Landesplanung*, ARL) sees potential for post-growth to develop into a 'paradigm in the economy, society and planning' (Akademie für Raumforschung und Landesplanung 2017: 4, translated from German). In 2019, the Association of German Architects (*Bund Deutscher Architekten*, BDA) heralded the end of growth as necessary for survival, elaborating on this in ten postulates (Bund Deutscher Architekten 2019).

On the level of neighbourhoods, urban districts, towns and cities, several examples of alternative practices and criteria have the potential to lead to new ways of thinking and modes of living. On the regional, federal-state, national and global levels, the debates largely remain niche topics (very markedly in Denmark, Galland 2012). Indeed, the post-growth discussion has been split into, on the one hand, concrete and often radical demands directed towards established institutions and, on the other hand, a focus on self-organised projects and niches (Schmelzer/Vetter 2019: 217). Throughout, calls are made for new (positive) social visions which can break down the supremacy of a growth orientation, or even the 'growth fetish' in economy, society and urban and spatial planning.

Roles in an active transformation

The post-growth debate does not lead to a single role suitable for planners in public administrations or in private planning agencies. This seems particularly undesirable considering demands for diversity, pluralism and critical debate in large parts of the field. A set of roles can help daily planning practice to become more reflexive and active in face of the challenges and limits that the post-growth discourse identifies. Bringing together social, cultural and ecological issues in a broad discourse (as in Schmelzer/Vetter 2019: 15) provides a good basis for an integrative planning perspective on space. It is therefore especially helpful to identify impulses that receive little attention in the classical definitions of urban and spatial planning.

The six propositions of post-growth planning proposed by Lamker and Schulze Dieckhoff (2019) show the need for new roles from a post-growth perspective. New roles are intended to act as a bridge to bold action that sees current developments as being changeable, right down to their fundamentals. It is essential to use various types of communication including playful approaches for taking people with their personal and emotional dimensions seriously in open processes (Innes/Booher 1999: 19; similarly also Schneidewind 2018). Roles must provide a robust basis for communication, an immediate link to transformative action, and anchors that can be used in shared responsibility by every individual planning actor. Although social change has been occurring in many initiatives and micro-practices since the 1990s, spatial planning seems increasingly challenged by these approaches. Demands for rapid construction and the rapid development of land come up against the clear limits to growth and the real-world housing situation, mobility opportunities and quality of life. Debates about services of general interest, equivalent living conditions and the social divide are accelerating at all spatial levels and require a new perspective (Bundesinstitut für Bau-, Stadt- und Raumforschung 2017; Hagelüken 2017; Terfrüchte 2019). Is it impossible to effect large-scale and even systemic changes through collective decision-making?

Urban commons, cooperative kinds of urban development, civic neighbourhood concepts and spatial associations are already changing neighbourhoods and urban districts (Schneidewind 2018: 301–475). Although these approaches can be described using planning vocabulary, they focus on direct action, on collective forms of organisation and on the concrete improvement of the spatial environment. In addition, a new generational conflict is emerging. On the one hand, degree programmes, conferences and initiatives reveal a great interest in urban and spatial planning among young people from many backgrounds. On the other hand, there are problems with the representation of younger generations in democratic bodies. In the public debate, awareness and appreciation of demands for change – made visible, for example, by the Fridays for Future movement – are met with uncertainty or even rejected by established planning actors in research and practice. The long-term goals are well accepted, as seen, for example, in the transfer of the Sustainable Development Goals to all policy levels (Bundesregierung 2018). However, it is difficult to take the necessary courageous steps and to create a breakthrough with innovative solutions and new institutionalisations (Schneidewind 2018: 30). Part of the post-growth discourse fundamentally questions the way in which our modern society is organised, while other strands of the discourse actively direct their appeal to existing institutions (like, for instance, Fridays for Future). Post-growth calls for the stronger politicisation of social and thus also spatial issues (Schmelzer/Vetter 2019: 226).

In the context of a broader 'turn to action' in spatial and planning sciences (Lamker/Levin-Keitel 2019: 112), roles should be developed that provide inspiration and motivation for change. The established roles as a facilitator and coordinator of spatial processes have not so far opened up the necessary opportunities for a broader and more political process of change. They seem too passive and conservative to introduce and motivate a new perspective. Integrating post-growth into urban and spatial planning requires action-based roles that can inspire a positive vision of a growth-independent world (Lamker/Schulze Dieckhoff 2019: 8). As a discipline, urban and spatial planning is, however, characterised by the ability to use changing roles to repeatedly establish connections between people and spatial development and to envisage alternative futures (Lamker 2016: 323).

An open process is important to connect the integrative and long-term perspective with bold and immediate action. Planners should trust themselves (and be given the necessary scope by others) to develop ideas and even radical alternatives, offering them for public discussion. As inspirers, motivators and leaders, it is possible to help develop a link between concrete proposals within established institutions and the hope connected with self-organised forces in civil society, thus supporting a dual (or shared) transformation strategy. It should not be forgotten that the long tradition of urban and spatial planning in Germany and Central Europe has produced many valuable ideas and instruments that can also be used for changed goals and new success criteria.

Outlook

The greatest challenge is to collectively organise spatial development and at the same time to release it from its growth orientation. With their overview of modes of action and interrelations in space, planners can help by questioning apparently unquestioned assumptions. They can consider the long-term effects of individual decisions in the context of the diverse impacts of our uses of space. And, with the help of a broadened repertoire of roles, they can take an active and leading part in developing growth-independent spatial change. They should not enter into a cycle of avoiding critical discussion, but actively take responsibility within their own field, translating this responsibility into collective action with other stakeholders. The post-growth debate underscores that structural social changes are necessary if dependence on growth is to be overcome (Schmelzer/Vetter 2019: 26). It is not a question of whether the conditions or individual actions have to change first. Both are intricately linked and can only be fundamentally transformed if different groups of players simultaneously act together in new understandings of their roles (as in the transformation model in Schneidewind 2018: 477; also see Kristof 2017: 169–171).

Leading processes of sustainable transformation also means that planners must engage responsibly and actively. Combining post-growth with urban and spatial planning involves focusing more closely on shared and bold engagement. Ecological boundaries and social movements especially demand fast and dynamic action. In the future, planners should also adopt the roles of inspirers and motivators. An important step in this context is to combine existing approaches, to enter into creative discourse and to jointly embark on even those steps that initially appear almost impossible.

Spatial organisation is a collective matter where planners can take a key position precisely because of the level of complexity and dynamism. They thereby become leaders in developing the spatial conditions for a growth-independent society. At the same time, suitable social and political conditions must be created for collective action to have a lasting effect. This can provide fertile ground for the emergence, growth and activation of new roles in a growth-independent post-growth planning.

Cited literature

Abbott, J. (2005). Understanding and managing the unknown: The nature of uncertainty in planning. *Journal of Planning Education and Research*, 24(3), 237–251.

ARL – Akademie für Raumforschung und Landesplanung (2017). *Forschungskonzept 2017–2022*.

BDA – Bund Deutscher Architekten (2019). *Das Haus der Erde. Positionen für eine klimagerechte Architektur in Stadt und Land. Auf dem 15. BDA-Tag am 25. Mai 2019 in Halle/Saale*. https://www.bda-bund.de/wp-content/uploads/2019/04/20190819_DasHausDerErde_Monitor.pdf (2019, December 10).

BBSR – Bundesinstitut für Bau-, Stadt- und Raumforschung (2017). *Raumordnungsbericht 2017. Daseinsvorsorge sichern. Vorlage des Bundesamtes für Bauwesen und Raumordnung zur Unterrichtung des Deutschen Bundestages*.

BMU – Bundesministerium für Umwelt, Naturschutz und Reaktorsicherheit (2007). *LEIPZIG CHARTA zur nachhaltigen europäischen Stadt. Angenommen anlässlich des Informellen Ministertreffens zur Stadtentwicklung und zum territorialen Zusammenhalt in Leipzig am 24./25. Mai 2007*. https://www.bmu.de/fileadmin/Daten_BMU/Download_PDF/Nationale_Stadtentwicklung/leipzig_charta_de_bf.pdf (2020, February 24).

Brand, U., & Wissen, M. (2017). *Imperiale Lebensweise. Zur Ausbeutung von Mensch und Natur in Zeiten des globalen Kapitalismus*. oekom.

Brenner, N. (2014). *Implosions/explosions. Towards a study of planetary urbanization*. Jovis.

Bundesregierung (2018). *Deutsche Nachhaltigkeitsstrategie. Aktualisierung 2018*.

Deutscher Bundestag (2013). *Schlussbericht der Enquête-Kommission „Wachstum, Wohlstand, Lebensqualität – Wege zu nachhaltigem Wirtschaften und gesellschaftlichem Fortschritt in der Sozialen Marktwirtschaft"*.

Ekardt, F. (2017). *Wir können uns ändern. Gesellschaftlicher Wandel jenseits von Kapitalismuskritik und Revolution*. oekom.

Felber, C. (2018). *Gemeinwohl-Ökonomie*. PIPER.

Fromm, E. (2005). *Haben oder Sein. Die seelischen Grundlagen einer neuen Gesellschaft*. dtv.

Galland, D. (2012). Is regional planning dead or just coping? The transformation of a state sociospatial project into growth-oriented strategies. *Environment and Planning C: Government and Policy, 30*(3), 536–552.

Gunder, M., & Hillier, J. (2007). Problematising responsibility in planning theory and practice: On seeing the middle of the string? *Progress in Planning, 68*(2), 57–96.

Hagelüken, A. (2017). *Das gespaltene Land. Wie Ungleichheit unsere Gesellschaft zerstört – und was die Politik ändern muss*. Knaur.

Hahne, U. (2017). Die Region in der Postwachstumsdebatte. In J. Knieling (Ed.), *Wege zur großen Transformation. Herausforderunge für eine nachhaltige Stadt- und Regionalentwicklung. Ergebnisse des Interdisziplinären Doktorandenkollegs Dokonara*. oekom, 49–64.

Heinrich-Böll-Stiftung (2017). *Geteilte Räume. Strategien für mehr sozialen und räumlichen Zusammenhalt*. Writings on economy and social affairs 21.

Hunecke, M. (2013). *Psychologie der Nachhaltigkeit. Psychische Ressourcen für Postwachstumsgesellschaften*. oekom.

Hüther, G. (2013). *Kommunale Intelligenz. Potenzialentfaltung in Städten und Gemeinden*. Körber edition.

Hüther, G. (2018). *Würde. Was uns stark macht – als Einzelne und als Gesellschaft*. Knaus.

Innes, J., & Booher, D. (1999). Consensus building as role playing and bricolage. Toward a theory of collaborative planning. *Journal of the American Planning Association, 65*(1), 9–26.

Jackson, T. (2017). *Wohlstand ohne Wachstum – das Update. Grundlagen für eine zukunftsfähige Wirtschaft*. oekom.

Janssen-Jansen, L., Lloyd, G., Peel, D., & Krabben, E.V. (2012). *Planning in an environment without growth: invited essay for the Raad voor de leefomgeving en infrastructuur(Rli)*, the Netherlands.

Kallis, G. (2018). *Degrowth*. Columbia University Press.

Konzeptwerk Neue Ökonomie e. V., & DFG-Kolleg Postwachstumsgesellschaften (2017). *Degrowth in Bewegung(en). 32 alternative Wege zur sozial-ökologischen Transformation*. oekom.

Kristof, K. (2017). Change Agents in gesellschaftlichen Veränderungsprozessen. In J.-L. Reinermann, & F. Behr (Eds.), *Die Experimentalstadt.*

Kreativität und die kulturelle Dimension der Nachhaltigen Entwicklung. Springer, 165–179.

Lamker, C. (2016). *Unsicherheit und Komplexität in Planungsprozessen. Planungstheoretische Perspektiven auf Regionalplanung und Klimaanpassung.* Rohn. "Planungswissenschaftliche Studien zu Raumordnung und Regionalentwicklung" 6.

Lamker, C. (2019). Planning in uncharted waters: spatial transformations, planning transitions and role-reflexive planning. *Spatial Research and Planning,* 77(2), 199–211.

Lamker, C., & Levin-Keitel, M. (2019). Planung im Wandel – von Rollenverständnissen und Selbstbildern. Editorial. *Spatial Research and Planning,* 77(2), 107–113.

Lamker, C., & Schulze Dieckhoff, V. (2019). *Sechs Thesen einer Postwachstumsplanung. FRU-Preis 2019, Sonderpreis.* http://www.postwachstumsplanung.de (2019, July 6).

Latouche, S. (2010). Degrowth. Editorial. *Journal of Cleaner Production,* 18(6), 519–522.

Needham, B., Buitelaar, E., & Hartmann, T. (2018). *Planning, law and economics. The rules we make for using land (= The RTPI library series).* Routledge.

Paech, N. (2012). *Befreiung vom Überfluss. Auf dem Weg in die Postwachstumsökonomie.* oekom.

Piketty, T. (2016). *Das Kapital im 21. Jahrhundert.* C.H. Beck.

Raworth, K. (2018). *Die Donut-Ökonomie. Endlich ein Wirtschaftsmodell, das den Planeten nicht zerstört.* Hanser.

Rosa, H. (2016). *Beschleunigung. Die Veränderung der Zeitstrukturen in der Moderne.* Suhrkamp.

Rosa, H., & Henning, C. (2018). Good life beyond growth. An introduction. In H. Rosa, & C. Henning (Eds.), *The good life beyond growth. New perspectives.* Routledge, 1–14.

Rydin, Y. (2013). *Future of planning. Beyond growth dependence.* Bristol University Press.

Savini, F. (2019). Responsibility, polity, value: The (un)changing norms of planning practices. *Planning Theory,* 18(1), 58–81.

Schmelzer, M. & Vetter, A. (2019). *Degrowth/Postwachstum zur Einführung.* Junius.

Schmid, B. (2019). Degrowth and postcapitalism: Transformative geographies beyond accumulation and growth. *Geography Compass,* 13(11), 1–15.

Schneidewind, U. (2018). *Die große Transformation. Eine Einführung in die Kunst gesellschaftlichen Wandels.* Fischer.

Schreyögg, G., & Geiger, D. (2015). *Organisation. Grundlagen moderner Organisationsgestaltung. Mit Fallstudien.* Springer.

Schulz, C. (2018). Postwachstum in den Raumwissenschaften. *ARL Nachrichten, 2017*(4/47), 11–14.

Stein, S. (2019). *Capital city. Gentrification and the real estate state.* Verso.

Terfrüchte, T. (2019). Gleichwertige Lebensverhältnisse zwischen Raumordnung und Regionalpolitik. *Wirtschaftsdienst, 2019*(99), 24–30.

van Assche, K., Beunen, R., & Duineveld, M. (2017). Witchcraft, oracle, and magic in the kingdom of planning. A reflection on planning theory and practice inspired by Ernest Alexander. *Planning Theory, 16*(2), 223–226.

Welzer, H. (2013). *Wege aus der Wachstumsgesellschaft.* Fischer.

Wissenschaftlicher Beirat der Bundesregierung Globale Umweltveränderungen (2011). *Welt im Wandel: Gesellschaftsvertrag für eine Große Transformation.*

Wittmayer, J., Avelino, F., van Steenbergen, F., & Loorbach, D. (2017). Actor roles in transition. Insights from sociological perspectives. *Environmental innovation and societal transitions, 2017*(24), 45–56.

The Bauhaus as a designer of transition
Post-growth approaches in East Germany after reunification – between false growth and unwanted non-growth

Heike Brückner

In the upheaval following the German reunification, spaces and initiatives emerged that launched alternative approaches to sustainable and independent regional development: post-growth initiatives, although they were not yet known as such. Much of what was trialled and tested is today discussed as part of post-growth approaches. Since the 1990s, the Bauhaus in Dessau has proved itself an institution that provides important creative and cultural impulses for this transformation process. This thinktank and creative institution has accumulated knowledge on issues related to a 'different modernity', produced images and narratives of change and instigated concrete interventions for real change. With what is, in retrospect, amazing continuity, processes of change have been designed in keeping with a post-growth approach, setting an example for other cities, landscapes and regions. This chapter reflects on this experience, venturing to draw conclusions about the framework conditions, (planning) instruments and infrastructures that can support the development of a post-growth economy, using the example of an East German region, the Dessau-Wittenberg-Bitterfeld area.

Bauhaus and post-growth

In the midst of the weeks marking the fall of Berlin Wall in autumn 1989, the Bauhaus in Dessau launched a project named 'Industrial Garden Realm' (*Industrielles Gartenreich*), pursuing approaches towards a post-growth economy. Only nobody described it in this way, indeed the term did not yet exist. At that time, the concept targeted regional renewal, aiming to improve and utilise the endogenous potentials of the region and adhere to the ideal of sustainability. The goal was to initiate an 'Ecological Model Region' directly on the doorstep of the Bauhaus, in the triangle formed by the towns of Dessau, Wittenberg and Bitterfeld.

This idea was born in the 'Walter-Gropius-Seminar' that began on 4 November 1989, the day of the ground-breaking demonstration on Alexanderplatz in Berlin, and ended with the fall of the Berlin Wall on 9 November 1989. The rapid transformations kindled hope for a renewal of the region, one that would change the catastrophic ecological conditions, take care of the cultural heritage, prevent further decline of the inner cities and use architecture, landscape design and urban planning to create an environment worth living in.

The term 'Industrial Garden Realm' spatially and conceptually combined two historical reforms that had affected the region: the Garden Realm of the Enlightenment, and the Bauhaus and industrial culture of Modernity. Thinking about this reform heritage created a conceptual space in which approaches appropriate for the social challenges of the closing Industrial Age could be developed. The 'Limits to Growth' by the Club of Rome (1972) and the Brundtland report 'Our Common Future' (1987) were also read in East Germany (published by the state publishing house of the GDR as a book in 1988) and provided a backdrop for the model approach with its goals of sustainability and ecological improvement. The analogy to the reforms initiated by the historical Bauhaus, which had emerged in the upheaval following World War One, was quickly established: the end of the GDR represented another 'historical upheaval' that demanded and enabled reform.

That's right: the concept for this programme of independent – sustainable – regional development was conceptualised in the Bauhaus Dessau. Since the mid-1980s, the Bauhaus had once again existed as an institute of design, a 'Centre of Design' (*Zentrum für Gestaltung*) as it was officially called. In the early days, people were searching for spaces in which they could use planning and design to work towards change – despite political restrictions like the GDR's housing programme and in the face of dilemmas such as the decay of the inner cities, the catastrophic environmental problems and an inefficient economy. Concrete design issues of relevance to GDR society were negotiated, including design workshops, architectural projects intended to improve industrial housing, and urban planning issues. It should also be mentioned that from 1987 the Bauhaus again hosted students, who were 'delegated' to the foundation by universities with design disciplines (Weimar, Berlin, Halle, Dresden) and who became involved in the new Bauhaus design projects.

The self-image of the 'new' Bauhaus as a thinktank dealing with questions about the future found its way into the legal act that established the foundation in 1994. The goals recorded included not only conservation of cultural heritage and educational tasks but also 'contributions towards designing today's living environment' (translated from German). In line with the three objectives of the foundation, it has three departments: the Collection, the Academy and the Workshop. The Academy and the Workshop took an interdisciplinary approach from the very beginning and brought people from architecture, urban planning, landscape planning, regional planning and sociology together with cultural scientists, art historians and artists.

A popular rhetorical question intended to trigger discussion about current design tasks was: What would Gropius do today, what would the members of the Bauhaus do? While in the 1920s the Bauhaus found itself in a growing, up-and-coming industrial city with new tasks in housing development, serial design and urban development, in the present day it is confronted with the challenges of post-industrial change. Just like the historical Bauhaus helped to change society at the height of industrialisation, today it is called upon to help deal with problems at the end of industrialisation. Since 1989, highly politicised 'long-term projects', each planned to continue for about ten years, have been established to tackle urgent tasks and discourses:

- 'Industrial Garden Realm' (*Industrielles Gartenreich*') (1989-1999)
  Projects for sustainable and independent - sufficient - regional development in the Dessau-Wittenberg-Bitterfeld region
- The 2010 International Building Exhibition on Urban Redevelopment – (*Internationale Bauausstellung (IBA), Stadtumbau*) (2002–2010)

Research, expertise and experience from practice for planning without growth
- Post-fossil Spatial Design (*Postfossile Raumgestaltung*) (2010–2014) Scenarios and experiments with the model projects on the city, climate and landscape: Energy Landscapes 3.0 (*Energielandschaften 3.0*) / Active Mobility (*Aktive Mobilität*) / Productive UrbanLandscapes (*Produktive StadtLandschaften*)

In retrospect – and from the perspective of the post-growth discourse – it can be said that in all three project phases, growth-critical positions were adopted and strategies developed for alternative spatial development paths leading beyond growth. The projects opened perspectives for spatial development that focused on sustainability, regionality and a new concept of work that regarded individual fulfilment, creating and making as just as important as productivity and securing a livelihood.

From the very beginning, it was important not only to think in terms of concepts and scenarios, but also to use concrete projects to visualise how change could be possible – to try things out, to initiate a joint search for solutions. Such concrete project experience allows the process to become comprehensible for individuals, it then leaves the abstract canon and touches their own lifeworlds. People who are involved in this way become actors themselves.

Another important aspect was the creation of institutions, i.e. the institutionalisation of new spatial actors. Who negotiates which goals and how? The old institutions cannot successfully negotiate future goals. A whole spectrum of 'negotiating bodies' has thus been developed and implemented including planning workshops, charters, a contract for the area surrounding the waterbody known as '*die Goitzsche*', (regional) forums, a 'watershed master' and temporary advisory councils (for further reading see Scurrell 2002).

Interim conclusion

While the transformation of the old industrial REGION of Dessau-Wittenberg-Bitterfeld provided the spatial framework for the 'Industrial Garden Realm', the focus of the 'International Exhibition on Urban Redevelopment' was on the transformation of URBAN AREAS against a backdrop of demographic change. Finally, the scenarios of post-fossil spatial development were inspired by the idea of new URBAN-RURAL structures in which new spatial relationships are established, with more decentralisation, regionality and the self-empowerment of actors.

Post-growth approaches in the individual project phases

The Bauhaus project 'Industrial Garden Realm'
For sustainable urban and regional development

'Industrial Garden Realm' and 'Environment-Expo 2000' (Umwelt-Expo 2000) → Planning sustainable regional development, developing and testing methods and instruments for independent - sufficient - regional development

Growth vs. deindustrialisation
If you were a planner in the 1990s and started to talk about non-growth, independent regional development and sustainability then you were quickly sidelined. Everywhere was booming, growth was demanded (and promoted!) everywhere, fast growth moreover. Although much emerged in this time that we can be glad about (e. g. urban conservation, inner-city renewal), the 'Upswing East' programme also bore strange fruits: huge commercial areas and shopping centres in the suburbs and peripheries of the cities, a gigantic wave of suburbanisation accompanied by the construction of new residential estates on the outskirts of the city, the exorbitant expansion of transport infrastructure as an economic development measure, the designation of peripheral areas for – tax-incentivised – single-family homes, the construction of new swimming pools, leisure facilities and hospitals regardless of demand. This false growth has come at a high cost in some places, as is seen just a few years later. One extreme example concerns the suspension of planning laws, e. g. when construction was allowed in floodplains, developments that are now having to be demolished.

This false growth occurred at the same time as widespread deindustrialisation, which was accompanied by new ecological maldevelopments. Instead of investing in existing structures – and thus protecting them – the nature conservation provisions and regulations protecting historic buildings were often circumvented. Many of the new investments led to the sealing of new surfaces, interventions in the natural water regime and new environmental damage. Such measures were politically flanked by, for instance, 'investment facilitation laws'.

In everyday professional life, 'planning' then primarily involved forming alliances to fight against the destruction of the landscape or built heritage, to organise resistance and to avoid negative developments. It quickly became clear that the classical planning instruments like land-use plans or landscape master plans were not able to withstand the pressure of 'wrong' investments.

In face of the massive job losses and recognition that labour-intensive industries would no longer exist in the future, it was important, and indeed necessary, that an institution like the Bauhaus focused on 'new work' and new jobs in a deindustrialised society. This included all the issues associated with such a change and the development of new perspectives and concepts. Developmental and educational workshops focused on new professional prospects and new job profiles for an 'economy of sustainability' in which gainful employment and personal and community work were to be of equal status.

Employment figures for the Wolfen film factory

31.12.1989	15.380
31.12.1990	11.500
01.11.1991	7.050
01.11.1992	3.796
01.11.1993	1.300
01.01.1994	964
01.09.1994	799

Source: Stein 1996: 190

Figure 1: Protestors demonstrating against the closure of the Dessau rail-car construction works

Source: Jänicke, K.-D., *Lokalanzeige Dessau* on 24.12.1994, in: Stein, M. (1996): 193

Figure 2: Discarded excavator

Source: Stiftung Bauhaus Dessau, Archiv Industrielles Gartenreich, 1992

Figure 3: Wounds in the landscape, open-cast lignite mine Goitzsche

Source: Brückner, Stiftung Bauhaus Dessau, 1995

How can new developments be set in motion on the remains and traces of former industrial use? The following topics formed the programmatic cornerstones of the 'Industrial Garden Realm' project:

- 'New work'
- The ecological repair of wounds left by the industrial society
- The re-establishment of ecological cycles
- Dealing with industrial heritage
- A different economy focused on sufficiency

What emerged and how it continued

In the period between 1989 and 1999, 16 projects emerged, all of which were designed as experimental fields for sustainable regional development: large and small, investment and culture, constructional and conceptual, spectacular and common projects. While a great deal became clear and developed its own momentum, certain things had to be put on hold and are still waiting to be picked up again. Much has been successful and is now celebrated as positive transformation, e. g. FERROPOLIS, an open-air museum of industrial machines also used as an event location, and the renovation and revegetation of the open-cast mine Goitzsche.

There are also less well-known examples. For instance, the conservation and restoration of the factory housing estate in Wittenberg-Piesteritz, which was linked to a 'car-free' concept very early on (a concept that continues to be successfully applied today). Or the far-reaching plans that viewed the Dessau-Wörlitzer Garten Realm not only as a tourist attraction but also as a source of inspiration and impetus for ecological agricultural reform. Or the priority zones for wind energy that were designated at a very early stage in Saxony-Anhalt, so as to open up the prospect of a renewable energy supply after the closure of coal-fired power plants. The first wind farm was built in 1999 in sight of the Zschornewitz lignite-fired power plant and owes much to the commitment of the Bauhaus to new economic fields for the time after coal.

Other goals could not be realised due to a lack of political support but remain at the top of the agenda of post-growth regional development. These include the recultivation of an open-cast mine without artificial flooding with river water, and an ecological flood protection system for the Elbe and Mulde rivers.

In 1995, the 'Industrial Garden Realm' was accepted as an additional location for the Environment-Expo 2000 in Hannover. This gave the project a significant boost – and recognition beyond the region. With the resources provided by EXPO, many plans could be realised professionally and access to funding was made possible. It should be noted that in the process some developments or projects that aimed at slow and cautious recultivation were very quickly transformed into event locations, which was actually rather contrary to the idea of ecological sustainability.

The 2010 International Building Exhibition Urban Redevelopment

Less is More – Less is Future

The 2010 International Building Exhibition Urban Redevelopment Saxony-Anhalt: Planning non-growth. Research, expertise and experience from practice for planning without growth (including the research project 'Shrinking Cities' and the international exhibition 'Less is Future').

After the collapse of the old industries led to whole swaths of land falling into visible disuse in the 1990s, the problem of vacancies and decline spilled over into the cities in the early 2000s. Planners had pointed out that there was no long-term demand to justify the construction of a surplus of new offices, housing and commercial buildings, estates of single-family homes and shopping centres – all developed with (tax) subsidies. However, these warnings of the new problems being created were ignored. A change in approach was only seen once the housing industry itself came under pressure and in turn brought pressure to bear on politicians. An expert commission known as the 'Lehmann-Grube Commission' was established to consider structural change in the housing industry in the new federal states. They predicted a surplus of over a million vacant dwellings in East Germany. Politicians reacted and set up the 'Federal Programme for Urban Redevelopment in the East' (*'Bundesprogramm Stadtumbau Ost'*).

Reacting to an initiative by the Bauhaus Dessau, the state government of Saxony-Anhalt decided to hold an International Building Exhibition on the topic of urban redevelopment. The exhibition was based on investigations and studies by the Bauhaus workshop, which approached the topic of shrinkage not only in terms of demolition programmes to ensure housing market adjustment but aimed to change the urban planning and development paradigm to focus on greater sustainability and less consumption of resources.

How do we conduct planning without growth? Which instruments and methods must planning use and which spatial models result from this?

The contrast between a 'motorboat' and 'sailing boat' provides a powerful image here. The 'motorboat' symbolises the old system of unrestrained, constant growth. With the outboard motor – i.e. with external investment – I can reach any destination and determine my course very independently and precisely. If there is no external investment then development – moving forwards – must be organised very differently, by using existing resources. This is what the image of the 'sailing boat' symbolises. The course is not straight but needs to be repeatedly adjusted and adapted to the concrete situation. The passengers in the boat are part of the system. With their actions they rebalance the boat again and again – and they have to be very agile, react very flexibly and adapt to the circumstances (Oswalt/Overmeyer 2001).

Small and medium-sized towns as a focus of the International Building Exhibition

The federal state of Saxony-Anhalt is deep blue on the map of demographic change in Germany. Blue stands for a declining population – and thus for negative development, shrinkage. Apart from the two cities of Magdeburg and Halle, there are no areas that are not characterised by a shrinking population. However, if we look more closely at the settlement distribution it becomes clear that this is not an abandoned or empty space. On the contrary, it is an area that is characterised by many small settlement structures, creating a lively populated network of villages and small and medium-sized towns. And it was precisely these small and medium-sized towns that formed the focus of the International Building Exhibition Urban Redevelopment. Such settlements are often important anchors and support points for rural areas. With between 20,000 and 70,000 inhabitants, they house over half of the population of Saxony-Anhalt. In Germany as a whole, about two-thirds of the population live in small and medium-sized towns (BBSR 2007), a fact that receives insufficient attention both qualitatively and quantitatively in current political and strategic debates on social cohesion, and is not given the space it deserves in considerations of the future of urban areas.

Ultimately, seeing these shrinking small and medium-sized towns as pioneers of sustainable and post-fossil urban development was one of the core ideas of the International Building Exhibition, and resulted in three spatial scenarios. These scenarios for the future focused on the topics of urban areas, (agricultural) landscapes, and climate and energy. They aimed to create new urban-rural structures with 'cluster-cities' and 'rural republics' (MLV 2010).

Gaining new actors for sustainable spatial development

The traditional actors, however, tended to take a wait-and-see approach to these changes and tried to preserve their vested interests. New actors had to be found who saw an opportunity in the redevelopment processes and wanted to participate with openness, creativity and new ideas. This required a different kind of planning. Planning that targets invitation, activation and enabling. Planning that helps to initiate and shape processes, even ones with unclear outcomes. Planning that no longer prescribes something that just needs to be implemented but aims at the gradual cultivation of urban or rural spaces that have fallen into disuse.

This is well-illustrated in the example of Dessau, where one of the most advanced city-wide redevelopment projects was realised as part of the International Building Exhibition. As this is where the Bauhaus is located, it seemed obvious that the city and the foundation should together try out new paths. In addition to a long-term urban strategy based on the island theory, the focus was on new ways of mobilising the public to open up opportunities for direct participation. An 'Urban Redevelopment Planning Workshop' was launched, inviting new – different – stakeholders to become involved in the redevelopment process, such as the sponsors of cultural institutions or initiatives, the providers of supply and disposal systems, associations and private citizens.

Figure 4: Citizen claims '400 m² of Dessau'

Source: Reckmann, Stiftung Bauhaus Dessau 2006

The Bauhaus as a designer of transition 375

Figure 5: Pixels & Claims: for a culture of interaction and exchange

Source: Brückner (graphics: Faber), Stiftung Bauhaus Dessau 2004

Correspondingly, the spatial scale was 'broken down'. The city was symbolically pixelated. Using grids of 20 x 20 m, areas of 400 m² were created, which approximately corresponds to the smallest average plot size. The areas were given to private citizens, associations or firms to cultivate, no matter whether as a garden, as a three-dimensional business card or for sport and leisure etc. Analogous to the goldrush atmosphere that once characterised North America, these areas were named 'claims'.

Claims are important elements in the transformation of the city. Wherever an actor is willing to undertake something concrete then site ownership, usage contracts and design considerations must be clarified. This always accelerates the redevelopment process.

The grid used here is a method that can also be widely transferred – to other cities and other spaces. It gives structure and order to the emerging diversity and the spatio-temporal uncertainty. The structure of the pixel grid also creates an aesthetic but nonetheless systematic way of juxtaposing the planned and the unplanned, the small and the large, the conventional and the unconventional, etc. The uses and functions of the space are not programmed 'from above', rather its character is determined by the process of cultivation by the actors involved.

The claims were originally intended for temporary use, in the meanwhile a number of them have become long-term garden projects, educational sites or leisure areas, and some have been extended. The 'Urban Farm Dessau', which is in the process of establishing a 'neighbourhood farm' on brownfield sites, also sees itself as a further development of the claims, providing necessary infrastructure. With grow-your-own strategies and local supplies of renewable energy, water and food in the middle of the city, it aims to establish productive land uses in urban neighbourhoods.

Post-fossil spatial design

Urban areas, the climate, (agricultural) landscape

At the end of the 2010 International Building Exhibition Urban Redevelopment, three spatial scenarios were developed that outlined visions for a post-fossil society. They formed the starting point for further work by the Bauhaus Dessau on urban areas, the climate and (agricultural) landscape.

The Bauhaus Master Plan of 2011 states that 'the present is characterised by manifold crisis phenomena: the financial crisis, climate change and demography are indicative of the serious global structural problems of contemporary societies. They are at the centre of the upcoming design tasks...' And it continues: 'In order to strengthen the ability to shape the future, scenarios are being developed that reach far into the future and from there reveal possible paths for solutions to the present problems' (Stiftung Bauhaus Dessau 2010, translated from German).

The spatial scenarios are dedicated to the relationship between urban and rural, landscape and agriculture, climate and energy. Under the heading 'Less is Future', they demonstrate strategies for alternative spatial development paths beyond growth.

The focus is on the region, specifically the region with its interplay of urban and rural structures. One core idea is that the disintegration of society is reflected in space. We are dealing with the juxtaposition of growing urban areas and shrinking rural regions, with cleared agricultural landscapes and scattered villages whose inhabitants cannot find work locally and therefore have to commute to the nearest town or even really long distances. We are dealing with areas where the economy is booming and with leftover areas where nobody can earn a living and which are being abandoned as people move away. Linked to this is a spatial 'decoupling': the decoupling of production and consumption, of work and housing, of the cultivation of the land and the settlement of the land. 'Although 54 percent of the population in Saxony-Anhalt live in rural regions, agriculture provides employment for only about one percent of the people' (Veihelmann/Overmeyer 2010, translated from German).

Re-regionalisation

How can processes of reintegration be designed that include perspectives for sustainable transport, a renewable energy landscape and productive urban landscapes, as well as promoting strategies of renewal from within?

The old instruments are no longer sufficient: '... already in the past too much emphasis was placed on infrastructure and equipping structurally weak areas with transport infrastructure did not help to stabilise them. On the contrary, the reduction of spatial resistance actually accelerated the abandonment of the area. ... It sounds paradoxical, but it seems to make more sense to increase spatial resistance again and to look for endogenous development potential' (Rettich/Dolata 2010, translated from German).

The keyword in all three scenarios is 're-regionalisation': a regionalisation which relies on each locality's unique qualities and makes them productive in the most diverse ways. This is linked to an image of space organised in a decentralised manner, with structures for local supplies and self-sufficiency, where nature, resources and the landscape are protected, and where people negotiate with one another about what is done when, where and how in regionally anchored networks and forms of organisation.

Spatial models for the post-fossil society

These scenarios have managed to find strong images and terminology for spatial models that enrich the discourses on services of general interest, future sustainable energy supplies, a changed farming culture and the reorganisation of transport and mobility. They make existing knowledge accessible, also for non-planners and laypersons. The scenarios can be understood as a kind of 'visual thinking' intended to bring together technicians, designers and other experts, such as those specialising in climate and energy.

Working on new 'spatial images' for a post-fossil society helps to focus the discourse, while the scenarios demonstrate different options for action. They can open up spaces for models and experiments. Ultimately, they can strengthen relevant approaches, increasing their influence on society. They are not 'exclusive' truths based on research findings, nor are they 'target photos'. They are rather primarily 'images for communication'. If we assume that in a post-fossil society, prosumers (see Kurzja/Thiele/Klagge, Bürkner/ Lange and Lamker/Schulze Dieckhoff in this volume), who design their own life processes, will be the most significant actors for many areas of life and the economy, then this 'learning to design' will be an important educational challenge for the Bauhaus (Stiftung Bauhaus Dessau 2011).

The spatial scenarios serve to demonstrate what the status-quo is, what is going wrong and how things can be done differently:

- The status-quo: Energy Avantgarde Anhalt
- What is going wrong: Energy Landscapes 3.0
- How things can be changed: Productive UrbanLandscapes

The status-quo: Energy Avantgarde Anhalt

Saxony-Anhalt is a pioneering state in renewable energies. The first wind farm was established on a spoil heap of a former open-cast mine as early as 1999. In the same year, solar cell production was initiated in Thalheim near Bitterfeld. In July 2001, the first solar cells rolled off the production line at Q-Cells and continued until the slump in 2012.

However, not only large investments were made. The initiatives were primarily small ventures, organised privately or collectively, which – it should be emphasised – still exist today. They are remarkable in their continuity. Such initiatives include the revitalisation of a historical (protected) watermill, which today provides about 400 households with electricity. In Dessau there is also the first citizen-led solar power plant in Saxony-Anhalt, which has been supplying electricity to the grid as a 10 kWp system for over 15 years. Youth education projects have also been set up to encourage learning about the principles of self-sufficient energy supplies, as have a number of architectural projects involving showcase energy efficient buildings and solar modules integrated into buildings. One example is the Federal Environmental Agency in Dessau, a new build designed by the architects Sauerbruch Hutton. There is little public awareness of these projects, so the initial task was to map and make visible what is there. Re-evaluating what exists is often the first step towards initiating transformation processes.

Bringing together this wide variety of actors led to founding of the network Energy Avantgarde Anhalt. This network of artists, sociologists, private citizens, technicians and companies from the region was founded at the Bauhaus and has since established itself as an independent association. It focuses on working on a regional electricity system that makes it possible to turn private, public and civil society institutions and private citizens into producers and consumers of regionally generated energy. This provides an alternative to dicussion about major power transmission lines.

What is going wrong: Energy Landscapes 3.0

Revealing what is going wrong is also part of 'visible thinking'. Around 2010, the project DESERTEC hit the headlines. An international consortium planned to build enormous solar farms in North Africa and southern Spain and to transport the 'desert electricity' produced there via major transmission lines to Europe and elsewhere. Even at the time, Herman Scheer (2010) criticised the plan for creating a structure for renewable energies 'that would be even more centralistic than the conventional energy system, at least in part' (translated from German). A Bauhaus summer school took up the topic, focusing on the cultural, social and socio-economic dimensions because until then the issue had been viewed mainly from a purely technical perspective.

The opinion of the students at the summer school was unanimous: producing energy sustainably requires alternative economic approaches and lifestyles. 'Production with the goal of continuous capital accumulation cannot be social, sustainable and re-productive' (translated from German). They drew up concepts for decentralised supplies of renewable energies that involved as many actors as possible in a cycle of energy production, storage and use. They advocated the development of a prosumer culture in which reconnecting to social spaces, self-sufficiency, frugality and moderation would become the objectives of social action. The current energy supply model with its split between production and consumption is to be replaced by the model of prosuming, in which diverse actors enter into exchange with one another and practice new models of negotiation (Brückner 2011).

In contrast, projects like DESERTEC 'are conceived purely in terms of the energy business and not in terms of the overall economy, certainly not in terms of the regional economy. They reduce the number of actors producing renewable energy instead of increasing them' (Scheer 2010, translated from German).

Immediately after the summer school, the findings were communicated at a festival entitled 'On the art of living / Survival art' (*Über Lebenskunst*)'. Visitors to the festival could not get enough of the wonderful graphics, diagrams and maps. There was a great deal of animated discussion in front of the displays. This indicates the importance of visualisations of this kind that open up a space for discourse about the right and wrong approaches and allow joint learning.

How things can be changed: Productive UrbanLandscapes and Urban Farm Dessau

The Urban Farm Dessau project aims to produce healthy food and renewable energies where they are needed, in the cities and the urban neighbourhoods. The transition to non-fossil energy sources means that local supply strategies and self-sufficiency approaches are gaining significance. In the context of the 2010 International Building Exhibition Urban Redevelopment, unused spaces in Dessau were made available, initially temporarily, for new productive forms of land use, such as an energy crop plantation and 'claims' that could be used as gardens. This success of these claims and the increasing number of brownfields led to the vision of Productive UrbanLandscapes.

The aim of Productive UrbanLandscapes is to cultivate more and more green spaces in urban areas as gardens, making them productive for local economic cycles (for further reading see Brückner 2016). The Dessau urban development concept provides a good basis for this: in line with the island model the city was divided into a number of neighbourhoods (see Stadt Dessau-Roßlau 2013). Between these 'urban islands', a landscape runs through the city that can be used in a variety of ways: as a climate-productive space, for food production, as retention areas to provide protection against flooding, for energy bands, for community activities by urban actors. The products are processed and used in the neighbouring districts. Neighbourhoods become 'urban factories' where value is created.

In order for these goals to be realised and flourish, institutional support and structural opportunities are needed. 'Neighbourhood farms' provide the infrastructure for cultivating the surrounding land. They are the control centres that coordinate the economic activities, provide social exchange and organise negotiations about what should be done where and how.

The idea of initiating a 'neighbourhood farm' of this sort in a Dessau neighbourhood was born in the Bauhaus Dessau. With the support of the Robert Bosch Foundation and their Land Reclaimers programme, it was possible for the project to flourish and a network to develop with people from the neighbourhood. Since 2016, the project has been running independently and has been gradually extended both spatially and in terms of focus.

Figure 6: Future vision: Productive UrbanLandscapes

Source: Brückner, Stiftung Bauhaus Dessau/Urbane Farm 2014

What comes next: Post-growth and spatial planning

Here we come full circle: initiatives like the 'Urban Farm Dessau' are infrastructural projects that can develop and test post-growth economies in practice. What conclusions can be drawn from them for the spatial implementation of post-growth scenarios? What contribution can spatial development and the planning disciplines make to the emergence of a post-growth economy?[1]

---

1 Also see here Brückner 2020.

The Bauhaus as a designer of transition   383

Civil society actors are the drivers of a post-growth economy. Associations, co-operatives and private citizens are looking for alternative modes of living and alternative economic approaches in order to promote more sustainable development focused on the common good – in urban and rural areas alike. Actors and projects no longer want to wait for someone 'from above' (see Lange/Bürkner in this volume) to change course in order to tackle societal challenges such as climate change, the energy and food issue and social cohesion. Instead, they are taking action themselves, with their own resources, their own networks and their own alliances, in a very concrete and local way.

With their networks, these actors create real alternatives to the dominant economic system. The networks of eco-villages and transition towns, of Community Supported Agriculture (CSA) and permaculture, of repair culture and citizen-led energy co-operatives, social housing projects, etc. – all show ways of operating in a different economic mode, beyond the classic logic of exploitation and growth convictions. They abstain from consumption, operate in small cycles, develop step-by-step investments. They work in solidarity, collectively, ecologically. They act according to the principles of a post-growth economy – today.

The aim should therefore be to develop (management) instruments for spatial planning that support growth-critical approaches and open up spaces in which post-growth economies can flourish.

Projects led by private actors, initiatives and associations tend to be 'finegrained'. They are imaginative and creative. Rather than following a grand plan, they trigger creative chain reactions. Instead of big, spatially dominant investments, there are a multitude of small steps that focus on what is available and what can be made productive locally – so instead of the one big solution, there are a multitude of small solutions.

Citizen-led, civil society initiatives thereby develop a momentum that cannot be planned for or managed using conventional planning instruments. The classical plans are too sluggish, too formal, too functionally specific and divisive. 'Open planning processes' and 'informal plans' are needed instead, ones that are flexible in time and space and which allow the repeated renegotiation of goals, tasks and wishes so that interaction between actors is encouraged. Instead of a finished plan that describes a final vision, we need planning tools that are understood as part of the processes being managed and designed.

What I have learnt in the long-term projects at the Bauhaus is that developments of this kind can be stimulated, encouraged, guided and qualified with a structural impulse 'from above'.

What could that be? A federal ministry for the promotion of post-growth economies? Why not? Let us imagine that the federal government takes up our suggestion and creates a POST-GROWTH Ministry. What would it have to do, what tasks would we give it?

Planning shrinkage and growth together

Shrinkage in one place always produces growth in another place. Rural regions characterised by infrastructural weakness, outwards migration and a declining population stand in contrast to growing metropolises. People go where they can find work. This leads to a shortage of housing and land in the large cities. Life grows increasingly expensive there and new social inequalities emerge. As a result, more surfaces in urban areas are being sealed, which is not good for the climate or for human health. What is needed is to put both developments in the same context – the shrinking in peripheral regions and the enormous growth in the metropolises. Urban and rural then move closer together, become neighbours. And that occurs in smaller spatial units that are manageable and negotiable.

Keeping land available for reproductive economic activity

Local supplies and self-sufficiency in terms of water, energy and food are essential to post-growth. The prerequisite for this is that land is available that can be cultivated sustainably. However, current land speculation is an absolute obstacle to this – just like the sealing of urban land. While a great deal of public money continues to be used to demolish buildings in declining regions, the conditions in the cities are less and less suitable for reproduction. Here, active soil protection should be implemented, so that land can be deliberately and structurally kept free for climate protection, urban agriculture, water management and social interaction, especially in metropolitan neighbourhoods. These areas of a new urban commons could be cultivated, managed and negotiated by a communally run 'neighbourhood farm'.

Planning 'free spaces' for self-empowerment

My third thought relates to the many initiatives that are committed to the post-growth idea and, indeed, are already living it. They still receive too little attention in the guiding principles of spatial planning. The classic discourse on the provision of services of general interest focuses on the state ensuring equivalent living conditions. In parts of the post-growth discourse the focus is completely different: it is about strengthening structures for self-empowerment and creating conditions within which these structures can flourish.

One possibility is to use the coal phase-out programme here. Former mining areas can be recultivated so that the land and water is used for small-scale ecological agriculture and forestry and made productive again. In between, climate productive potential can be created with evaporation areas, a small-cell water regime and measures to build up humus in the soil. This also involves correcting mistakes made when recultivating the open-cast mining areas in the past and introducing measures that help to repair the entire water regime and allow it to recover.

Local initiatives and actors would gain access to resources like land but also to empty buildings. They should receive support if they pursue goals aligned with sustainable economic activity and focus on sufficiency and public welfare. Citizen support structures can help strengthen the projects initiated by local actors. This approach promotes people's ability to self-organise and cooperate and creates incentives for collective action – thus shaping a post-growth society from within.

The character of the area changes in such a process. It is not programmed by designations and uses assigned 'from above' but by what people actually do locally. This active appropriation grows out of the concrete behaviour of those involved and gains its value from the real actions of many. The area loses its static quality. It becomes more and more of a living structure in which different things happen simultaneously and design options emerge again and again.

Conclusion

There is no one master plan for post-growth. As it becomes clear that post-growth develops in small spatial units then the role of spatial planning also changes. It is no longer about an authority that prescribes (or regulates) and thus triggers reactions; planning rather becomes part of the processes. Process-oriented planning focuses on creating structures, occasions and opportunities in which creative spaces and creative forces can emerge. It is not about setting a linear course towards a final plan, but about continuously configuring and reconfiguring knowledge, forms and alliances. The planner then has the role of facilitating these processes, of providing focuses, aesthetic ideas and economic impulses – and of stimulating creative enthusiasm!

Figure 7: Creative enthusiasm

Source: Stiftung Bauhaus Dessau, Archiv Industrielles Gartenreich

Cited literature

BBSR – Bundesamt für Bauwesen und Raumordnung (2017). *Laufende Raumbeobachtung des BBSR. Raumabgrenzungen. Stadt- und Gemeindetypen in Deutschland 2017.* https://www.bbsr.bund.de/BBSR/DE/Raumbeobachtung/Raumabgrenzungen/deutschland/gemeinden/StadtGemeindetyp/StadtGemeindetyp_node.html (2020, February 14).

Brückner, H. (2011). Mit Gestaltung bilden. Energielandschaften 3.0 als Gestaltungsaufgabe. In Stiftung Bauhaus Dessau (Eds.), *Energielandschaften 3.0. Dokumentation zur Internationalen Bauhaus-Sommerschule 2011,* 44–47. https://www.bauhaus-dessau.de/2011-energy-landscapes-1.html (2020, February 13).

Brückner, H. (2016). *Produktive StadtLandschaft.* Stiftung Bauhaus Dessau; Landesenergieagentur Sachsen-Anhalt.

Brückner, H. (2020). Einen anderen Maßstab wagen. Kleinteilige Prozessgestaltung in der Raumplanung. *Politische Ökologie, 38*(160), 32–38.

MLV – Ministerium für Landesentwicklung und Verkehr des Landes Sachsen-Anhalt (2010). *Internationale Bauausstellung 2010. Weniger ist Zukunft. 19 Städte – 19 Themen.* jovis.

Oswalt, P., & Overmeyer, K. (2001). *Weniger ist Mehr. Experimenteller Stadtumbau in Ostdeutschland.* Studie der Stiftung Bauhaus Dessau.

Rettich, S., & Dolata, K. (2010). Republic of Harz: Rurale Republiken und urbane Cluster-Cities. In MLV – Ministerium für Landesentwicklung und Verkehr des Landes Sachsen-Anhalt (Eds.), *Internationale Bauausstellung 2010. Weniger ist Zukunft. 19 Städte – 19 Themen.* jovis, 830–841.

Scheer, H. (2010). Supergrids als pseudoprogressive Bremse. In H. Scheer (Ed.), *Der energethische Imperativ. 100 Prozent jetzt: wie der vollständige Wechsel zu erneuerbaren Energien zu realisieren ist.* Kunstmann, 139–140.

Scurrell, B. (2002). „Lernprozesse im industriellen Gartenreich". *Berliner Debatte Initial, 13*(4), 64–74.

Stadt Dessau-Roßlau (2013). Räumliches Leitbild Dessau-Roßlau 2025. In Stadt Dessau-Roßlau (Eds.), *Integriertes Stadtentwicklungskonzept INSEK Dessau-Roßlau 2025,* 55–57.

Stein, M. (1996). Eine neue Landschaft entsteht. In Stiftung Bauhaus Dessau (Eds.): *Bauhaus Dessau. Industrielles Gartenreich.* expose, 190.

Stiftung Bauhaus Dessau (2010). *Arbeitspapier zur Strategiediskussion, Oktober 2010.* Unpublished.

Stiftung Bauhaus Dessau (2011). *Konzeptpapier zur Programmplanung. Bereich Werkstatt, 20.10.2011.* Unpublished.

Veihelmann, T., & Overmeyer, K. (2010). Was blüht unseren Landschaften? Zum Beispiel Bitterfeld-Wolfen im Jahr 2050. In MLV – Ministerium für Landesentwicklung und Verkehr des Landes Sachsen-Anhalt (Eds.), *Internationale Bauausstellung 2010. Weniger ist Zukunft. 19 Städte – 19 Themen.* jovis, 842–853.

Lessons from Practice

Post-growth perspectives for the Lausitz lignite mining region? - Opportunities and challenges

An interview with Carel Carlowitz Mohn, conducted by Mai Anh Ha, Meret Batke and Bastian Lange

The civil society group 'Lausitz Perspectives' ('*Lausitzer Perspektiven*') is committed to positively shaping structural change in the Lausitz region and actively influencing the transition to a post-fossil economy. It views itself as a platform for exchange and understanding of what the future of the region could look like. Citizens should not be passive spectators but should act to shape and manage structural change.
www.lausitzer-perspektiven.de
Carel Mohn is a qualified journalist and holds a degree in political sciences. He became involved in the founding and work of 'Lausitz Perspectives' because he is convinced that it is possible to combine decent employment opportunities, industry and environmentally sustainable economic activity.

How long has the initiative been active?

Carel Mohn: It was in 2011/2012 that we began to look at the future prospects of the Lausitz. Over time this work led to the establishment of our organisation as a registered NGO, which works very closely with a group of initiatives called 'Lausitz Citizen Region' ('*Bürgerregion Lausitz*').

What was the idea behind the initiative?

Carel Mohn: In the early days, there was no sign of the coal phase-out but it was clear that sooner or later the Lausitz and the other lignite-mining regions would have to get out of coal because of the huge greenhouse gas emissions associated with lignite. The aim was to start a conversation in society and the region about what development opportunities there are beyond coal. This conversation was then actually set in motion.

Is this aim still relevant?

Carel Mohn: In the recent past, political developments have accelerated enormously. There's no longer a need to talk about the future in order to allay people's fears about the coal phase-out, because the decision about the coal phase-out has been made. Nevertheless, the development of the region should still be monitored. There are two points in particular that are central: first, the extent to which truly far-reaching decarbonisation is a guiding principle for this structural development and, second, how citizens and civil society organisations can participate and contribute to this process.

What are the processes that develop in a coal-mining region and what has changed since the coal phase-out was decided?

Carel Mohn: Coal regions have traditionally had one very dominant economic sector. This shapes the region, so that other industries, economic sectors and social spheres can hardly get past this giant – although the perceived importance of coal has actually always been much greater than its real economic weight. You could quickly get the impression that these regions define themselves only through coal. In the Lausitz, this led to the emergence of a kind of 'establishment' based on coal. This establishment included the mining operators themselves but also regional politicians, trade unions, chambers of commerce and business associations. For a long time, they protected coal and used scenarios of fear, even while the coal phase-out was still being negotiated. However, once there was the prospect of government funds to buffer the phase-out process, there was a very quick U-turn and a great deal of thought about what could be done with all that money. That's basically understandable and quite legitimate. However, you have to ask whether the people who for years and decades vehemently fought for a policy of carrying on and on with coal are or should be the best people to develop new perspectives.

The term 'establishment' implies that there are others who were left out...

Carel Mohn: The problem is that the people who proposed development alternatives for the region very early on aren't yet part of the circle of full-time, mostly paid officials involved in implementing new development perspectives today. This means that they also don't have access to the funding. But these are the people who years and years ago developed ideas about what could happen in the Lausitz, ideas that also involve civil society commitment. The question is whether these people should have a chance to be heard. What resources can they use to be able to play a role?

What other challenges have emerged in the region?

Carel Mohn: This is a region that has been traumatised by the experience of the post-reunification period and the collapse of 90 % of the coal industry and the heavy industry associated with it. Quite understandably, there's therefore been a lot of clinging to the remnants of this industrial complex. This includes all the sectors associated with coal as well as the energy-intensive industries grouped around it. However even 15 or 20 years ago, it was clear that this industry couldn't flourish forever, because there was the climate problem even then. My impression is that this saga of coal as the only anchor of stability has really blocked the region from developing alternatives for too long.

What are the impacts of these challenges for the local residents?

Carel Mohn: On the one hand, the traumatisation of the collapse of GDR structures hasn't been dealt with sufficiently; on the other hand, in the run-up to the national coal phase-out consensus adopted in early 2019, the state governments in Saxony and Brandenburg failed to show political leadership by preparing the population in the region for the phasing-out of coal at an early stage. Instead, they competed with one another in pledges of allegiance and commitment to Lausitz lignite. This combination continues to create a tense atmosphere to this day. In addition, many people from the Lausitz felt that the urbanites and climate protectors were badmouthing the Lausitz and jobs in coal – which actually offered very good working conditions. In conversation you can often hear the frustration about this. These negative experiences first have to be overcome, and of course many from the Lausitz struggle with the fact that the coal industry is coming to an end, because at least mentally this is also associated with a certain devaluation of the region.

What are alternative perspectives in the future?

Carel Mohn: At the political level, it's now clearer that something new needs to be developed in the Lausitz. The question is, however, whether attracting companies like Tesla (which is planning its largest European factory in Grünheide, some 50 kilometres to the north of the Lausitz), to use a current example, is really a good option in the long term. Or whether this isn't just people being intoxicated by the apparent success of an industrialisation model. It may work again to a certain extent, this attracting of large external investors, which creates many thousands of jobs in one go. What gets forgotten, however, is that this approach to economic and regional development is actually a course that hasn't really worked in the last 20 years.

How does this manifest itself?

Carel Mohn: The weakness of eastern Germany also has to do with the fact that there are too few small and medium-sized enterprises, too few research-based companies and too few corporate headquarters in the region. As a result, in the private sector generally there's a lack of research and innovation. Of course, building up this commercial landscape is extremely arduous and takes a long time but there are no real alternatives. Attracting a huge external corporation like Tesla fatally confirms the position of actors who have always hoped for large structures.

Are there examples of small-scale structures with small and medium-sized enterprises in the Lausitz?

Carel Mohn: Saxony and Brandenburg take different approaches here. In contrast to Brandenburg, the state of Saxony has focused more on promoting small and medium-sized enterprises in recent years. Of course, there are many examples of companies that are not active in the field of the coal industry. Some of these companies absolutely epitomise a pioneering spirit and entrepreneurship and also stand for very innovative approaches and concepts for the future. But you need many such enterprises and, importantly, state investment in science and research in order to create a small-scale, vital economic structure.

Is the term 'post-growth' one that comes up in this debate about a future perspective?

Carel Mohn: I don't think that this is a very helpful category in the Lausitz. My suspicion is that the model that's associated with it creates more fear than inspiration among most of the people affected by the phase-out of coal. The term 'post-growth' communicates too little about what could concretely change and improve in people's everyday lives. The region has very concrete problems, like keeping well-educated young people in the region and unfavourable demographics, and problems in offering and maintaining adequate local infrastructure, for example health care in rural areas, public transport or public amenities as banal as local grocery stores. These are the issues that concern and interest people. It's not really helpful to use buzzwords like 'post-growth' because it divides rather than unites society. Post-growth is a view that's strongly associated with left-wing values. It is important that we have value-based debates over the future of the region. However, if you want to convey new confidence in the Lausitz as a region strongly characterised by engineering and industry, then I don't think that the term is tremendously helpful.

Is there an exchange between different political camps in the debate on regional development in the Lausitz, especially with regard to the AfD [Alternative für Deutschland – Alternative for Germany] and its definition of the terminology related to post-growth?

Carel Mohn: The AfD relies on picking up on people's moods and playing on their fears. This can be clearly seen in the Lausitz region at the moment. However, it shouldn't be forgotten that the ground was prepared for the AfD over decades – by actors who didn't exercise political leadership responsibly but rather spread fear among the public.

Where have political leaders specifically failed to take responsibility?

Carel Mohn: The state premiers and numerous other state politicians in Brandenburg and Saxony didn't see the need to change, but rather spread fear about the coal phase-out. Instead of explaining to people that although there are well-paid jobs in the coal industry they unfortunately can't last forever. Instead of involving the public in ideas for the time after coal, thinking about how a soft exit could be made possible. Overall, there was an exorbitant lack of political leadership. This is what drove voters to the AfD. This is the historic failure of the SPD and CDU in this region.

What potential does the region have?

Carel Mohn: The region has immense potential because it's very centrally located between various metropolises in Europe and is also at the intersection of the three most dynamic economies in the EU, i.e. the Czech Republic, Germany and Poland. There are large areas of land, large open spaces available, and a population that can be described as open-minded. For example, there is a natural proximity to engineering and technology. The region also has a special cultural and industrial heritage, for example experience in textiles, glass and ceramics. These are valuable qualities and opportunities that other regions don't have. Agriculture has been completely marginalised by the coal industry to date, but it can also play an important role – Berlin, but also Leipzig and Dresden are huge markets right on the doorstep where regional, organic products are increasingly in demand. And when it comes to renewable raw materials, the bioeconomy and the circular economy, there's a natural link here to the technical expertise that has previously been in demand in the Lausitz region.

What suggestions or wishes do you have for the transformation to post-fossil regional development?

Carel Mohn: Above all, it's important to develop a concept about how the municipalities can be given more scope and greater autonomy. They would clearly have more options if they had more financial freedom. In addition, municipalities need the financial and political scope to promote initiatives, projects and local individuals who take on local responsibility. They also need to be able to apply for funding or to use their own resources. The whole issue of what municipalities could do if they had better resources and jurisdictions is neglected in the debate. The second point is that there are really many pioneers in the region who are involved in cultural projects, in associations, in village renewal. We need to think about how to make it possible for these actors to actually implement their ideas. It's extremely difficult to get funding and support to implement this non-profit work or even to participate at all – not because there is no money but because it's so time-consuming, bureaucratic and arduous to apply for just transition funds. It's not just about the paid officials in the chamber of commerce and the union, there are also others involved. It is neither fair nor economically sensible if these pioneers have to privately develop their projects in their spare time. A small proportion of the billions should be directed towards foundations and NGOs to find ways to improve the involvement of civic engagement.

Hacking Ulm
Open data, digital literacy and coding as practices creating space in the city

An interview with Stefan Kaufmann, conducted by Meret Batke, Mai Anh Ha and Bastian Lange

The *'Verschwörhaus'* describes itself as an 'experimentation platform for the world of tomorrow' intended to accompany the city of Ulm into the future. Ideas are developed in labs and at events. Equipped with 3-D printers, open workshops, lecture rooms and 'cyber, chaos and public disorder', this is a place where interested (young) people come together to experiment and to learn from one another.
www.verschwoerhaus.de
[Editorial comments and translations in square brackets]

What is the 'Verschwörhaus' and what does it do?

Stefan Kaufmann: My name is Stefan Kaufmann, I'm originally from the field of open-data activism, that's an environment where people use particular means and technical abilities to try to tackle things and problems in the city. Not necessarily directly to solve things but at least to indicate ways that they could be dealt with. The *'Verschwörhaus'* was founded out of this movement. It's actually divided into two – one part is a project run by the city of Ulm, the *'Stadtlabor'* ['Urban Laboratory'], which provides an administrative and organisational framework. The city rents the rooms and makes them available, but the content is provided by people involved in 'digital volunteering' – where people give their time because of intrinsic motivation, i. e. not because they want to earn money with this but because they want to exchange ideas and do things and make a difference and are strongly influenced by a creative idea.

How can the project context for the city of Ulm be explained?

Stefan Kaufmann: The context was that there had been an open-data working group in Ulm for a very long time, one that was predominantly made up of students. The group dealt with mobility and public transport issues, for example, partly because that was a major problem that affected them personally. And relatively early on this voluntary work made it clear that if you want to make something like this permanent, you need a youth section so that the issue is also taken up and continued. In 2015, after we implemented various organisational formats to create exchanges between the administration and the public and to work on these issues, the group got to know the '*Jugend hackt*' ['youth hacks'] format from the 'Open Knowledge Foundation' and '*mediale pfade*' ['media paths'].

We made an effort to bring this format to Ulm as a youth development programme. We wanted to bring young people together for a weekend, young people who don't have much chance of meeting people like themselves as they come from the rural areas of southern Germany. We used the motto 'Improving the World with Code', and the young people could exchange ideas and work on problems about how to improve people's everyday working lives. And this led to us saying that it would be good to have such formats not only once a year at the university, where everything has to be set up, but with a permanent space for them in the city. The model of hacker and makerspaces, which is really nothing new, also exists in other places and has already existed for twenty years.

How did you implement the project in Ulm?

Stefan Kaufmann: There was only a problem in Ulm if we wanted to do this under our own steam. Ulm is too small a city, there's not much space and few vacancies and also not the physical mass of people who can support something like this and also pay for it and finance it. So there's something like the '*Freiraum*' ['Free Room'], a very small space with two rooms, where something like this was set up with relatively close links to CCC [Chaos Computer Club – Europe-wide decentralised groups and associations of hackers], but getting a really large space, one with exciting machines and devices too, is hardly possible to finance on our own. And then came the idea of approaching the city to create space, also against the background that it's a positive location factor if young people who like to tackle the topics have a contact person and a contact point where they can spend time. This led to a municipal council resolution in 2016, and now we will soon be in our fourth year.

Where did the name 'Verschwörhaus' ['Conspiracy House'] come from?

Stefan Kaufmann: The house had a range of names first, ones that changed again and again, partly because a lot of different actors wanted to join in who were primarily business-oriented and worked in the areas of design and entrepreneurship. But we as a group specifically wanted to implement a citizen-centred approach, one that comes from civil society and is also a bit rebellious and non-conformist and sometimes makes itself heard if it doesn't like something.

The name was a relatively obvious choice as the historical *Schwörhaus* (Oath House) is next door and is linked to the medieval tradition of the *Schwörbrief* [a historical document of the city of Ulm from 1397], which is (among other things) about staying true to yourself and following through. The name *'Verschwörhaus'* was also google-distinct, in contrast to *'Stadtlabor'* ['Urban Lab'] – which was the municipal title for the project and is a generic name like 'chemist' – and this meant that the name continued to be used.

What is the relationship between hardware infrastructure and software?

Stefan Kaufmann: We have about 500 m^2 of space that we can use. This includes a large lecture room, where large projections and lectures are possible. We can also record and livestream lectures. We have an electronics lab with quite extensive equipment – hardware can be developed there and wireless measurements for sensor networks, for example, can also be recorded. There are multi-purpose rooms that can be used in different ways, and two workshops, one with classic fab lab equipment, i. e. laser cutter and several 3D printers etc., and a large metal workshop with several circular saws, tools and a permanent project – a CNC metal milling machine [Computerised Numerical Control for the automatic production of parts].

Who uses the 'Verschwörhaus'? What do you provide?

Stefan Kaufmann: We're open mainly in the evening hours, because people do this mainly on a voluntary basis and not full-time. And there are different groups, there is an association that you can become a member of, but you don't have to, and in this association there are different specialist areas, e. g. the sensor network group, which meets every fortnight and then sometimes gives public lectures or simply works on things together, and almost everyone is organised in groups like this. Among other things, there's also a sporadic sewing cafe, which is organised by a sustainability group from the university, and *Generationentreff* [Generations Meeting] organises events on digital literacy with elderly people. And in addition, there is a programme aimed at young people, such as the *'Jugend hackt'* ['youth hacks'] lab, where young people come together under supervision, and individual events such as weekend *Jugend hackt* events or events with 'Wikimedia Germany' and the 'Open Knowledge Foundation'.

What backgrounds do the users have?

Stefan Kaufmann: We're well aware that this is predominantly used by white people with academic backgrounds, who are mostly male and not necessarily poor. We know that and this is always a problem with such places. We try to set up specific formats that counteract this, for example, together with Caritas we have a job application cafe for refugees, so that we also reach other target groups. But I think the majority of those active here are mainly people with an academic background between 16 and 36, although the bell curve continues to shift and the person who is mainly in charge of the workshop in the basement is a retired 63-year-old electrician.

How do you deal with material and data flows?

Stefan Kaufmann: We work with a lot of electrical and IT equipment and, self-critically, we have to say that we also order and install things from China via 'Ali Express'. We reuse a lot of IT equipment that has been taken out of service elsewhere and is then used here instead of being scrapped directly.

We see ourselves very strongly as being less on the material level and with more of a user-centred focus as opposed to profit-making. Mobility is still one of the core issues that many people are tackling, and we always try to focus on reusability with free software, free licences, free concepts, in order to set a contrast, to show that it's possible to do something that could help the public but that thinking of everything too much in terms of profit-making puts obstacles in the way. Here the approach is one of generating maximum profit for society as a whole.

Can you describe an example of the transport project?

Stefan Kaufmann: One topic that has preoccupied people for a decade is open data in the area of networked mobility. The approach here is to say that transport providers should provide the data needed for the use of services as barrier-free as possible, so that any third party can use them to build information and so develop intermodal mobility that is no longer dependent on the car. There's been a lot of resistance to this in Germany, especially from the transport associations, which believe in the nonsensical comparison that data is like oil and can be monopolised. In the meantime, more transport companies and transport associations are providing data, also thanks to EU regulations. What we can do in the '*Verschwörhaus*' is prototyping, in a larger context we're trying to find ways of moving beyond the pure concept stage. A concrete example is the free software 'digitransit' in Helsinki [an open-source trip-planning solution that combines several open-source components in a route-planning service]. From public transport to rented bikes, the software integrates mobility options from different sources to provide information. Because it was free software, several people here were able to port it to show how it works. At the time the city had an EU project which it fitted in with, so it was possible to appoint people as fellows who normally would not have ended up in the administration. The aim was to show what it could be like to think not of viability, but of maximising benefits.

Where is the link to a scaling perspective?

Stefan Kaufmann: What is important to me about people's personalities, especially if they have an IT background, is that [when it comes to the products] they are not open to economic exploitation, because this would destroy the basic principle of the common good. With a good annual salary in an IT company, I tend to be more focused on overtly doing something good in my free time.

Another example is 'Open Source Bike Sharing', which could be undertaken by municipalities themselves. This looks at how something can be implemented as an operating model instead of as a business model. Profit maximisation is not the priority here, but the focus is rather a model with minimal losses, which can perhaps be made self-sustainable and shows how this could function if organised cooperatively.

What are the interests behind such solutions, does it have something to do with the common good?

Stefan Kaufmann: Because of the networking of voluntary actors who want to further develop the networks and find new people to continue working on them, you have to be careful about how you understand your role. What is already run by the city? Where is the space occupied by the volunteers in complete freedom, where they themselves say where we are heading? My role at the interface is rather one where I tell the stories as well as possible, so that afterwards the political decision-makers want to pursue things like this. But of course I can't make the targets, can't say what the guidelines are, I don't have that leverage.

What are your hopes and vision for the future of the 'Verschwörhaus' in ten years time?

Stefan Kaufmann: I hope that in ten years I no longer have to sit here. I've been working to do away with my role since day one, and that has to be the target. This is a space that's by the people for the people, it's a basic principle to distribute the keys of the kingdom and to share them with many people. I hope that those who are active get funds from various sources so that they're not dependent on any one place, for example on the city, something that must be seen critically. And that good cooperative ways and means can be found for the city to adopt and integrate and transfer the ideas that emerge here.

Glossary

CCC: Chaos Computer Club e.V., the largest European association of hackers, consisting of different decentralised local associations and groups; annual event: Chaos Computer Congress (CCC)

CNC machines: Machines that use modern electronic control technology (Computerised Numerical Control), which enables the automatic production of parts

Digitransit: Open-source trip planning solution that combines several open-source components to create a route planning service.

'*mediale pfade*': Agency for media education with a focus on political education

'*Jugend hackt*': Educational programme promoted by '*mediale pfade*' and ('Youth hacks') the NGO Open Knowledge Foundation. Very different to '*Jugend debattiert*' (Youth debates) and '*Jugend musiziert*' (Young musicians) competitions etc., as the format is deliberately non-competitive and creates networking opportunities.

'*Schwörbrief*': Historical document of the City of Ulm from 1397 ('*großer Schwörbrief*' [large Oath Letter]), which extended the rights of the guilds and regulated legal relationships.

Designing living spaces together in open-ended approaches
Participation in spatial development for a good life

An interview with Torsten Klafft, conducted by Martina Hülz

Torsten Klafft is an architect and sociologist-in-training. He works in the architecture agency 'nonconform', which states that it is 'technically an architectural firm. But only technically'.
https://www.nonconform.at/

How are post-growth or ecological, sustainable aspects of designing space – i.e. growth-critical planning in the broadest sense – reflected in your work?

Torsten Klafft: They're reflected in our core themes. In principle, the current 'nonconform' came about in reaction to the sudden resistance from the public that we encountered in projects – resistance to planning by us and by those responsible. That puzzled us because we actually thought we were doing something good: using land frugally, focusing on local and urban centres or open-use building for communal utilisation to conserve resources. Why is there opposition to such approaches when they should be in everyone's interest? Then we had the idea of involving the residents from the outset and letting them discuss what should actually be planned. The *'nonconform ideenwerkstatt'* ['nonconform ideas workshop'] was then developed and has since been implemented dozens of times. Participation in combination with sustainable planning principles has become a self-sustaining field of work.

We often deal with development in rural areas. For us, this primarily involves the development of village or town centres. Communities regret that their town centres are wasting away, the small shops are closing, the main street is more and more deserted, and the church is seldom able to bring life into the surrounding square. And then we're asked to contribute our expertise. Our initial recipe is quite simple: we invite the locals to talk to us about these developments and to develop solutions. The *'nonconform ideenwerkstatt'* is a form of participation that's kept very concise. It has a sort of event character: we arrive, are on site for three days and invite everyone to our open 'ideas office'. Anyone can come and join in the discussion and develop strategies in various formats that we facilitate. The goal is to find a solution path that's individually tailored to the village or small town.

Is it reasonable to assume that, with the focus on the development of local town centres, there's already a certain awareness of sustainable spatial development among your clients and the local residents?

Torsten Klafft: Many of the municipalities involved do already know about town-centre development, and we're brought in to accompany them on this path. We can add the experiences of other municipalities to the process and there is much that can be learned here. Improving what exists is often not as 'sexy' as creating something new on a greenfield site. We provide answers about how it is possible to take the public along the path to sustainable town-centre development.

But the starting point is never the same twice – in terms of what motivation and ideas are available locally, what projects have already been implemented. Sometimes people are aware that the town centre has a problem, but this hasn't been linked to the new retail park on the outskirts that's attracting people out of the town centre. Or not everyone accepts these conclusions yet. Often there are local protagonists who've already initiated a few good projects and now want to take the next step with us, together with the local residents. Then it's our task, depending on the situation, to adapt the process appropriately. We have to accept what we find at the time. After all, the idea is to engage and convince people, we want it to happen *with* them. There's no universal recipe for this.

What exactly do you want to achieve in these places, what motivates you? Participation is actually the instrument or the method that you use, which has proved successful.

Torsten Klafft: I think that, on the one hand, it's the instrument we use to get necessary transformative processes going. But, on the other hand, it is in itself precisely what we think is important: it's about what people have in common in the village or town – around it and within it – because they live together in one place. That's always the central idea behind it. How can local people improve their lives and shape them together?

So your philosophy is the joint search for a good life with local people? What message do you bring with you?

Torsten Klafft: We bring our experiences from other places with us: that in fact there are always many local people who get involved very constructively. Even if one person says: 'I don't need the village, I just want a bit of peace in my own home', there is always someone else who thinks the village or town centre is important because it connects people. You can trust in the power of shared stories if everyone's involved in the process. Then many more ideas come together about what can be done for the town centre. There's simply a lot of potential that we can filter and process. To do this, we look for good examples that have worked elsewhere and put these approaches together with the images that exist locally. Together, we then create a local story, one that emerges from that place.

There's a general feeling that rural areas are once again being perceived as living spaces for very many people and are seen as important. That's why more funding is being created to encourage participation. There's often still a strong idea of community in rural areas. This makes it possible to tell a different story. If this is then linked to committed, open-ended participatory work, it also makes it possible to hold more difficult discussions. Too often, the critics don't get their message through when plans are being made for the next development of single-family homes. With the '*nonconform ideenwerkstatt*' we create a space where people can openly discuss the future of the village, encourage each other and develop new energy locally so they can then move on together. This doesn't always work, but often. At first, it's 'only' about the town centre, but active communities can grow out of this, ones who continue to discuss their plans together and perhaps also convince others with their reflections on spatial development.

Are people always willing and open? Or do you sometimes encounter resistance and scepticism? Or do you meet a certain type of person who's open to topics related to sustainability?

Torsten Klafft: It's more a case of having individual proponents in the towns, people who support the process and say: 'I've understood this for myself and I believe in it and think it's good'. If that's the mayor or members of the local council, then it's very helpful of course because they're the ones in charge. And even if some people are sceptical at first, most of the participants quite quickly say: 'Ah yes, that's right, it's kind of fun to discuss this together with everyone else, and I hadn't seen it like that before'. Spaces of possibility are opened up and often a spirit arises that overcomes any initial doubts or inhibitions. And then comes the real challenge, because people have to stay on the ball and those responsible locally have to implement the ideas – even if there are then discussions because the car park next to the church is moved out of the very centre. It's then important that the focus continues to be on the jointly developed vision of a lively church square as a meeting place and that this motivates people and gives them the courage to implement even unpleasant decisions because they believe in the *goal*. Especially at such moments, it helps a lot if the vision was not only passed by the local council but was worked out by many people together.

Do you follow up on further development or what happens afterwards?

Torsten Klafft: First we document our work, write a concept and hand it over to the municipality for further follow-up. In the best cases, there's an immediate opportunity for further cooperation, perhaps because small workshops have been arranged or because a competition is planned that we can help with as process designers and facilitators. Or we support the work of a local individual who has taken on responsibility for the process, like in Trofaiach in the Steiermark region. There we agreed to communicate closely with them, and if there were any problems, we worked together to find a solution. If this spirit flows into continued joint work, then of course we're closely involved in the process, but that's not decided or fixed from the outset – it may just develop. It's up to the people on the ground whether they want us involved.

All of the projects are potentially exciting, and we could spend ten years working on each of them because town-centre development requires continued work, even if you usually don't see the results for a few years. In an ideal scenario, we're invited for the awarding of a prize for rural building culture. But many communities continue on their path without us, although even then we always keep an eye on them, following developments and staying in touch.

The topic of 'participation' has become increasingly important in recent years and has been legally anchored in planning processes, so that public participation has become a necessity. Would you say that this is basically the right way to approach more sustainable spatial development? Or what are your experiences? What else is needed?

Torsten Klafft: We are very much in favour of participation being more strongly anchored, especially in spatial development processes – but not only anchored, it must be practised! Because, on the one hand, these are the topics that can encourage people and arouse their interest. On the other hand, we still too often see that it's only half-hearted and descends into a kind of 'alibi participation'. That can be counterproductive. I'm always amazed when people talk about the 'spectre of participation' or about the negative effects that can emerge. There are events where the visitors, the participants, are asked almost fearfully: 'What do you say to this?' Is the storm about to break? There's a risk that inviting the public is only seen as a duty and that the dominant emotion is one of fear that the work of recent months is going to be destroyed. This shouldn't become the defining experience, because good participation is important, even if it involves really demanding challenges. The language of planning must be translated in a way that everyone can understand. But the needs and statements of citizens must also be properly understood and translated into possible planning interventions for those responsible. In other words, in both directions. Many citizen participation processes are still affected by an attitude of getting them done because they're prescribed by law. If planners try to push through the plans or only half-heartedly involve the public, then this tends to lead to more doubts about the plans. If the procedure is only intended to let people get to know the planning process and the arguments, then this must be clearly communicated. If people are lured to an event with false promises so that as many of them as possible take part in an elaborate public participation process, then this tends to be counterproductive.

So, are you now taking away our hope for post-growth, sustainable spatial development through citizen participation?

Torsten Klafft: No! For the highest political level to say: 'Participation in such procedures is important' is a significant political statement. There's space, time and funding available to try out many things. But we have to ask ourselves how we go into such processes with our planning language. Do we really want to engage people because that makes the processes better? There are processes that are just understood as fulfilling requirements, but there's increasingly a belief that projects are really improved by participation. Some people enjoy using walks or cooking dialogues as formats. We have to try out new things and tackle them wholeheartedly, but also have the courage to accept there may be failures. We already have a few good recipes, and we're not the only ones who have repeatedly used them successfully. For example, people don't always have to be seated like an audience facing the organiser. Sometimes you need to liven things up a bit so that everyone moves around and comes together in different constellations. Some people might like to stand in the middle and talk in front of everyone, but many others say: 'Well, if there are a hundred people sitting here, I don't need to add my two cents'. In smaller groups of six or seven, discussing around a table, everyone gets a chance to contribute. It's important to find these ways of reaching participants. Our 'ideas office' is one access point, where anyone can drop by during the day and look at what was discussed the evening before on the flipchart. In a personal conversation, these people then also say what they think and what they want for their hometown.

You're so convinced that you're convincing me! Where does that come from? Did your training as a planner and architect equip you to do precisely this job with such motivation?

Torsten Klafft: After studying architecture, I worked as a traditional architect for two years and found that I didn't know anything at all about what constitutes social space. That's why I started to do a master's degree in sociology, to understand how society actually functions, the society that uses the spaces that we blithely design. Architects actually always design society, but it often looks different from the utopian image of society in magazines, where everyone happily walks around with a pram and a parasol. In reality, questions are rarely asked about how people are supposed to get there or why they should go to the glitzy magazine places designed in the isolated offices. I've become very critical of planning and planners' discourse. Many discourses about the people who use the spaces – who live in them – take place among planners' circles. I think it takes a lot of courage to say: 'Alright, let's find out *how* to find out if people want this or if people agree with the needs we're designing for or what spaces they want to use or maybe what spaces they need to design their own living space'.

In retrospect I find it rather shocking to think how little attention my training gave to such questions, because there's a lot of knowledge about this available. I think a great deal can come from broader exchanges between architecture and the humanities. As well as considering the functionality of spaces, it should from the outset be more important to ask how the newly planned space will be used, whether it will work well and how it fits into a holistic sustainability debate – the appropriation, repurposing and diversity of spaces for different user groups who create the place for themselves and make it their place. Urban planning is already a bit ahead in this area.

This is a fundamental problem of science and practice and of linking the two and also of the old debate about universities doing science and not training.

Torsten Klafft: Yes, but I studied architecture at a technical college. There we were trained to deal with the practical demands of an architect's job, i.e. the requirements encountered in an architect's office. But the professional image of an architect in practice that was reproduced at my architecture school was one that was limited to architects carrying out planning for the clients. Of course, it's difficult to implement social ideals in everyday life or to negotiate them with clients, but I think it's important to develop a position on this and to include it in the planning processes. In retrospect, for example, I would have liked to have had critical discussions at university about established housing standards. Does a flat that you can get with a housing entitlement certificate have to comply only with the minimum standards, when findings in social research show that these minimum construction standards are rather arbitrary definitions that actually contradict how people deal with spaces? If you want to develop 'good' social housing as a young architect, you don't just need courage and conviction, but you also need access to critical discourses – and these are still not heard enough at many architectural colleges. It often seems to me that architecture is a little slow to discuss scientific findings that contradict its self-image. Often, architecture training is characterised by a very generalist habitus of modernism, which also means that many of our most exciting colleagues initially had to deal very critically with their own training. There is still a lot of potential here, which could lead to more young planners being able to identify with their work and to many innovative approaches emerging.

With this society-centred view that you've just highlighted, I would like to make the connection to post-growth, sustainable spatial development and sustainable spatial design: How can geographers, planners and architects implement these ideas?

Torsten Klafft: First, we need courageous planners who believe that collaborative approaches are a good way of designing coexistence. Then we need courageous people in positions of responsibility who support this and who provide the instruments – such as funding – that make it possible. We need open processes and experiments. Each place needs its own experiment, but it has to be possible to put these experiments into the necessary funding forms. And of course, the best thing would be if the regulars in the pub held active, differentiated and heartfelt discussions about post-growth ideas – in language that doesn't exclude anyone from the discussion – and talked about how we would like to live together.

At 'nonconform' we like to talk about the 'best common denominator' between local citizens, those responsible, the administration and everyone with an interest, basically all the stakeholders. When people don't just talk about what they're *against* but try to understand the needs of the other party, you get more than the lowest common denominator. If it's possible to bring everyone together and develop a solution together, then there's added value for everyone. The 'best common denominator' is greater than a grudging compromise.

That fits in with post-growth, which is not fundamentally about less growth but about growing the right things, like in your case with finding not just a common denominator but actually the best common denominator for a good life. This attitude fits into this debate very well.

Torsten Klafft: Exactly. What can we all gain if we all focus on our commonalities?

That's a nice conclusion. Let's keep experimenting to find out and then spread the message. Thank you very much, Torsten.

Opening up spaces of possibility with artistic experiments

An interview with Viola Schulze Dieckhoff and Hendryk von Busse, conducted by Christian Schulz

As graduates of urban and spatial planning, they both took an artistic approach to questions of urban design and urban policy at a very early stage. Schulze Dieckhoff works at the TU Dortmund and is also active in *'die Urbanisten'* [The Urbanists] e. V., Dortmund. Von Busse is involved in and co-founder of the *'Freiraumgalerie – Kollektiv für Raumentwicklung'* [Open Space Gallery – Collective for Spatial Development] in Halle/Saale.
https://dieurbanisten.de/
https://www.freiraumgalerie.com/

In your six theses on 'post-growth planning' you, Viola, write together with Christian Lamker: 'Post-growth planning needs experimental and artistic action!' What exactly do you mean?

Viola Schulze Dieckhoff: Christian Lamker and I have always tried to bring together post-growth and planning and have noticed that it is not always socially acceptable to talk about post-growth. And so, through what can be said and what cannot be said, through 'do-able' and 'not do-able' things, we came to realise how important experiments and art are. It is actually clear that the growth mantra of economic activity doesn't work and must be abandoned. There's enough scientific evidence that shows that life satisfaction doesn't increase with more money and more consumption, there's also no direct link to social justice, and GDP also grows through climate disasters and through diseases. Those are the facts but it's not always easy to talk about them and to link things up with them because you can then quickly find yourself socially 'offside'. And let's just say that through 'experiments' it's possible to open up a kind of protected space – many people also say: to open up windows of opportunity or to create spaces of possibility – in order to consider what we actually want, how we want to live, how we want to work. And this space is not dependent on private economic interests or political calculations (e. g. thinking about the electorate) and is thus without any social path dependencies. Art also takes this up, firstly as an experiment or laboratory. However, art is also anchored in the Basic Law, and artistic freedom is protected. This goes beyond the fact that individuals can think about art to include the notion that people can also do what they have thought about, and that they can exchange ideas about it and also empower new discourses. Art is therefore centrally important because it also ends in a product and materialises, perhaps in a way beyond what has been previously thought of and worked out as a socially accepted norm. But artistic creation also changes things, through performances such as theatre or even when you design facades. Just looking at others triggers something in the viewer and changes something in the viewer's relationship to his or her environment – and can thereby create something new. Art and experimentation are therefore a possible way to 'fuel' the socio-ecological transformation, perhaps we can find transformative practice through the transformative actions of art and experimentation. The point is to show that changing, wanting to change and being able to change are also part of what we do, not just maintaining, preserving and preventing.

Where do you, Hendryk, see references to the topic of 'post-growth' in your recent projects? What role does art play in the imagination of post-growth living worlds?

Hendryk von Busse: I would simply use the example of the mural. The mural itself, as an urban design tool, has no direct relation to post-growth. But by investing resources, time and empathy, urban surfaces are enhanced or given life and identity, and thus become more than purely functional design. Otherwise, it depends very much on how you do this urban art, what you do with it. Where I see a connection is, for example, with our work on the 'civic neighbourhood concept'. In Halle-Freiimfelde, we used murals to revitalise vacant buildings and to provide a better identity and image for the neighbourhood, which also had an impact on quality of life. Thanks to the increased attention, it became clear that a plan was needed for this forgotten district. It was then courageous of the city to say: 'OK, we didn't do anything about this upgrading, the public did that, so the public should also design the neighbourhood concept, i.e. the future of this neighbourhood'. So this neighbourhood concept came about as a result of art, and it has many components that have to do with post-growth planning, for example, planning not from the outside through investors or redevelopment programmes but from the inside with the ideas, input, wishes and needs of residents. In this neighbourhood concept – based on the wishes of residents – there are many areas for artistic and experimental activities. So there's a citizens' park where people can garden, but which is also available for other projects. Besides classic post-growth activities like urban gardening and street art, there are also just open spaces and workshops where no one has defined what has to take place, and which are intended to remain flexible – even in the long run.

This civic neighbourhood concept also includes some guidelines for property development, e. g. how owners can come together to design cooperative property projects. In the process of developing the neighbourhood concept, a close network of residents and property owners was created; this neighbourliness was an important basis for further discussion.

So art is also a vehicle to promote social participation and democratic participation in the design of urban districts. Can you elaborate on that?

Viola Schulze Dieckhoff: I remember we did our first Street Art Festival in 2012, and afterwards Benjamin Davy wrote: 'Ms Schulze Dieckhoff, you have created such a great *'Gemeinsamhaben'* ['having together']!' And that was exactly what we created back then. There were no economic interests, we were fresh graduates, financing ourselves with small jobs, and we had a big network. So we could put a lot of voluntary work into a vision, by saying that we would like to paint in the neighbourhood, also together with the local residents. We financed that festival with far less than 30,000 euros and created over 5000 m² of wall designs. That was a process of exchange. We didn't have much, but we were able to give something artistically – the design of the facades, the use of urban space. We traded this with local companies (e. g. providers of lifting platforms), with the economic actors in the neighbourhood, and everyone gave what they could. We were then able to create a little world in its own right. It was precisely this democratic aspect that made it clear to me again that art can be used in different ways. Art is used or even instrumentalised in representative democracy in order to integrate and involve different parts of society, so rather to initiate somewhat controlled creative processes that can also be useful for planning. But there is a more anarchistic form of art, like uninvited contributions to spatial design – e. g. through graffiti or street art, which is often very critical of growth. The beginnings of the Street Art Festival had a lot to do with self-empowerment, this joint creation in the neighbourhood and the awareness that I can and want to help shape my city. Back then, we also used the facades to shake things up. A small civic initiative was quickly formed, and they didn't like our pictures much and emphasised that the local problems had more to do with cleanliness and safety on the streets. And so there was a second group, and the pluralism of opinion in the city also became publicly visible.

So you managed to mobilise a lot of local people. How did the planning authorities react to this?

Hendryk von Busse: In the case of the '*Freiraumgalerie*', it was indeed initially the case that the urban planning authorities tried to prevent it because the word 'graffiti' was used far too often rather than the term 'murals in participatory urban design'. Because of the negative association of 'graffiti', there was concern at the time that the image of the neighbourhood would deteriorate further – become even more stigmatised.

Viola Schulze Dieckhoff: In addition, at that time all activities were being directed towards Halle city centre, and the east of Halle was more or less written off. Efforts were supposed to be concentrated elsewhere.

Hendryk von Busse: Back then, the city had no development concept for the district. Accordingly, there were no plans that our plans maybe *didn't* fit in with, which is often a way of legitimising the prohibition of other plans. The city's failure to tackle the neighbourhood therefore left it basically unable to act.

So when we arrived with our approach, there was at first a certain amount of tolerance. The neighbourhood developed very well and also grew strongly. Many houses were renovated, many people moved in, more citizens became actively involved in the area. The city also noticed this and came under pressure because things quickly became embarrassing – as the neighbourhood became more visible so too did the city's failure to act and this was also discussed by the media. I think this is why attitudes changed in Halle's urban planning, so there was a willingness to say that we're now going to do something special, not simply designate a redevelopment area and not simply hire a classic urban planning office to produce a development concept. Now we'll take the step of trying a civic neighbourhood concept in order to test public participation as a maxim and also to learn from it. This laboratory, which we had initiated, could then be continued in this way.

What would you like to see in the planning from the point of view of the creatives and artists?

Viola Schulze Dieckhoff: What planners from the administration keep telling me behind closed doors is that if they wanted to do something different, it would be overturned by the city council, if not before. They're always at the mercy of the political process and the city council decisions. I believe that planning could or should act differently and contribute more to the political opinion-forming process. In my opinion, the professional field of planning should not only include consensus building, but should also communicate more facts, bringing out what actually needs to be done in the city and thus fuelling the discourse. With a vigilant urban society, there would then be more opportunities for progressive city council decisions to be made. And art and artistic creation are also good starting points so planners can see that it's necessary to promote places of creation more, because art is an essential building block of democracy, important for democratic negotiation.

We've often discussed the idea of the '*Bannwald*' [protected area of woodland], that is, an area where you leave things so that something new can naturally develop. Transferring something like this to the city could mean creating a kind of 'cultural conservation area' and introducing a corresponding land-use category into formal planning, at the regional and municipal levels. Land could also be set aside as commons and for the community economy. Planners could become opinion leaders in a negotiation process.

If you were awarded an unconditional grant for an art project related to post-growth and space, funding you for a year and providing all the resources you needed, what kind of project would you be most excited about?

Viola Schulze Dieckhoff: I'd be particularly interested in a project on the very current issue of 'climate adaptation and mobility'. I'd find it very interesting to make the analyses and plans we've discussed visible in urban space. Which areas will particularly heat up, where there's a danger of flooding, etc. – and to present this artistically, perhaps with street markings, but also to use formats of exchange with the public to inform and reflect on the issues and to collect people's impressions. And this is linked to the question of how a change in mobility can be promoted. My creative place, the one that I'd then like to have, would be a mobile container unit in a car park, symbolising that every parking space we provide free of charge could alternatively be a place of productive creation that generates value for society. From my office in this car park, numerous artistic projects should then emerge that serve to pass on knowledge and trigger discussion.

Do you see a general tendency for art to be increasingly recognised by planning, politics and science as an important element in the social debate about space?

Hendryk von Busse: Initially, I'm inclined to say yes, people are interested and the role of art is recognised. By the way, I also think that all forms of growth criticism have become socially acceptable and can be found in journalistic opinion pieces of all political persuasions. But actually, I think that overall the answer is rather no, because only 'good' art is recognised and promoted. Street art, unwanted graffiti and tags, on the other hand, are considered defacements. There are standardisations and designations for them that are really below the belt. We need to ask which art is wanted and recognised as engaging with space. My feeling is: the current discussions further emphasise the value of beauty and thus narrow understandings of art.

Authors

aus dem Moore, Nils, Dr, is an economist, journalist and Head of the Berlin office of the research group 'Sustainability and Governance' at the Leibniz Institute for Economic Research (*Leibniz-Institut für Wirtschaftsforschung, RWI*) in Essen. Contact: nils.ausdemmoore@rwi-essen.de

Batke, Meret, is in the eighth semester of her bachelor's in geography at Humboldt-Universität zu Berlin, focusing mainly on urban sociological and economic geographic aspects of human geography. Since 2018 she has been a researcher with 'Multiplicities' in Berlin. Contact: batke@multiplicities.de

Bauler, Tom, Prof. Dr, is Chair of Environment and Economy at Université Libre de Bruxelles (ULB). He conducts research on the socio-ecological transition, questions of environmental governance, alternative indicators of social welfare and social innovations. Contact: tom.bauler@ulb.be

Brückner, Heike, is a landscape architect focusing on research, planning and experimental design projects on the topics of 'post-industrial cultural landscapes' and 'productive urban landscapes'. Since 2010 she has been working on post-fossil urban and regional development and initiated the 'Urban Farm Dessau'. Contact: brueckner@bauhaus-dessau.de

Bruns, Antje, Prof. Dr, is a geographer and Head of the Governance and Sustainability Lab at Trier University. Her research on society-nature relations addresses questions of global sustainability and justice, resource governance and political ecology. Contact: brunsa@uni-trier.de

Bürkner, Hans-Joachim, Prof. Dr, is an economic and social geographer at Potsdam University and the Leibniz Institute for Research on Society and Space (*Leibniz-Institut für Raumbezogene Sozialforschung, IRS*) in Erkner. He is currently researching new forms of work in makerspaces, labs and open workshops. Contact: buerkner@uni-potsdam.de.

Dörry, Sabine, Dr, is a Senior Research Fellow at the Luxembourg Institute of Socio-Economic Research (LISER). Her research focuses include the transformation of international financial centres through sustainable and tech-based financial activities and financial institutions. Contact: sabine.doerry@liser.lu

Eichmann, Hubert, Dr, is a sociologist at the Working Life Research Centre (*Forschungs- und Beratungsstelle Arbeitswelt, FORBA*) in Vienna. His research focuses include transformation of the world of work, quality of work and life, urban and regional development and transformation research. Contact: eichmann@forba.at

Ha, Mai Anh, works on critical urbanism and historical justice in agglomerations. She is studying geographical sciences and historical urban studies in Berlin. Since 2017 she has been a researcher with 'Multiplicities' in Berlin. Contact: ma.ha@multiplicities.de

Hesse, Markus, Prof. Dr, conducts urban research at the University of Luxembourg on questions of urban and economic geography, spatial planning, governance and the interface between research and practice. Contact: markus.hesse@uni.lu

Hofmann, David, is a social economist and research associate at the Institute for Ecological Economy Research (*Institut für ökologische Wirtschaftsforschung, IÖW*) in Berlin. He is working on post-growth, the platform economy and economic policy. He is editor of the blog www.postwachstum.de. Contact: david.hofmann@ioew.de

Hülz, Martina, Dr, is a geographer and Head of the Academic Section for Economics and Mobility at the Academy for Territorial Development in the Leibniz Association (Akademie für Raumentwicklung in der Leibniz-Gemeinschaft, ARL). Contact: huelz@arl-net.de

Jarvis, Helen, Prof. Dr, is Professor of Social Geography Engagement at Newcastle University, UK. Her research focuses include the compatibility of family and work, the significance of public spaces and the 'social architecture' of new collaborative living arrangements. Contact: helen.jarvis@newcastle.ac.uk

Kaufmann, Stefan, studied media informatics and completed his thesis on open data in public transport in Germany. He has been involved in the field of open data since 2011, with a particular focus on mobility. On behalf of the city of Ulm he has, since 2016, actively supported the '*Ver-*

schwörhaus', a networking space for digital volunteering. Contact: stefan.kaufmann@verschwoerhaus.de

Kettner, Le-Lina, is a human geographer (M.Sc.) and research associate in the working group Spatial Planning and Sustainability in the Institute of Geography at Münster University. Her research interests include alternative economies, post-growth planning and feminist theories. Contact: l_ketto5@uni-muenster.de

Klafft, Torsten, is an architect and is studying sociology. With the agency 'nonconform', he implements participative processes in rural and urban areas. He also conducts research on participating amateurs. Contact: klafft@nonconform.at

Klagge, Britta, Prof. Dr, is Professor of Geography at Bonn University and Head of the Economic Geography working group. Her work focuses on energy and infrastructure, financial geography and critical capitalism research. Contact: klagge@uni-bonn.de

Kurzeja, Matti, is studying for his master's in geography at Bonn University. His bachelor's thesis was on makerspaces in North-Rhine Westphalia. He is involved in various self-organised, socio-cultural and political projects in the field of DIY culture. Contact: matti.kurzeja@posteo.de

Lamker, Christian, Dr, is Assistant Professor for Sustainable Transformation and Regional Planning at Groningen University in the Netherlands. He researches and teaches on roles in planning, post-growth planning, planning theory, regional planning and leadership in sustainable transformation. Contact: c.w.lamker@rug.nl

Lange, Bastian, Dr, is a lecturer at Leipzig University. He researches on the cultural and creative economy, alternative geographies, governance and urban planning. With 'Multiplicities' in Berlin, he provides consultancy for politics and business in the European context on ways to create urban regions fit for the future. Contact: bastian.lange@uni-leipzig.de

Lange, Steffen, Dr, works at the Institute for Ecological Economy Research (*Institut für ökologische Wirtschaftsforschung, IÖW*) in Berlin, where he researches how economies can be managed sustainably. His research focuses include the decoupling of economic growth and environmental consumption, rebound effects, digitalisation and concepts for economies without growth. Contact: steffen.lange@ioew.de

Langlinderer, Martin, is an industrial engineer who, with other volunteers, founded the first open workshop in Stuttgart in 2015. His primary concern is to develop an open-source concept for the spread of open workshops. Contact: martin@hobbyhimmel.de

Mayer, Heike, Prof. Dr, works in the Institute of Geography and Center for Regional Economic Development (CRED) at Bern University on the topics of innovation, entrepreneurship, the development of rural and mountain areas and regional policy. Contact: mayer@giub.unibe.ch

Mössner, Samuel, Prof. Dr, is Head of the Department of Spatial Planning and Sustainability in the Institute of Geography at Münster University. He conducts research on topics related to the social sustainability transition. Contact: moessner@uni-muenster.de

Mohn, Carel Carlowitz, lives and works as a journalist in Berlin. He is the founder and deputy chair of the civil society group 'Lausitzer Perspektiven e. V.'. Contact: carel.mohn@cleanenergywire.org

Petschow, Ulrich, is an economist and research associate at the Institute for Ecological Economy Research (*Institut für ökologische Wirtschaftsforschung, IÖW*) in Berlin. He conducts research on post-growth, transition strategies and technology assessment. Contact: ulrich.petschow@ioew.de

Pissarskoi, Eugen, Dr, works at the International Centre for Ethics in the Sciences and Humanities at Tübingen University, focusing on the field of ethics in sustainable development. Contact: eugen.pissarskoi@uni-tuebingen.de

Pütz, Marco, PD Dr, is a geographer and research group leader at the Swiss Federal Research Institute WSL. He works on urban and regional development, spatial planning, environmental governance, and adaptation to climate change. Contact: marco.puetz@wsl.ch.

Rydin, Yvonne, Prof. Dr, is Chair of Planning, Environment and Public Policy at Bartlett School of Planning, University College London. In her research on sustainable development, she focuses on planning processes, democratic participation, political power and governance, and the role of civil-society organisations. Contact: y.rydin@ucl.ac.uk

Schmelzer, Matthias, Dr, works at the Laboratory for New Economic Ideas (*Konzeptwerk Neue Ökonomie e. V.*) in Leipzig and at Friedrich Schiller University Jena. He is actively involved in the climate justice movement. Contact: m.schmelzer@knoe.org

Schmid, Benedikt, Dr, is a post-doctoral researcher at the chair Geography of Global Change at the University of Freiburg. His research focusses on the role of community initiatives and social enterprises in processes of transformation towards post-growth economy. Contact: benedikt.schmid@geographie.uni-freiburg.de

Schulz, Christian, Prof. Dr, is an economic geographer in the Department of Geography and Spatial Planning at the University of Luxembourg, with particular interest in sustainability transitions, alternative economies and post-growth approaches. Contact: christian.schulz@uni.lu

Schulze Dieckhoff, Viola, is a spatial planning engineer and works in the Department for Spatial Planning and Planning Theory in the Faculty of Spatial Planning at TU Dortmund University. She researches and works on post-growth planning, transformative action and the commons and is actively involved in 'Die Urbanisten e. V.' in Dortmund. Contact: viola.schulzedieckhoff@tu-dortmund.de

Seidl, Irmi, Prof. Dr, works at the Swiss Federal Research Institute for Forest, Snow and Landscape (*Eidgenössische Forschungsanstalt für Wald, Schnee und Landschaft WSL*) in Birmensdorf, Switzerland, on rural development, the economics of nature conservation, energy cooperatives and post-growth. Contact: irmi.seidl@wsl.ch

Szumelda, Anna Urszula, Dr, is a research coordinator and project worker at the Stanisław Karłowski Foundation (*Fundacja im. Stanisława Karłowskiego*) in Juchowo, Poland. Her main areas of work and interest are the social and structural transformations of rural areas and agriculture in Poland, organic farming (in Poland) and the sustainable development of rural areas from a socio-ecological perspective. Contact: anna.szumelda@posteo.de

Thiele, Katja, is a research associate in the Department of Economic Geography at Bonn University. Her PhD thesis is concerned with the development of public libraries in a European comparison. Her research focuses are (municipal) social infrastructures and the crisis of public services. Contact: kthiele@uni-bonn.de

Tschumi, Pascal, works in the Institute of Geography and Center for Regional Economic Development (CRED) at Bern University. His research concerns topics of social innovation (in the field of health), (regional) growth (in)dependence and regional development in rural areas and mountainous areas. Contact: pascal.tschumi@giub.unibe.ch

Vetter, Andrea, is a transition researcher and journalist. She is press officer for the Laboratory for New Economic Ideas (*Konzeptwerk Neue Ökonomie*

e. V.) in Leipzig. Her main interests are in degrowth, (eco-)feminism, care, convivial technology, digitalisation and the commons. Contact: a.vetter@knoe.org

von Busse, Hendryk, is an urban and regional planner and freelance artist. He works, inter alia, at the 'Open Space Gallery – Collective for Spatial Development' (*'Freiraumgalerie – Kollektiv für Raumentwicklung'*) in Halle/Saale, which he co-founded. Contact: hendrykvonbusse@gmail.com

Winiger, Andrea, works in the Institute of Geography and Center for Regional Economic Development (CRED) at Bern University on the topics of social innovations, post-growth, growth (in)dependencies, the construction industry, mountain areas and socio-economics. Contact: andrea.winiger@giub.unibe.ch

Wirth, Samuel, works in the Center for Regional Economic Development's Tourism Research Unit (CRED-T) and the Institute of Geography at Bern University, focusing on the topics of social innovations, tourism and the development of rural and mountainous areas. Contact: samuel.wirth@cred.unibe.ch

Wohlgemuth, Olivia, researches regional economies, spatial planning, settlement development and housing development at the Swiss Federal Research Institute for Forest, Snow and Landscape (*Eidgenössische Forschungsanstalt für Wald, Schnee und Landschaft, WSL*) in Birmensdorf, Switzerland. Contact: olivia.wohlgemuth@wsl.ch

Ziehl, Michael, Dr., Dipl.-Ing., is an Urbanist and Urban Researcher with focus on the Co-Production of Urban Resilience and user-driven project development. From Hamburg, Germany he is running Urban Upcycling – Agency for Urban Resources. Contact: kontakt@urban-upcycling.de

Zimmermann, Jan, is a qualified horticultural engineer and owner of a company offering ecological garden services in Dessau. He is one of the initiators of the 'Urban Farm Dessau' and has been involved as a leader, gardener and visionary since the beginning of the project. Contact: kontakt@urbane-farm.de

Social Sciences

kollektiv orangotango+ (ed.)
This Is Not an Atlas
A Global Collection of Counter-Cartographies

2018, 352 p., hardcover, col. ill.
34,99 € (DE), 978-3-8376-4519-4
E-Book: free available, ISBN 978-3-8394-4519-8

Gabriele Dietze, Julia Roth (eds.)
Right-Wing Populism and Gender
European Perspectives and Beyond

April 2020, 286 p., pb., ill.
35,00 € (DE), 978-3-8376-4980-2
E-Book: 34,99 € (DE), ISBN 978-3-8394-4980-6

Mozilla Foundation
Internet Health Report 2019

2019, 118 p., pb., ill.
19,99 € (DE), 978-3-8376-4946-8
E-Book: free available, ISBN 978-3-8394-4946-2

**All print, e-book and open access versions of the titles in our list
are available in our online shop www.transcript-publishing.com**

Social Sciences

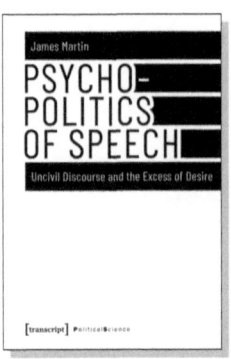

James Martin
Psychopolitics of Speech
Uncivil Discourse and the Excess of Desire

2019, 186 p., hardcover
79,99 € (DE), 978-3-8376-3919-3
E-Book:
PDF: 79,99 € (DE), ISBN 978-3-8394-3919-7

Michael Bray
Powers of the Mind
Mental and Manual Labor
in the Contemporary Political Crisis

2019, 208 p., hardcover
99,99 € (DE), 978-3-8376-4147-9
E-Book:
PDF: 99,99 € (DE), ISBN 978-3-8394-4147-3

Ernst Mohr
The Production of Consumer Society
Cultural-Economic Principles of Distinction

April 2021, 340 p., pb., ill.
39,00 € (DE), 978-3-8376-5703-6
E-Book: available as free open access publication
PDF: ISBN 978-3-8394-5703-0

**All print, e-book and open access versions of the titles in our list
are available in our online shop www.transcript-publishing.com**